The Second D-Day

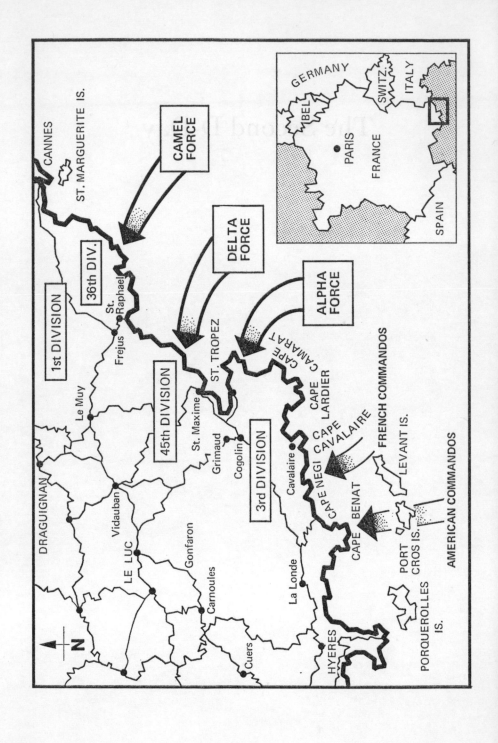

THE
SECOND D-DAY

Jacques Robichon

Translated from the French by
Barbara Shuey
for Army Times Publishing Company

WALKER AND COMPANY
New York

Contents

Illustrations

Introduction

IN THE EARLY MORNING HOURS of Tuesday, 15 August 1944, amid the velvety blackness and stillness of a warm Provençal night, the vanguard of an invasion army of nearly 300,000 combined American, French, Canadian, and British troops were preparing to land on the Mediterranean coast of France, somewhere between Toulon and Cannes. The first shot rang out shortly after midnight in the darkness around the sheer cliff at Cap Nègre, near Le Lavandou. D-Day in Provence had begun, two months and nine days after the landings in Normandy on 6 June.

The invasion of the south of France had a specific purpose. It was part of a swooping pincers movement designed to snap shut on the maximum number of German troops in France as a prelude to the final great sweep of General Dwight D. Eisenhower's forces toward their supreme objective, the heart of Germany itself. Half of the pincers jaw had been taking shape for sixty-nine days and was already operating; the other would be formed by the men who were to land in Provence. In the light of Allied estimates and planning, there was a slim likelihood that the Germans could put up even a token resistance to this doubled-edged assault.

For the German forces, many things had changed drastically in the nine weeks since 6 June. On all sides the *Wehrmacht* generals were issuing withdrawal orders that affected troops in every direction – in the west, the south, and the east – and certain of these officers, including the most experienced and renowned of Hitler's veteran military leaders, had been ruthlessly stripped of their commands – like Field Marshal Gerd von Rundstedt – or had become casualties themselves – like Field Marshal Erwin Rommel – and were definitely out of the fight.

Those nine weeks had been grim for yet another actor in the drama – Hitler. There had been the conspiracy of 20 July – the generals' plot, the attempt on his life, and the burns he suffered in the bomb explosion at the

East Prussian headquarters in Rastenburg. Hitler was no longer the impetuous, rabble-rousing Führer with the unruly brown forelock; no longer did he draw himself up, wiry, taut, ramrod-straight, 'like an Alpine tree.' Instead, he had deteriorated into an aging, white-haired, stooping figure, his body wracked with nervous twitchings, a strangely withdrawn dictator given to long, disconcerting silences. This latest Allied assault, the landings in Provence, forced his hand and compelled him at last to take the step that he had steadfastly refused to take in the aftermath of Stalingrad and Monte Cassino, even in the days that followed 6 June. He now had no alternative but to order a general retreat. He would have to sign the document acknowledging total defeat on the Western front. But he had not realized any of this yet. On this dawn, Hitler was still sound asleep.

Night was fading over the Mediterranean, shedding its blanket of darkness, and the growing light was erasing the last lingering stars from the August sky, in which a late-risen crescent moon still hovered hesitantly. From the nearby mainland, the earthy night air flung all the heady, untamed fragrances of the Mediterranean summer out to the waiting men on the 1,200 ships of the huge armada standing by off the beaches of Cavalaire-sur-Mer, Sainte-Maxime, and Saint-Raphaël. The ships were strung out along the more than thirty miles of sand and rocks that were to be attacked at H-Hour by the fighting troops that had converged from all over the Mediterranean.

Thousands of human beings were breathlessly awaiting this hour. In addition to the assault troops, the combat infantry, the airborne battalions, the military staffs, and the crews on the ships and landing barges, there were the countless men and women in Provence whose hopes were focused on the events of the coming dawn. Yet none could match the intense yearning, the glorious pride and the restless anxiety of the men in the French divisions – the bulk of the invasion forces – as they ticked off the minutes and hours aboard ship, eager to be home again after four years of exile. In the hush of night, broken only by the occasional eddying and slapping of the surf against the rocks and sand, the first Allied soldier to land on the coast of Provence was going to be a Frenchman. The first man killed would also be a Frenchman.

Dawn was at last about to rend the shroud of darkness, in the wake of the night fighting. H-Hour had been set for 8 A.M. But the battle would not be truly over and won until the troops that had landed in Normandy and the armies from Provence had finally joined forces and could stand together.

Part One

PRELUDE

1

THE DAKOTA HAD TAKEN OFF right after lunch from the Capodichino airfield a mile from Naples. As the plane gathered altitude and began leveling off over the pale waters of the Tyrrhenian Sea, the pilot headed west toward the Sardinian coast. Southern Italy was smothering in the August heat wave that had produced another airless summer afternoon under a glinting, bright sky.

One of the Dakota's passengers sat wrapped in scowling silence, hunched back in his seat. He exuded taciturn disapproval, his great frame topped by a tousle of thinning wisps of hair, his gloomy countenance making him look for all the world like a massive bulldog as he stolidly exhaled deep puffs of smoke from an outsized cigar. Peering out the window, the passenger stared indifferently down on a cloud-wreathed Mount Vesuvius, on the sprawling suburbs of the dark mass of the city, and on the ruins of what had once been wharves and docks, now disemboweled and exposed to the sun's merciless rays. After the plane had started out to sea, he could glimpse the outline of the Isle of Capri looming up like the misshapen back of a maimed sheep. This Dakota was the one permanently assigned to General Sir Henry Maitland Wilson, the Allied commander-in-chief of the Mediterranean Theater of Operations, but it was not flying in the lane prescribed by those responsible for air security. Planes that followed the recommended route flew over the Pontine marshes, and did not venture out over the water until somewhere near the island of Elba. However, the pilot of this C-47 had set his course due west, and was steering straight for Sardinia.

His septuagenarian hulk propped up in one corner of the cabin, Winston Churchill was not proffering a word of conversation. As a matter of fact, his face – with its strongly protruding underlip and the ever-present cigar jutting out defiantly – did not even register a flicker of interest until the plane veered right at a 45° angle, abruptly shifted

3

course, and began heading toward Corsica. The hands of Churchill's watch pointed to 2.40 P.M.

At that moment, less than 200 miles away, the ships of an immense war fleet, gathered from staging areas throughout the Mediterranean, was assembling off the Strait of Bonifacio. Minute by minute, the seemingly limitless expanse of smooth water was filling up. New convoys continually heaved into view, and combat vessels of all shapes, sizes, and descriptions, flying the various flags of the Allied fleet, edged in to take their places in the formation. As one of the participants in this gathering later described it,[1] 'the ships' white wakes seaming the blue water looked like the pattern of a vast, intricate spiderweb etched into the flat surface.'

Twelve hundred ships – troop transports, aircraft carriers, mine sweepers, tugboats, cruisers, battleships, destroyers, destroyer escorts and drop-ramp landing craft crammed with equipment and ammunition – were churning through the sea on a radiant day that would have been perfect had it been a little less hot. Some of the convoys had taken more than five days to reach their destination. They were nearing the coast of Corsica after setting sail from Malta and southern Italy, from Algeria, Tunisia and Sicily, by incredibly devious routes, in compliance with the strict itineraries and schedules of an over-all plan meticulously conceived to prevent a naval traffic jam in the narrow, mine-infested Strait of Bonifacio.

Hardly a breath of air was stirring as they steamed in from all directions, pennants fluttering proudly from mastheads and signals flashing from deck to deck under a massive umbrella of antiaircraft balloons. There were ten of these widely strung-out convoys, breasting the waves in a profusion of hulls and superstructures daubed with camouflage, as many classes of vessels as there were countries of origin. All of them were headed in the same direction, toward Cape Senetosa, west of Bonifacio, as if making their way to a rendezvous.

The date was Monday, 14 August 1944, two months and one week after the Allied landings in Normandy. It was nearing 3 P.M.

2

ABOUT AN HOUR had passed since two British officers, Admiral Sir John Cunningham, commander-in-chief of Allied naval forces in the

[1] Jean Meirat, French naval signalman.

4

Mediterranean, and General Wilson, had sailed on the destroyer *Kimberley* from Ajaccio on Corsica, to keep their rendezvous with the fleet.

In the Dakota, Winston Churchill had arrived too late over Ajaccio to catch a glimpse of the assembled armada. By the time his plane was ready to land, the *Kimberley*, flying two halyards of flags, had steamed back to port. Churchill swore to himself that he would make up for lost time the following day. This thought helped dispel his cranky mood and helped him overcome the deep grudge that he had been nursing for weeks against Eisenhower, Harry Hopkins, President Franklin Delano Roosevelt's political adviser, and against the President himself.

Churchill had arrived from England via Algiers three days earlier, on Friday, 11 August. At the Villa Rivalta, a grandiose but somewhat down-at-the-heels Neapolitan mansion, one of the British Prime Minister's first visitors was a figure resplendent in an eye-catching blue and gold uniform, complete with a tight-fitting collar, 'singularly unsuited to the blazing heat,' as Churchill later commented. The uniform boasted two distinguishing features. First, it had been made in the Soviet Union and was a gift from Stalin himself. Secondly, the gold stripes and braid that adorned it had come directly from the United States. Churchill's visitor was escorted by two bodyguards armed with automatic pistols and a forbidding demeanor. The man for whose security they were responsible was Josip Broz, known as Marshal Tito.

The Yugoslav marshal, who had come over from the island of Vis, where he was staying under British protection, assured his host emphatically that, despite the splendid uniform from Moscow, he entertained no intention of setting up a Communist régime in his own country. The ensuing conversation centered on other topics, including the delivery of British ammunition and arms to the Yugoslav troops who were battling the Germans. The interview continued throughout a *tête-à-tête* luncheon under the watchful eyes of the two bodyguards, with the Bay of Naples and Mount Vesuvius as a backdrop.

When Tito had left, Churchill indulged in a brief siesta that was soon interrupted by the arrival of Rear Admiral John Morse of the Royal Navy. His launch could be heard, its motor idling down among the rocks near the Villa Rivalta's landing pier. Churchill suggested a jaunt to Ischia.

Since 1 October 1943, when the Allies had entered the city, the war had been lingering about Naples and scarring the skies over the surrounding countryside; it had continued through the interminable winter of mud and snow that drove the rivers, the *fiume*, out of their beds, transforming olive groves and highways into unrecognizable bogs, trapping

5

Allied troops in the hostile mountains. It was the winter of the Abruzzi, the Volturno, and the Belvedere, the winter of the Rapido, and it had lasted until the end of the siege of Monte Cassino. In Naples, the intense activity had not let up for a day.

On this summer afternoon in 1944 under the sultry sky, every square foot of seaside, all the docks, the piers and the wharves gave the appearance of a frantic beehive. The LSTs[1] were loading matériel, and the rows of LSIs[2] tied up in the harbor were taking on the endless lines of troops presenting a discouraging picture to watchful German intelligence agents. Vast concentrations of vessels filled the bay all the way to Sorrento and Massalubrense. As one Allied military leader observed, it was a scene reminiscent of 'Vulcan's forge installed at Capua.'

Admiral Morse's launch bounded at a fast clip over the blue waters toward Cape Miseno, carrying on board a thoroughly relaxed and jovial Churchill, wearing a white linen suit, cigar clenched between his teeth, delighted to be combining business with pleasure far from the madding sessions of the War Cabinet in Downing Street.

When they returned from Ischia, the sun was beginning to sink, and the Bay of Naples was swarming with departing convoys whose maneuvering made navigation tricky for the Admiral's launch. Most of the ships in the convoy were American-built heavy tank transports that, before arriving in the Mediterranean, had been diverted to England for the Normandy operations.

Among the ships in a convoy of American troops was a unit of twenty-five LSTs under Commander O.F.Gregor. The men leaning against the railings had just recognized the passenger on the launch flying the Royal Navy ensign, a heavy-set, bareheaded civilian who was smiling up at them and stretching out his hand in the 'V for victory' sign.

The troops – part of Lieutenant General Alexander M. Patch's Seventh Army – jostled one another for places near the handrails so that they could cheer 'good old Winnie,' the aging lion with his sparse mane tossing in the wind.

From the crowded decks there rose the traditional rousing three cheers, followed by shouts:

'Winnie! It's Winnie! It's the old man himself! Hey, how about that? Nice work, Winnie! Good show!'

Among the men in the convoy was a young second lieutenant from the Free French forces, one of the few Frenchmen to embark with the United States 3rd Infantry Division's assault troops. He watched, considerably moved, as the old man 'progressed across the bay like a pilgrim.' The

[1] Landing ship tank.
[2] Landing ship infantry.

lieutenant, the internationally known screen star Jean-Pierre Aumont, reflected to himself that 'it was as if Churchill had come out to bestow a personal blessing on each one of us.'

Aumont could hardly have suspected that at the very moment, aboard the launch speeding over the waves, Churchill was grumbling to Admiral Morse:

'These men don't realize that if I'd had my way, they'd all be heading in a completely different direction. . . .'

Churchill was right. They didn't realize, and it had not even occurred to them to wonder. And while the launch proceeded to weave its way through the convoys of the most redoubtable armada ever to sail the waters of the Mediterranean, the 3rd Division's troops broke into their marching song, *The Dog-Face Soldier*.

This was the music that, one week earlier, had greeted the arrival of General Patch, in over-all command of the ground troops of the landing forces, on the occasion of his final inspection of the division at Pozzuoli.

In addressing the veterans of the fighting in North Africa, Sicily and Anzio, Patch had said:

'Men, I am not at liberty to disclose your next destination to you . . . Even your officers don't know. However, I *can* say this much. There are still a lot of battles ahead of you to be won before you'll see the end of them!'

Lieutenant General Lucian K. Truscott, Jr., the division's former commander, then spoke to the troops assembled in the huge olive grove where the division's tents were pitched. To everyone's surprise, he shouted:

'Boys, I'm not asking you to hate the Germans! I'm only telling you that you've got to win this war! Win it, I tell you, win it!'

And then he added:

'The same way that you'd win a baseball game!'

Scarcely had these visitors turned their backs when Major General John W. O'Daniel, the division commander, nicknamed 'Iron Mike' by his troops, stepped out in front, the set of his forehead somehow more stubborn than ever and his jaw more firmly set, and began pounding the air with his fists:

'You can take it from me, boys! I'm telling you to hate the Germans! Hate 'em, hate 'em!'

While they had been enthusiastically acclaiming Churchill, General Mike O'Daniel's battle-toughened warriors could not for a second have imagined that the old lion who appeared to be giving them his benediction had actually been the most fanatic opponent, the most overt and

7

resolute adversary of the very operation that they were getting ready to undertake.

Through the last weeks and days before the decision, even up to the very last minute, the lion had fought tooth and nail to prevent the Allied forces from landing on the Mediterranean coast of France.

3

NINE MONTHS EARLIER, at the end of November 1943, the chiefs of government of the Soviet Union, Great Britain, and the United States had gathered in Teheran one evening to confer on the possibility of opening a second 'second front' against Hitler's Europe.[1] The time was about 6 P.M.

Franklin D. Roosevelt had just emerged from one of the last and most exhausting plenary sessions of the conference, held at the Soviet Embassy, and was contemplating his youngest son, Elliott, who was drawing a bath for him.

The President suddenly spoke up:

'It's settled at last.'

And everything had indeed been settled, or at least so it appeared. There was to be a large-scale invasion in the west, scheduled for May 1944,[2] concomitant with an attack on the German war machine in the south of France.

'Everything will be timed simultaneously – from the west, from the south, and the Russians from the east,' Roosevelt continued. 'I still say the end of 1944 will see the end of the war in Europe. Nobody can see how – with a really concerted drive from all sides – the Nazis can hold out much over nine months after we hit 'em.'

Although events worked out differently, the result was pretty much as Roosevelt had anticipated – a result that he himself was doomed to miss by only a few weeks.

'Elliott,' the President went on, explaining with suddenly increased vehemence. 'Trouble is, the PM is thinking too much of the postwar.... He's scared of letting the Russians get too strong. . . . Maybe the Russians will get strong in Europe. Whether that's bad depends on a whole lot of factors.'

[1] The first 'second front' had been formed the previous July with the invasion of Sicily, followed by that of continental Italy in September.

[2] 1 May 1944, was the date originally agreed on in Teheran for the Normandy landings.

Relaxing in his warm tub, the President fell silent before resuming:

'Elliott, our chiefs of staff are convinced of one thing. The way to kill the most Germans, with least loss of American soldiers, is to mount one great big invasion and then slam 'em with everything we've got. . . . Now Winston is talking about two operations at once. I guess he knows there's no use trying to argue against the western invasion any more.'

'What does Churchill mean, Pop, two invasions at once?'

'One in the west and one up through guess where.'

Elliott Roosevelt reflected briefly.

'The Balkans?'

'Of course.'

The President chuckled, probably remembering the meeting that had just put Churchill and 'Uncle Joe'[1] at loggerheads. Roosevelt closed his eyes. Silence descended on the two men, and the only sound was the ticking of the big Russian clock in the adjoining room.

Roosevelt's somewhat hoarse and fatigue-edged voice picked up again as he massaged his body.

'Whenever the PM argued for our invasion through the Balkans, it was quite obvious to everyone in the room what he really meant. That he was above all else anxious to knife up into central Europe, in order to keep the Red Army out of Austria and Rumania, even Hungary, if possible. Stalin knew it, I knew it, everybody knew it. . . .'

Churchill's obsession was exactly as Roosevelt described it to his son. The British leader contemplated victory over Nazi Germany less from the military standpoint than from the political. What was the point of wiping out Hitler's power, sacrificing all those lives and all that energy, if the war's outcome were ultimately to promote in Eastern Europe a Soviet empire that might prove even more redoubtable than the German? Was Stalin to reap the lion's share of a victory that had been so hard won and so dearly bought? Churchill indignantly rejected this prospect; furthermore, he had never condoned the British habit of 'doing other people's dirty work for them.' There was only one way to stem the Soviet tidal wave; only a single solution for neutralizing the threat of Stalin's imperialism to the postwar world. That was a massive sweep of the Allied forces toward the Balkans – striking Europe in its 'vital organs' and rushing into Vienna one jump ahead of the Soviet tanks.

This was Churchill's theory, which he tirelessly expounded in Roosevelt's presence. However, Roosevelt displayed only a limited concern with 'real or fancied British interests on the European continent.'

'We're at war,' the President repeated to his son, 'and our job is to win it

[1] Stalin.

9

as fast as possible, and without adventures. I think – *hope* – that he's learned we mean that, once, finally, and for all.'

In making this statement, the President was greatly underestimating the lengths to which the Prime Minister in his stubbornness could go. Franklin Roosevelt asked his son to fix him his favorite cocktail, an Old Fashioned.

4

WHILE CHURCHILL WAS CONTINUING to nourish the illusion that his ideas would prevail and that he would get his way, preparations for the simultaneous invasion of France in Normandy and in the Mediterranean were proceeding amid the utmost secrecy.

On a sunny February morning in 1944, out in the country about two miles from Algiers, a French naval officer, Commander Yann Le Hagre, was making his way through an impressive number of barbed-wire barriers guarded by military policemen. At length, Le Hagre found himself near a cluster of neo-Moorish buildings in a setting of palms, aloes, cypresses and yew trees. The Bouzaréa Normal School stood perched high up on a hill overlooking on one side the Algiers roadstead and on the other, Cape Sidi-Ferruch, where French troops had first landed in 1830. They had been followed over a century later, on the night of 8 November 1942, by the first Anglo-American contingents of Operation Torch. Since January 1944, the Bouzaréa buildings had been the most carefully guarded sanctuary in the whole of North Africa.

Commander Le Hagre next found himself shut up in a room piled with documents. A letter addressed to him in a sealed envelope informed him drily that he would be summarily shot if he revealed any of the secrets entrusted to him. His period of solitary confinement lasted three weeks, during which nobody paid him the slightest attention. At the end of that time, a Scottish major threw open the door of his room and asked him point-blank:

'You're familiar with the French coasts?'

'That's part of my job,' Le Hagre replied.

'The Mediterranean coasts?'

Receiving an affirmative answer, the Scot relaxed his peremptory manner and led Le Hagre to a stray hut set apart in the grounds. The room was empty except for a huge file lying on a desk. The file contained a detailed description, mile by mile, of the coast of France from Port Vendres to Menton, the designations and positions of the German defense installations over every inch of ground, the possibilities of access by sea, and the features of the surrounding area. Topography, hydrography, climate, tides and currents, types of soil, means of communication, industrial resources, electric power and plants, water supply – all the information had been classified, indexed, and numbered, down to the most insignificant concrete dugout, the most unobtrusive machine-gun nest, the tiniest patch of mine fields. Everything had been noted, checked, and cross-checked by the innumerable photographs taken by Allied reconnaissance planes.

Although Le Hagre was stupefied and dumbfounded by some of these discoveries, he did not let on. As he leafed through the pages, he ventured various observations, expressed criticisms, or refuted certain bits of information – specifically about a 13.4-inch gun battery, one of the most formidable on the entire Mediterranean coast of France, situated on the Saint-Mandrier Peninsula, opposite Toulon and commanding all the coastal approaches from La Ciotat to Le Lavandou.

Seeing that the Scottish major had begun to display polite skepticism, Le Hagre nonchalantly remarked:

'It so happens that I built it and armed it. That was a good twelve years ago, in 1932.'

A few seconds later Commander Le Hagre found himself being whisked by his 'mentor' through a maze of corridors until finally, as he gazed incredulously, there swung open in front of him the door to an enormous air-conditioned office guarded by two military policemen armed with machine guns.

The man who stepped forward to greet Le Hagre, his hand out-stretched, only his eyes smiling, was tall and lanky, past fifty years of age; he had sharply accentuated features and was bald. He wore a purple silk scarf, and on the shoulder-tabs of his battle dress uniform were the three silver stars of a lieutenant general in the United States Army.

This man had commanded an army corps on Guadalcanal in the Pacific. One story concerning him went clear back to World War I, when he was commanding a machine-gun battalion in 1917 in France. At the time, he needed a dentist, but had been able to locate only a veterinarian.

'Have you ever pulled teeth?'

'Horses' teeth, yes,' replied the veterinarian.

A pair of pliers was promptly produced and the new patient opened his mouth wide.

'O.K.,' he said, 'now you can pull one of mine.'

On this day in 1944 the searching gaze of his keen blue eyes was appraising Yann Le Hagre. It was the Frenchman's introduction to General Alexander M. Patch.

5

SINCE DECEMBER 1941, following the attack on Pearl Harbor, the strategic command of the Allied forces at war with Germany and Japan had been in the hands of the Combined Chiefs of Staff, made up of the Commanders of the British and American armies, air forces and navies. On Tuesday, 6 December 1943, a few days after the end of the Teheran conference, the Combined Chiefs of Staff informed General Eisenhower, soon to be designated Supreme Commander, Allied Expeditionary Force, that concomitant with Operation Overlord (code name for the Normandy landings) there would also be an attack on the Mediterranean coast of France, designed to establish a beachhead that would assist the Channel invasion by compelling the *Wehrmacht* divisions still on the coast between Port Vendres and Menton to remain in the south of France.

Since then, the Mediterranean landing was referred to by the code name Operation Anvil, and in the next eight months the exchange of information about it grew into a formidable pile of telegraphic correspondence. If all went as planned, there would be invasions of both the north and south of France, the south serving as the Allies' base for penetration into the heart of Germany. The German armies would be caught in a vast pincers movement. Although Anvil's exact date had not been fixed, it was supposed to be closely synchronized – no more than a few weeks intervening – with the launching of the Channel invasion, on the most favorable date in May 1944.

Theoretically, as in the case of Operation Overlord, final responsibility for Anvil rested with the Supreme Commander, Eisenhower. In reality, it devolved upon a Briton, General Sir Harry Maitland Wilson, known as 'Jumbo' to his friends, to whom in 1942 Churchill had entrusted the defense of Cairo against Rommel's Afrika Korps. As matters stood, Wilson would act as the Supreme Commander's 'delegate' on the Mediterranean front until the transfer of operation control would come about automatically, after Patch's Seventh Army and the French Army under General Jean de Lattre de Tassigny had joined forces with the

Normandy invasion troops. Eisenhower would then resume supreme command over all the Allied forces.

A further problem had arisen and been added to those that faced the leaders of the invasion forces who were hoping to land simultaneously in Normandy and at some other point on the French coast. In 1944, General George C. Marshall, the United States Army's Chief of Staff, went to London to inform Churchill of his concern with this problem. It was the first the British had heard of it.

'In our camps in the United States,' Marshall began, 'we have some forty or fifty divisions ready for the European invasion. These divisions will have to be sent into the battle with all possible speed. The trouble is that neither your British ports nor the Normandy ports – much less those of the Atlantic coast, assuming that we take Brest fairly early in the game – are in a position to handle and process such a mass of troops and matériel. . . . However,' he stated, 'Eisenhower will begin to need these reinforcements pretty fast.'

Marshall could see only one way of solving this crucial problem – capturing new bases in France. The question was, which ones?

The American Chief of Staff and the British Prime Minister gazed over the map of France.

Churchill's wide thumb came to rest on the hollow of the Bay of Biscay. Not unintentionally, the British statesman then pointed out the Atlantic coastal areas of France that would first be reached by convoys from the United States. But when Marshall shifted his gaze to the Mediterranean area, Churchill remained silent.

When Eisenhower was consulted, he repeated what by then had been his theory for weeks and months.

'The port of Sète,' he stated, 'which is the only one on the Languedoc coast, obviously has the immense advantage of being only 215 miles from Bordeaux. It enjoys the additional advantage, as far as our landings are concerned, of presenting no serious mountainous obstacles. Unfortunately, its daily unloading capacity is barely 7,500 tons.'

The Supreme Commander added that, furthermore, the waters around Sète were definitely too shallow for the Liberty ships with their heavy cargos.

'The only other possibility,' Eisenhower continued, 'is Toulon. Despite the fact that it has an entrenched camp, its prospects are far more promising.' (Toulon had a daily capacity of 10,000 tons.)

'No,' continued Eisenhower after a silence, 'what we really need . . .'

Churchill's fleshy underlip accentuated its pout of utter disapproval of what the Supreme Commander in Chief was getting ready to suggest.

'There's no doubt about it,' Eisenhower concluded. 'What I need is Marseilles, as a transit base for our reinforcements and supplies.'

And he flashed one of his irresistible smiles at the two men.

Just before the outbreak of World War II, the over-all freight capacity of the port of Marseilles had been nearly ten million tons, and its gross capacity nearly thirty-three million tons. As a result, with its docks and wharves, a daily unloading capacity of twenty thousand tons, seven types of drydocks and an interior railway system, Marseilles was France's foremost seaport, and – as the people of Marseilles are fond of pointing out – also the Mediterranean's foremost seaport.

Eisenhower eventually carried the day with his persistence in wanting Marseilles as the main base for the Allied forces engaged in the battle of Europe, and he won out over the unconcealed hostility of Churchill and the British Chiefs of Staff, who were resolutely against any attempt to land in southern France. Marshall energetically seconded Eisenhower.

From then on, as the Allied plans gradually took shape, the capture of Marseilles became the principal objective of the landings in Provence.

While Eisenhower had to reckon with the tides in Normandy, Wilson in the Mediterranean had no such problem. The sea is in a state of virtually permanent slack water, with a maximum of eight inches of tide at Marseilles. And although its stiff, short waves with their fast-moving, tightly packed undulations can make navigation difficult in heavy weather, the ground swell of the Mediterranean Sea is very slight, and, except for the winter months, the barometer rarely drops very low.

Meanwhile, the question nagging at the minds of the experts at Bouzaréa with increasing urgency was the choice of landing sites. At first glance, the Provençal coast, which is wild, rocky, and sharply indented along almost its entire length, appears to be impassable. Once the assault troops had landed – assuming that they managed to establish a beach-head – were they not likely to run up against insuperable obstacles? Would it not be almost impossible for them even to begin an advance that could only be laborious, discouraging, and costly in human lives? They would have to overcome tortuous mountain *massifs* that, in some places for dozens of miles at a stretch, plunge sheer down to the water's edge like a wall? But no other part of the coast of southern France lent itself so well to a landing. The immense advantage of the Provence shoreline lay in a 'shallow water line' one hundred yards wide, quite near the shore. It began drawing closer to the shore at Marseilles, and beyond the Iles d'Hyères it lay at an average distance of only one mile from the beach. It thereby ensured the invasion fleet of anchorages that would make it possible to move naval guns forward without too much risk from mines. In addition, nearby Corsica, which had been transformed into an advanced airbase for Allied bombers and fighter planes, made tactical air support readily available, almost within arm's reach. It would have been unthinkable to hesitate any further; the landing had unquestionably to take place in Provence.

There is a thirty-five mile stretch of coast extending from the wide, pine-tree-bordered beach at Cavalaire-sur-Mer, at the foot of the Monts des Maures, over to the roadstead of Agay tucked between the rocky promontories of the Esterel chain.

'It was a tempting idea,' De Lattre remarked afterward, 'to try to establish a beachhead by landing on the Iles d'Hyères, or on the shore at Le Lavandou, for example, or even at Cavalaire itself. But this could not have been done without risking the deadly fire of the 13.4-inch guns on the Saint-Mandrier Peninsula, which had a range of twenty miles.'[1]

It was these four guns, the most dangerous of all those of the French Riviera – capable of sweeping the beaches with eight volleys a minute and protected by ten-inch steel plate – that Commander Le Hagre had called to the attention of the staff at Algiers. He had succeeded in proving that it would be impossible between then and D-Day, even with the most accurate and persistent aerial bombardment, to knock these guns out completely.

Under the circumstances, there was no option but to choose a landing zone protected from the Saint-Mandrier guns – somewhere between Saint-Tropez and Saint-Raphaël.

6

AS THE WEEKS WENT BY, the problems General Wilson had to cope with increasingly resembled a Chinese puzzle, and no invasion was ever

---

[1] The existence of the Saint-Mandrier battery played a decisive role in the choice of landing beaches. This battery had two double turrets (four 13.4-inch guns), which had been blasted when the French fleet scuttled its ships on 27 November 1942. However, as noted by Admiral Paul Auphan and the French historian Jacques Mordal: '... in the excitement of the moment, the same demolition technique had not been applied to both turrets. In one of them, the explosive charges placed in the barrels had split the guns, putting them hopelessly out of commission. In the other turret, although the guns had been temporarily knocked out ... the damage was *not beyond repair*.' In 1943, the Germans managed to replace the two damaged 13.4-inch guns, 'and the battery would have been *completely operational* again at the time the Mediterranean landings took place if a few courageous people from the Toulon Arsenal (notably a foreman named Richelme) had not intervened discreetly but efficiently and sabotaged one of the guns.' (Mordal and Auphan: *Histoire de la marine française pendant la seconde guerre mondiale.*)

so constantly challenged as that scheduled for Provence. In fact, it was only by a hair's breadth that this invasion escaped being scrapped before it ever began.

It was already obvious that the Normandy landings would not take place on 1 May. Operation Overlord had been postponed to 15 May, then to 30 May, and was finally set for early June. The exact date would depend on atmospheric conditions favorable to both the naval and the air forces. Operation Anvil suffered the inevitable backlash of the delays and postponements, for the two operations were closely interrelated and interdependent. And then, suddenly, the very question of their synchronization became a problem.

In their offices behind the Moorish windows of the Bouzaréa school, officers in the American Seventh Army headquarters assigned to charting each movement of *Wehrmacht* troops all over France, continued their daily posting on huge maps representing the future assault area. Up to the end of March, these special officers had recorded a dozen German divisions south of Lyons and Bordeaux; by early April and in the ensuing weeks, this figure had risen to fourteen, including three *Panzerdivisionen* (armored divisions) and eleven infantry divisions. However, the Allied experts expected the Normandy landings to reduce these figures, so that the forces in Provence would eventually have to face only nine divisions, or perhaps as few as eight.

In the meantime, three men and their staffs were working day and night on the elaborately detailed planning of an invasion for which the starting signal might never be given. These men belonged to the staffs of the Allied navies, air forces, and army ground forces; they were also part of Force 163, which included all the invasion units assigned to establishing a beachhead in southern France. An American, Brigadier General B.F.Caffey, was in charge of ground-force planning; another American, Brigadier General G.P.Saville, who was to assume command of the XII Tactical Air Command in the Mediterranean – the entire air force involved in the Provence landings – was busy with the complex details of the systematic aerial bombardment in the days immediately preceding the attack and for the Second D-Day itself. And of all these officers devoting their days, and part of the their nights, to poring over reports and endless columns of figures, doubtless the unhappiest of all were those in the little group from the personal staff of Vice Admiral Henry K. Hewitt, commander of the Eighth Fleet, whose Western Task Force would participate in Operation Anvil.

Hewitt was aware that he need no longer fear the danger of an operational enemy fleet in the Mediterranean – since the previous summer, marked by Italy's surrender, matters had changed considerably for the Axis. Hewitt had commanded the Allied fleet at Salerno, and this experience, which should have been one of his claims to glory, remained one of the most unhappy memories of his life. This veteran navy officer, who was built like a good-natured Hercules with a slight paunch, could not put from his mind the recollection of a September morning in 1943, when the Fifth Army's assault troops had narrowly escaped being thrown back into the sea. Hewitt was praying that this nightmare would not be repeated in France, for he and his officers had the sole responsibility for the landings.

He knew that when the troops started to board ship, before the first convoy was under way, the scenes of that September dawn would surge up in his memory. He doubted whether the prospect of victory could ever really ease his torment.

His role would end with the actual landing of the invasion army's headquarters on the French coast, when Patch would resume command of the assault troops. Until then, the entire responsibility for consolidating the beachhead would devolve upon the navy, as well as the responsibility for commanding nearly 100,000 assault troops until the Seventh Army commander finally took over. Besides, had not the final choice of the landing beaches been made on the strength of the navy's recommendations? And was it not Hewitt's staff that would have to prepare the itineraries and the navigation charts for the convoys, organize the supply of reinforcements, and, until the beachhead had been firmly established, support the infantry and tanks with naval gunfire? It was the ships' guns alone, as Hewitt and his officers well knew, that had been able to prevent the landing at Salerno from turning into a disaster. Furthermore, it would be his own carriers, aboard which would be the planes of Rear Admiral T.H. Troubridge of the Royal Navy, that would be called upon to provide air cover for the armada and to stand ready to intervene on the beaches in case the going got really rough.

Just as Hewitt and his staff were beginning to feel that their task was nearly over, and with it long months of worry and anguish, a thunderbolt struck.

They could not exactly call it a surprise. Despite his attitude of typical British phlegm toward the Provence landing, Wilson had steadfastly believed that this particular thunderbolt would not strike, that somehow matters would reach a satisfactory solution. He was wrong.

For Hewitt and his men it was like a deathblow. Despite all the careful calculations, despite all the complex planning, which had been revised and checked point by point, the operation was going to require such a staggering number of assault vessels – particularly LSTs, not to mention

17

the LSIs necessary for pouring forth the swarms of troops onto the beaches – that the planners had to face the hard facts – the Allied nations simply had not been able to produce enough ships.

The supply of LSTs depended upon a strict manufacturing schedule in the United States, and this schedule, already tight, allowed absolutely no flexibility for fulfilling the requirements of the risks and variations of an amphibious attack. Not only were there not enough ships left over for the landings in Provence, but even those that were assigned to the Mediterranean would now have to proceed at full speed to England to participate in the Normandy operation. An impasse had been reached.

From that moment, everyone in Algiers realized that it would be impossible to stage landings simultaneously in the Channel and in the Mediterranean. The deadline for the landing in Provence was forty-five days after the Normandy landing, or around 20 July, assuming that Eisenhower would attack across the Channel on 5 or 6 June. But because of the problem created by the shortage of landing craft, this deadline could no longer be met.

They would now have to wait until a beachhead had been firmly established in Normandy so that the landing craft that survived the fire of the batteries defending the Atlantic Wall, could then be dispatched to the Mediterranean to help assault the *Südwall*.[1] For the time being, the feebleness of the Allies' amphibious resources doomed Eisenhower's hopes and forced the unalterable separation of Operations Overlord and Anvil. Back in London, Churchill felt sure that he was about to score a point.

7

ON THE RADIANT JUNE MORNING in the Italian countryside outside Rome, a young French noncommissioned officer named Jacques Morieux, assigned to the Seventh Tank Destroyer Regiment, had just had his efforts rewarded. As his gaze strayed down over the expanse of bomb-torn vineyards below the little town of Frascati, Morieux was twirling the dial of the receiving set in his scout car, seeking the wave length of Radio Algiers, which was supposed to be broadcasting a program of light variety music.

[1] The *Südwall* (South Wall) was the name given to the German fortifications along the Mediterranean coast of France. Sometimes also called the Mediterranean Wall.

The tank crews were busy filling up with fuel and ammunition, but Morieux knew, from a message that had come in a few minutes before, that his unit would not be alerted until early afternoon. Still he could not help reflecting that, for more than twenty-four hours now, things had been happening pretty fast. The evening before, at 7.15 P.M., spearhead detachments of the United States 88th Infantry Division had reached the Piazza Venezia in the center of Rome.

On the pocket calendar he had bought in Naples, Morieux had circled 4 June in blue.

After the endless winter in the Abruzzi and along the Rapido River, spring had finally put in an appearance on the Liri plain. And there had been the memorable night of 11 May when, with two thousand Allied guns firing all the way to the sea, the Garigliano nightingales had begun pouring forth their defiant song of love, filling the Italian night with lilting tenderness. After a siege that had lasted four months, Monte Cassino had surrendered in a single morning. In turn, Rome, too, had just capitulated, and Morieux felt convinced that this was certainly the beginning of the end and that nothing now could interfere with the triumphant Allied rush to Austria – to Vienna, Prague and Berlin. Even though all this did not bring Jacques Morieux any closer to Paris, the heady air of the Roman spring imbued him with the feeling that he would be home in Montmartre by Christmas.

Morieux suddenly froze. While his mind had been straying fondly to thoughts of all the pretty girls who might be strolling along the Rue Lepic at that moment, he had not been paying close attention to the voice of the announcer, who had just interrupted the melancholy strains of Charles Trenet's song *Les Oiseaux de Paris*. Morieux snatched off his earphones.

He raced back to the command post, where Lieutenant André Soudieux, squinting into a mirror hung from the stripped branches of a war-torn olive tree, was finishing his shave. Lieutenant Soudieux – in prewar days a schoolteacher in a small Lorraine village – was thinking yearningly about a certain young woman, widowed like himself, with two children. He had met her in Tunis, and firmly intended to marry her.

'Any news, Morieux?' he asked.

'News, news? Oh, yes, Lieutenant. There's . . . there's news!' Morieux stammered.

But he could only stand there with his mouth open, oblivious to the tears streaming down his face.

He had just become one of the first Frenchmen on the Italian front to learn that the Allied landings had taken place in Normandy that morning, 6 June 1944.

The following day, Wednesday, back in Algiers in the spacious Operations Room at Allied headquarters, Lieutenant General Sir James Gammell, 'Jumbo' Wilson's chief of staff, saw his superior's face suddenly light up. The commander of the Mediterranean area, whose appearance and uniform were reminiscent of the officers in Britain's Indian army, was contemplating a huge map of Western Europe that covered one entire wall. Wilson turned toward Gammell.

Although he spoke with apparent composure, his words and the sudden brief flush on his cheeks belied his gruff impassivity.

'James,' he announced, sliding his thumb under his shoulder belt, 'I believe that we can now plan to land in France on 15 August.'

Returning to his desk, Wilson set about compiling the report he would dispatch to the Allied chiefs of staff in London. He paused only long enough to issue instructions to Gammell to proceed immediately with checking on the troop transports available in the Mediterranean and seeing to their equipment and personnel. With that, he resumed his task of drawing up the detailed list of the landing craft and combat vessels that would be urgently needed.

Although Jacques Morieux's hunch about his Christmas homecoming turned out to be accurate, he had been wrong on one score. For him, the road to Paris was not to lie through either Prague or Vienna; he would not be going to Berlin, nor would he see Florence. Less than forty days after the Allies entered Rome, not one French regiment on the Italian front would be in contact with the enemy, and all the French divisions would have been redeployed toward the south.

Already, the troops of the American 45th Infantry Division, followed closely by those of the 3rd and the 36th had been withdrawn from the front and diverted toward Naples and Salerno. For two days they would hold the Riviera beaches by themselves until the bulk of the French troops could catch up with them.

But a number of important considerations that had seemed negligible or totally insignificant were yet to come into play. One fact remained unknown for quite some time to the troops who would be spending most of the last weeks of July and early August rehearsing landings along the beaches at Salerno and Naples in anticipation of the invasion of Provence. And many of them never did learn of it. In order to throw German intelligence agents off the scent (they were swarming all over southern Italy and North Africa), it was decided to discard the code name for the landing in southern France. Operation Anvil ceased to exist, and became Operation Dragoon.

8

MEANWHILE, THERE WAS A MAN in London who could not acknowledge that he had lost out, who refused to accept the inevitable and channeled all his energies and will power into an attempt to prevent it from happening. This man was Winston Leonard Spencer Churchill.

With dire foreboding, Churchill had resigned himself ('letting a battle die,' as he termed it) to the end of the battle of Italy. The first of the Allied attacks against Hitler's fortress Europe, sagging under the heavy toll of casualties at Salerno, Anzio and Monte Cassino and stripped of its troops, was doomed to the slow decomposition of dead battles.[1] The old bulldog did not yet consider himself vanquished, and on Friday, 4 August, he resumed the discussion with a renewed attack on Roosevelt.

That day, Rear Admiral Don P. Moon, who was to direct the assault against the Saint-Raphaël coast, also did something he had been putting off for several days. He knocked on Admiral Hewitt's door. Two months earlier in Normandy, Moon had commanded Assault Force 'U' at Utah Beach, and his long hours of overwork and strain brought about by the coming landings in the Mediterranean, as well as many long, sleepless nights, had deeply disturbed him both physically and mentally. By now, his morale had reached its lowest ebb. Inside Hewitt's office, Moon made no attempt to conceal his anxiety, freely confessing his concern over the 'unreadiness' of Operation Dragoon and begging his superior to postpone the Second D-Day. Hewitt listened patiently and succeeded in calming him. To appease Moon, he promised that he would discuss the matter with General Wilson if further investigation of the Allied plans confirmed these apprehensions.

The interview had ended to Moon's satisfaction, or so Hewitt believed. But Moon had only partially retrieved his peace of mind. The minute he was alone, his misgivings assailed him anew and he slumped into a gloomy, final meditation. The next morning, Rear Admiral Don Moon committed suicide.

On this same 4 August, Second Lieutenant Philippe de Rochambeau, who was descended from a hero of the American Revolution, was

---

[1] Nine months later, at the end of the hostilities, when the Soviet army was holding four-fifths of Berlin, the armored units of General Sir Harold Alexander were still nineteen miles from Venice.

champing at the bit in an Adriatic port off Brindisi. Rochambeau, in command of a four-tank detachment of the Algerian 3rd Infantry Division, had just seen his vehicles safely aboard the troop transport *Fort Gaspereau*. For him, as well as for most of his men, the abrupt withdrawal from the Italian front did not necessarily mean that they were going to land in France. But wagers were mounting on board the *Fort Gaspereau*, and most of the men were betting on Yugoslavia as their likely destination.

On the other side of the Mediterranean, near Oran, another French soldier, Master Sergeant René Michelet, assigned to the 1st Battery of the 68th Artillery Regiment, was also biting his nails. For two days his unit had been placed on alert and confined to barracks. Michelet later recalled that 'only by going swimming could the men calm their nerves and keep from going crazy.' To help while away the time, they had also spent many hours on the cliffs over Fernandville, watching the convoys coming and going from Oran and Mers-El-Kebir.

Everywhere on that day, in the ports of Algeria, Tunisia, Corsica, Malta, Sicily and southern Italy, thousands upon thousands of men were waiting. Radio Quartermaster Sergeant Gabriel Battut was aboard the French sloop *Commandant Bory*, which had just dropped anchor off Taranto. Battut had spent the last eight months escorting convoys from one end of the Mediterranean to another. He was in Haifa when he learned about the Normandy landings. Battut had hoped that after all the constant hard work of these recent days, he and his crew might be permitted shore leave. Instead, everybody was confined to the ships, and he began wondering what the powers that be were up to now, letting the troops 'stew in their own juice there in the hot sun.'

While this fantastic concentration of men and matériel was being organized, while the huge number of vessels – over one thousand ships of all kinds – were riding at anchor or still picking their routes through the mine-infested waters, while the swarm of activity continued in all the ports, air bases, vehicle depots and ammunition dumps that were being stripped before one's eyes, while the top-secret orders were being issued from the Allied headquarters – now transferred from Algiers to Naples – to the more modest staff headquarters to direct the over-all movements of nearly 400,000 troops to their ultimate destination, a dramatic dialogue was going on between London and Washington, reviewing and reassessing the hand that was about to be played in this deadly game.

In the White House, Harry L. Hopkins had just placed on the President's desk what he would describe as a 'stupefying' cable from Churchill. After reading it, Roosevelt decided that he would not answer it – at least not right away.

General Charles de Gaulle shakes the hand of Lieutenant General Alexander
M. Patch, Jr., over-all commander of the ground troops of the landing forces in
southern France, after awarding him the Commander of the Legion of Honor,
Knight of the Legion of Honor, and the Croix de Guerre with palm. He also presented
him with the Knight of the Legion of Honor for his son, Captain Patch, who was
killed in action in France on October 1, 1944. (*Photo U.S. Army*)

Lieutenant General Alexander M. Patch, Jr. (left), commanding general of the Seventh U.S. Army, and General Dwight D. Eisenhower, Supreme Commander, AEF, during General Eisenhower's visit to the U.S. Seventh Army in France. (*Photo U.S. Army*)

Although Churchill had now abandoned his efforts to get the Provence-bound troops diverted to the Balkans, he had dreamed up a new destination for Admiral Hewitt's LSTs – 'Saint-Nazaire, or some other port along the coast of Brittany.'

Roosevelt simply could not believe his eyes.

'Winston's gone stark raving mad,' he commented to Hopkins.

And, for two days, Churchill vainly awaited a reply to his cable.

On 6 August, his message still unanswered, Churchill sent another, this time addressed to Hopkins. Although time was running out, for Churchill it was never too late. The reply that reached him the following day was, he judged, 'far from encouraging.' Roosevelt's adviser had failed to be stirred by the reminder that Saint-Nazaire and Nantes had been 'your major disembarkation ports in the last war,' nor by the port of Bordeaux's potential facilities 'for the fullest importation of the great armies of the United States still awaiting their opportunity.' Nor was he moved by the remark concerning the splendid victories that Britain and the United States had won jointly over the preceding two years, victories that, nevertheless, 'do not bring us together in strategy.'

Whatever the case, Hopkins's answer displayed hardly a trace of deference, and Churchill read it with a measure of resentment.

'While there has been no reply as yet from the President . . . I am sure his answer will be in the negative.'

The tone of this exchange in no way deterred Churchill in his determination to divert the attack planned for southern France, and the old warrior still preserved the illusion that all was not yet lost. On 7 August he paid a lunchtime call on Eisenhower's headquarters near Portsmouth. Operation Dragoon 'had to be stopped.'[1]

Since it was no longer possible to halt the boarding of troops and loading of matériel in the Mediterranean ports, Churchill was inclined to let them continue. But, once the ships set out, the convoys could swerve westward through the Strait of Gibraltar and turn north to land at Bordeaux. However, Eisenhower remained inflexible, and made it clear that he was firmly opposed to any alteration in the plans that were already being carried out.

With that, Churchill realized that he had no further recourse. On Tuesday, 8 August, when he had received Roosevelt's cable confirming the 'veto' issued by the American chiefs of staff, the Allied armada was already prepared to set sail over the ten Mediterranean sea routes laid out by the naval planners. By 10 A.M. on 9 August, the first LSTs of the tank convoy had weighed anchor off Naples and began sliding through

[1] Winston Churchill.

the water, over which a light heat mist was shimmering. Nothing was now going to prevent Operation Dragoon from being carried out.

9

FOR THREE WEEKS, an extra load of work and a whole swarm of new worries had beset General Walter Botsch, chief of staff of the German Nineteenth Army, and his aide, Lieutenant Colonel Schulz, at headquarters in Avignon.

In addition to the bad news from Normandy, which was getting worse by the hour, scarcely a day went by without the wailing of the town's air-raid sirens, followed by Allied bomber squadrons flying over and 'laying their eggs' in the midst of the ancient papal city. On Monday, 17 July, the personnel of Nineteenth Army headquarters had had to scramble for their lives out of the Dominion Hotel, on which the waves of Liberator bombers had vented their fury, and take refuge in a suburban villa that was a less prominent target.

Botsch remembered every detail of the raid – the planes had begun coming in just as he was about to sit down to a meal. The antiaircraft batteries had immediately opened fire on the B-24s, which were flying in a wide, sweeping formation at an altitude of less than 10,000 feet. One plane, hit by flak, had dropped out of the group and started to turn and spin, 'its wings glinting like those of some giant dragonfly in the sunlight,' as Botsch saw it. Almost in the next instant, a second plane had been brought down, trailing a whitish streak as it spiraled toward the earth. But the apparently endless waves of Liberators came on relentlessly, pounding the bridges over the Rhône and the Durance rivers, the railway yard, the Saint-Chamand quarter, and the burning ruins of the Dominion Hotel. Following the raid, the civilian authorities announced a total of four dead and thirty wounded.

Today, however, Botsch's uneasiness was sharpened by a more specific anxiety, one that was extensively shared by his superior, the brilliant infantry general Friedrich Wiese, whom Hitler had put in command of the Nineteenth Army, assigned to defend France's Mediterranean coast from Menton to Port Vendres.

Yet, over the last twenty months, since the beginning of the total occupation of France, things had not been going too badly. On that dawn of 11 November 1942, when Hitler had chosen to violate the

Franco–German armistice by sending his armored units clear to the Mediterranean, he had encountered only one setback – but that setback had been serious. Sixteen days after this Hitlerian display of force, the French fleet at Toulon was scuttled to prevent it from falling into German hands. The fearful din of the explosion had been followed by a fatalistic silence that, like an endless night, was to enshroud and weigh upon France for another year and a half, until the first Allied soldier set foot on the soil of Normandy.

By the end of November 1942, Germany and Italy had organized the occupation of southern France according to a strict allotment. The *Wehrmacht* had dug itself in from Port Vendres to Marseilles, and General Mario Vercellino's Italian Fourth Army was stationed along the Riviera as far as Menton.[1] By September 1943, Mussolini's arrest, the downfall of the Fascist regime, and Field Marshal Pietro Badoglio's capitulation had altered this situation by extending the *Wehrmacht*'s domination over the entire coastal area, including Corsica.

But as early as 7 June 1944, with prospects of success for the Allied forces that had begun to land on 6 June, the situation of the *Wehrmacht* began to deteriorate, particularly for the German generals and marshals who were caught up in the whirlwind of madness blowing from Berlin, and who had been forced to execute an intricate and bewildering dance that probably remains without precedent in history.

On Sunday, 1 July, Lieutenant Colonel Borgmann, who was Hitler's second-ranking aide-de-camp, paid a visit to Field Marshal Gerd von Rundstedt's headquarters at Saint-Germain-en-Laye, just outside Paris. The field marshal received from Borgmann the oak leaves of the Iron Cross and a letter signed by Hitler relieving him of his command. Von Rundstedt, the senior marshal in the *Wehrmacht*, was replaced as *OB West*[2] by Field Marshal Günther von Kluge, who had formerly commanded the German forces in the Soviet Union.

Less than two weeks later, Rommel, riding in his staff car in Normandy, was hit in an attack by three hedge-hopping Allied observation-fighter planes. Thrown into a ditch and almost given up for dead, Rommel was critically injured – he had a fractured skull, shrapnel wounds in his head, and an injured left eye. He survived, but not for long. The almost legendary former commander of the Afrika Korps, the Desert Fox, did not return to his command. At Hitler's order, Von Kluge was assigned to command both the German forces in the West and those of Army Group

---

[1] With the exception of the 'entrenched camp,' or fortified area, at Toulon, which remained under German control, with Rear Admiral Scheer in command.

[2] *Oberbefehlshaber*, or Commander in Chief, West, of the *Wehrmacht*. (Translator's note.)

B, which had been under Rommel. This state of affairs was not destined to last very long either.

The news of Rommel's accident had scarcely reached the Führer's headquarters at Rastenburg when a time-bomb exploded a few feet from Hitler during a military conference there. Although several were killed or wounded, Hitler managed to escape with burns and his uniform in shreds. The Führer's revenge was swift and merciless. The investigation revealed that, although doubtlessly Von Kluge had had no direct hand in the attack of 20 July, he most certainly knew of the plot and its perpetrators.

On Sunday afternoon, 13 August, General Botsch and Colonel Schulz were poring over a map of southern France. The two men anxiously scanned the winding line representing the 300 miles from Italy to Spain along which the divisions of the Nineteenth Army – some 250,000 troops – were spread out.

Botsch had been at his post for barely four months, and his commanding officer, General Wiese, for an even shorter time. In assigning Wiese to Provence to replace General Georg von Sodenstern, Hitler, as usual, had ordered him to hold out at all costs if anything happened along the French Riviera. Since then – early in June – the already meager reserves of the Nineteenth Army had been further reduced by regular, massive withdrawals of troops, artillery, antitank weapons, and service units. Within a few weeks three infantry divisions and two Panzer divisions had been removed from the Pyrenees to the Italian frontier for immediate shipment to Normandy.

Wiese was understandably concerned about what he could do if, by a stroke of bad luck, anything happened in his sector.

From the outset, the coast of southern France had been occupied only sparsely, unlike the rest of the country, and despite the obvious threat to his security since early in 1944. Of the Nineteenth Army's original thirteen divisions, Wiese now had only eight, including the under strength 11th Panzer, which, moreover, was directly attached to the *OKW*.[1] And the garrisons controlling the coast were made up mainly of the remnants of infantry divisions (the 716th, 198th, and 353rd) that had suffered heavily in the battle of Normandy and had been sent south. The very composition of these troops presented a new and distressing problem for the Nineteenth Army's commander.

Mixed in with the regiments that had been recruited in Germany were gradual additions of a miscellaneous assortment of battalions whose fight-

[1] *Oberkommando der Wehrmacht*, or High Command of the Armed Forces, with Hitler as its Supreme Commander.

ing capacity had not been proved, non-German troops with low morale. They were auxiliary troops of Caucasian origin – Armenians, Georgians, Ukrainians, Azerbaijanians, Poles, and still others – recruited among war prisoners and people living along the Eastern Front, and serving under German officers. General Wiese, for whom they were a never-ending source of anxiety, had been obliged to entrust these unreliable *Ost Legion* forces with the defense of the installations thrown up along the hastily fortified Mediterranean coast. Wiese wished that he had never seen the reports describing the impossibility of assigning guard duty to some of these 'recruits,' who did not even know German and were incapable of pronouncing the passwords.

The question that constantly plagued him was what would happen if an Allied landing took place in the area?

The Nineteenth Army commander feared that he knew the answer only too well. Wiese's apprehension had just assumed a tangible form. All the items of intelligence that had been transmitted since the end of July were in agreement on one point – the enemy had withdrawn troops from the Italian front and was getting ready to attack by sea along the Mediterranean coast, most probably in France.

There could be no doubt. The 185 Luftwaffe planes remaining out of the previous spring's 240 would not be adequate to repel an Allied attack on the beaches of Languedoc or Provence. In the threatened area, the *Kriegsmarine* (navy) itself could muster only eight submarines, half a dozen destroyers, the patrol boats of the Sixth and Seventh Fleets – fifteen altogether – and about thirty torpedo launches. German intelligence reports calculated at well over two thousand the number of Allied bomber and fighter planes based in Corsica and Italy. As for the invasion fleet that the Allies held ready to launch against the coast, it was considered more discreet not to estimate its strength.

As in Normandy, the fighting on the beaches would be decisive. And the defense sectors assigned to each of the eight divisions of the Nineteenth Army sometimes stretched for more than sixty miles.

General Botsch had just put through a call to Lieutenant General Johannes Bässler at Brignoles, near Toulon. Bässler commanded the 242nd Infantry Division, the only one that still had three complete regiments available. The 242nd controlled the French Riviera between Sanary-sur-Mer and Agay. This was the division that would bear the full brunt of the assault by the United States VI Corps two days later.

It was late afternoon on Sunday, 13 August. Bässler assured Botsch that, except for the routine bombing raids by the Allies, his sector was completely quiet. Because of the continuing hot weather all along the coast, his men were enjoying themselves on the beaches, along with the local French population. However Bässler had not thought it necessary to grant any leaves for the 15 August holiday.[1] Jokingly, Botsch reminded Bässler that 15 August also happened to be Napoleon's birthday.

When Botsch called General Hans Schaefer, commanding the 244th Division near Aubagne, he received an answer along similar lines. Schaefer, assigned to General Baptist Kniess's LXXXV Corps, had nothing to report. The Nineteenth Army's chief of staff was nonetheless assailed with misgivings.

After he had hung up, Botsch seemed oblivious of Schulz's presence and proceeded to lose himself in deep meditation, his head resting in his hands.

Schulz went about his duties, going and coming busily, but Botsch still did not move. The open windows let in the distant hum of the city, mingled with the shrill chirping of the birds. The first part of the day had been punctuated by two air-raid alerts, followed by a third at lunchtime. The cooler evening breezes of Provence were now wafting in a southerly direction the smoke that was blowing up from the fires still burning in the bombed areas of the Boulévard Monclar.

The shrill jangle of the telephone suddenly shattered the silence in the vast office. Schulz picked up the receiver and listened a moment before handing it to his superior.

'Army Group, General,' he said.

The calm voice of General Heinz von Gyldenfeldt, chief of staff of Army Group G, came over the wire, informing Botsch that after ten days of waiting, Hitler had at last authorized the transfer of the 11th Panzer Division stationed in the Albi and Carcassonne area. This division was now assigned to the Nineteenth Army sector.

General Botsch already knew that the order had come too late.

10

SOME 250 MILES AWAY, near Toulouse, messages were pouring into the communications center at Army Group G. They then found their way, along with the piles of reports and accumulated dispatches from the previous few days, on to one corner of General Johannes Blaskowitz's

[1] August 15, the Feast of the Assumption of the Virgin, is a legal holiday in France. (Translator's note.)

desk. The general, after looking them over, passed them on to his chief of staff. These messages contained nothing new; they were merely predictions about the imminence of an Allied landing at some point on the Mediterranean beaches.

Blaskowitz, who operated from headquarters in Rouffiac, felt that he could believe everything he read but could not be sure of any of it. He was responsible to only one superior, von Kluge, and his command covered all the *Wehrmacht* troops south of the Loire river. Blaskowitz was biding his time and awaiting developments.

As he had remarked to his officers, 'Considering the reconnaissance and intelligence means at our disposal, it must be realized that only landing itself can end any doubts by providing the answer to our question about where it is going to take place.'

And until the landing began, an occurrence that ninety-five per cent of the estimates predicted would happen in his sector, he was recommending a policy of wait and see.

For two weeks, bets had been made, speculation had been rife, and the wildest possibilities had been considered. In the beginning, the sudden increase in the number of Allied aircraft carriers in the Mediterranean had led to the belief that a landing was to be made in Turkey; however, other, more reliable intelligence pointed to an attack aimed at the Adriatic coast (Tito's visit to Naples had not gone unnoticed by German agents). By now, more serious predictions were beginning to gain favor, particularly in Berlin, where the Allied raids against Italian air bases and the systematic pounding of communications installations between Nice and Genoa made opinion veer toward an invasion of the Italian Riviera, with the purpose of attacking the rear of Field Marshal Albert Kesselring's forces. It was the favorite theory propounded by Ribbentrop's intelligence bureau on the Wilhelmstrasse. For its part, the *Kriegsmarine* G-2 (Intelligence) office was not going to be caught napping. It was convinced that only one possible interpretation could be given to the withdrawal of the French divisions from the Italian front – a landing in France. On 10 August, the *OKW* had summarily concluded that 'large-scale operations were certainly not being contemplated by the Allies for the time being.' But the very next day, German agents in Madrid and Gibraltar reported that large Anglo–American naval formations had sailed from North Africa with troops and matériel 'for an unknown destination.'

What might that destination be? As late as 11 August, the predictions of the German naval command centered once again on the Adriatic. However, everything now seemed to indicate that if a landing were actually going to take place, it would be in the Mediterranean, although it was difficult to say whether it might be near Genoa, or in southern France, or maybe in both places at once. At all events, it seemed highly unlikely that anything would be happening in the Bay of Biscay or elsewhere on the Atlantic coast.

At dawn on Saturday, 12 August, two planes of the *Luftwaffe's* IV Corps, after a reconnaissance flight over Corsica, had returned to their bases to report 'two big convoys, with seventy-five or one hundred troop transports, south of Ajaccio and proceeding toward Ajaccio . . .' The two pilots had been able to pinpoint part of the convoy – some fifty ships riding at anchor at Propriano, on the far side of the Gulf of Valinco. The Focke-Wulf pilots did not realize that they had just been flying over the first troops who, sixty-five hours later, on the night of 14 to 15 August, were to come ashore on the French mainland.

At headquarters of Army Group G, the time was now past for the often groundless speculations that had been making the rounds in the meal-time discussions of General Blaskowitz's staff officers. From intelligence relayed by double agents in the Resistance movement it appeared that the Second D-Day would be 15 August, and Blaskowitz now realized that the Allied invasion was going to take place in his own sector.

At the same time, as a general security measure, Field Marshal Kesselring's headquarters in Italy ordered the state of alert along the Italian coast changed from the second degree to the first degree. It was 12.21 P.M. on 13 August.

11

AT RASTENBURG, THE FÜHRER's military conference had just broken up when a teletype message arrived reporting Kesselring's emergency measures. But the item got lost in the shuffle of events that had been going on without let-up since early morning.

The Allied divisions in Italy were attacking Florence, and Kesselring had been ordered to blow up all the bridges over the Arno river, a mission he carried out, sparing only the oldest, the Ponte Vecchio. In Warsaw, the heroic uprising that had been launched prematurely by General Komorowski Bor was continuing under *Luftwaffe* bombardment, while planes of the RAF were trying to drop provisions and ammunition to the Polish patriots. Between the Vistula and the Neman rivers, between the Danube and Lake Peipus, in the Carpathians, on the mountain

heights and on the steppes, the Soviet attacks were relentlessly continuing, pushing back the *Wehrmacht*'s rear guard on all sides. In
Normandy, Field Marshal von Kluge, successor to Rommel and Von
Rundstedt, was experiencing the most dramatic hours of his Western
command – despite Hitler's reiterated orders, there was no longer the
remotest possibility of his breaking through toward Avranches. The
Germans had lost the battle of Normandy.

In the minds of the German High Command there was no more doubt
about what the intentions of the Allies had been since the end of July.

The aerial activity in the Mediterranean area had never before reached
the pitch of intensity that it had attained during the last few weeks. From
Sète to Genoa, in the valleys of the Rhône and the Po, highways, bridges,
railroad tracks and installations, airports, harbors and docks, radar
stations, coastal and island fortifications, beach dugouts and blockhouses, mine fields – all were being methodically pinpointed and
pounded, day and night, by squadrons of Mitchells and bomber-fighter
planes, just as they had been in Normandy during the weeks leading up
to 6 June.

Although Eisenhower had been able to effect what amounted to a
surprise attack across the English Channel, circumstances were not the
same in the Mediterranean. For weeks the *Kriegsmarine*'s G-2 and Axis
intelligence agents had been reporting innumerable troop concentrations
in North Africa, Italy and Corsica, the continuous influx of ships and
landing matériel, the presence of an airborne division in Italy, reconnaissance off the French coast, and, for two days now, the departure of a
huge attack fleet from Algerian and Italian ports, notably Oran,
Brindisi, and Taranto. This time there could be no doubt whatever.

Among the reports submitted to Nineteenth Army headquarters in
Avignon during the morning was the first specific information concerning
the route taken by the Allied armada. A group of warships that had first
been reported south of Corsica had just veered sharply north.[1] In the
opinion of Field Marshal Wilhelm Keitel, Chief of the Armed Forces
High Command (*OKW*), and the armchair strategists at the headquarters in Rastenburg there was no further question that the target was
the French Riviera.

Less than one hour after the information had reached Avignon concerning the advancing Allied convoy, Von Kluge's headquarters at
Saint-Germain-en-Laye called the *OKW* operations bureau.

---

[1] In the direction of the Gulf of Genoa, as Nineteenth Army headquarters was to believe
for some time. In all likelihood, this was an LST convoy that had left Naples at 10 A.M. on
9 August and stayed over at Ajaccio on 12 and 13 August before setting out for its ultimate
destination. Subsequent Nineteenth Army reports for 14 August also confirmed that the
convoy was bound for the Italian coast.

Since 1941, the *Wehrmacht*'s operations bureau (*Wehrmachtführungsstab*) had served Hitler as the principal military agency for the conduct of operations in the West. Walter Warlimont, an artillery general, answered the phone. He could not know that this was going to be one of Von Kluge's last calls. The caller's sudden silence twenty-four hours later was going to cause Hitler keen anxiety.

Although the attention of *OB West* was centered on the greatest peril, with the Normandy front still continuing as his main concern, Normandy was no longer Von Kluge's sole source of worry. Thus, on this Sunday morning of 13 August, Warlimont was informed that, 'on the basis of irrefutable information,' a landing in Provence might be expected any day. *OB West* even specified the area that was threatened – between the Rhône and the Var rivers.

Warlimont hastened to transmit this intelligence over the direct line that connected him with his superior, General Alfred Jodl, Chief of Operations of the *OKW*.

As often happened, Jodl that day was a long way from his headquarters. He had gone once again to join Hitler, to whom he clung like a shadow. But for the last four days Jodl had not been able to bring himself to remove from his desk a set of orders made out by Warlimont that lacked only Hitler's signature. They were orders concerning the situation in France. The truth was that, although these measures were designed simply to prevent matters from deteriorating into catastrophe, Jodl disapproved of them. And the most valid reason for his disapproval was his conviction that Hitler would not sign the orders.

Since 1 July, following the latest developments in Normandy, the operations bureau had been waging a bitter battle against its own chief and – over Jodl's head – against the Führer's strategic views and 'brilliant inspirations.' Warlimont realized there was no way out of the impasse, but calmly continued to deluge Hitler's headquarters with 'orders for signature,' which Jodl just as calmly tucked away in his desk drawer – when he did not just return them to their sender.

So, for a month, Warlimont and his staff had been pursuing a clearly defined goal – to save the pieces by ordering the withdrawal of the German forces toward the Swiss and German frontiers. But to prevent this massive operation – involving troops all over France – from degenerating into a chaotic retreat, time was of the essence. It had to be carried out before the complete collapse of the *Wehrmacht* divisions in Normandy, and certainly before an Allied landing in southern France. The only troops not affected by the withdrawal order would be those on the Mediterranean coast occupying the forts and fortified camps at Marseilles and Toulon; Kesselring's army would be assigned the defense of the Italian frontier.

Obviously, Hitler was never going to agree to sign such an order, and Jodl knew this better than anyone.

Since 2 August, he had been giving only evasive answers to Warlimont's insistent questions about the proposed withdrawal. As Warlimont later observed, 'Like Hitler himself, Jodl tended to feel that plans of this kind were designed only to be kept in a drawer.' On various occasions between 2 and 8 August, Jodl made it clear that he could not 'bring himself to accept them.'

The morning and afternoon of 13 August went by unmarked by any major changes, except that by now information was available on when and where the Allies would strike. According to Warlimont, the exact date 'was no longer a secret for anyone.' The *OKW*'s unanimous opinion was that it would be 15 August.

12

SUNDAY WAS DRAWING TO A CLOSE in the long summer twilight. At headquarters of Army Group G in Rouffiac, General Heinz von Gyldenfeldt was still awaiting a teletype message from the *OKW* permitting him to order the 11th Panzer Division to roll toward the Rhône, to cross the bridges with its tanks before it was too late. The 11th Panzer was the only armored reserve unit available to intervene immediately in southern France and, like all the other *Wehrmacht* armored detachments, it was commanded directly by the Führer.

Since the beginning of the month, as soon as it had become obvious that a landing was going to take place in the area, the Army Group had been urgently requesting the order that would authorize the tanks to rejoin the sector of the threatened Nineteenth Army. But for ten days no answer had been forthcoming from Hitler.

Jodl, 1,200 miles away, still had not been able to make up his mind to intervene with the Führer. Since mid-July, Hitler had been holed up in his East Prussia headquarters, waiting, exactly as he had done two months earlier, on that fateful 6 June. In the Toulouse-Carcassonne-Albi area, the Panther tanks of the 11th Panzer were on permanent alert, ready to start rolling on three hours' notice, but neither the headquarters at Rouffiac nor the command post of General Wend von Wietersheim, commanding the division, knew whether the order would come through in time.

In a small Languedoc village, Colonel Werner Drews, chief of staff of the 11th Panzer, rapped his cane angrily against his highly polished boots as he railed against the disastrous concept introduced by Hitler, a stultifying system that made the outcome of operations dependent on the Führer, who was hundreds of miles from the fighting fronts. Hitler's decision to assume personal direction of even his farthest-flung reserves dated back to the outbreak of hostilities. By now this totalitarian method of command, which kept his generals' hands tied by remote control and forced them into a kind of humiliating paralysis, had become an obsession.

Night had begun to fall, and it was cool and slightly misty around the lakes and forest of East Prussia as darkness shrouded the Rastenburg headquarters, the *Wolfschantze* (Wolf's Den), its green painted walls and rooftops covered with camouflage netting. The place had its own airport and was complete with a network of electrified barbed-wire barricades, mine-trapped woods, and guard posts bulging with sentries spaced every hundred feet. General Jodl suddenly decided not to wait until the next day's military conference, but to submit to Hitler then and there all the plans that his staff had worked out over the past month as instructions for the future conduct of operations in the West.

The scene that followed was what Jodl had long been anticipating. Hitler glanced through the 'plan for general withdrawal in France,' cast it aside without comment, began reading the other plans, and finally paused as he came to Order Number Three, which provided for 'resistance by all available means' along the coast of southern France. Hitler had just decided that the battle of Provence was going to be fought on the beaches.

Hitler's decision touched off a chain reaction of orders down through the echelons of command. In the Landes area between Dax and Bordeaux, the 198th Infantry Division, which had escaped from Normandy, was placed on alert, with instructions to proceed immediately toward the Rhône and Var rivers, behind the 242nd Division, which was controlling the coastal region. At Rouffiac, Von Gyldenfeldt's phone finally rang, and moments later he rushed into General Blaskowitz's office clutching a paper in his hand.

'Here's the order! It's just come through!'

He handed the message to his chief. Order Number Three, ten days late, authorized the release of the 11th Panzer's tanks and placed them under General Wiese in Avignon.

Blaskowitz heaved a sigh. He did not for a moment believe that Von

Wietersheim's armored division would be capable of driving the Allies back into the sea. What was more, he sensed that, in a way, the long-delayed go ahead signaled the beginning of an arduous ordeal for him. But his conscience was clear, and it seemed to Blaskowitz that the nervous tension that had gripped him and his staff over the preceding weeks had at last begun to relax.

Night had set in, and for the next hour, in the Toulouse-Carcassonne-Albi area, the 11th Panzer Division's sector, the tanks continued to roar along the line of departure. The engines of the light armored vehicles and the dispatch riders' motorcycles sputtered through the sleeping towns and hamlets under the frail light of the August moon. The deep, sustained roar, which was the sound of war itself, the metallic clanking of weapons, the hammering of countless boots, men's voices calling as they set out, filled the night, echoing from one end to the other of the 120 miles of the division's assigned area.

The armored cars adorned with skulls and black crosses set out from three assembly areas. It was an ideal time for traveling, in the tepid warmth of the Langeudoc night suffused with the fragrance of blooming wisteria and syringas. Old houses with venerable, mellowed façades literally shuddered as the noisy columns jolted past. Wherever possible, the division veered off on to side roads, bypassing the heavily populated regions. All vehicles were camouflaged under leafy foliage, and they proceeded in long, thinly drawn-out formations. Heading east, the hulking, low-slung steel mastodons bore down on the back-country lanes, while staff officers' armored cars and huge trucks loaded with fuel plunged at full speed along the road to Béziers and Montpellier in their race against the arrival of the dawn.

They had orders to proceed only under the protective cover of darkness, in order to elude Allied air attacks. But it did not take Von Wietersheim long to realize that even this elementary precaution had to be discarded. And he ordered full speed to Nîmes, having resolved that the division would proceed in scattered groups and by daylight.

Colonel Drews, who was to become a general, later gave his recollections of the 11th Panzer's mad dash to the banks of the Rhône, with 'the vehicles bristling with foliage, speeding along the main highways in broad daylight, leaving ample space between them, darting from one place of concealment to the next.' The idea of taking only the secondary roads had long since been abandoned, and the separate columns of tanks and cars, some of them completely isolated, and hence more vulnerable than ever, plowed steadily along France's *Route Nationale 113*. The tank commanders of Colonel Hax's 110th Regiment maintained a

35

constant alert, their guns aimed forward, ready to return instant fire against possible attacks by local resistance groups.

By the time the leading units drew near the Rhône, fifteen miles out of Avignon, it was late afternoon on 14 August. Von Wietersheim had decided to set up his command post for the night at the junction of the Nîmes and Avignon highways. He had reached Remoulins, with its suspension bridge spanning the Gard river.

Von Wietersheim fully expected to be at the banks of the Rhône and to get his tanks across the river by dawn.

13

AT ABOUT THE TIME that the 11th Panzer's leading elements were looming into sight near Remoulins, a French girl, Andrée Riccioli, was pedaling her bicycle under the sweltering August sun. She had set out from her comfortable villa at Croix-Valmer near Saint-Tropez, and was cycling on *Route Nationale 559*, along the seashore, trying to keep in the shade of the pine trees as she headed for the sleepy little resort town of Cavalaire-sur-Mer at the far end of the bay. She was bareheaded, and occasionally she panted as she bent over the handlebars of her bicycle with its worn, patched tires.

Suddenly she heard an all too familiar noise roaring out from behind the wooded slopes of Les Pradels, and a wave of bombers ripped through the sky. Andrée could make out the five-pointed American stars on the fuselages as they passed directly over her, 'like thunderbolts zooming in fast and low,' giving the alarmed girl the feeling that they were about to bear down on her and crush her to the earth.

Although she realized that this deserted, isolated road made an ideal target from the air, none of her apprehensions was fulfilled. A series of explosions rocked the summer afternoon. With fiendish accuracy, the planes had just dumped their load of bombs on the resort's one anti-aircraft battery, and already they were streaking off to disappear beyond the horizon.

Within the space of three and a half months, from 28 April to 10 August, planes of the Allied Strategic Air Forces – Lightnings, War-hawks, Mustangs, Thunderbolts, Mitchells and Liberators – had carried out no fewer than 10,000 raids, raining down 12,000 tons of bombs (twenty times more than it had taken to pulverize Monte Cassino in one day) over southern France and the Mediterranean, and causing the gradual disappearance of what remained of Germany's submarine fleet. General Sir Henry Maitland Wilson subsequently reported that of all the targets assigned to the Bomber Command, 'communications lines suffered the heaviest beating, followed by ports, factories and airfields.' The first air raid in preparation for the Second D-Day had taken place on Friday, 28 April, with an all-out foray by United States four-engine planes over Toulon. Beginning in July, the bombings in the south became intensified, and were directed particularly against the coastal areas. On 6 August – a date that the people of Toulon will long remember – 360 tons of bombs rained down on the entrenched camp in Toulon and the strategic Saint-Mandrier peninsula during an eight-hour raid aimed mainly at the docks, the port facilities, and the submarine shelters. This was one of the most devastating attacks that the *Kriegsmarine* sustained in the period leading up to D-Day. The bombers sank four submarines of the eight assigned to the 29th Fleet, and sent two tugboats and a submarine chaser to the bottom.

The total number of Allied planes concentrated in the Mediterranean amounted to some five thousand, including three thousand based on Corsica and Sardinia. In the last ten days before 15 August, the United States 12th and 15th Air Forces took turns pounding mainland France and northern Italy. Several months earlier, extensive work had been done to transform Corsica into an attack base for the Allied planes. The area around Bastia, which was ideally flat but also unhealthy, was infested with malaria-bearing mosquitoes, vigilantly fought by the medical corps. This region eventually became, as Lieutenant General Ira C. Eaker, air commander in chief in the Mediterranean theater, phrased it, the 'vital aerial platform' for the invasion. Brigadier General Gordon P. Saville had his United States XII Tactical Air Command based here, on fourteen airfields stocked with a massive reserve of bombs and ammunition of all calibers and types, and for all purposes – for night raids, for the British Spitfires, for American heavy bomber squadrons, and for the French reconnaissance and fighter groups.[1]

The big preliminary D-Day attacks began on the night of 4 August and continued without let-up until 3.30 A.M. on Tuesday, 15 August.

As General Wilson stated later: 'It had been agreed that the bombings should begin relatively early, but that they would be combined under a wider over-all program designed to inflict extensive damage in the attack

[1] The French air groups that were placed under the XII Tactical Air Command included seven groups of Spitfires and fighter planes, four groups of Marauder medium bombers, and a group of P-38 (Lightning) reconnaissance planes. In addition, French naval aviation had mustered its 2nd, 4th, and 6th Squadrons – the first two from Oran, the last from Agadir, Morocco.

area, the idea being that the final coup de grâce on D-Day would, by and large, be a relatively simple affair.'

Hence, the strategic preparation for the Provence landing began in the Rhône Valley, to prevent German reinforcements from reaching the invasion front. Air bases in Italy, in Udine, and in the Po Valley, as well as in southern France, were bombed to knock out the *Luftwaffe*'s planes.

On 7 August, three hundred four-engine bombers flying in close formation dropped bombs from Nice to Montpellier. The following day they carried out the same mission over Imperia and the Italian Riviera. On 10 August, a raid by 510 two-engine planes against the rear of the German armies retreating toward Florence sent the entire Italian coast into a state of alert and convinced Field Marshal Albert Kesselring that the Allies were preparing to land within the next few hours somewhere between Genoa and San Remo. On 11 August every radar station on the Mediterranean was bombed; the German naval command acknowledged, among other losses, the destruction of the stations at La Ciotat, Mont-Rose, and Cap Camarat, south of Saint-Tropez. On 12 and 13 August, from Sète all the way to Menton and Genoa, along the entire coast and the Rhône Valley, no one left the air-raid shelters; people ate their meals there and slept with their clothes on. Operation Nutmeg, the 'softening-up,' had entered into its terminal phase.

The heavy waves of planes streaking through the blue August sky were no longer confining themselves to flying with that majestic indifference, which thus far had merely caused local heads to look skyward in idle curiosity. The entire Côte des Maures was now taking a beating and was being attacked point by point. According to Dr Jean Verdier of Sainte-Maxime, 'The detonations gradually came closer and thick clouds of black smoke rose up threateningly behind the mountainous peaks' above Cap Camarat and the villages of Gassin and Ramatuelle. The Thunderbolts and Liberators were having a field day over Cap Saint-Pierre, in the bay at Canebiers near Saint-Tropez. 'The most fantastic air shows were being staged,' Dr Verdier recalls, 'from the terraced hills of Sainte-Maxime.' The Allied planes seemed to be 'making sport' of the coastal batteries at Les Issambres; they were pounding the mine fields and blockhouses from La Gabelle to Saint-Pons-les-Mûres.

Over the entire length of the anticipated invasion area, the sore points that had been pinpointed by Allied intelligence became the favorite targets of General John K. Cannon's bombardiers. At the entrance to the Gaillarde woods near the small seaside resort of Saint-Aygulf, the Germans had converted a road surveyor's house into a fully-fledged pillbox – the walls still had a sign saying *Ein Reich, ein Volk, ein Führer*! – but the house itself was soon gutted after a raid by the XII Tactical Air

Command; according to one witness, 'the guns lay sprawled out on their backs.' One evening, the little local train known familiarly as the 'Pine Tree Special,' a wheezy old electric conveyance running between Toulon and Saint-Raphaël, had been singled out by low-flying planes and machine-gunned as it wound its way through the Monts des Maures.

This incident, more than any other event, inspired the passengers who alighted at Beauvallon to exclaim, with no pun intended:

'By God! There's a landing in the air, all right!'

In the town of Le Lavandou, lying between Hyères and Cavalaire-sur-Mer at the foot of the Monts des Maures, there was no air-raid siren; the church bell was used to sound the alarm. The local priest, Father Arthur Hélin, had noticed that over the last few days the German garrison troops were in a state of agitation, borne out by the fact that the *Kommandantur* (headquarters) had decreed a dusk-to-dawn curfew, going so far as to forbid Father Hélin from paying visits to ailing parishioners. From the presbytery windows, the priest could see the Cap Bénat railroad signal tower 'wreathed in the fire and smoke of exploding shells and torpedoes' dropped by the Allied planes. On Sunday, two days before the landings, he had celebrated early mass at 7.30 A.M., and had been pleased to note a larger attendance than usual; but, he remembers, 'just as high mass was beginning, Colagnon, the town policeman, started ringing the church bell alert again.'

Gustave Roux, a resident of Hyères, recalls that since the end of July 'they hadn't even been bothering to sound the air raid alarm because they were in a permanent state of alert.' An eighteen year old student named Nicole Ciravegna, who had taken refuge in the basement of a building between Marseilles and La Ciotat, scribbled in her notebook:

'Bombs! Bombs! Nothing but bombs! If we don't all get killed, we may live to see Aubagne liberated!'

Between waves of planes, Nicole listened enviously to the 'song of the cicadas out in the gardens, while we are down in the cellar, passive witnesses of a battle that for us is more sound than spectacle.'

At the other end of the Côte d'Azur, near Cap d'Antibes, was a young mother, Francine Duclos, whose baby had been expected on 15 August; but little Jean-Pascal had come into the world a month ahead of schedule, on 12 July. As matters stood, Mme Duclos was glad that her son had been born prematurely, even though his natal day, too, had been marked, she remembers, by a 'terryifying air raid on Saint-Laurent-du-Var, with bombs falling right near the hospital.' Off Cap Bénat, a fisherman from Le Lavandou, Raymond Forneron, had been hit by low-flying planes attacking the Iles d'Hyères and 'had had a tough time getting back to port' in his small boat.

Irène de Morsier, who lived in Boulouris, had felt the police surveillance getting tighter around her house on Boulévard Mimosas. But she took comfort in the fact that at least the bombing raids were discouraging the Gestapo from searching her home, in which she was hiding an American intelligence agent, Allen Dimmick. Mme de Morsier's nephew, a young scientific draftsman named Alain Born, was enjoying the most glorious hours of his youthful career. Although his plans to escape through Spain had failed, Alain had managed to elude the massive requisitioning of personnel for the compulsory labor camps by working as a chauffer for a German officers' unit, and he regularly delivered to the local Resistance his sketches of German fortifications and batteries installed along the Côte des Maures. On Monday, 14 August, Alain Born could hardly contain himself for joy; every one of the guns he had reported had been hit by Allied bombers.

A few miles away, in Trayas, the postmaster, Canale, was one of the town's few residents who had not been evacuated. Now he was beginning to wonder whether this was good or bad, because the Allied bombardiers aiming at the Anthéor viaduct invariably unloaded their missiles some five miles off to the east, right where Trayas lay. As he recalls it, the 'viaduct was strong, and the marksmanship of the American bombardiers wasn't all that accurate.'

The Allied air raids had not disrupted the activities of Gabriel Cotel, a young sculptor who had escaped from a prison camp in Germany and was now hiding out, camping up in the hills above Collobrières. During his adventure, he had met one of the first Allied participants in the Provence landing, a French officer who had been parachuted over by the British. He assured Cotel that the landing was set for around 15 August on the coast of the Department of the Var.

In Hyères, after one of those alerts that she recalls 'kept coming along one right after another,' Mme Pascotto who had made a quick trip out of the shelter to pick up some food in her apartment, saw 'huge columns of dark smoke rising high in the sky over the Ile de Porquerolles and Ile de Port-Cros.' A short distance away, at Le Canadel, a quiet little beach that seemed destined to remain lost in the anonymity of all the other little coves that punctuate the coast between Le Lavandou and Cavalaire-sur-Mer, Joseph Cherrier, a gardener, distinctly saw one afternoon 'bombs falling out of planes' and striking their target – right on top of Cap Nègre.

On the far side of the Saint-Tropez peninsula, from his vantage point on the terrace of the Cogolin Hospital, Dr Joseph Salvetti was also able to make out without binoculars the bombs falling on the tiny hamlet of Saint-Pons-les-Mûres. As he watched the planes describing semicircles over his head, he could not help wondering why the American bombers so consistently spared Cogolin.

On the afternoon of 14 August, a German soldier from Berlin named Kurt Schroeder, a member of the 148th Division, was looking on from a distance while the Gulf of Fréjus underwent a heavy bombardment, with great smoke clouds mushrooming above it. With four companions from the 15th Communications Company, he was taking a dip in the sea near the rocks, occasionally harpooning whatever stray fish might happen along.

Paradoxically, Schroeder felt himself to be secure. In his unit there was no more talk of an Allied landing and the war itself seemed to have assumed an almost incongruous aspect – as if nobody quite believed in it any more. His company was suffering from a shortage of vehicles, fuel and ammunition; the batteries in the radio transmitters were dead, and of the two machine guns that were still able to fire, one was of Czechoslovak make and the other of British. But the young German's morale was high. His only regrets were for his erstwhile companions, most of whom, since the beginning of 1944, had been sent either to the East or to Normandy. Most of Schroeder's fellow soldiers were Poles and Armenians, some of whom could speak only a few words of German.

The case of Leopold Bobinski, for example, was the strangest of all. He was a mechanic whose father had died in a concentration camp, whose mother and sister had disappeared, and one of whose brothers was fighting with General Anders's forces.[1] But as far as Schroeder was concerned, the worst fate of all would have been to be sent to the Russian front. So far, his 8th Infantry Regiment had managed to slide through, and had not moved from the French Riviera. But within a few hours everything was going to change, and Schroeder would find himself hurled right into the midst of the chaos of war, débâcle and death.

For the time being, however, he was happy and without a care in the world as he splashed around among the rocks. The sun was high in the sky, the temperature was still hot, and the Mediterranean was as smooth as glass. This was really living it up, and Schroeder felt himself completely '*wie Gott im Frankreich*.' Meanwhile, the planes continued dropping their bombs over the Gulf of Fréjus.

A short distance away, Warrant Officer Karl Heinz Riecken, assigned to a coast artillery battalion, saw planes bearing down on him.

Riecken had been tensely awaiting the landing, and for the last three weeks the thirty men under him had been anything but idle. As he

---

[1] General Wladyslaw Anders, who was taken a Soviet prisoner early in the war, led Polish forces recruited among prisoners in Soviet camps. He fought in Italy, joined the II Polish Corps, and had a distinguished record at Monte Cassino. (Translator's note.)

expressed it, 'If the Allies happen to come anywhere near me, everything is ready to receive them!' Near the railroad tracks between Saint-Raphaël and Cannes, between the beaches of Agay and Le Dramont, antitank trenches and ditches had been dug, a flame-thrower solidly ensconced in its concrete pit, four battery positions prepared for 20-mm. Oerlikon guns, and, as a finishing touch, there was a machine-gun nest covering the position. Riecken was proud of himself and sure of his fortified battery.

At about 5 P.M. he had come out for a last look around. Then, feeling that he more than deserved a leisurely swim, he removed his boots, undressed, and ran down to the water's edge. He had barely had time to get his toes wet when the throbbing din of a wave of bombers filled the air. Riecken thought he had never seen so many at one time. With a fearful howl, the first string of bombs started coming at him, the machine guns of the Thunderbolts crackled, and streams of tracer bullets ricocheted off the rocks. Under this onslaught, it seemed to Riecken that the sea was boiling and that the earth was heaving; whirlwinds of fire and smoke were whipping up wherever he looked along the shore. Dazed and half-blinded by the explosions, Riecken managed to get to the beach and ran stumbling for shelter. The bombardment seemed to be growing heavier ever second, and Riecken clenched his fists in helpless, frustrated anger because the antiaircraft guns that he had been promised were still sitting in Toulon. (As it so happened, he learned later, these guns had already been smashed to smithereens.)

When the planes had finally dropped their last bomb and turned back, Riecken crept out from the big, jagged rock on the beach under which he had taken refuge. Still clad in his bathing trunks, he ran all the way to his battery. A glance told him everything. Although the blockhouses had held up – none of his thirty men had been injured – the mine fields and trenches were an unrecognizable mass of craters, and not a trace remained of the gun batteries; the flame-thrower pit had been wiped out, and the nearby railroad tracks had been chewed up like so much mincemeat.

After taking in the extent of the disaster, Riecken did not let himself give way to discouragement. He gathered his men together, grabbed a shovel, and pitched in to help clear away the debris and rubble.

The bombing raids were not the only form of attack. Late one morning, when the sun had already climbed high overhead, two planes flaunting American stars had boldly come in, flying low over Sainte-Maxime, stupefying the villagers with their daring, and striking terror into the hearts of the civilian 'conscripts' who were at work on the concrete pillboxes on the beach at Nartelle under the supervision of Todt Organization foremen.

However, on this occasion, the planes released only a few empty belly tanks, which the terrified onlookers at first took for delayed-action bombs. Then the twin-boom Lightnings, the world's fastest reconnaissance planes, soared up and away and vanished over the horizon.

The French pilots of the 6th Squadron were taking turns with the Americans under Major General Cannon in these forays over France. As they sat in their plexiglass-enclosed cockpits, flying Lightnings from which the guns had been removed to make room for five automatic cameras, they could not resist a feeling of nostalgia. Here they were, flying over the blessed region of France, a true earthly paradise, and antiaircraft batteries now marred the wide beaches on which carefree bathing beauties had once preened themselves.

As a French pilot declared, 'For everybody who was streaking around through the skies here, these missions had gradually become sheer hell.'

On a Monday in the latter part of July, a Lightning from the French 2/33 Reconnaissance Group had taken off from Borgo, near Bastia, in Corsica. The weather was fine and warm.

The pilot, who was alone, had pulled on over his flying suit a 'triple, stifling poultice' consisting of his Mae West life jacket, a parachute, and a bullet proof vest to protect him from flak. He knew that his was his last take-off, that this mission over France was to be the last one of all those for which, over the preceding two months, he had managed to get his commanding officers' consent. He had long ago passed the age limit and was scheduled to go on reserve duty. In fact, it had required nothing less than the personal intercession of General Eaker, commander of the Allied air forces in the Mediterranean, to get him special authorization for five flights. He had already made eight. This would be the ninth mission for this forty-four year old Frenchman. He was Major Antoine Marie Roger de Saint-Exupéry.

The P-38 steadily pursued its course to the rhythm of its two engines, out over the Mediterranean toward its objective, which was the region of Grenoble and Annecy. Saint-Exupéry had taken off from Bastia around 8.30 A.M. with enough fuel for six hours; the deadline for his return was 2.30 P.M. On the morning of 31 July 1944, Saint-Exupéry and his fellow flyers did not yet know that the landing for which all these preparations were going on would take place in Provence, nor that the Allied forces would be attacking within two weeks. What he was even farther from dreaming was that, in order to keep him pacified until the big day, his superiors had decided to let him in on the secret. On his return from

43

Annecy, Saint-Exupéry was to be called in for a briefing by the squadron leader. More important still, the invasion was going to take place in the Department of the Var, where Saint-Exupéry's sister, Mme d'Agay, lived.

It was now past 1.30 P.M., and the Lightning, with only one hour of gas left, had not returned to base.

Later that afternoon, First Lieutenant Vernon V. Robison of the Army Air Forces put his daily report sheet into his typewriter and typed the date in the upper right-hand corner – 31 July 1944. On the left side he entered the pilot's name, Major de Saint-Exupéry; after it, the take off time, '0845, time out.' But the space opposite 'time in' remained blank.

At the bottom of the page, in the space provided for 'general observations,' Robinson added: 'Pilot did not return, is presumed lost.'

Tonio de Saint-Exupéry, the aviator-novelist, did not return.

On the aerial photographs developed by the Allied intelligence laboratories, the three light-colored coaches of the little Toulon-Saint-Raphaël train stood out clearly against the dark background of the woods at Les Maures. On closer scrutiny through a magnifying glass, what looked like a train actually turned out to be camouflaged German fortifications and blockhouses. When this ruse was disclosed, the Allied experts began examining with suspicion every slightest anomaly that occurred on the thousands and thousands of photographs in their files. It was discovered that the Germans had taken the trouble to paint what resembled entire convoys of *Wehrmacht* trucks along the highways and byways of southern France.

The aerial photographs turned in daily by the reconnaissance flyers soon provided a staggering mass of accurate information, including no fewer than twenty-three photographic 'mosaics' representing the German defenses that would confront the assault troops on D-Day. By the end of July, complete sets of top-secret staff maps had been printed for the unit commanders, to whom they would be distributed on the basis of sectors and times of operating assignments. These maps contained, over-printed in red, artillery positions, machine-gun nests, bunkers and pill-boxes, mine fields, and the categories of roads able to accommodate the various types of vehicles – jeeps, DUKWs, the big 2½-ton General Motors trucks, and the tanks of the invasion forces. However, it was expected that the Allied bombers would have wiped out the bulk of the fortified positions before the D-Day landings and attacks began.

Monday, 14 August, marked the terminal phase of the action assigned to the Strategic Air Command. On that date, D-Day minus 1, fighter and bomber planes carried out a last raid against all the coastal radar stations, and the 47th Bombardment Group again attacked all the air bases from which the Dornier 217s, the JU-88s, and the Focke-Wulfs might try to take off the following morning. The RAF's Halifax and Wellington planes staked off the port of Marseilles as their own private hunting preserve, while Liberators of the United States 12th Air Force poured down a deluge of blockbusters on Genoa and the surrounding area.

The waves of medium Mitchell and Marauder bombers – 244 of them – began looming up in the August sky over the Iles d'Hyères, the Monts des Maures, and the Esterel heights. And suddenly, as if the fires of the Apocalypse were blazing up to make an inferno out of the entire coast, flames and huge columns of black smoke and whirling dust spouted forth from the craters hollowed out by the bombs and the explosions. On a forty-five mile front, squadrons of Allied planes defied the *Kriegsmarine*'s vicious flak and pounded away at the beaches, on which, at the dawn of the next morning, the troops would be wading ashore.

14

IN SAINTE-MAXIME, Father Célestin Buisson was walking sadly along in front of his venerable church, which stood in one corner of the port. He could not go inside because of the bristling network of obstructions and barbed-wire entanglements. Like all the buildings along the waterfront, the parish church, which was dedicated to a young seventh-century Provençal saint, had been evacuated by order of the *Kommandantur*. But what made the priest's cup of bitterness run over was the fact that his beloved church was being used as an arsenal by the Germans. Father Buisson refused to let himself even think what might happen to the beautiful seventeenth-century marble altar if by some ghastly mischance the Allied bombs came hurtling down to make a direct hit. For the last six months he had had to resort to holding his services in a room in the municipal casino, on the stage of which the local Philharmonic Society's orchestra usually performed. It was beyond Father Buisson's wildest dreams to imagine that his humiliating exile was about to draw to a close, and that, within the next twenty-four hours, the bell tower of the Sainte-Maxime church was going to be the setting for a tragi-comic incident in the fighting that would free the little town from the Nazi yoke.

45

Nearby, between La Nartelle and Pointe-des-Issambres, in the pine woods at Val d'Esquières, stood the comfortable home of Maximim Rivaud, a local lawyer. Although he had so far managed to stave off the requisitioning of his property Rivaud was conscious of the tightening vice. Networks of barbed wire surrounded the neighboring houses, and for several hours now, a far more ominous threat had been menacing the sixty-five year old president of Sainte-Maxime's bar association. On 14 August, two German soldiers had come with a bucket of paint and a clumsy brush and smeared a black cross over one corner of his wall.

This was their way of informing Rivaud that his villa, which formed part of a group of buildings slated for demolition, would be dynamited on 17 August.

Monday afternoon was scorchingly hot, and at times the air seemed almost suffocating. Many of the people living near the shore were making the most of the brief respites between air raids to go swimming off the rocks and beaches that had not been mined. And it was obvious that the German soldiers had had the same idea.

In her house on Cap Nègre, Suzanne Ferrandi[1] was not suffering too much from the heat. A light sea breeze kept finding its way to the high sheer cliff, bringing a refreshing coolness. The Ferrandis owned a large estate, one of the most prominent in the area because of its location and because of the exquisite taste and lavish comfort that characterized it. The steep, rocky face of Cap Nègre, plunging down from vertiginous heights, extended out into the deep waters between the beaches of Cavalière and Pramousquier. On this 14 August, a bluish haze hovering over the entire Mediterranean made it impossible to distinguish with perfect clarity the neighboring Iles d'Hyères.

André Ferrandi, an overworked businessman, was at his desk in his library on the ground floor of the villa, which somehow resembled a vast, luxurious dove cote nestling amid cypresses, sea pines and feathery mimosa foliage, its wide bay windows opened out toward the Mediterranean. Ferrandi had always had a consuming interest in everything connected with aviation, and close friends knew that he had distinguished himself in World War I as a member of the famous 'Stork Squadron.'

Suzanne Ferrandi heard her children scampering down the stairway that led to the miniature port and the small private beach. She hesitated a moment, wondering whether she would go out to join them. Behind the

---

[1] A few of the witnesses to, and involuntary participants in, the Second D-Day – six altogether – requested not to be personally identified in this book. These people have therefore been designated under fictitious names. They include, among others, Suzanne and André Ferrandi.

house, Nicholas, the Russian maître d'hôtel, stepped quietly over the gravel around the pool. The fragrance of the rose laurels and the last stalks of blooming stock basking in the August sun was as strong as a concentrated scent. To the casual observer it might have been a day like any other, at siesta time. But, since the day before, the Allied planes seemed to have had it in for the Ferrandis' estate.

Father Hélin, the priest in Le Lavandou, recalls that, for twenty-four hours, Cap Nègre, which local residents were fond of comparing to a 'big policeman's hat,' had become a 'sort of bald mountain tonsured by bombs.' Some weeks before, the attention of Allied intelligence had been drawn to the fact that Cap Nègre contained a formidable battery of three 155-mm. guns overlooking the beaches on which the French commandos were to land. So far – and this seemed incredible to the Resistance fighters who had transmitted warning after warning – this battery had been spared. However, since 13 August, the situation had changed, and the feverish activity around the rocky promontory was a sure sign that the planes of 12th Air Force had hit home.

As Mme Ferrandi was joining her children on the beach, the troops from a *Kriegsmarine* detachment had just finished setting up a battery of 77-mm. field artillery pieces on one slope of Cap Nègre.

Back in Trayas, the postmaster Canale, sitting at his desk, felt a surge of elation. Allied planes had finally scored a direct hit on the Anthéor viaduct. However, since only two of the structure's nine arches had been damaged, Canale could not help thinking that the planes would be returning to finish the job. He did not know that, for several weeks, a few Resistance workers had also been vainly attempting to destroy the viaduct, which overlooked one of the landing beaches.

In Saint-Raphaël, at the far end of the Gulf of Fréjus, Father Jean Latil found himself in nearly the same predicament as Father Buisson in Sainte-Maxime. His big Church of Our Lady of Victory, a modern, neo-Byzantine structure, was situated within the vast perimeter of the German fortified camp. It had been closed off to its parishioners, and the priest had taken refuge in the Church of St Peter. At this moment, with the help of some of the little girls, the 'servants of Mary' in his flock, who were bringing in armloads of fresh flowers, he was decorating the old altar as best he could. The girls seemed to have organized some sort of plot, and the church was beginning to resemble a hothouse. It was, as he recalls, as if 'all of Saint-Raphaël's gardens had been innocently plundered so that the shrine could be decked with flowers' for the following day's religious celebration, the Feast of the Assumption. However, on this 15 August, there would be neither a procession nor altar stations,

47

and although Father Latil planned to hold a few services, he was anxiously wondering whether he would have time to get around to performing all of them.

In Le Lavandou, Father Hélin did not intend to have any service. In Saint-Tropez, the members of the congregation who dropped by the church were told that Father Joseph Massel was planning no special religious service for the Feast of the Assumption. Like most of his parishioners, Father Massel expected to spend most of the day staying under shelter, but he did not dream that this day would begin much earlier in Saint-Tropez than elsewhere along the coast.

Between Saint-Raphaël and Boulouris, a short distance from the beach at Le Dramont, the tiny locality of La Péguière lay drowsing under the heat, shaded by eucalyptus and palm trees. La Péguière was the home of only a few hundred people, and even they, as in almost every other settled area in the vicinity, had been evacuated the previous spring by order of the Germans. The Born family had been evacuated like everybody else, and, in a sense, more so than anyone else.

However, the Borns had been lucky enough to remove most of the furnishings from their comfortable seaside villa, which commanded a view over most of this stretch of coast. Suzanne Born had hastily dug a trench in which she had buried the collection of porcelain and bronzes inherited from her father. Immediately afterward, a detachment of twenty troops from the German 242nd Division, all of Slavic origin except the *Feldwebel* (sergeant) who commanded them, had barricaded all the roads leading into La Péguière and entrenched themselves in the town.

What kept preying on Suzanne Born's mind was that the Saint-Cyr cap,[1] the shako belonging to her brother Martin, who was serving with the Free French forces, had been left in the attic of the old mansion. Suzanne had virtually lost all hope of ever seeing the Allied troops land on this bit of the Esterel coast, which she described 'so steep and so difficult of access.' She could not suspect that, for the last several weeks, in the Bay of Naples, a unit composed of eighty assault craft under the command of an American naval officer, Captain Robert Morris, had been rehearsing in detail every phase of a landing in front of a model of La Péguière and the beach of Le Dramont, which were destined to be the stage of some of the most intense activity on this second D-Day.

Lidia Airaud, her husband, and their two children had been living for four years on a farm in the back country of the Department of Var, near

[1] Saint-Cyr was formerly France's military academy, the equivalent of West Point. It was destroyed in World War II and is now Coëtquidan Guer. (Translator's note.)

Fayence, in the township of Tourrettes, amid vineyards, cork-oak forests and pine trees.

On the evening of 14 August, Airaud returned to Fayence from Saint-Raphaël. In 1939, he had been granted an army discharge for poor eyesight, and since then the Germans had not bothered him. However, in late July he had been summoned to appear before the Compulsory Labor Organization Board,[1] and now he was about to be sent off to Germany. On this Monday night Lidia set out to meet her husband along the Fayence road. At the entrance to the town, on the left side of the boulevard, stood several villas, one of which belonged to the mayor of Tourrettes, Fleury Giraud. He smiled pleasantly at Mme Airaud, whose thoughts were concentrated on the dismal prospect of having her husband taken from her.

'Don't worry, Madame Airaud,' said the mayor. 'Before then plenty of things are going to happen, and I feel that I can tell you a secret . . .'

Giraud stepped forward and whispered in Lidia's ear:

'It'll be pretty soon now!'[2]

At the Airauds' farm up on the hill there was no electricity, and no radio. Aside from the local papers, which could publish only Vichy-managed news, there were only the rumors and gossip handed on from one neighbor to the next. Lidia Airaud continued on her way, feeling her spirits lifted in spite of everything. True enough, for some time now there had been talk of an Allied strike in the south, but Fayence was remote from the sea, and certainly this tiny stray hamlet tucked in between Grasse and Draguignan had not attracted the attention of the Allied staffs.

Lidia Airaud was right. There was no mention of Fayence whatever in the Allied invasion plans except perhaps as one of the innumerable Provençal villages through which General Patch's Seventh Army might pass. Things were going to happen quite differently before sunrise on 15 August, but no one could have predicted it.

The estate of Valbourgès, twenty miles south of Fayence, was lying somnolent under the late afternoon heat, although the sun had now begun to set. James Stevens's gaze rested on the calm surface of the large elliptical pool behind his house. Although he had lived most of his fifty-four years in France, Stevens had retained his British citizenship.

The château of Valbourgès, a handsome big building with an ancient

[1] Known to the French as the *STO*, or *Service du Travail Obligatoire*. (Translator's note.)

[2] Mayor Giraud was doomed to be the first Frenchman killed in Tourrettes, during the German garrison's counterattack against General Robert T. Frederick's First Airborne Task Force. There was no carpenter available to make a coffin for his body, and the local farmers built one out of a few old wooden planks.

chapel and two wings housing the servants' quarters, stood on a hilltop overlooking the valley of Nartuby, between Draguignan and Le Muy, amid wooded hillocks that were the favorite haunt of cicadas.

Stevens was thinking about his friend Pierre Fradin, who was expected to come over from Sète for the holidays. He wondered whether Pierre could make it by nightfall. In any case, Stevens would wait up, assuming that his friend would disregard the curfew. The great house at Valbourgès was filled with relatives and friends, refugees from Marseilles and other places on the coast, not to mention the families of the local farmers. Like Lidia Airaud in Fayence, Stevens had no idea that within a few hours everybody around him would be thrust abruptly into the heart of the fighting, nor that the hamlet of La Motte, on whose territory his property was situated, would be the first Provençal settlement to be liberated by the Allied forces.

Not far away, at Le Muy, François Jacquemet, a foreman in the local cork factory, and his wife were wondering whether they would ever see their son Claude again. The youth had just turned twenty in February. The last they had heard was that he was in a small Algerian town called Staouéli; the name did not mean much to the Jacquemets. They were unaware that this was the location of the training center of the First Shock Battalion, which was being given special instruction including paratroop training, in carrying out sabotage missions on the enemy's rear. By now, however, Corporal Claude Jacquemet had left Algeria and was somewhere in Italy, south of Rome. For seventeen hours now, on this 14 August, Claude had known that by the following evening he was going to be able to give his mother the greatest and happiest surprise of her life.

'Just think! No – you can't imagine how it's going to feel!' the young paratrooper was saying to a fellow soldier from Provence, Corporal Jean Folliero de Righi. 'I'll be knocking on the shutters of my own house, just about the time the old man'll be starting out for the factory!'

Events were going to turn out differently from what Jacquemet imagined. But there on the Italian seashore, at the air base near Ostia, the young soldier could think only about the extraordinary bit of luck that fate had reserved for him.

That same afternoon, the Countess de Saint-Exupéry, the pilot's sixty-nine year old mother, had made a short trip to Grasse, less than two miles from the hamlet of Cabris in which she lived. Marie de Saint-Exupéry's husband had died in 1904 and her younger son, François, during World War I. Since then, the aging woman had had her full share of troubles. Her elder son, Antoine, had given her plenty of cause for concern, and it had been four years since she had seen him – not since he had gone to the

United States at the end of 1940. But now she had reason to believe that this separation would soon be over.

The Countess was on her way to pay a call on a worker's family in Grasse to whom she secretly gave a large share of her food ration coupons. At the corner of the big square, the Place du Patti, she ran into a friend who, in contrast with her usual habit, kissed her.

'Don't give up hope, my poor Marie,' said the friend. 'I heard the news over the radio, but that doesn't mean we mustn't hope . . .'

Countess de Saint-Exupéry instinctively placed her hand on her heart. The intuition that had never failed her whenever her son was involved, had just given her a warning, once again.

She stood there barely able to draw a breath, her eyes downcast, lips pressed together.

'And anyhow,' the friend continued, 'maybe Antoine's only been injured, or taken prisoner. Anything's possible, you know. We mustn't despair . . .'

The other members of Antoine de Saint-Exupéry's family had heard through a BBC broadcast in early August that he was missing. Mme d'Agay, one of the pilot's sisters, had concealed the news from her mother. Who could say whether Tonio had been captured by the enemy? Perhaps he had just been shot down and had found refuge with a Resistance group. There were so many unverified rumors making the rounds . . .

When she returned from Grasse, Marie de Saint-Exupéry went out into her little garden and sank into a chaise-longue, where she sat facing the sunset. That was where her daughter found her, and the mother had only to clasp her daughter's hands in her own, without uttering a word, her eyes shining with a single light of infinitesimal hope.

That same evening, François Onorati met with some other members of his Resistance group in Le Lavandou. From now on he was to be just one more anonymous figure among all the others – and furthermore, he was in hiding. Until the day before, Onorati had been the assistant to Amiel, the head keeper at the Titan lighthouse on the Ile du Levant. For eight months, since the mass evacuation of the population, the two guardians and their families had been the island's sole inhabitants, except for the German garrison stationed there.

And for the two preceding days things had become utterly impossible. Onorati knew that in the event of an Allied landing the *Kriegsmarine* troops, who maintained an unceasing vigil, would blow up the lighthouse. They would set off the two detonators connected to the two containers of cheddite and to the explosives in the magazine. Under the circumstances, Onorati knew what his duty was, and his mind had long since been made up.

By his calculations, in under ten days the Ile du Levant had been subjected to fourteen air raids by the Allied planes that flew over to spread their carpet of bombs on the Titan promontory between the lighthouse and Pointe-de-la-Reste. In mid-morning on 12 August, the sky was once more filled with the ear-splitting roar of the Lightnings and the Mitchell bombers coming in over the Iles d'Hyères. One bomb fell on the underground shelter in the Ile du Levant, into which the guardians' wives had fled as soon as the planes were heard. Mme Amiel had panicked at the idea that she might be buried alive and had dashed back out of the shelter, despite the low-flying planes that were bombing and strafing everything that moved on the island. The frightened woman kept running about aimlessly, and was finally struck by a bullet in one shoulder; a German sailor near her was killed by the fire of the Lightnings.[1]

The following day, five more violent raids occurred on the island. François Onorati realized that his wife and children would go mad if they did not escape from the bombardments. From time to time a few fishermen from Le Lavandou came to cast their nets in the waters around the Ile du Levant. On the morning of 13 August, Onorati began keeping an eye out for them. When one eventually approached, the lighthouse assistant hailed its occupant. The fisherman agreed to take some passengers on board, and Onorati ran back to get his family.

He also did something else. While the German troops were occupied elsewhere, he managed to get into the magazine, where he removed the pin that primed the explosives and put the two big detonators out of commission. He then hurried his wife and children over to the cove and got them safely embarked on the fishing boat. It was a glorious summer day, and if it had not been for the maddening cycle of the planes returning hour after hour to smash the coasts and the islands, Onorati could almost have imagined that he and his family were setting out on a joyful picnic. But he was fully aware that he was merely trading off one danger for another. François Onorati had now become a fugitive, a hunted man.

For several days a big gazogene[2]-equipped Buick kept breaking down on *Route Nationale 74* near the small village of Puligny, to the south of Dijon. Each time this occurred, two men and a woman would clamber

---

[1] As a result of the intensive air raids on the Ile du Levant in July and August, Amiel and his wife required extensive treatment at the psychiatric hospital in Pierrefeu-du-Var.

[2] Gazogene is a transformer of coal or wood into combustible gas. (Translator's note.)

out onto the road and get busy. When the repairs were completed, the Buick would chug off again amid the din of its 'gazo.'

Before the war, Paul Cabanon had been a manufacturer of kitchen stoves; subsequently, he had converted his factory to produce incendiary bombs for the French War Ministry. Since the armistice, he had been confining himself to running his small estate at Corpeau, on the Côte-d'Or.

On Monday, 14 August, toward the end of the afternoon, Cabanon's Buick again stopped dead on the way out of Puligny, this time on a bridge spanning a slender stream. The breakdown routine was again re-enacted. Cabanon was putting on an impressive display of raging temper.

'This goddamned jalopy!' he stormed. 'Always giving out in the middle of nowhere! It's that blasted "gazo" again!'

Mme Cabanon alighted from the rear door just as two Feldwebel started over the bridge on their bicycles. They did not even cast a backward glance. Cabanon whispered to the car's third occupant:

'Armand. Make it snappy! Quick, hand me the oil can! And whistle when you're ready!'

Armand Plat, once a foreman in Cabanon's factory, crawled under the car. A few minutes later he whistled softly, and Cabanon crawled under with him. On the arch of the bridge, Plat had laid bare the lead sheathing of a telephone cable containing 450 long-distance lines over which calls were put through between northern and southern France.

A few years before the war, Paul Cabanon had happened to witness the laying of the Lille-Marseilles underground coaxial cable. Later he had begun manufacturing explosives, and since April 1944, he had been a member of the Resistance. He had suggested to his group leader, Jean Régnier, that they sabotage the telephone cable, which was vital for liasion between the German armies in the south of France and the general headquarters of Von Kluge – *OB West* – in Saint-Germain-en-Laye.

The cable lay along the arch of the bridge over the stream at Puligny, and Cabanon had instantly realized the opportunity it afforded. Except for the garrison of mediocre troops occupying the village, there was no special surveillance over the little bridge at Puligny-Montrachet, despite the fact that over it, for some twenty feet, there ran the only long-distance cable used by the occupation forces.

Régnier had willingly agreed to Cabanon's suggestion, but instructed him to do some preliminary work by opening up a hole in the span so that the cable would be ready for sabotage when the time came. Régnier and Cabanon had adopted a code word, to be used in the course of an ordinary conversation, for launching the final phase of the operation. On the afternoon of 14 August, Cabanon found out that it was to be for that very night, and that the landings in the south were only a few hours away.

After exposing the lead covering, Plat and Cabanon used the oil can to pour in twelve gallons of dilute sulfuric acid, designed to short-circuit 165 feet of cable. The two men next attached to the cable an explosive charge with a delayed-action fuse. Mme Cabanon kept watch. When they finally climbed back into the car, she was white as a sheet, and both men were sweating as they had never sweated before. Cabanon's watch pointed to 7 P.M. By his reckoning, the explosion would not go off for six hours.

Right on schedule, at 1 A.M., a dull boom shattered the calm of the August night, and then all was silent. After the initial alarm, the Germans did not notice anything amiss. Even the next morning, the team of engineers sent to repair the line thought at first that it was just a simple break. When the Germans finally realized the extent of the damage, which would necessitate replacing 230 feet of cable, they were furious. Angèle Protoy, the daughter of the café-keeper in Corpeau, was about to cross the bridge when she stopped short in stupefaction. As she started back, three German soldiers set upon her and began beating her, without the poor girl's even knowing why.

The cable repairs required forty-eight hours, during which time direct communication between the *Wehrmacht*'s headquarters near Paris and the German troops in Provence was disrupted. Service was not resumed until dawn on 17 August. By then the Allied beachhead had been firmly established.[1]

15

IN MARSEILLES, ON THE SECOND FLOOR of a building on the Rue de la Darse, a man was enduring the most anguished evening of his life. He knew that the Allied landing was imminent. Everything that he had been preparing for, at the risk of his life, was now about to come into being.

---

[1] For four days, Paul Cabanon thought the Germans were off his trail. On the night of 18 August, he went out to pick up some arms that had been dropped by parachute. He still had not returned by the morning of the 19th when the Germans came to his house. They found Mme Cabanon alone and took her away in place of her husband. His house and factory in Corpeau were burned down, but Cabanon had been warned in time. Meanwhile, a convoy of women deportees – Madame Cabanon among them – was en route to the Ravensbrück concentration camp.

Prime Minister Winston Churchill, Under Secretary of War Robert P. Patterson, and Lieutenant Commander J. W. Rylands (commanding officer of the *Kimberley*) watch the progress of the invasion. (*Photo Imperial War Museum*)

The British battleship *Ramillies* bombarding the coast. (*Photo Imperial War Museum*)

A night shot of the air raid on Saint-Tropez harbor, southern France. (*Photo U.S. Army*)

And yet, an implacable order, one from which there could be no appeal, had just cut him off from the realization of his finest victory. The entire high command of the Resistance movement in southern France had been reorganized.

The man's name was Louis Burdet, but few of those around him – not even his closest friends – knew his true identity. Among the members of the Provence underground, Burdet was known as 'Circumference,' and he was the London-appointed chief of 'R-2,' the area of the French Forces of the Interior (FFI) in which the Second D-Day landings were to take place. Louis Burdet had sweated it out in England for months waiting to be parachuted into France. At last, on a February evening in 1944, a plane had dropped him on a plateau in the Jura. The first bed occupied by the chief representative from London for the seven departments of the south coast of France was to be in a Lyons brothel.

Burdet was forty-four years old. The dramatic episode in his career as the Provence Resistance leader occurred on Monday, 5 June, the night before the Normandy invasion. On that evening, the BBC had continued transmitting for longer than usual the customary personal messages that thousands of French people waited for and listened to in secret. Just before he left London, Burdet had been given five intricately devious sentences. They had been devised by a French officer on the London staff, Captain Mamy, and when they were broadcast, they would be the signal for the immediate execution of various sabotage operations and uprisings throughout France. On the evening of 5 June, the five sentences had been broadcast. Yet Louis Burdet was assailed by misgivings.

The Allies had not yet landed, and in only a few hours Resistance fighters were to rise up and attack German garrisons all over France.

Burdet wondered anxiously what would happen if Eisenhower's forces were hurled back into the sea. Suppose the landings failed?

And even if one adopted a less pessimistic outlook, how could one conceive of small handfuls of men and women fighting, harassing the Germans, in places that were hundreds of miles – *several* hundred miles away, as far as the underground in southern France was concerned – from the real battlefield? Was it possible that General Pierre-Joseph Koenig, who was Eisenhower's special aide and the commander-in-chief of the FFI, could have deliberately issued such an order when everything about it pointed to total disaster?

It was not long before events confirmed Burdet's forebodings. While the Normandy landings were taking the Germans by surprise, while the supposedly invulnerable Atlantic Wall was crumbling before Eisenhower's attack, while the British and the Canadians were occupying Bayeux and the Americans were advancing on Cherbourg, Burdet transmitted to his local Resistance chiefs, in accordance with a long-established plan, the orders from London. The guerrilla fighting in Provence was to last five exhausting days.

The *Wehrmacht* garrisons quickly pulled themselves together and launched powerful counterattacks, which the Resistance fighters – far fewer in number and poorly armed – were unable to repulse. Many of them carried out to the letter the orders for the uprising, and rashly fought out in the open, with no attempt at concealing their identities, whereupon the Germans mercilessly tracked them down and the Gestapo took over. This was the signal for a new period of reprisals and atrocities. Hundreds of men, women, old people and children were shot, tortured and deported. In Toulon, when the news of the 5 June messages arrived, many arsenal employees abandoned their jobs to join forces with the *Siou-Blanc* Resistance group in the mountainous back-country forests. This group was hastily dispersed, but from then on the former arsenal workers, the teams of naval engineers, the armed clandestine fighters, had no choice but to continue in hiding in the deep woods and to change hideouts constantly in order to elude the Germans. A large number were taken prisoner, and their bodies soon filled the common graves at Château-Bourgeois in Castellet, near Bandol, and the ditches at Signes and in the woods at Cuges.

Louis Burdet recorded item by item the news of how his fighters were wiped out, transmitting the communiqués to London. Not until 15 June did he receive Koenig's telegram ordering the cessation of hostilies and cynically instructing all those who had been mobilized prematurely to 'return to their homes.' For Burdet, as for countless other Resistance leaders, the counter order had arrived too late.[1]

On Wednesday, 28 June, at 7.30 A.M., in his room in Marseilles, Burdet was awakened by what sounded to him like footsteps outside his door. The next instant, German plainclothesmen brandishing pistols burst into the room. Burdet was caught. On top of a tall Provençal dresser near the window lay a locked briefcase stuffed with several million francs' worth of French treasury bonds and papers that had

---

[1] From 6 June on, the situation of the French Resistance was catastrophic. The premature alert and the anticipated uprising by the underground precipitated crises throughout France, the responsibility for which, in the light of the investigation carried out by Raymond Aron, would appear to lie with Eisenhower's staff. On 4 June, acting on orders from their superiors, two Allied officers – a Briton, Major General Sir Colin Gubbins, and an American, Colonel David K. Bruce – asked Koenig whether he 'saw any reason to prevent the BBC from broadcasting messages corresponding with the general launching of all the plans.' Actually, at the time this request was made, Koenig was already faced with a *fait accompli* – the decision to broadcast the messages had been made and the orders had been issued. Counter orders were not telegraphed to the Resistance leaders in France until six days later, on 10 June. Burdet's telegram did not reach him until the 15th.

arrived two days earlier from London. Burdet was interrogated closely for two hours and his room was ransacked from top to bottom, but the Germans overlooked one thing. It did not occur to them to climb up on the mantel, from which it was possible to reach the top of the dresser. Burdet was arrested and handcuffed, but as he was marched out of the building on his way to Les Baumettes prison, he heaved a sigh of relief because his hiding place had not been discovered. There was still a good chance that it might be if the Gestapo decided to do a more thorough job, and during the ten days he spent in jail Burdet's nerves were constantly on edge. On the morning of the eleventh, a French agent of the Gestapo entered Burdet's cell. The agent – with large, globelike eyes protruding from a weary face – had a sinister air about him, one that Burdet felt could be only ominous. He was now sure that the game was up. He was wrong. No evidence against him had been found, and for some reason he found himself again a free man.

But even as he strode out of the prison gates, Burdet realized that he was no longer the same person, at least as far as his own Resistance agents and chiefs were concerned. Although he had been released, the very fact that he had been arrested would compromise his activities, and he did not have to wait long for proof of this.

The officers who were parachuted into France to prepare the landings in Provence had received orders from the French G-2 in Algiers to make no contact with him. The leader of 'R-2' was now 'hot.' Burdet was not the least surprised when, on 19 July he received his first message from London since his release from prison: 'Consider change of air indispensable. Sending in mid-month new regional military deputy as replacement. Await your arrival as soon as contacts established. Stop.'

What alternative had he but to comply? Burdet submitted with a sinking heart. It was not until two weeks later, twelve days before D-Day in Provence, that the new 'R-2' chief, Widemer ('Cloître'), fresh from Algiers, was parachuted into the Vauclus area. Up to the last day before the Provence landings, a whole new set of Resistance leaders infiltrated into the Drôme, the Basses-Alpes, the Alpes-Maritimes, and the Var regions.

By the evening of 14 August, Burdet had still not received any news of his successor, who had made no contact with him. In the end, he never did receive any word from him.

16

THE RESISTANCE MOVEMENT in southern France resembled a huge spider's web woven with the threads of an infinite number of clandestine networks whose goal was to run the Germans out of France and whose immediate assignment was to harass the *Wehrmacht* troops and keep them on edge.

To this end, there were no holds barred. Everything was allowed – attacks, sabotage, assassination of enemy agents, espionage and the transmission of intelligence to the Allies. Everywhere, on the coasts, in the towns and cities, out in the countryside, in the forests of Esterel and Les Maures, in the tiniest villages and remotest hamlets, the men and women of the Resistance bided their time in the shadow of the occupier and watched for their chance to strike.

The secret networks had names that were as variegated as they were conventional – *Alliance* (under Marie-Madeleine Méric, who made a sensational escape, half-clothed, from the Aix-en-Provence prison in the middle of the night); *Jean-Marie* (its leaders were Yves Bertin for the Var and the Alpes-Maritimes, Jean Bonavia for Monaco, and Georges Doyen for the coastal area, from Perpignan to Sète); *Mithridate* (under Colonel Herbinger, one of the first groups in all France); *Gallia, Jade-Fitzroy, Kasanga, F-2* (under Jean Charlot); *Franc-Tireur, Libération, Duquesne* (under Frank Arnal, who was also the regional chief of the Resistance Sector for Free France); *Combat* (led by Sarie, the executive secretary of the Toulon subprefecture); *Marine,*[1] *Ritz-Crocus, Etoile*, the *ORA* (an armed Resistance unit staffed by former officers of the regular French army), and many others.

A society for the preservation of the forest at Les Maures, recognized as being in the public interest, had been set up in 1943 by Lieutenant Boudouresque, who was in the army at the time of the 1940 armistice.

[1] Since 1943, the Toulon Naval Security Services had maintained clandestine radio connections with the French Special Services in Algiers. It was by this means that, on 7 August 1944, one week before the Second D-Day, the following telegram was sent to Admiral André Lemonnier:

'In event of invasion, formations have orders to place themselves under naval authority in Algiers, while preserving appearances, in order to forestall reprisals against nonliberated naval units'. Signed: 'Jack' (Commander Jacquinet).

According to Lemonnier, he never received this message. During this same period, a secret radio transmitter in Paris maintained connections with Algiers.

The group's members were 'forestry engineers,' a designation that, in most cases, was a disguise adopted by young men who were trying to avoid being conscripted for the forced-labor camps in Germany and who scratched out a living by doing deforestation work and digging trenches for forest-fire prevention. They were scattered around the countryside in groups of three, and on 15 August they became the shock troops for several Free French units. On 29 April 1944, an RAF plane shot down by a German fighter had crashed in flames in the thick of Les Maures, at La Font-de-Truie. Its pilot, a twenty year old Canadian who went by his *nom de guerre* Pepino (no one ever learned his real name), parachuted to safety and was taken in by the local *maquis*. He had been working for three months as a lumberjack in the forest, and was still at it on the morning of 15 August. Three days later, Pepino was killed in the attack on the fort at Mauvanne with the African Commandos.

The men and women in the Resistance, whether they were acting as isolated individuals or were organized into scattered groups and mingling with the population in the big cities, were constantly on the lookout for opportunities to harass the enemy and also to protect their fellow citizens from the arbitrary decrees of the occupier. The pillaging of the German 'Employment Services Office' (for forced-labor conscription) in Hyères naturally caused quite a stir, and the records and documents that were taken in this raid met a picturesque fate – they were used for lighting the fire in Paul's bakery for the first batch of morning loaves. But it was usually in the after-dark hours that clandestine activities went into full swing.

Under cover of darkness, a little group of Resistance fighters, the most vulnerable of all, sat by their radio transmitters – sets ranging in size from that of a large cigar box up to a suitcase – and relayed to London and Algiers hundred of coded messages, asking for money, weapons and ammunition, and also transmitting whatever intelligence they might have picked up during the day. At this time of the evening the men and women of the Resistance no longer felt quite so alone. In Aix-en-Provence, a radio operator named Lévêque, belonging to the *Alliance* group, was able to broadcast in virtually total security because of the zone of silence surrounding his location, one that the Germans in Vice Admiral Paul Wever's headquarters were never able to pinpoint. This immunity eventually had highly dramatic consequences for the 11th Panzer Division's armored vehicles. But Aix-en-Provence was an exception. Theoretically, no transmitter was supposed to operate more than three times from the same location, and in order to thwart the *Wehrmacht*'s direction-finding devices, orders had been issued to all the operators to send their messages from a different place practically every day.

59

Never has an anonymous army been more accurately described. This was a true army of the shadows, a secret force whose soldiers, minus uniforms or insignia and assembled behind bolted shutters or in deep forests, transported orders and arms at the risk of their own and their families' lives, and noted the strength of German units, the positions of batteries and of mine fields, and the direction of enemy movements. Their activities also often included helping prisoners to escape from the Gestapo's jails and attacking convoys headed for the concentration camps.

Many of these men and women were totally ignorant of one another's true identities[1] and the leaders themselves knew only their immediate subordinates. Only a few persons were fully informed of the over-all ramifications of the vast clandestine organization, so as to be able to step in and repair the damage should one of the units be compromised. These 'hermetically sealed' compartments had to be maintained between the members of the different networks or else general annihilation would surely have ensued. Despite all these precautions, mistakes did occur. A Resistance worker known as 'Grand-Duc,' and also as 'The Killer' (alias Hélin des Isnards), belonging to the *Alliance* group, was for a long time confused with another one called 'Archiduc' (alias Rayon), who operated in an adjacent area.

But even at the highest levels of responsibility, the leaders deliberately chose to remain ignorant of one another's identities, and fierce rivalries with respect to both clans and doctrines persisted among these men, even though they were committed to the same struggle and were pursuing the same goal – the elimination of the maximum number of Germans by every means available.

On the eve of D-Day in Provence, the Allied staff estimated at some 24,000 people the strength of the Resistance movement. As a matter of fact, there were barely 15,000, fewer than a third of them armed. Besides being woefully inadequate, their weapons were notoriously nondescript. The Resistance fighters in the Var region, where the invasion was to take place, had arms ranging from parachuted Sten guns and pocket revolvers to ancient French army muskets and Italian rifles captured from Badoglio's troops. Following the Normandy invasion, Eisenhower personally saw to it that the parachuting of arms to Resistance members in southern France was stepped up. Several hundred thousand containers of weapons and ammunition were dropped over Provence during the weeks preceding 15 August. Yet, despite the all-out

---

[1] 'The regulations required that Resistance groups operate under a strictly compartmentalized set-up. Each member of the Resistance occupied his own "fox-hole"; he did not know who his neighbours were, and his horizon was strictly limited.' (Henri Michel, *Second International Congress on the History of the Resistance*, Milan, March 1961).

efforts of the II Tactical Air Command based in England, the parachuted supplies were insufficient, and failed to equip the Resistance groups adequately.

On the afternoon of 14 August, Honoré Dumaine, a member of the Draguignan Resistance group, received a hasty visit from his sector chief, Marchesi, who came rushing in, red in the face and out of breath.

'My car's parked over on Avenue Carnot with two crates in it. Grab them, Honoré, and take them with you on the train for Lorgues.'

And Théotime Marchesi, who ran a small tannery on the banks of Nartuby, gave Dumaine the exact instructions that he was to carry out.

Since the previous April, Draguignan had been the headquarters for a large German staff. But a few of the local citizens realized that the *Wehrmacht*'s sleek Mercedeses driving through town, were carrying the officers of General Ferdinand Neuling, commander of the LXII Corps, who had recently been withdrawn from the Eastern front. It did seem to Honoré Dumaine that the Germans were busier than usual that afternoon, but he failed to attach any particular significance to their activity. He was concentrating on catching the first train for Lorgues as he registered his crates to be put in the baggage car. The train made its scheduled stop at the Flayosc station. At Lorgues, the person waiting for Dumaine claimed the crates in a businesslike fashion. They were then loaded on to an asthmatic truck which came to a halt at a bakery. Dumaine's crates were conveyed downstairs to the oven room, where their contents were unpacked. They contained British machine guns that had been parachuted over the Broves plateau for the Lorgues Resistance group, in preparation for D-Day. The Sten guns were quietly distributed that night, after the 7 P.M. BBC broadcast. And then the people gathered around the radio set at the Lorgues bakery began their long vigil.

In Callas, too, north of Draguignan, the day had been hot and sultry. Robert Aymard, the manager of a big local cork works, noticed 'members of the Resistance going off in the direction of Le Muy,' and his intuition was correct, as he thought:

'Tomorrow's the day.'

Aymard remembers that 'the evening of the 14th was as stifling as a hothouse, enough to set your nerves on edge, with something else in it, an undefinable uneasiness, like when you've been waiting too long for a storm that's been gathering but hasn't broken yet.' Taking leave of his family at home in Callas, he, too, set out for Le Muy, ten miles away. Although the coast was fairly far away, Aymard realized that the Germans must have had some reason for planting sharpened spikes all over the countryside, in all the *pouvadous*,[1] as a defense against para-

---

[1] A Provençal word meaning a barren spot in which nothing grows.

troopers. Disregarding the curfew without a second thought, Aymard hopped onto his bicycle. He was going to reach Le Muy just in time to have his suspicions confirmed.

In far-off London, there was a man who knew the hour was imminent and would have given anything to be 'right there on the spot at Saint-Raphaël.' Louis Marchand was a native of Luxembourg who had joined the intelligence service four years before, and now had good reason to feel impatient. The members of his family for generations had been quarrying porphyry in Belgium, and around the end of the nineteenth century they had founded the Saint-Raphaël quarries, overlooking the beach at Le Dramont.

Since late in 1943, Marchand had become an especially valuable agent to the Allied staff in charge of preparations for the landings in Provence. His superiors had issued him a specific order that only he could carry out, and a large share of the success of the Provence invasion would depend on his ability to accomplish his mission – to prevent the German engineers from planting mines on the beach at Le Dramont, which was in the trickiest sector of the attack zone.

For months Louis Marchand had been fighting, foot by foot, his weapons being the rivalry and the conflicting requirements of his two main opponents, the engineers in General Johannes Bässler's 242nd Division and the men in the Todt Organization; he alternately played one group off against the other. Since the beginning of the occupation of southern France, the Todt people had been trying to get the Vichy authorities to let them have quantities of crushed rock from the Saint-Raphaël quarries. They were especially anxious to lay hands on all the supply of rock at Le Dramont in order to speed up completion of the Mediterranean Wall. Marchand had managed to get the deadline extended, but he realized that it would not be possible to evade the requisition order much longer – it was being energetically pushed by Vichy's Minister of Production and Transport, Jean Bichelonne. And then he received another item of news – the German engineers were getting ready to mine the beach.

The beach at Le Dramont – called Camel Green on the Allied invasion maps – stretched for over a quarter of a mile at the base of the quarries filled with the bluish-gray porphyry (which had been used to pave the streets of Marseilles), less than a mile from Boulouris and about the same distance from the little port of Agay. Marchand well knew that the presence of great quantities of rock on the beach would not be an insurmountable obstacle to the sowing of mines. A few steam rollers would do the trick, and these the Germans had at their disposal.

From that time on, Louis Marchand's mission, perilous as it was, took on a drastically different aspect. His only resource was to let the Germans wrangle among themselves in a mad tangle of priorities and rival agencies, hoping that the leaders of the Todt Organization in Marseilles, who were insatiable in their demands for materials, would win out. By the evening of 14 August, Marchand's maneuver had borne fruit beyond all expectations.

He had just been able to confirm to headquarters in London that Camel Green would not be mined. In the space of several months, all that the Todt Organization had been able to accomplish was to set up a few rock-crushing machines along the shore, and the amount of rock actually quarried had been insignificant. Marchand had also brought with him to London photographs of the bunkers flanking the critically important beach at Le Dramont. These had indeed been completed, but as of 14 August the Germans still had not managed to equip them with guns.

One of the zones that was scheduled to see some of the heaviest activity was also one of the most weakly fortified.

17

THE HEADQUARTERS OF THE UNITED STATES EIGHTH FLEET in Naples was operating out of a building on the Riviera di Chaia, whose eight stories, until Italy's capitulation, had contained the offices of the Tyrrhenian Shipping Company. These quarters now accommodated all the Allied administrative units concerned with the personnel of the invasion forces, the liaison missions of the British Tactical Air Force, the United States Strategic Air Command, the British, American and French armies, all the departments responsible for naval matériel for the landings, and a laboratory for the photographic intelligence detail that kept a day-to-day map of all enemy defense installations in the invasion area.

Since July, every morning at about 8 A.M., a pile of top-secret photographs taken the previous day and processed overnight by the laboratory had been arriving on the desk of a French naval officer, Lieutenant Commander Raymond Payan. Daily, Payan painstakingly pored over the results of the Allied bombardments along the coast of Provence. He had no trouble in identifying the light patches of freshly poured cement, which represented the blockhouses and batteries that the Germans were hastily throwing together but had had no time to camouflage.

By noon each day the pictures had yielded all their secrets, and before going to lunch, Payan turned them over to a French Navy signalman, Jean Meirat, who immediately consigned the lot to the building's furnace. Every day as he went about his mission, Meirat found himself thinking about what went on behind the scenes of these photographs, pondering the 'ruses and efforts of the French civilians, who weren't necessarily born spies.' Yet these amateurs managed to smuggle in to the Allied headquarters 'explosive little scraps of paper' that were mixed in with the stacks of aerial views of the *Südwall,* 'often accompanied by short, ceremonious forms of greeting.' For example, a Côte d'Azur contractor begged to inform the Allied headquarters politely that the Germans had just placed an order with him for several hundred concrete pyramids, and 'had signed a contract for bombproof shelters to be constructed immediately and fast.'

On the afternoon of Tuesday, 2 May 1944, a line of cars flying the flags of the *OKW* had sped through the sparkling garden city of Hyères-les-Palmiers, east of Toulon, on their way to the coast, headed for the beach at Ayguade. The cars drew up alongside a brand-new railway station, whose special equipment included an electric hoist for conveying the sand and gravel used in building the great concrete pyraminds that were to be planted in the Hyères roadstead. As far as the eye could see, the shore bristled with steel and wooden spikes, looking as if they would stop the sea itself from surging up on to the beach.

An officer alighted from one of the front cars. He was fiftyish, somewhat on the lean side, his jaw firmly set, one hand held up to shade his eyes against the brilliant sunlight. His uniform bore the insignia of the highest rank in the German army. The officer was Field Marshal Erwin Rommel, freshly arrived the day before from his headquarters in La Roche-Guyon for a quick inspection tour of the south. Rommel was accompanied by his naval aide, Vice Admiral Friedrich Ruge.

This was Rommel's second trip to southern France since the beginning of 1944. His first visit – although the Mediterranean sector lay completely outside his jurisdiction – dated back to the first week in February. Rommel had no intention of lingering. General von Sodenstern's staff had scheduled him to be back at the Nineteenth Army's command post at Avignon for dinner after a brief stopover in Aix-en-Provence, where he would drop in at the naval headquarters. Rommel planned to return immediately afterward to Paris.

In the spring of 1944 the consensus among German staff officers was that the Hyères roadstead, which was spacious and studded with sandy beaches, and not far from the fortified camp at Toulon, was one of the most likely spots for an Allied invasion. Consequently, extra attention had been given to building up the local defense installations, and tl mine fields both on the land and under the water were undoubtedly the most formidable of all. A *Kriegsmarine* report submitted to Rommel stated that the number of submerged mines planted in this zone, between the Giens Peninsula and Cap Bénat, totaled over 60,000. And Rommel's mines were by no means the whole story. Serried ranks of pillboxes equipped with heavy machine guns and antitank artillery rimmed the shoreline and the area beyond, guarded the intersections, menaced the highways, and loomed over the secondary roads. The entire area was crawling with barbed-wire entanglements, gun pits embedded in the surrounding hills, antitank ditches, and underground shelters like rabbit warrens with connecting passages to various concrete structures.

All these defenses notwithstanding, on this day in early May, Rommel was far from satisfied. From November, 1942, to September, 1943, the Italian troops had occupied this stretch of coast; but, even before that, General Mario Vercellino's garrisons had been replaced in their work on the Mediterranean Wall by *Wehrmacht* engineering troops and Todt Organization teams. Before 1942 the Mediterranean Wall had not even existed; it had been wrested out of the earth, like the others along the North Sea and the English Channel. Spanking new railway tracks wound through the Provençal landscape, freshly cut highways sliced through the Monts des Maures, new bridges hastily spanned age-old streams, and observation posts spiked the landscape with ungainly towers. Miles and miles of beachfront and endless lengths of wharves and docks had been shut off by big signs with the laconic warning '*Minen!*'

Rommel was acutely aware that, despite the intensive recruiting of local labor, despite the high wages paid to requisitioned workers (from 120 to 150 francs, with certain skilled workmen earning up to 900 francs a day),[1] despite the intensive work of the last eighteen months, there was still much to be done here, as everywhere else on the Atlantic coasts and on the English Channel. There would never be enough mine fields nor enough obstacle traps to repulse a seaborne attack, enough flame-throwers or machine-gun nests to rake the assault troops, enough pill-boxes on the beaches, enough antitank ditches and heavy batteries inshore to prevent the enemy from establishing a beachhead. More buildings would have to go up, more pits would have to be dug, more concrete poured, new obstacles stuck into place, new mine fields and barbed wire planted, more traps sunk into the water, more men and women requisitioned, more fortifications thrown up everywhere, and still more fortifications.

Rommel's visit set off, over the ensuing weeks, an avalanche of orders

[1] The French franc in 1944 was in a state of high inflation. (Translator's note.)

and instructions along the entire Mediterranean coastal area, aimed at reinforcing the *Südwall* defense. This activity reached a new pitch of intensity early in June, when the Allies landed in Normandy and won the first decisive invasion battle, the battle of the beaches. The frenzied building of fortifications attained its height during the first three weeks in July.

All over the Riviera's beaches Rommel's 'asparagus stalks' were thrusting up their ugly spears. Rows of sawed-off beams were laid down along the shore, and each beam contained a 75-mm. shell rigged to an antenna fuse, which would be triggered by the slightest contact. (Many of these shells to which the German connected fuses had been made for the French army.) Farther up from the water line, cement tripods were anchored in the sand and equipped with Teller mines the size of large pie pans. Then began the barbed-wire networks, which were connected to still more mines and to those special traps on which the Germans particularly prided themselves. In addition to all the German devices, there were the mines planted by the Italians. Supersensitive, weighing only five ounces, booby-trapped and laid out in staggered rows, they were designed to explode at waist-level and rip open a man's guts. Behind them stood the concrete pillboxes with their machine guns and cannon commanding the beaches and all the approaches to them.

From Cavalaire-sur-Mer to Anthéor, a distance of some thirty-five miles, German engineers and Todt Organization crews had pooled their efforts to convert into blockhouses practically all the private homes that were situated on the strategic routes, their inhabitants having long since been evacuated. All the beachside buildings in all the seaside towns, especially in Cannes and in Nice, were to be heavily fortified and transformed into bastions.

On the beach at Fréjus, between Saint-Raphaël and the Argens river delta, on the site of the future Camel Red landing zone where the United States 36th Infantry Division would fail in its attempt to establish a beachhead, the innocent-looking pavilions, gaily colored refreshment stands and bright little cabanas were excellent camouflage for a formidable array of long-range coastal batteries. Although most of the original French-built fortification had been put out of commission in November 1942, there still remained – east of the Rhône, from Marseilles to Nice – about six hundred isolated pillboxes or artillery positions equipped with guns ranging in size from 13.4 inches to the 75-mm. long rifle. In the sector between Cavalaire-sur-Mer and Agay, in the 242nd Division's defense area, over 150 guns were ready and waiting for the Allied fleet.

And the Germans had also thoughtfully prepared for an invasion other than by sea. The needlelike points of thousands of carefully filed spikes were strategically planted throughout the landscape, in the vineyards, in the flowering fields, over every last bit of open space. This had involved neither concrete nor metal, only the felling of a few forests. The 'asparagus stalks' – less than twelve inches in diameter – had been made with pine wood from Les Maures forest. They had been devised to impale the paratroopers and glider pilots who would be bringing in equipment and reinforcements for the airborne units.

Since the end of July 1944, the Germans had been priming themselves for a potential airborne invasion around Draguignan, twenty miles from the coast. Every morning for three weeks, on his way to work, Jean Ramella, who lived in La Motte, had seen some thirty people of all ages – requisitioned by the *Kommandantur* – making wooden spikes about twelve feet long and from ten to twelve inches thick and loading them on to wagons. The spikes were then transported to various places and planted in holes dug about fifty feet apart. Whenever the German supervisors were not paying too close attention, the conscripted workers assigned to digging the post-holes deliberately dug them shallow. These obstructions were invisible at night and formed a complete network over the Argens Valley and in the plains around Le Muy, Les Arcs, and Trans-en-Provence, precisely where the paratroopers of General Frederick, in command of the airborne forces for Operation Dragoon, were going to jump on the Second D-Day.

The people of the hamlet of La Foux, near Saint-Tropez, will long remember a Sunday in the spring of 1944, about one month after Rommel's visit. For generations, one of the local attractions to which the villagers liked to point with pride had been a line of about thirty parasol pines standing majestically along the Saint-Tropez racetrack at the mouth of the bay.

During siesta time on this sleepy June afternoon, a flurry of explosions followed by a series of rumbling jolts shattered the air. Occupied with their game under the shade of the plane trees, the *pétanque*[1] players, startled, looked up to see thick columns of smoke spiraling into the sky.

'Some more ammunition dumps gone to blazes,' was the first thought that occurred to Dr Joseph Salvetti, half-dozing in his garden.

And the physician imagined resignedly that 'the Germans would soon be coming around again to take a few hostages' from the local population. For once he was wrong.

A battery had been built some time before on the heights of Les Parys, overlooking the beach at La Foux. The local Resistance had informed Algiers about these guns, which commanded the entrance to

[1] A form of bowling game popular in southern France.

the Gulf of Saint-Tropez. It did not take long for the Germans to realize that the parasol pines at La Foux constituted a serious obstacle to the line of fire, and the township was notified that the trees had to go.

Dr Salvetti was summoned to the *Kommandantur*, and somehow managed to keep his temper, but protested to the officer impassively sitting behind a desk:

'If those trees are blasted, it'll take another hundred years to grow some more anywhere near that height.'

Afterward, nothing more had been said about the trees, and Dr Salvetti was lulled into a sense of false security. Then, early in June, he placed only slight importance to an occurrence that should have aroused his suspicions. At this time, a group of high-ranking *Wehrmacht* officers appeared on a surprise inspection tour. The order was again given to destroy the trees, and this time the Germans meant it.

Twenty-four hours later, dynamite had the last word, and the thirty pine trees at La Foux toppled to the ground with an ear-splitting crash that raised a blinding dust.[1]

Two and a half months later, the village's 2,500 residents were preoccupied with more urgent matters, notably the question of food, which was becoming harder and harder to obtain. On D-Day minus 1, Dr Salvetti's feeling was that the guns at Les Parys would not be firing many rounds. Most of the German fighting troops had left the area two weeks before, and the story was that they had been sent off to the Italian Alps.

18

BY MID-AFTERNOON ON MONDAY, 14 August, there could be no more doubt about it. The ten huge convoys were proceeding toward a definite rendezvous on their various routes from Naples, Sicily, Malta and North Africa as they sailed at full steam off Cap Senetosa, near the western shore of Corsica.

Aboard the command ship *Catoctin*, Admiral Hewitt was peering through his binoculars at a small Royal Navy destroyer that had left the coast far behind and was speeding to catch up with the convoys. The

---

[1] Contrary to the rumour that was widely believed at the time, the pines were not used in the making of the thousands of 'asparagus stalks' that bristled over the adjoining Cogolin plain, and for a very good reason. As Dr Salvetti has pointed out, their trunks were some twenty-five inches in diameter, and hence too thick for this purpose.

admiral's white flag hoisted high on the mast meant that the commander in chief of the Mediterranean naval forces, Sir John Cunningham, was on board. The destroyer was the *Kimberley*.

As he stood at the handrail of the *Catoctin* looking through the binoculars that he was sharing with a companion, Sylvain Bernard, the young French signalman Jean Meirat also saw the *Kimberley* plowing toward them. Meirat correctly read the message that was being conveyed by the double halyard of flags fluttering from the British ship:

'Good luck! Good luck to all you who are on the sea today!'

Hewitt, on the bridge with two aides, returned the *Kimberley*'s salute, and the British destroyer steamed off toward the other convoys. As Meirat later described the scene, 'the sight of the *Kimberley* threading its way in and around the LSTs, the cargo ships, and the destroyer escorts cutting through the open sea, the admiral's white flag flying, created in the minds of the onlookers a vision and a concept that were as ancient as the long-vanished memory of the Viking ships.'

The time was 3 P.M. On the waters of the world's most beautiful sea, it was the Mediterranean's most glorious hour as the invasion fleet passed in review for the last time. Everything was sparkling under the brilliant August sun – the hulking United States battleships, looking almost as if they were sliced in two where the deep blue of their hulls met the light blue of the superstructures, the sleek British cruisers, camouflaged by grays, greens and blues, the British small destroyers and corvettes, the bulky American destroyers, the trawlers, the dark dredgers bulging with coal, the Italian cruisers and destroyers,[1] extremely pretty to watch, perhaps too pretty, with their sea-green superstructures. All these mighty lords of the sea were arrayed on the smooth waters, blending with the most motley assortment of transports and tankers, Polish, Greek, and Norwegian cargo vessels, and countless other craft from many countries.

The convoys did not slacken speed while the *Kimberley* cruised about, displaying its message of good luck to all the formations in the armada.

Rear Admiral André Lemonnier, chief of staff of the French Navy, was standing a few feet from Meirat, who watched as the horizon off Ajaccio 'gradually swelled with the proud silhouettes of the French ships gliding stealthily along like a pack of wolves eager for their prey.'[2] There were the *Montcalm* and the *Georges Leygues*, followed by the *Fantasque*, the *Terrible*, and the *Malin*, all of them sleek and swift, corsairs of the high seas. They in turn were saluted by the *Kimberley*, where General Wilson and Admiral Cunningham were standing on deck side by side.

And then they were off.

[1] These were the spoils from the Italian fleet's surrender in September 1943.
[2] Meirat.

'Course due north ...'

At crack of dawn they were due in front of the landing beaches, well ahead of the landing craft and the transports.

19

BRISTLING WITH TRANSMISSION ANTENNAE and bursting with generals and other officers from all the services, the *Catoctin* had weighed anchor and cast off from Naples the evening before with the last of the invasion convoys.

The *Catoctin* had been designated as the supreme headquarters for the invasion forces at sea, and in a few hours she would be issuing final landing orders for the men and equipment going ashore. Her crew enjoyed bragging about the fact that their ship had been specially assigned and sent from the United States for this historic occasion. Indeed, the *Catoctin* was worthy of anything conjured up in the visions of an Edgar Allen Poe or a Jules Verne. Her radar equipment was the most accurate in the fleet; her aircraft identification devices, her radio transmission center, complete with several dozen sending sets, her teleprinters with luminous screens for announcements, her gangways and passageways alive with loudspeakers, made her the last word in technical perfection. She was in fact a fantastic 'floating factory,' equipped with the latest refinements in the modern techniques of directing amphibious operations.

Although almost wholly devoid of guns or armor, the *Catoctin* had radar screens powerful enough to enable her to maintain virtually total aerial surveillance.

The atmosphere in the ship's radio room, where all calls were received and hundreds of messages reproduced on the teleprinters, resembled less a naval communications post than it did the offices of a bustling international bank at rush hour. The *Catoctin*'s operations switchboard enabled the invasion staff to follow minute by minute every detail of the action, both on the sea and on the beaches, and the huge luminous dials provided a continuous record of the positions of all the amphibious forces, down to the smallest assault craft, as well as of the aerial situation. Every conceivable contingency had been thought of, including a special weather forecasting service that kept Admiral Hewitt, commanding the invasion forces, informed every four hours about local weather conditions.

This was by no means all. For the first time in the history of amphibious operations, including the Normandy landings, the invaders had in the *Catoctin* a ship that was not just the headquarters for the naval forces alone, for those responsible for the actual landing of troops. It also had on board General Saville and the entire staff of the 12th Air Force, who would be coordinating their orders with the navy's and lending their support to the divisions on the beaches.

On this last afternoon before D-Day, the *Catoctin*'s decks and ladders were crammed with airmen, sailors and soldiers, nearly one thousand of them.

As one of the ship's Filipino stewards remarked afterward, 'It was simply incredible that so many guys could all be piled in together on that big creaky tub!'

A clutch of American generals, combat boots gleaming, necks adorned with bright silk scarves that on closer inspection turned out to be printed with colored maps of the landing area, were packed in among the admirals and a tight little group of war correspondents.

In the crush and the heat, few people had recognized an unobtrusive man dressed in a simple khaki shirt. His eyes held a cold light, his lips were a thin gash across his face, and he had once had his nose flattened by a blow from a fist, making him look rather like a boxer. But it was an arresting face, one that no one could forget once he had seen it. The man seemed to be making a point of going unnoticed, and although crowded in with three other men in a little stateroom, he was succeeding pretty well. Lemonnier, who sat next to him at Hewitt's table, assumed that he was a vague diplomatic adviser attached in some capacity to the invasion headquarters staff.

Lemonnier's neighbor was James Vincent Forrestal, United States Secretary of the Navy. This was the man who had personally worked out all the details of the plans for assembling the immense fleet of landing vessels that, since 1942, had been serving the beaches of North Africa, the Pacific and the English Channel. In less than seventeen hours they would be disembarking the troops on the beaches of the French Riviera, from Cap Nègre to Le Trayas.[1]

---

[1] By the end of World War II, Forrestal had supervised the building of 65,000 combat ships and 110,053 planes for the Navy. This August day in 1944 was by no means his baptism under fire as a statesman face to face with the realities of war. A few months earlier, Forrestal had been on Kwajalein at the time of the American attack in the Central Pacific; in 1942, he had been at Guadalcanal. In 1945, at Iwo Jima, he became the first Secretary of the Navy to land under Japanese fire. Four years later, after having been appointed Secretary to Defense by President Harry S. Truman, Forrestal suffered a nervous breakdown as the result of years of overwork, and leaped to his death from a hospital window. A bronze bust of Forrestal stands at the entrance to the Pentagon.

20

FROM ONE END OF THE HORIZON to the other the Mediterranean was shrouded under a slight heat mist. Not a breath of air was stirring in the garish summer light. The ships, swathed in the mingled fragrances of the sea and the stench of fuel, determinedly pursued their course north, at an average speed of twelve knots.

Captain Robert Morris's assault group had long since left the convoy's assembly area far behind. His fourteen LCTs, bound for Saint-Raphaël, were spearheading the invasion fleet. His orders read that he was to arrive offshore by 5 A.M. the following morning. As the great procession of ships wended its way through the waters off Corsica, Morris was not aware that his convoy had been spotted by reconnaissance planes from the *Luftwaffe*'s IV Corps and that the Focke-Wulf pilots, in their planes adorned with black swastikas, had already radioed his position and from it had deduced the direction the rest of the Allied Force, was taking.

The group of officers – Morris's best friends on the staff of the Eighth Fleet – who had the task of maneuvering some 1,200 ships transporting six assault divisions across the Mediterranean, had found themselves up against a succession of thorny problems. Half of the ships would still be at sea more than a day and a half after the attack had been launched. But the 200,000 invasion troops, coming from over half a dozen main ports, would be converging simultaneously on their objective, a relatively limited assault zone barely forty miles long.

For the Normandy invasion, Eisenhower had been able to wait until only twenty-four hours before D-Day before issuing the send-off order. Such an arrangement was not feasible for the landings in Provence. The Channel crossing had required only a few hours, whereas the distance to be covered on the Mediterranean, the numerous ports of departure, and the type and number of the convoys were factors that raised completely different problems.

Morris knew that General Patch's assault troops were scheduled to arrive opposite the French shore in the last hours just before dawn, and that the convoys were to have maximum air cover along the full length of their routes, from the moment they got under way. Moreover, they were to navigate in channels that had been cleared by the mine sweepers. But Morris wondered just how – even assuming that the strict timetable assigned to each formation could be adhered to – it was going to be possible to prevent the congestion and the overlapping of routes that seemed to threaten all the convoys.

Each type of ship had taken on its load at a different port. There were LCTs, and there were vessels that carried only infantry assault craft; there were troop transports filled until their hatches overflowed with men, and long lines of combat cargo ships and fire-support ships, which would be raking the beaches with their artillery before and during the landings. And, last but by no means least, were the reinforcements – General de Lattre de Tassigny's French First Army, the B Army – traveling aboard the merchant marine ships of the Free Nations. In the Italian ports, the troops had been drilled and drilled again in loading and unloading the assault ships, and this training had had to be completed no later than 9 August.

The first convoys had set out from Naples that same morning. By the following night there had begun the fantastic concentration that was to reach its culmination four days later. On 10 August, the French divisions, which had the hardest and longest route to cover, began pulling out of the Italian ports. The following day, the battleships, cruisers and destroyers bound for the beaches off Cavalaire-sur-Mer and Sainte-Maxime got under way from Taranto and Naples; at the same time, in Oran, the First Special Service Force's transports, carrying Colonel Edwin A. Walker's Canadian and American commandos – whose destination was the Iles d'Hyères – put out to sea at full speed in order to get into position at the head of the armada, 550 miles away in a small Corsican bay. At 12.30 P.M. on 12 August, the column of 118 ships laden with the assault barges that would be taking the ground troops ashore on the three invasion beaches, began slowly pushing away from the port of Salerno. In the meantime, the majority of the landing troops, the men of the United States 3rd, 36th, and 45th Infantry Divisions, were confined to quarters and waiting to sail that afternoon.

Admiral Troubridge's nine aircraft carriers – seven British, two American – had already left Malta, and were advancing steadily over the Mediterranean in the direction of Sardinia. Forty-eight hours later, after lunch on Monday, every ship of the largest flotilla ever assembled in this part of the world was at sea and moving.

After drawing near the Corsican coast, which they had reached after following one of thirteen charted and mine-swept routes, these ships of all sizes had proceeded to occupy their assigned position. Under the broiling August sun, they trailed a great wake of foam across the Mediterranean. As Brigadier General Aimé Sudre described it, they were 'lined up with the same meticulous care that a boy uses in lining up his toy soldiers for battle.' In exactly twenty-four hours, Sudre would be the first French general to land on the soil of Provence with his First Armored Combat Command. Sudre had embarked at Oran aboard the British troop transport *Winchester Castle*, and had lost no time striking up a friendship with the ship's captain, 'a big, hearty Englishman with a deep suntan, a veteran mariner of the Cape route' who couldn't speak 'one damned word of French.' He and Sudre managed to get along quite satisfactorily in Spanish.

On another ship, Pierre Rigal, a radio operator and interpreter attached to the French 68th Artillery Regiment, was still wondering whether they 'were really on their way to France.' In the same convoy was a chief warrant officer, René Michelet, who had felt he was almost going out of his mind while waiting to embark near Oran. He had no more doubts concerning his destination. He even knew that the First Armored Combat Command was to land on 15 August at 6 P.M., near Saint-Raphaël. Michelet, of course, could hardly know that the strongly entrenched troops of the German 242nd Division were going to prevent every one of the assault boats from even getting near shore there. But Michelet possessed information that many of his battle companions did not. He knew that the beach at Fréjus was defended by a 'concrete wall $4\frac{1}{2}$ feet high,' that 'antitank mines lay planted like potatoes all around,' and that 'the German guns in position behind enormous trenches could easily sweep the entire area for a distance of twelve miles.'

Second Lieutenant Jacques Moine, a veteran of the Tunisian campaign attached to the same outfit, the only French armored unit slated to land on D-Day, had embarked with his platoon of Sherman tanks on a flat-bottomed LST that had set out from Mers-el-Kebir. He had a crew of Polish sailors. Three days later, Moine had still been firmly convinced that they were on their way to reinforce the army in Italy; now he was busily poring over the landing-zone maps that had been distributed to all the officers of the 2nd Armored Regiment. Moine was worrying about how it was all going to be in a few hours from now. He was thinking about the water proofing of his four tanks and about how their ventilation systems were going to function when the long-anticipated order sounded:

'Man the tanks, start 'em up, loose the cables!'

Pierre Rigal on board the *James Parker*, recalls how the ambulance nurses were getting into mischief 'fooling around with the gas cartridges used for inflating their safety-belts, and finally had to be called to order by the American ship captain.' Warrant Officer Joseph Lacrampe, on board LST 914 in the same convoy, was occupied with more serious matters. On the afternoon of Monday, 14 August, he begged out of the card game that his tank crew had been going at continuously since morning; a former French prisoner named Martinet, who had escaped from the Germans, immediately slipped into his place.

Lacrampe stood staring out over the waters of the Mediterranean, paved with ships as far and the eye could see, and wondered what had become of one of his friends, Foissac, attached to the African Commandos. He would have given anything to know whether Foissac was on one of those ships out there. Lacrampe had just learned that Lieutenant Colonel Georges-Régis Bouvet's commandos had been assigned to open the beach a few hours later somewhere on the coast. The commandos would go into action all by themselves – a group of fewer than eight hundred men picking their way through the enemy defenses before the first of the main assault waves began coming ashore – and would be on their own for eight hours.

An atmosphere of calm and sober optimism prevailed aboard virtually all the ships in the Allied armada. This was true notably of the *Montcalm* and the *Georges Leygues*, two cruisers in Rear Admiral Robert Jaujard's 4th Division. Their French crews had stood by for nearly four years, and two months earlier, on the dawn of 6 June in Normandy, they had amply demonstrated their ability and courage.

However, this Mediterranean crossing was anything but a pleasure jaunt for Jaujard. He was assailed with misgivings about the haze that had been obscuring the horizon since they left Taranto, and his mind kept straying to thoughts of the German batteries in the Gulf of Saint-Tropez, and particularly to the formidable guns on Pointe-de-Rabiou. Jaujard was worried that the persistent fog might seriously interfere with his ship's 6-inch guns. He was praying that his men would not once again have to live through the long, fearful hours that they had experienced in the English Channel, off Omaha Beach, which for thousands of sailors and soldiers had become 'gory Omaha.'

Jaujard's anxiety was eased somewhat by the reflection that although his ships and men were the same ones as in the Normandy landings, the assault conditions were going to be radically different. He was understandably haunted by the thought that once again, it was against their own native land that his men were going to unleash their fire. The most crucial moment would come when they arrived near the beach, when the troops would be going ashore, after the saturation air and artillery, pounding which was supposed to wipe out the enemy batteries. Still Jaujard was not experiencing quite the same trepidation as during those hours of anguish that had preceded the Normandy landings seventy days before.

The sight of the convoys 'like a continuous procession of great gleaming caterpillars' gave seaman Manuel Navascuès, aboard the *Tunisien*, part of the French 2nd Destroyer Escort Division, 'an immense feeling of security and strength.' The *Tunisien* and her sister ship, the *Marocain*, were carrying out their watch-dog duties, a chaperoning assignment that could hardly be described as heroic. The 2nd Division's ships were part of those that had had to cover the longest distance for their rendezvous with the invasion fleet – Navascuès had left Casablanca in early August. As he gazed out over the group of ships that it was his job to protect, the young sailor felt that they 'all looked like one big family headed towards home.'

A radio operator, Carré had left his listening post on the light cruiser *Le Fantasque* and gone up on deck, still wearing his earphones. He, too, was deeply stirred with emotion and pride as he contemplated the French tricolor flying alongside the flags of the free nations of the world. But he also felt that 'they'd had to scrape the bottom of the barrel and drag in everything they could find' from the French fleet. He noted a random sampling of all sorts of vessels, from the small destroyers that had 'spruced themselves up a bit' to the 'matronly figure waddling in bulky petticoats,' the *Lorraine*, which was 'keeping up appearances and doing a decent job, although she did rather look like an ostrich heading into the wind, with a few ack-ack guns hastily stuck on her.'

The 10th Light Crusier Division had cast off from Bizerte only the previous day, just before noon. Like three beasts of prey crouching for the final lunge, fur bristling and fangs bared, the three grayhounds of the sea, the *Fantasque*, the *Terrible*, and the *Malin* had had to maintain full speed in order to join the main fleet. Within a few hours, engines churning, the three ships had caught up with and outdistanced the heavy American cruisers with their star-spangled banners flying.

According to Chief Petty Officer Joseph Cochard, a radio operator on the *Terrible*, 'we had to change direction every once in a while in order to thread our way around all sorts of things floating in the sea.'

But it seemed to Cochard that the hull of the *Terrible* was 'quivering with joy, as if she knew exactly what the glorious mission was that she was carrying us to.'

The *Malin* was also hurrying as fast as she could with what her captain, Lieutenant Commander Ballande, described as a 'game leg.' An accident had almost kept her from being part of the Allied armada. Off Tripoli, the *Malin* had struck a sunken ship that had cost her one of her propellers, and Ballande was dismayed at the prospect of being left behind because of this mishap. Over the past months, this ship had been roving ceaselessly over the Mediterranean, her guns firing and her powder magazine being emptied over and over again. At the last minute, there had been just time enough to outfit the ship with new guns to replace the old ones, which were worn down to their last groove, but none of the arsenals or foundries in North Africa had been able to provide a propeller for the 'seashorse.' But, with her single propeller, she was still maintaining twenty-eight knots. The expedition to Provence was to earn the nickname 'gimpy' for the *Malin*.

21

THE 250 COMBAT SHIPS of the Allied fleet were moving like a giant steel carapace, crawling along behind the mine sweepers under the protective umbrella of the antiaircraft balloons hovering five hundred feet above, pennants and flags flapping against halyards whipped by the wind. Behind the veil of haze that by now was hiding the Corsican coastline, Cap Senetosa gradually faded from view.

Although the venerable British battleship *Ramillies*, skippered by Captain G.B. Middleton, had been in service for twenty-eight years, her 15-inch guns ranked with the most redoubtable in the invasion fleet. The French cruiser *Gloire* was in the same convoy, escorting the American 3rd Infantry Division, and had finally been able to repair the turbine trouble that had kept her out of action during the Normandy invasion. Commander Adam was priming his 6-inch guns for readiness against the beaches of the Côte des Maures.

Among the many other veterans of the Channel invasion the American cruiser *Quincy*, the British *Black Prince*, and the *Ajax* (a participant in the famous River Plate battle of December 1939, when the *Graf Spee* was scuttled) had already done their fair share of work against the German coastal batteries on the Atlantic Wall. Two other aging battleships, the *Texas* and the *Nevada*, had also been present on that morning of 6 June, off Omaha and Utah beaches – and the *Nevada* could reminisce even farther back, to 7 December 1941, when she had been part of the fleet caught by the Japanese planes at Pearl Harbor.

Another salty veteran was also heaving through the Mediterranean. The cruiser *Tuscaloosa* had been 'repatriated' from the Channel. She, too, had borne part of the brunt of the battle for Utah Beach, and in August 1942, she had been part of the most famous of the Allied convoys, the one that set off for Murmansk to bring supplies to the Russians. Now, two years later, the sturdy *Tuscaloosa*, with seventeen other firing-support ships headed for the Camel beaches of the heavily fortified

Saint-Raphaël sector, was sailing under the command of Captain J.B.W.Waller and escorting the troop transports and cargo ships of Texas's 36th Division. The *Bayfield*, a troop transport and attack ship, had also seen action at Utah Beach; it had aboard Major General John E. Dahlquist, in command of the 36th Division, and was following close behind the *Tuscaloosa*, escorted by two French cruisers, the *Emile Bertin* and the *Duguay Trouin*.[1]

The convoy that was bound for Sainte-Maxime, where it would be landing its troops and vehicles on the beaches the next morning, included *Biscayne*, an American converted seaplane tender, which had flown Rear Admiral Frank J. Lowry's flag at Anzio. Today the *Biscayne* had aboard it the entire staff of the 45th Division, including its commander Major General William C.Eagles. Lowry, whose flag was still flying a short distance away on the *Duane*, was in charge of Alpha sector, the westernmost part of Operation Dragoon, from Cavalaire-sur-Mer to Saint-Tropez.

One formation had by now outdistanced all the others and, with engines at maximum speed, was leading the Allied fleet. The men in this convoy, who were the most lightly armed of all the invasion troops, were to land well before daybreak on 15 August. In the plans of the Allied staff these assault units, less than a full division in strength, were designated as 'Sitka Force' and 'Romeo Force.' They were composed of French, American, and Canadian officers and men specially trained for night fighting and hand-to-hand combat. Their mission was to knock out the German defenses on the Iles d'Hyères and on the coast west of the landing zone before the combat fleet began firing its first volleys. Among them was a forty-seven year old French officer who would be the first man to splash ashore on the beaches of Provence, Marcel Rigaud.

About a dozen British and American cruisers and destroyers – including the *Somers*, the *Gleaves*, the *Sirius*, and the *Lookout* – were providing an escort for the small troop transports. The Canadian and British ships had on board the First Special Service Force and the African Commandos. The lead ship was the heavy cruiser *Augusta*, which flew the flag of Rear Admiral Lyal A. Davidson, commanding one of the naval assault forces. Nearly two years before, on 8 November 1942, Davidson had led the American landings at Safi, in Morocco, and the *Augusta* –

---

[1] The *Jeanne d'Arc*, the third of Rear Admiral Philippe Auboyneau's cruisers, did not take part in the Provence landings. She took aboard the members of the French Provisional Government at Algiers and brought them to Cherbourg. According to Jean Meirat, the *Jeanne d'Arc* won quite a name for herself when she returned to Algiers in a blaze of glory with a huge cargo of Camembert cheeses from Normandy. Her crew had bought them up in wholesale lots, figuring that the French in Algiers had been deprived of this gastronomic delicacy for quite some time.

before becoming the flagship of the Normandy invasion – had taken President Roosevelt to Newfoundland in 1941 for his meeting with Winston Churchill.

The coast of Corsica was still sending out lines of small amphibious vessels proceeding under their own steam to their various landing areas, their routes frequently intersecting those of the big convoys. Not a breath of wind was rippling the Mediterranean waters. The only grudging bit of cool air that came to the fleet's crews and the troops, now huddled on the decks after having stuffed themselves with mostly ineffective seasickness remedies, was produced by the speed of the ships themselves. Far behind, dominating the beach at Ajaccio, stood a bronze statue that looked as if it were scanning the horizon for the columns of departing ships – the statue of Napoleon.

At about 4 P.M. the *Kimberley* veered sharply about and began heading at full speed back to Ajaccio, drawing near the *Catoctin* as she passed.

The British destroyer's semaphores began flashing busily, and Admiral Hewitt received the following message, the last he would receive before the landing:

'I have just sailed round all the convoys. Everything is shipshape and in position. Good luck! May God be with you!'

By then, the entire attack fleet, from the heaviest, slowest ships down to the tugboats, the beacon buoy boats and the most modest of the small craft, was carrying out its sailing orders. These formations, some of which had been assembling for days from all corners of the Mediterranean, were now following the course designated for all the convoys, a course designed to throw enemy reconnaissance off the trail. They were sailing in a general northerly direction, for all appearances toward the Gulf of Genoa, and would hold to this course until nightfall.

As a matter of fact, many of the ships' captains and unit commanders had not been let in on the over-all plans. When General Sudre questioned the captain of the *Winchester Castle* about the route he was steering, he received a laconic reply:

'I'm mainly concerned with not losing sight of the ship ahead of me.'

And so, during the afternoon of Monday, 14 August, until about 8 P.M., the *Montcalm*'s log recorded that the course followed by Admiral Jaujard's French cruisers 'oscillated between 345° and 15° – a due north course.'

22

THAT EVENING THE PILOT of an RAF Dakota was circling for a landing at the Ajaccio airport. The landing strip was narrow and tricky to negotiate. As the plane started to lose altitude, it suddenly found itself between two steep rock walls, one of them less than fifteen feet from its left wing. While his passengers were clinging to their seats, the pilot managed to come in safely. Winston Churchill heaved himself out of his seat, beaming and jovial, the ever-present cigar clenched between his teeth.

The flight from Naples had been uneventful, for by now German fighter planes had virtually been wiped from the Mediterranean skies.

Although Churchill had not yet regained complete peace of mind, he appeared to all intents and purposes to have overcome his hostility toward Operation Dragoon, the 'expedition fraught with peril' that he had vainly tried to stop. The old lion had become resigned to the inevitable, and was wishing Operation Dragoon and its participants all success.

At Ajaccio, a car bearing the insignia of the commander-in-chief of the Mediterranean naval forces was waiting for Churchill. Admiral Cunningham and General Wilson greeted him as he alighted. On the short drive to the port, Wilson described the vast amount of work that had been required since the beginning of the year to transform the island into an advance airbase for strategic bombing.

The general also explained the plan for providing reserve supplies of ammunition to the combat ships for the following day.

'The whole stock of shells for the attack fleet is here in Corsica,' he said. 'In only a few hours, the ships can report to one of the nearest ports that have been equipped for this purpose.'

More specifically, two French transport ships, the *Quency* and the *Barfleur*, which were riding at anchor off Ajaccio and Propriano, were set up to transfer their reserve of ammunition – everything from 3-inch shells to 13.4-inch shells – to the ships that would come in periodically for supplies. The transports would, in turn, take on more supplies themselves during the off hours.

Arriving at the port, the Admiral and the General immediately whisked the Prime Minister aboard the *Kimberley*, on which Churchill was going to sail during the night in order to see for himself how the Second D-Day landings were faring.

23

THE TIME WAS 7.15 P.M. on the French mainland. René Girard, an engineer, was in his house at Saint-Tropez, seated by the radio. Over the noise of German interference, he could barely catch the words of the BBC announcer. Since 1943, Girard had been heading a large Resistance group in the Monts des Maures, and his men had been on an alert status for the last twenty days. He had just heard two messages announcing the landings on the Mediterranean coast.

Like most of the Resistance group and section leaders, Girard did not know exactly where the Allies were planning to strike. However, he did know how he was to act when the messages began coming through, what his men were to do, and where he was to assemble them. He bent closer over the radio, turned up the volume as high as he dared, and listened intently.

But the messages that were coming over the air – some days there were as many as sixty-five of them – neither concerned him nor had any meaning for him. There were all sorts of colorfully contrived phrases: 'The hour is redolent with fragrance, and bells are ringing over the river . . .'; 'the yellow of the crocuses is staining the acid meadows . . .'; 'carp fishing is not done from a ladder . . .' The announcer paused for an instant and then resumed: 'Attention, here is an important message for Samuel and Arthur.' Girard sighed. None of this was intended for him. Once again, as he had so often done, he reflected sadly that 'tonight wasn't the night.' Still, as he had been doing for the last three weeks, he continued listening to the rest of the broadcast.

Suddenly there came the words 'Gaby is going to lie down on the grass. Nancy has a stiff neck.'

Girard held his breath and felt as if his heart had stopped beating. He could not believe his ears. The voice from London was continuing, repeating the first part of the message . . . which meant that the Allied landing in Provence was imminent:

'Nancy has a stiff neck.'

Girard really did not expect anything more. He thought it highly unlikely that the remainder of the message – the all-out signal for the entire Mediterranean Resistance – would be forthcoming that evening. He was reassuring himself that he still had all the time in the world to organize his men for the fighting and to attend to the final details.

To his astonishment, he now heard the announcement:

'The hunter is starving. The hunter is starving.'

The words were repeated twice.

This time Girard was almost unable to catch his breath again. There was no more doubt about it. Those brief sentences that he had just heard coming from his loudspeaker meant only one thing – the Allied landings were to take place the following day at 7 A.M.

Yet Girard felt a little hesitant. He went out his front door and walked calmly through the streets to visit his section leaders. They were all going to listen to the second broadcast at 9 P.M. Girard dispatched one man, an Alsatian who was employed as an interpreter at the *Kommandantur*, to find out what was going on with the Germans. The personnel at the *Kommandantur* had such confidence in their interpreter that the officers entrusted him with their most secret communiqués.

When the Alsatian returned, he could report only that there did not seem to be anything out of the ordinary going on, nor were there any special orders being issued for the night. As it turned out, this night the Germans in Saint-Tropez were going to foil most of the plans of Girard and his small band of men.

In Draguignan, another Resistance leader, Cazelles, had tuned in to the broadcast at 7.30 P.M., too late for the messages. But he had been in time to hear a warning from the Allied command:

'London speaking. You have just heard a few personal messages. Now please listen to this message from the Allied Supreme Commander ... The armies of the liberation are fanning out over France, and the enemy is actively shifting his troops and his defense positions. The enemy must be tracked down and destroyed everywhere, his weapons demolished, and his supply sources with withdrawal routes cut off. Your locality may be a target, whether or not there are any Germans in it. When you see the Allied planes approaching, take shelter. They may have to strike close to your home.'

At that instant the air-raid sirens began to moan. Cazelles hunched down closer to the loudspeaker. The announcement from London continued:

'Stay off the main highways. Don't linger under the bridges. Don't ride bicycles. If you must stay in town, remain in a shelter. If there are no air-raid shelters, stay under a staircase; lie flat on your face, keep away from windows and from all glass surfaces. Stay under shelter,' the voice went on. 'Make sure that your children are wearing identification tags with name and address on them. The fighting that has to be carried on against our mutual enemy is causing the deaths of many men today, of soldiers as well as civilians. It is impossible . . .'

Here the faint voice trailed off and became drowned in static. The warning had struck Cazelles as decidedly strange, and he made up his mind to listen in again two hours later. This time he, too, heard all the messages. It was now 9.15 P.M., and Girard, back in Saint-Tropez, had received the confirmation of the earlier messages that he needed. One by one his group leaders slipped out into the warm night on their way to alert the other men.

In La Motte, two local intelligence agents belonging to the *Mithridate* group, Jean Ramella and André Bauchière, hurried to Maurice Leycuras's house. Their total armament consisted of three shotguns and two pistols, but it was not the dearth of weapons that worried them most. What they needed desperately were some tricolored armbands, the identification by which they could make themselves recognized by the Allied troops who, as they had just learned, were to be parachuted during the night. Leycuras's father had been a tailor for the French army, and the two men immediately pounced on him. As Ramella describes it, 'every pair of scissors in the house as well as the sewing machine was sent into action to turn out those armbands.'

In Le Lavandou, Father Hélin, although active in the Resistance, had missed the 7 P.M. and the 9 P.M. broadcasts and so knew nothing of the messages. However, through some intuition, he had gone to bed fully clothed, for which he was later grateful. Ulysse Richard, who lived near the presbytery, had been a member of the *Alliance* group for the last two years, but he, too, had failed to listen to the broadcasts. On 2 November 1942, with the assistance of a fisherman, Richard had arranged the escape of General Henri Giraud, who subsequently made his way by submarine to Gibraltar in time for the Anglo-American landings in North Africa. In the spring of 1944, Richard had been arrested and imprisoned in Les Baumettes in Marseilles. By an inexplicable stroke of luck, his file had been destroyed. But when he returned to Le Lavandou, he found his house empty – both his wife and daughter had been deported.

In Valescure, a few miles from Saint-Raphaël, on this evening of 14 August, Agent ATE 163, a Belgian whose real name was Georges Dewaël and who was the man best informed about the German defenses on the invasion front, was putting away the tools in his welding shop. He had not received any notification, nor had he heard the radio. Like Father Hélin, Dewaël was planning to retire early and get a good night's sleep. Many other Resistance members, as it turned out, had also planned just a quiet evening at home. . . .

Of all those who had caught the clandestine announcements of the landings, perhaps the only person to whom they were not news was Michel Chrestien. For him, the message meant only that what he had been hoping for so long, against all probability, was finally about to happen. In March 1944, Chrestien had been arrested by the Toulouse police and thrown into the Saint-Michel prison. In early July, Darnand's[1] men had delivered him and his companions to the German authorities. Chrestien had had it – the abrupt summons in the dead of night, the SS men barking out orders, the brutal blows from rifle butts, and the sinister last march to the freight cars of the last shipment bound for Buchenwald. All things considered, the young man's spirits should have been completely dashed by the time the cold light of dawn broke. Yet something kept telling him that all was not yet hopeless.

Chrestien had managed to escape three times, four times, while the convoy was winding its way through the Rhône Valley under the bombardments, with bridges torn down and tracks ripped up by the Resistance fighters. Each time, he had been captured again and beaten. Chrestien recalls that, in his delirium, the name of one place kept haunting him, 'Golfe Juan.' 'Maybe,' he says, 'it was only because of Napoleon and the return from Elba.' During the entire time he was a prisoner, as each succeeding day made his liberation seem more remote, he kept telling himself that 'it was inevitable that the Allies should eventually stage a landing in the south,' and that such a landing would occur in the normal order of events after 6 June in order to drive the maximum number of Germans as far out of Normandy as possible. Cooped up in the death train, his body a mass of bruises, half-dead from starvation, tortured by thirst by day and by the cold at night, he still would not abandon hope.

Near Montélimar, Chrestien finally succeeded in escaping for good. He found himself in a little settlement called Homme d'Armes, where members of the local Drôme Resistance group took care of him for ten days. When he had recovered, he joined the Resistance group, and on the evening of 14 August he was thinking to himself that 'anything can happen as long as a train just keeps on running.'[2]

The warm Mediterranean evening was drawing to a close. For many

---

[1] Joseph Darnand, the Vichy Secretary of State for Maintenance of Order, was known as 'the French Hitler'. Executed in October 1945 (Translator's note.)

[2] The next evening, Chrestien saw a column of tanks turning on to the Montélimar highway, and he jumped into a ditch. As the tanks drew near, he realized that they were American Shermans. They were with General O'Daniel's 3rd Infantry Division, which, on the night of 14 August, had been loaded on to the LSTs that were to proceed to the beaches of Cavalaire-sur-Mer. Chrestien wound up his wartime career by serving in a 3rd Division reconnaissance unit.

of the men and women who had heard and interpreted the BBC messages the night that was now falling over Provence was going to be both one of the shortest and also the longest. Certain of these people were faced with overwhelming problems and had considerable trouble rallying their forces around them. Others, like René Girard in Saint-Tropez, were seriously wondering whether the task confronting them was not beyond their capacity and doubted whether they were sufficiently well-armed and organized.

Still uppermost in many minds was the memory of the bloodbath that had marked the reprisals following the abortive uprising of 6 June. But as of one mind, all were concentrating their hopes on the approaching dawn. The long night of exile, defeat and humiliation was at last coming to an end.

24

WHILE THE ALLIED ARMADA was still steering its course, ostensibly bound for Genoa, the stars gradually began to twinkle in the darkness. The night over the sea was serene.

Several times just before dusk enemy planes had flown over the convoys. They were isolated planes, probably from an observation unit stationed on the Ligurian coast. Their appearance had, of course, provoked furious bursts of gunfire from the antiaircraft artillery on the Allied ships, but each time the planes had managed to gain altitude and drop out of sight. These sporadic incursions could not really be said to disturb the invasion commanders. In fact, Admiral Hewitt seemed rather pleased.

The diversion plans designed to put the enemy off the scent had been carefully worked out by the staffs in Algiers and Naples. The officers responsible were not content with merely counting on German reconnaissance planes flying over – if they had been able, they would have provoked the flight deliberately! Hewitt, of course, had never entertained any illusions that the 1,200 ships and his force of flattops might slip by undetected by German intelligence. The important thing was to keep the enemy ignorant, up to the very last minute before the actual landings, of the exact sites at which the attack would be launched. For this reason, once it had set its course toward Genoa, the Allied flotilla did not deviate from its path. This was but one of many ruses cooked up by the staff of the Eighth Fleet to confuse the enemy; more were to follow, well in advance of H-Hour.

Aboard a ship of the Special Operations Group, whose assignment was to strike panic among the Germans, was an officer in the United States Naval Reserve who had been entrusted with a mission that was destined to produce repercussions all the way to Berlin within a few hours. He held the rank of lieutenant commander, and his face stirred memories in the people who saw him. At this moment, in the middle of the Mediterranean, Douglas Fairbanks, Jr., one of the most famous film stars of the between-wars era, was nonchalantly shod in sneakers as he stood on the deck of the *Stuart Prince* watching the soft darkness fall about him. He was wondering whether his mission – code-named 'Rosie' – would be successful, whether the Germans were really going to swallow the deception in store for them. By contrast with his experience making movies, in this particular assignment it was far more important to make oneself heard than seen.

Few of the men drifting along under the star-spangled August sky even cared about getting any sleep; anyhow, for most of them the night was going to be short. Standing at the bow of the *Joseph T. Dickman*, one of the 45th Division's transports, Corporal Carl B. Tenant, who had just marked his twenty-third birthday, was softly singing the words of a popular song, a sweet and slightly melancholy tune. Although Tenant's deck companion, a French master sergeant named Emile Bresc, did not understand the words, the melody was to linger a long time in his memory. Bresc had embarked with the American infantry troops to serve as a guide during the 180th Infantry Regiment's assault. He still had not had time to grasp the full extent of the adventure in which he was participating. Ten days earlier he had still been in Corsica with his 4th Senegalese Infantry Regiment, whose members were veterans of Elba. On 3 August, Bresc and three other men had been notified that they were assigned to a special mission. A plane had spirited them off to Naples, where they were immediately confined to quarters in the fort at Castelnuovo. Finally, three days later, Bresc was briefed on the reason for his abduction and on the mission for which he had been selected. He was informed that he would be landing in France a few miles from his birthplace, Roquebrune-sur-Argens. The officer who conducted the briefing was, in Bresc's word, 'a strapping fellow, fiftyish, full of all the fighting spirit of a West Point cadet.' He was Colonel Robert L. Dunaley, commanding the 180th Infantry. His men, survivors of the campaigns in Sicily and at the Volturno, were to land on the coast of Sainte-Maxime.

Bresc spent nearly all his time aboard the *Joseph T. Dickman* with Dunaley and the other officers, poring over aerial photographs of the

General Jean de Lattre de Tassigny,
commander of the French First Army.
(*Photo courtesy Robert Laffont*)

The French cruiser *Montcalm* in action.
(*Photo courtesy Robert Laffont*)

Infantry troops of the 45th Division surge ashore near Sainte-Maxime.
(*Photo U.S. Army*)

Parachutes "blossom" as troops descend to begin the liberation of southern France. The 10,000 paratroopers were commanded by General Robert Tryon Frederick.
(*Photo courtesy Robert Laffont*)

beaches that were to be assaulted by the regiment and studying a long, foam-rubber model of the areas around Val d'Esquières and Saint-Aygulf. But Bresc had been away from home since 1940, and occasionally he found his thoughts straying. He kept trying to picture how it would be to be reunited with his wife for the first time in four years. What stirred him most deeply was the prospect of seeing his little boy, Henri, who was now four and a half.

All the officers on all the convoy ships had by now opened the sealed envelopes marked 'top secret' that had been delivered to them under armed escort before the departure of the armada. The contents listed the positions and code names of the beaches. The Cavalaire-sur-Mer and Pampelonne sector, along which the American 3rd Division's troops would be landing, had been named 'Alpha'; the central landing area, around Sainte-Maxime, was 'Delta'; and the invasion zone farthest to the east, at the base of the dark red rocks of the Esterel heights, was 'Camel.' These were only three of the general landing areas along the stretch of some thirty miles between Cavalaire-sur-Mer and Anthéor; there were ten landing beaches in all, each identified by a name and color. 'Alpha Red' was the beach at Cavalaire-sur-Mer and 'Delta Blue' that of Val d'Esquières; 'Camel Green' indicated the beach of Le Dramont, while 'Camel Blue' was at Anthéor, on the right flank. Because of the many landing places strung out over a relatively limited distance, it was some time before many of the American soldiers, hailing from all over the United States, knew at which spot they had come ashore.

With the American troops that evening was a group of about twenty French navy men who maintained their vigil far into the night, continuing their study of the highly detailed invasion maps. They had caught up with the invasion fleet and boarded the convoy at the very last minute. They were thoroughly acquainted with the various landing sites, and had been assigned to guide the American units once the attack got under way on land. On board the *Dilwara*, Ensign François de la Fargue was smiling to himself over the overwhelming surprise he would give his father the next day by showing up, if his luck held, at the garden gate of his home near La Nartelle. La Fargue was assigned to the staff of Rear Admiral Bertram J. Rodgers, commanding the Delta area forces. Lieutenant Gisquet, on board the *Bayfield*, the command ship of the Camel zone troops, knew only that he would be landing at Le Dramont and that his mission was to proceed immediately, with Lieutenant Toop and a group of American navy men, to capture certain German documents in the semaphore and radar station at Cap Dramont. Since 5 August, Gisquet had been undergoing continuous interrogation by Toop and other officers about everything concerning the invasion coast around Saint-Raphaël. The question that had surprised him the most was one asked by Captain Thayer of Rear Admiral Spencer S. Lewis's[1] staff:

'Take a look at this map, Lieutenant. Tell me, what's wrong with it?'

Gisquet refused to let himself be disconcerted, even though he had noted something very strange. Intelligence reports in July had indicated extensive German mine fields at Le Dramont, whereas these latest maps failed to show the presence of any mines at all.

As he leaned against the railing of one of the twenty-five LSTs under the command of Commander O.F.Gregor, Lieutenant Jean-Pierre Aumont now knew where he was going to land – at the far end of the Bay of Cavalaire. Aumont wanted to tell his companion, Lieutenant King from Los Angeles, that the first of all the D-Day attacks would be occurring within a few hours on the estate of an old friend of his, Suzanne Ferrandi, at Cap Nègre, where he had spent a vacation in 1939.

But King had begged Aumont not to mention women again until they were back on land. The American officer was still reliving pleasant memories of a good-looking Neapolitan girl, 'the most gorgeous Italian creature that ever lived,' with whom he had spent much time over the past month. Aumont now stretched out in his sleeping bag and watched the stars come out above him in what seemed the most beautiful night he had ever seen, at the end of which he would be back home in his native land. Aumont had left France in 1941.

Signal lights pierced the darkness through which the Allied ships were slipping, and the signals were repeated from several ships at once, like the twinkling of thousands of stars, only to vanish instantly along the dark sea waters.

As suddenly as they had appeared, the lights blacked out. But already, at that instant, the 1,200 ships and troop transports had just changed course. The entire Allied fleet, over a thirty-five mile front, had set its sights on France. The time was 10.18 P.M.

The order had been carried out almost automatically, the convoy captains having been informed of the change in course two hours earlier. In two maneuvers, the assault fleet had shifted its direction 60° to port and was now steering a northwest course.

At the same time, a small cluster of British and Canadian ships, the first of the armada to sight the French mainland, had shut off their engines in the waters near the Iles d'Hyères.

---

[1] Lewis took over command after Moon's suicide.

25

ON THE EVENING OF 14 AUGUST, three reconnaissance ships of the German Sixth Security Fleet had sailed out of Marseilles harbor. It was shortly after 10 P.M., and the coast was already enveloped in deep night.

For the last two months, Lieutenant Commander Hermann Polenz had been getting his orders directly from Aix-en-Provence, the general headquarters of the navy's commander-in-chief for the coastal areas of southern France, referred to in the jargon of the *Kriegsmarine*'s higher echelons as *Admiral Südküste*.[1] Polenz found himself in command of some thirty ships that, although they were manned by German crews, enjoyed the peculiar distinction of not having been German-built. They were all spoils salvaged from the enemy – from the French in November 1942, and from the Italians in September 1943.

Under cover of night, two submarine chasers, former Italian sloops now flying the German flag – the *UJ-6081* and the *UJ-6082* – accompanied by the fast escort vessel *SG-21*, had steamed past Fort Saint-John at the entrance to the Old Port in Marseilles harbor and proceeded out to sea.

The *SG-21* was about to be the first German warship to face the Allied invasion fleet. She had been christened *Le Chamois* when she slid down the slipway into the murky waters of the Scorff at the French arsenal in Lorient. From the moment she hit the sea, *Le Chamois* embarked on a lively career. Until the June 1940, armistice, she had done escort duty with Allied convoys in the Mediterranean and the Bay of Biscay, had busily pursued German U-boats, and convoyed the troops of the Anglo-French Norwegian expedition to the coasts of Scotland. On the night of 3 July 1940, the *Chamois* was in North Africa, on her way out of Oran, when Admiral Sir James Somerville's British squadron, which had just attacked the French fleet anchored at Mer-el-Kebir, let go half a dozen broadsides in her direction – short ones, luckily. Two years later the *Chamois*'s luck was not holding up so well. On 27 November 1942, she

---

[1] In September 1943, Vice Admiral Paul Wever had been appointed to command the German naval forces in the south of France, from the Spanish frontier to the Italian frontier. But on the evening of 14 August, these duties were being assumed by Vice Admiral Ernst Scheurlen, who had just taken over; Wever had succumbed to a heart attack three days earlier.

was tied up at the Cronstadt wharf in the open basin at Toulon when her crew received orders to scuttle the ship. The *Chamois* keeled over on her side. Within the next year and a half she had been set afloat, abandoned, and sunk once more, during the Allied raid on Toulon on 24 November 1943.

Just a few weeks before this balmy August night in 1944, the former sloop *Chamois* had been made seaworthy again, and, as the *SG-21*, she was one of the four fast escort ships of the Sixth Security Fleet. The *SG-21* was headed south through the light offshore breeze. Her aging engines, which had not benefited from their two immersions in the sea, were still managing to do a respectable twenty knots.

26

THE DARKNESS WAS IMBUED with the fresh fragrance of the sea, mingled with the stench of machine oil. But now the air had caught and was holding a subtler scent emanating from the mainland – and Lieutenant Colonel Georges-Régis Bouvet's seven hundred African Commandos could not be wrong, even though they were understandably gripped by a strong emotion as their native shores grew nearer.

They were not the only men standing by for the attack signal as they waited off the Côte des Maures, a few miles from the steep rocks of the Ile du Levant. But they would be the first group to plunge into action in the predawn of this D-Day. Seven more ships of the American, Canadian and British navies, including the *Prince Henry* and the *Prince Baudouin*, transporting Colonel Edwin A. Walker's First Special Service Force, were standing by, their engines shut off, their bulky silhouettes looming against the somber starlit sky. In the silence, the low, murmuring voice of chaplains could be heard giving their blessings to the troops, to the 3,000 men who were going to lay the groundwork of the mission.

The ships' public address and loudspeaker systems had fallen silent. On board the *Prince David*, Bouvet stood lean and taut, his khaki cap smartly in place over his angular features. He took a last glance at his watch. The hands pointed to 9.57 P.M. and he knew that the long-awaited time was finally at hand, the moment that had been planned for all those months and years. But a lingering apprehension made him slightly uneasy. The moon, in its last quarter, was due to rise at 3.15 A.M. Bouvet wondered whether, by that time, he and his men would be able to accomplish all the tasks that lay ahead of them on the soil of France.[1]

In the darkness, Bouvet had trouble distinguishing the faces of his men who were gathered on deck to await orders to board landing craft. But this anonymity was deliberate, and was integral to the mission that awaited the African Commandos. Their orders were to work separately in the black of night, into which they would blend invisibly, behind the enemy lines.

Roger Font, an eighteen year old commando, was passing the time by listening to the light music with which the loudspeakers were flooding the decks and catching an occasional nap while stretched out on the boards that would serve as gangplanks for the men loading into the landing craft. Like all Bouvet's men, Font had volunteered for this assignment and had nurtured the hope that the Second D-Day would be in France – a country in which, as it happened, he had never set foot, Font had never been out of his native Algeria.

On board the *Princess Beatrix*, skippered by Captain J.D. King of the Royal Navy, Quartermaster Sergeant Georges du Bellocq, a rugged sportsman and expert mountain-climber, had regained his composure after a row earlier in the day with his close friend, Master Sergeant Noël Texier. They had almost fallen out over the drawing of lots for their landing assignment, which was to be one of the first on the D-Day time-table. Near them was a young midshipman, Albert Maury, who was feeling more anxious and uncertain as the minutes went by. He felt as if he were staggering under the burden of an overwhelming responsibility for 'everything that lay ahead of me.' Now that the convoy had halted, Maury was assailed by a great doubt, and was casting his lot with his men, as he reviewed all the instructions he had been given.

In preparation for their night attack, the seven hundred commandos, selected on the basis of a strict screening, had been given the toughest kind of training, one that strained their physical endurance to the limit. Even though they had already had a rough first-hand 'rehearsal' two months before in the hard fighting on Elba, Bouvet demanded even more of his men and placed them under iron discipline. Week after week they had had everything in the book thrown at them – cliff-climbing and rock-scaling, weaving their way through mine fields in pitch darkness, attacking pillboxes, even attacking ships, and engaging in combat under fire from live ammunition. The amphibious phase of their training had been particularly arduous, but the African Commandos took it all in their

[1] Bouvet's fears proved to be groundless. Although the moon did rise at 3.15 A.M., it failed to constitute the slightest hindrance to the Allied fleet in its approach to the coast, to the French commandos, or to Walker's troops on the Iles d'Hyères. With the exception of a few German aerial observers and navy men, no one noticed anything amiss.

stride – even the battle against seasickness! To toughen his troops against encounters with German armored vehicles, Bouvet had ordered each man to hollow out a narrow ditch and lie down in it, and then had sent vehicles rolling over the ditches – light tanks at first, followed by medium and heavy ones. There may have been a few cave-ins, not to mention attacks of colic, but in the end everyone had emerged safe from the ordeal.

These men, whose mission was one of very great danger, whose routine existence consisted of surprise attacks and slipping undetected through the enemy's defenses, would not have to rely solely on their sharp-edged knives for too long. Once the success of their mission was assured, they would be followed by a strong, fully motorized detachment and heavy covering fire, jeeps, trucks, antitank guns, an imposing array of automatic weapons, and some 2,000 pounds of British and American explosives.

But their success depended on the elements of surprise and secrecy. When the commandos, exhausted by their forced night marches and drilling on the beaches of southern Italy, were told that the Allied staff was planning to have them land in Yugoslavia, their morale sagged sharply. Bouvet's desk was piled with photographs and minutely detailed maps of the Adriatic, and several of his officers were requesting transfers to some other combat unit in which, as they put it, 'people won't be trifling with us by methodically pushing us farther and farther from the front lines.' The enlisted men were griping, too, as they collapsed wearily on to their blankets after the day's maneuvers. Colonel Ruyssen, Bouvet's adjutant, recalled that 'everybody was astonished that there weren't at least a few deserters.'

Meanwhile, one man was spending the major part of his time in Naples, in the innermost circles of the invasion staff. He was the only one in the African Commandos who knew the real target, the ultrasecret mission for which his men were training so strenuously. Each day a Piper Cub deposited Bouvet at the Capodichino airport, from which he made his way unaccompanied into Naples, to a big building that had been spared by bombs and was surrounded by barbed wire and military policemen. This was the Flambeau Building, in which General Patch had set up his Seventh Army headquarters. Bouvet's difficulties began at the moment when, after reaching the second floor – the inner sanctum of the invasion staff – he still had two more barriers to pass and had to show a different identification card for each. This was the famous 'XO' card that admitted its bearer into the 'double secrecy' of the operations room, a vast, airy office equipped with an alarm that would automatically sound the alert throughout the headquarters should anything interfere with the window-closing system. The walls were plastered with enormous blow-ups of aerial photographs, but the 'secret of secrets' occupied an outsize table in the middle of the room. This was a model comprising the twenty-three 'mosaics' that represented the landing area. The fantastic foam-rubber map, or mosaic, was a large-scale, amazingly accurate relief map depicting the coast between Le Lavandou and Cannes – every last detail of the terrain was faithfully reproduced.

Bouvet was interested in only a fraction of the mosaic – a narrow rocky strech of beach, barely $1\frac{1}{2}$ miles long, from Cavalière to Rayol. But in this bit of the Provençal shoreline there was plenty for him to worry about. From it projected the 350-foot-high sheet face of Cap Nègre, which his men would be attacking before H-Hour. The honor of bearing the brunt of establishing the first Provence beachhead by dawn devolved upon the commandos, and this meant that they had to knock out the three German 6-inch guns and the electrically operated flame throwers that defended the position. After they had landed at Rayol and occupied Cap Nègre, Bouvet's men had as their next job holding, by themselves and with no prospect of reinforcements, the coast highway at Cavalaire-sur-Mer until tanks of the American 3rd Division could catch up with them. Another part of their mission consisted of capturing a height one mile from the shore.

Bouvet's plan of attack had been set up long before. But never did he carry any notes or papers on his person, not even in his headquarters at Agropoli, near Salerno, where the commandos swapped the wildest rumors concerning their destination, and no one could have guessed that the young colonel had been assigned the awesome responsibility of leading the first of the D-Day assaults. No one else was in on the secret except Patch himself and a forty-seven year old commando officer appointed by Bouvet to spearhead the French landings.

Bouvet had originally requested that incendiary bombs be dropped on the thickly planted wooded area surrounding Cap Nègre. General Wilson flatly refused, declaring that the commando leader was out of his mind. Photographs taken in early July disclosed new pillboxes lining the beach at Rayol. Bouvet's immediate reaction was to request permission to take off by submarine on a personal reconnaissance, but Patch adamantly opposed him.

'Look here, Colonel! By any farthest stretch of the imagination, do you honestly believe for a single minute that I could risk letting the Germans get hold of an officer who's in on the whole invasion business?'

Bouvet bristled, but Patch gently reminded him that the agents of the *Abwehr*, Nazi military intelligence were masters of the art of extracting information no matter how strongly one resists. The impetuous French colonel realized that he would have to fall back on his own devices.

Those were definitely slim. However, one day in mid-July, a Piper Cub made an 'emergency' landing at Biguglia, on Corsica, after running into a storm over the Tyrrhenian Sea. As Bouvet alighted, he coolly gambled his whole hand by displaying his precious 'XO' card – and managed to get a Boston plane to fly him over his landing area. Off Genoa the plane ran into flak from German batteries, but the flight went off successfully. On this sultry July afternoon, the people in the little Mediterranean resort of Rayol could hardly dream that the Allied plane cruising low over their sleepy town was carrying a French officer who was craning his neck in order to etch on his mind an image of his forthcoming battleground.

It did not take long for Patch to get wind of this breach of discipline. But after an initial outburst, he subsided.

'Colonel,' the General said, 'at this minute either you should be a prisoner of the Germans or I should be relieving you of your command. You just happen to be damned lucky – and by God, I do believe that's one of the things I like best in a fighting man!'

And so, one evening, the African Commandos stationed in Agropoli failed to show up at the houses in which they were quartered. Their Italian hosts were used to this; on several occasions during the past month the men had not returned on schedule, sometimes not for days at a time. But this time they had gone for good, leaving all their possessions. Off the shores of Campania, three Canadian merchant marine cargo ships were slowly heading out to sea, and to the men on board, the tiny port of Agropoli, sheltered behind its breakwater, was rapidly becoming a speck on the horizon. The date was Saturday, 12 August. The following day, in the Gulf of Valinco in Corsica, the time came for Admiral Davidson to authorize Bouvet to brief his men.

Roger Font remembers the beach 'with the big, marvelous pine trees at Propriano, where we were being kept in quarters. Even when we went to get water in the village, we had to be accompanied by an officer.' Like his fellow commandos, Font was still under the illusion that they were going to be given a tough job in Yugoslavia to lend a hand to Marshal Tito. All the same, he had not given up hoping that their destination might yet turn out to be France, since, after all, nobody knew anything for sure.

Lieutenant Bernard Girardon of the First Commando Group was also hoping that the much-talked-of landing in the Adriatic was just so much eyewash. Girardon had been wounded on Elba while he was in the landing craft, but had managed to carry on long enough to knock out a blockhouse, whose fire was mowing down the men on the beach, and to finish off the battery by hurling the Germans' own grenades back at them. He had almost bled to death by the time they got him back to Ajaccio. Now he was hoping that his escape from his hospital room to join the others had not been for nothing. Girardon's wish would be fulfilled, but he himself had only a week more to live.

After Bouvet had mustered his men near the beach, he began speaking, his voice choked with emotion:

'Men ... My friends ... Boys ...'

(His words had caused a ripple of surprise; Bouvet was not known for informality.)

'All of you have been waiting for this announcement. There couldn't be any higher honor than the one that's been given to the African Commandos. By tomorrow night we'll not only be in France – we'll be the very first ones there!'

As Font recalls it, the colonel added that their diversionary tactic would be to 'constitute a nucleus that would cause all the Germans in the area to converge on them, so that the Allies could land and encircle the enemy, catch them in a trap.'

Davidson had not authorized Bouvet to reveal any more details than that to his men. Because of the need for absolute secrecy, they would not know the exact time or landing place until all were aboard ship.

Aboard the *Prince David*, the loudspeakers were sputtering, and then a great prolonged whistling was the signal for silence as the voice of a Canadian officer came through. Standing to attention side by side, Midshipman Albert Maury, Quartermaster Sergeant Portejoie, and a sixteen year old commando named Georges Bonnet, with his friend Pépion, listened to the carefully enunciated message. They felt as if the eyes of hundreds of men whom they had never met and whom they probably never would meet were fixed on them. This made Maury feel that everything was going to be all right.

At the end of the broadcast aboard the *Princess Beatrix*, Quartermaster Sergeant Georges du Bellocq of the First Commandos turned to his friend Master Sergeant Noël Texier. They had been singled out to spearhead the landings with only nine men apiece, and their job was to capture the blockhouses at Rayol before the arrival of the main commando group one hour later.

Du Bellocq realized that the right-hand side of the beach was by far the more dangerous, and he wanted it for his men. But when they drew straws, he had drawn the left. Now he was trying to work on Texier again, but the latter would not give in.

'Not on your life! It's all set now, so forget about it.'

'Damn it, you're going to let me have the right side. You'll see – everything'll work out all right.'

Texier shook his head, and Du Bellocq could see the suggestion of a gloating smile hovering about his friend's lips.

'Noël!' he shouted. 'You're going to let me have that right side, or I get real nasty! You'll be sorry!'

Texier's smile faded.

'O.K., have it your way, if you want it so bad. But remember, you asked for it.'

And that was how the left side of the beach fell to Noël Texier – who became the first casualty of the Second D-Day landings.

27

A BRITISH VOICE was now sounding over the loudspeaker:

'Attention! Attention! French Commandos! Be ready to move into the landing barges in ten minutes. Over.'

After a short pause the voice added: 'Commandos, all the best to you!'

The hands of Colonel Bouvet's watch pointed to 10 P.M. Like huge bunches of grapes, the men slid smoothly down the ropes hanging over the sides of the transports and lowered themselves into the twenty-four flat-bottomed assault craft. In one LCI,[1] Texier's and Du Bellocq's men pushed off in the darkness toward the PT[2] boat that was to tow them toward shore. The only visible guide light was a red signal casting a dull glow at the sterns of the launches.

Each LCI had three benches. Sergeant Préat straddled the middle one, between his second in command, Renévier, and two other men, Menière and Roland, who were armed with the group's only machine gun. Texier and Du Bellocq sat facing each other on the two other benches, leaning against the bulwark. Thus packed in, they would see nothing but the starry, moonless sky. Most of the men promptly fell asleep.

[1] Landing craft infantry.
[2] Patrol torpedo.

They were not interested in the operations involved in making the LCIs fast to the tow launches. Then came the jolt as the ropes became taut, and then they were off. The visibility was somewhere from four to six miles, and the haze that had covered the Mediterranean for two days was still persisting, hiding the distant mainland. The PT boats and LCIs had a good two-hour ride ahead of them. It took a little while for all the convoys to assemble, and Roger Font recalls that as he was pulling away from the transport, the LCIs and PT boats were still milling around 'in a kind of frenzied dodgem-car pattern.' In the midst of it all, out of the deep silence of the night, the ships' bells sounded eerie, like something out of another world.

'At one point a plane came over flying low and made several passes,' Font says. 'Each time, the little bells tinkled again and the LCI stopped moving.'

Many of the men were oblivious to what was going on around them as they droned across the water. In the account given by Bosun's Mate Vilmot, the first thing he knew was that someone's elbow was jabbing him awake, causing him to spring to his feet like a jumping-jack. It was only then that he realized the PT boat had vanished. And the next moment brought a further realization, 'a clearly discernible band, colored deeper than the night, stretched through the darkness right ahead of me; we were close to the coast.' Not a sound was uttered on any of the LCIs. Every man had his own job to attend to and knew exactly how to go about it in dead silence. The scenario had been rehearsed so carefully and so often that, as a First Commando rifleman named Henri has described it, when 'I felt a slight pressure from the hand of Sergeant Guillaume beside me,' that was the signal to launch the two rubber rafts[1] that were to float them ashore.

And so, like semi-automatons, exactly as they had been trained to do during all those days and nights in Italy and Corsica, the twenty men slid quietly into the rubber boats. As a sign of farewell, when each man climbed past, he gave a friendly tap on the shoulder of the British sailor who was standing by.

It was time for Du Bellocq and Texier to go their separate ways. They bade each other farewell without a word – just a familiar punch on the shoulder. If anyone could have looked into their eyes at that moment, he would surely have read the excitement kindled by the imminent combat, in which they were the very first fighters. Here the two men's paths separated, never to meet again.

Half a mile away, well in advance of the other units, the subdued putt-putt of an electric motor was throbbing through the night. To the two

[1] A rubber raft could accommodate ten men. These rafts generally had to be rowed.

men stretched out in the bottom of the narrow rubber dinghy, the faint noise of their engine sounded like a string of giant firecrackers exploding.

The craft was carving a straight furrow as fast as its tiny two-horse-power engine could take it, right to the beach at Rayol. A young American naval officer, Ensign Johnson, was steering. His fellow 'sailor' was a French officer twenty years older than he, Major Marcel Rigaud of the African Commandos. Together they were about to embark on the first mission of D-Day. For Rigaud, H-Hour was less than thirty minutes away – 5 A.M.

The only weapons aboard were two Colt revolvers and a Thompson submachine gun. The mission assigned to Johnson and Rigaud was not supposed to involve any actual fighting. As a matter of fact, they were being relied on to avoid it. On paper, it had all looked simple enough. They were to land at the little bay at Rayol, to the right of the redoubt-able Cap Nègre – without, of course, arousing the German sentries. There they were to set out a line of signal lights to mark the attack area and to guide the two leading patrols – Texier's and Du Bellocq's. One hour later, in the same manner, they were to guide the main landing force – Bouvet and his seven hundred commandos, who were to cut off the highway between Le Lavandou and Cavalaire-sur-Mer to prevent German reinforcements from reaching the assault area before daybreak.

However, events were to turn out rather differently. Rigaud had been briefed on his mission a month before, after having successfully replied to a series of interrogations and tests at headquarters in Naples concerning his knowledge of the Côte des Maures. (It happened that he was the owner of a small villa at Croix-Valmer, on the bay of Cavalaire. Fifteen months earlier, Rigaud had been an infantry reserve captain. At the age of forty-six, he had escaped from France through Spain and had joined the fighting on the beaches at Elba, on the previous 17 June.)

On the horizon, with the sea as smooth and motionless as a lake, the shoreline suddenly began to emerge out of the blackness. The Monts des Maures were silhouetted faintly against the night sky. The Frenchman could not resist whispering to his companion:

'Look, Johnson – France!'

Rigaud was compelled to utter those words, so deep was his emotion – his rejoicing stabbed him like physical pain. He even felt just a little ashamed, although deep down he knew that his American friend would understand and sympathize with his feelings. Years afterward, he still remembered Johnson's reaction – a silent grip on his shoulder and an almost equally silent whisper:

'Old fellow! . . . God bless you!'

Enveloped in blackness, the men scanned the dim shore line that now seemed to be rushing dizzily toward them. The beach was now only three hundred yards away.

It was only then that Rigaud realized, incredulously, that somewhere, somehow, they had gone off course. The beach lying directly ahead of them was not at Rayol.

28

THE MEN ABOARD the invasion fleet at sea noted midnight on their watches. The submarine chasers, patrol ships, cruisers and destroyers had maneuvered to form three groups offshore from the small beach towns of Cavalaire-sur-Mer, Sainte-Maxime, and Saint-Raphaël, and now they were going into position in front of the Alpha, Delta, and Camel beaches. Behind them lay the troop transports and the LCIs of the 3rd, 45th, and 36th Divisions.

At about the same time, on ten airfields in the area around Rome, 396 Dakota C-47s and C-53s were warming their motors on take-off strips made of long lengths of Summerfield lattice-board or perforated steel, fitted end to end and laid over thin beds of gravel. Under some of the strips even the gravel was lacking – there was just sand.

In the glare of the floodlights, the dark stripes stood out on the Dakotas' wings, the familiar marks that they had borne during their missions in North Africa, Sicily and the long siege of Monte Cassino. They were transporting over 5,000 airborne troops, mainly Americans and Britons, but including some Frenchmen.

At the Follonica military airfield, a formation of DC-3s carrying twelve special crews belonging to the 596th Airborne Engineer Company had just roared up and away from the wide strip. The job of the men aboard was to mark the dropping zones with ground lights. They were escorted by a group of night fighter planes, which in turn were accompanied by anti radar protection planes. The entire formation set its course toward the northern shore of Corsica. Allied ships would be waiting there, whose assignment was to set out lighted buoys outlining the air corridor. The last buoy would have been set out nearly opposite Cap d'Antibes, a few minutes' flight time from the dropping zones.

The planes rose up into a moonless night, but the 596th's scouts were hoping that the moon would appear on schedule, just when they would be arriving over the drop zones. The swarm of planes roared through the darkness until, to the watchers on the ground below,[1] it became a dim blur in the sky.

---

[1] Among the soldiers at this take-off was a twenty-four year old corporal from Marseilles named Jean Folliero de Righi, one of the sixteen Frenchmen assigned to drop over Provence with General Frederick's First Airborne Task force. He had been sent from North Africa and Corsica to carry out his mission, which was to act as guide and liaison for the paratroopers. At this moment, de Righi could barely contain his anger and disappointment – at the last minute he had been ordered to turn over his parachute and jump suit to an American war correspondent.

Part Two

THE ATTACK IN
THE NIGHT

1

THE ONLY SOUND now cutting through the stillness of the night was the faint murmur of the waves lapping at the shore. Ensign Johnson shut off the motor of the dinghy as it slithered and shuddered to a stop on the sand. Nothing was stirring, no flutter in the deep shadows betrayed any enemy presence. Around the narrow semicircular strip of beach with its overhanging mass of woodland, dotted here and there by the walls of houses, everything seemed utterly calm and silent.

Major Rigaud leaped on to dry land. He and Johnson had just wasted a precious half hour getting their bearings, about one mile west of their target. They had had to retrace part of their route, hugging the shore line, and fearing every minute that the noise of their motor would carry to enemy ears. Finally they had reached their destination an inlet shaped like a small natural amphitheater backing up against a wooded slope. This was it. Rigaud was now sure of his location and had nothing more to worry about on that score.

That tangled profusion of eucalyptus trees and palms, of Alep pines intermingled with terraced gardens set amid lush vegetation above a sandy beach – this was unmistakably Rayol, where he used to come to swim for so many years before the war. In passing, Rigaud had also just identified two rocks barely emerging from the water. The local residents called them the *Rochers de la Seiche*, although the maps listed them as the *Rochers Malpaigne*. It had never occurred to Rigaud to be concerned about these rocks. In the excitement of the moment, he could not have suspected that his confidence was ill-founded.

He busied himself preparing to carry out his task. The most important thing was to make certain his flashlight was in good working order. Pulling it out of its waterproof case, he shielded it with one and flicked it on. Three brief green flashes rewarded him. The batteries were all right. The next instant, pointing the flashlight toward the sea, he began sending

103

the series of signals that were to guide the commandos. What with the delay due to a navigational error, it was now time for the commandos to start arriving. As the minutes ticked by, two agonizing questions began nagging at Rigaud – Had the two spearhead patrols perhaps also been the victims of a similar miscalculation? And what about the rest of the forces waiting to come in behind them?

As Rigaud stood there flashing, watching and waiting, his anxiety reached its peak. As far as his eyes could make out, straining through the obscurity, there was nothing to see but the empty, dull-black water, nor was there any noise but that of the waves slapping restlessly against the sand. The waiting grew interminable, and the two men, wondering and worrying, felt their tension approaching breaking point as they stood helplessly in the dark. And still nothing was happening, or even appeared about to happen.

Baffled and perplexed, Rigaud and Johnson kept on flashing signals until the batteries finally petered out. Just then, to their left, the sky lit up in a violent conflagration high above the treetops and rocket flares began streaking the night amid the din of exploding grenades and the furious barking of machine guns. The battle of Provence had just begun, but Rigaud's mission, like many others slated for that important night, had been to no avail. Not one LCI came into sight, and Rigaud heaved a bitter sigh.

He was able to pinpoint the spot at which the fighting had broken out and was now becoming a full-fledged, all-out engagement. It was at Cap Nègre. The time was 1.30 A.M.

2

WHILE JOHNSON AND RIGAUD were desperately flashing signals, the two commando groups whose mission it was to knock out the pillboxes at Rayol were peering through the blackness just as desperately, vainly seeking those green flashes. From the outset, fate had had it in for the two patrols, and was reserving a double-barreled load of bad luck for them.

Rigaud's intuition had been correct. As he had feared, the successive waves of convoys that he was to guide safely to the shore had been the victims of the same navigational error, for which the Canadian navy men were responsible and which had nearly been fatal for him. He could not have foreseen that a cluster of rocks barely protruding above the water near the beach were to wreck all the plans to which those many months of laborious and minutely detailed preparation had been devoted. As it turned out, not one commando boat reached its destination. The LCIs were doomed to land at irregular intervals, sometimes very widely spaced as the result of errors of calculation, and they were consistently off to the west of their assigned areas.

Luck was definitely against the ill-fated African Commandos. Unaware that they were off course, drifting in utter blackness toward a beach that did not even appear in the invasion plans – below the ridge at Le Canadel – they were prevented by rocks from spotting the narrow opening of the Rayol inlet. Everything had been in vain – Rigaud's anxious signaling, their agonized waiting. Not one flash of light ever reached them. Rigaud, who had been entrusted with what was probably the most glorious mission of D-Day, had to face the awful fact that all had been for naught. There was no consolation.[1]

Sergeant Du Bellocq's nine men in the first group of commandos began pulling on the oars in earnest when they saw the shore looming up ahead of them. They were to land on the eastern edge of the bay at Rayol, the right-hand objective that Du Bellocq had almost forcibly wrested from his friend Texier. However, it did not take Du Bellocq long to realize that they had not come in at the proper place. The beach looked longer, more open and less sheer than the one he had memorized from the 'mosaic' model. Besides, Rigaud had provided additional details:

'You'll see a flight of steps with four arches, leading straight up in the middle of the beach. And believe it or not, it's the only one of its kind on the whole coast.'

And then he had added:

'And anyhow, I'll be there waiting.'

But now that he had landed, nothing was as Rigaud and the model had led him to expect. What was worse, there was no sign of Rigaud himself.

Du Bellocq's direst suspicions were being borne out only too well. Busy with the oars in the rubber boat, his men were unaware that anything had gone amiss. But their hardy, battle-toughened leader, who was ready for anything from fierce skirmishing on mountainous terrain to bitter hand-to-hand fighting in the darkness, was oppressed with the feeling that 'this unknown patch of land was fairly bristling with all kinds of hostility.'

[1] Following their long wait, isolated amid the German defenses, Rigaud and Johnson set out to sea again in black despair. Their craft's storage batteries eventually gave out, and they were picked up in the open sea by an LCI. Rigaud subsequently landed with an American infantry detachment at Cavalaire-sur-Mer that morning. Even by then he had not been able to find out what had gone awry.

The rubber boat suddenly lurched forward on a breaker, and Du Bellocq knew that they were almost on the beach.

He afterwards learned that the spot on which he and his men touched land bore the coy name of the Bay of Nymphs. In fact, they had landed on the beach at Le Canadel, near the railway tracks of the little coastal train. While Rigaud was helplessly searching for the commandos landing craft in the darkness, Du Bellocq was 'getting the hell out of this nameless beach,' making his way toward the nearby Monts des Maures. The commandos' objective, which they were to reach by D-Day morning, was Mont Biscarre, a wooded height northeast of Rayol.

For months the commandos' daily routine had consisted of instruction in the art of invisible, stealthy approaches and how to detect and slip through enemy posts. Exactly as they had rehearsed it so many times, Du Bellocq and his men immediately got into their stride, blending with the night. Sturdily, purposefully, almost mechanically, they set about scaling rock after rock, their bodies melting into the blackness. Suddenly, far above their heads, the beam of a powerful flashlight swept the darkness. Du Bellocq caught a quick glimpse of a *Feldwebel*'s helmet and uniform, peering anxiously as he leaned cautiously out over the rocks, trying to pierce the blackness before he, too, withdrew back into the night.

The ten men crossed through a garden redolent with all the summer scents of the Mediterranean before reaching a secondary road. They followed this for a while and then plunged into another garden, in which not a leaf was stirring. Here Du Bellocq, at the head of his men, abruptly plowed into some barbed wire. The sharp barbs pierced his thighs and stomach, and he could feel the warm blood trickling from his hands, but, as he commented later, 'at least now I knew what I was up against.' The members of the First Commando Group had just reached the outer defenses of the Provence coast.

As they began using their heavy wire cutters to open a breach in the tangled mass, they fully expected to be blown to bits by land mines. But nothing of the sort happened, and by dint of perseverance they nudged their way through the night. Only now they were being even more stealthy and cautious – if that was possible. A tree branch made a slight snapping sound overhead, pine needles slid with a silky rustling under their feet, and the men paused, alert for the slightest noise that might come from the gardens and houses that looked so peacefully asleep. A few moments later they found themselves on the brink of the first network of hillside trenches, but the trenches were empty.

That was when, a few yards to the left, a voice called out. The suddenness of it nearly caused Du Bellocq to leap into the air. With bated breath he stood motionless, waiting, his hand firmly gripping his knife.

'Ludwig! Ludwig!' the voice repeated.

Bending down in the shadows, the Frenchman flicked open his knife blade. The voice continued to call out, sounding increasingly nervous and anxious, although the German sentry kept walking toward the men hidden in the darkness. He stopped shouting and halted. Du Bellocq could hear the slight sound of the German's hand reaching for his Mauser, but the Frenchman beat him to the draw. The commando's submachine gun briefly shattered the silence, his knife slid back into its sheath. The German screamed once, before slumping down amid the sound of murmuring leaves and crackling twigs. A second burst of fire finished him off – 'he gurgled and then shut up,' the Frenchman recalls.

Du Bellocq felt reasonably sure that he had just killed the first German on D-Day in Provence.

3

MEANWHILE, ONE MILE TO THE LEFT of this group, a second rubber boat had landed on the coast. Its occupants too, had been the victims of the Canadians' tragic navigational error. They were the second sabotage group of the African Commandos, with Sergeant Noël Texier leading them. The error was to cost Texier his life.

He, also, lost no time taking in the situation, soon realizing that he was nowhere near his objective. Straining through the darkness, he tried to get his bearings. The dark, forbidding-looking mass that reared sharply up between the sea and the sky left no doubt of where he was, he had just landed in front of Cap Nègre itself, an objective that he was in no way prepared to reach.

He hesitated for a fraction of a second, just long enough to reflect on this predicament and then had his men disembark. They formed a handful of ten men at the base of a cliff some 350 feet high. As Texier knew, the position was strongly defended by three big guns and was further protected by an extensive and complicated system of electrically operated flame-throwers, as well as machine-gun nests planted strategically over the rocky promontory. The best-defended stronghold of all was Cap Nègre itself, whose steep drop automatically ruled out the danger of a seaborne attack. How could he expect to knock out the battery and overpower its crew with but one submachine gun and the light weapons that his nine men had on them? And even these noise-producing weapons were not to be used except as a last resort. Texier did not hesitate any longer.

The French commandos made fast the rubber boat and then began scrambling up the cliff, agile and supple as cats. After slashing their way through the first barbed-wire barricade, they dug into the rock on the east face of Cap Nègre, opposite the tiny bay at Pramousquier. A short distance farther, the men in the lead came upon some felled trees, booby traps, most likely, which they cautiously skirted.

The going was rough, but months of rugged training had inured these men, and it was almost as if they were leaping from rock to rock, pulling and pushing one another along, arching their backs to inch themselves upward, their weapons slung over their shoulders, digging footholds with their knives in order to cling to the rock. As they neared the halfway point, they came upon a forbidding encirclement of rocks that had been filed and sharpened, like the chards of broken bottles cemented on the top of walls. Here, instead of a wall, there was a sentry path, the Cap Nègre path, which had been fortified by the Germans, and along it ran the twisting tube of a flame-thrower that could sweep out over the two hundred feet of rocks dropping straight down into the sea. Texier, pressing his body against the rocky surface, wriggled his way up, the sharp stone edges now slicing deeply into his hands and wrists. As he grasped at the next rock, a piece suddenly gave way and went clattering down the cliff. But Texier had managed to hang on.

What happened next must have goaded him to a final fury. One can only imagine the black despair that seared his soul when a shower of grenades cascaded down from the sentry path in a roar of explosions that shattered the night. Noël Texier, mortally wounded, released his grasp and began falling, his body hurtling from rock to rock and finally coming to rest on a small ledge. He lay there bleeding, moaning faintly.

This was one of the most frightful moments of Sergeant Préat's life. Texier lay dying only a few feet away, yet no one could go near him lest the entire patrol be annihilated. Texier had issued the strictest orders for just such an eventuality.

In accordance with their instructions, the nine survivors of the commando group scattered as best they could over the recesses in the Cap Nègre cliff, making no attempt to answer the enemy's fire. Sick at heart, they had no choice but to abandon Texier to his solitary agony. The grenades had caught him full in the head, and now he lay still, his blood ebbing away, quietly giving up his life for a target that had not even been assigned to him. At best, death is only ironic, and Texier's death was cruelly so. He had reached the age limit for his rating, and furthermore, having been wounded in Tunisia the year before, he had been ready for his discharge. With only a few weeks of active service still ahead, he had not been able to resist the urge to return to his homeland. He had volunteered for this night mission, a spearhead mission entrusted to a handful of Frenchmen – and now he had been the first to die.

Resuming their scrambling along the vertiginous face of the sheer rock, the patrol managed to find refuge in the slight protrusions along the cliff. The nine men were now crouching there in the darkness, waiting for the H-Hour signal, which would mean the arrival of Colonel Bouvet and the main body of his African Commandos, scheduled to land around 1.30 A.M. at Rayol. Neither Préat nor the others had any inkling that the landings of the other commandos would also end in disaster. Nor by the the wildest stretch of the imagination could it have occurred to them that, although the plans for the attack on the Cap Nègre had been totally disrupted, it was going to succeed in spite of everything, and thanks to them.

The unnatural silence that followed the German outburst and the lack of any further reaction from the attackers stirred anxiety and bafflement in the defenders of Cap Nègre. Helmeted silhouettes surged out of the darkness, dashing about aimlessly, colliding with one another on the eastern slope of the cliff. Men's voices rang out, calling from the heights above the tenuous hiding places of the nine Frenchmen clinging for their lives to the rock. Shots from Schmeissers ripped through the night and roused the neighboring garrisons at La Fossette and Le Canadel.

Corporal Renévier of the First Commandos has since described it as it seemed to him from his cramped position underneath a providential ledge on Cap Nègre's cliff:

'There was plenty of commotion going on up there, all right! Those Germans were really having fits, going all to pieces, running around like chickens with their heads cut off !'

The ruddy glow of warning flares disrupted the tranquility of the sky. Guns went into action on all sides, even from places a few miles from Cap Nègre – and Germans were shooting at other Germans in the darkness and confusion. According to Du Bellocq, 'from that moment on during the whole rest of the night, the Jerries hardly left off shooting at one another.' The next day he and his second in command, Sergeant Guillaume, rounded up thirty-five injured soldiers, mostly Poles and Armenians from the 918th Grenadiers, who had been wounded by bullets from their own troops.

Préat and his commandos remained motionless in their hard-won footholds, biding their time. It was all they could do for the moment. If worst came to worst, they would at least have the satisfaction of knowing that the enemy had paid dearly for their lives. In fact, it was the misfortune of these nine men that they had attracted most of the German garrison toward their position. But now the various batteries were dangerously undermanned, stripped of most of their crews. If these guns were not knocked out before Bouvet and his six hundred men arrived, the landing of the commandos was going to wind up in a bloody disaster. The deadly fire of the German guns commanding the beach would simply wipe out every man at the water's edge.

4

WHILE THIS MAELSTROM WAS RAGING on the eastern face of Cap Nègre, a man was groping his way through the night with sixty more commandos behind him. They, too, had strayed from their course. This was the unit assigned to capturing the gun batteries. They had sixty minutes in which to complete the job, and had already wasted thirty merely trying to get their bearings and locate their objective.

Captain Paul Ducournau of the First Commandos had spent his time while crossing the Mediterranean in going over every detail of his mission, although he had already committed it to memory. When – after a moment's disbelief, followed by a fleeting instant of consternation– he had had to face the fact that the mammoth shape of Cap Nègre was not sticking up where it ought to be, he proceeded to take stock. His two LCIs filled with thirty men each were in view of the shore, but they had drifted off course, far to the west of their destination, and were near the beach at La Fossette. The ominous mass of Cap Nègre lay a considerable distance to the right, its sharp ridge and steep slopes – studded with the guns that he was to wipe out – barely discernible through the gloom. (By a stroke of luck that was almost as sheer as the sides of the cliff, Ducournau had, shortly before the outbreak of the war, been assigned to a naval training course on this very stretch of coast between Toulon and Saint-Tropez.) Keeping his wits about him, Ducournau quickly ordered his LCIs to make a U-turn and head back in the direction from which they had come. But this maneuver, executed in complete silence, was going to cost him half his men.

The second boatload of thirty commandos, led by Midshipman Jeannerot, clearly saw the captain's LCI turn sharply around, but Jeannerot thought that the LCI had unloaded its men and was now returning toward the open sea. Consequently, he and his group continued on their course, and by the time the young officer realized what had happened, it was too late; he and his men were completely isolated. After hastily transferring to their rubber assault rafts at a spot several miles from their objective, they found themselves caught in a murderous hail of machine-gun fire and tracer bullets. Schmeissers mercilessly raked the commandos crouching low in the small boats, and red repeater rockets rained down on the rocks along the beach. In the darkness Jeannerot and his group had stumbled upon another of the batteries that the Germans had set up at La Fossette, a rocky eminence planted with the *Kriegsmarine*'s artillery and barbed-wire obstacles; in the Allied plans, this was one of the positions that had been earmarked for capture during the day of 15 August.

Meanwhile, Ducournau had been following his altered course, never realizing that Jeannerot was not trailing along. The leader of the second LCI had of course withdrawn under the enemy's fire, but was unable to get anywhere near Cap Nègre, which by now lay over a mile away. He decided to take cover on the beach, and for the rest of the night the brave young officer and those of his men who had not been hurt went back and forth from rock to rock transporting their wounded companions, often wading through water up to their waists. Jeannerot's iron nerves stood him in good stead, and he was able to rescue most of his commandos, who ultimately managed to reach their assigned objective.

Ducournau and his thirty men were now preparing to climb the sides of Cap Nègre by themselves. If things had gone according to plan, it would have taken them half an hour to reach the batteries – a distance of about one-third of a mile – with an extra fifteen minutes allowed to cover possible encounters with German patrols and sentries. As matters stood now, these plans had to be scrapped.

Dimly silhouetted against the night sky, the cliff top seemed to tower up to fantastically inaccessible heights, with all the odds against the little group below. But Ducournau and his commandos, each man weighted down with eighty-eight pounds of weapons and ammunition, began ascending the rock as if their very lives depended on it – as in a sense they did – with all the grimness born of desperate determination. But they were preoccupied with the thought of those great guns waiting in the concrete blockhouses, and now it was beginning to seem almost impossible for them to achieve everything in the limited time allotted for their mission. No one, not even Bouvet, could be positive that the Allied bombers had succeeded in demolishing the huge guns. In a sense, it was almost better for them not to know. Although the three 6-inch guns had indeed been destroyed, the Germans had had time to set up new ones that, while less powerful, would still represent an all-too-real threat to Bouvet and his battalion when they landed.

Sergeant Daboussy, who was leading the silent band of advance scouts, finally reached the top of the cliff. With blood oozing from his hands and face, as a result of scraping against the rough rock, but with his courage and coolness intact, he set about finding a strong anchorage, around which he quickly and deftly secured a long, stout rope, which was then lowered along the length of the cliff. One hundred and fifty feet below, the men caught it. Breathing hard, occasionally swaying under the weight of their packs, the hardy commandos got a firm grip and slowly began hoisting themselves up. They could hear the murmur of the surf splashing against the rocks growing dimmer farther and farther below them in the summer night.

When all had safely reached the top of the rock, Ducournau gave the signal for the attack, and the thirty men were off.

As they made their way toward the battery, they crossed over a terrain in which the vegetation appeared increasingly sparse, almost as if a tornado had cut a swath through what had once been a heavily wooded area. The earth was punctured with bomb craters and covered with a tangle of mangled bushes and wrenched-off branches, all strewn amid uprooted trunks and twisted stumps. No lunar landscape could have been more desolate or chaotic. The men forged steadily ahead, snipping their way through barbed wire, alert to all the obstacles and mined traps that lay in their path. Finally, against a patch of wooded ground, right in the midst of this wilderness of churned-up rubble, gaping holes, and bristling barbs, Ducournau was able to discern through the darkness the ugly, unmistakable shapes of two big guns – two of the three that he was expecting to find.

The commandos, as if moved by a single impulse, sprang out of the shadows, sprinted forward and waded into the thick of the fight, their captain leading. The Frenchmen's submachine guns spat fire, their grenades exploded, while German bullets began whistling all around and orange flares burst over their heads, lighting up the battlefield more garishly than the brightest Mediterranean sun.

The ensuing few minutes were an uproar, a scene straight out of the Apocalypse. The fighting went on amid a clamor of yelling and shouting, the French commandos calling excitedly to one another, the Germans, bewildered and caught off guard, howling out orders, running and shooting wildly all over the clearing. The deep rumbling of the detonations tore at the roots of the night, punctuated by sharp fusillades from all directions along the cliff top, merging into a great screaming confusion. The French commandos continued pumping their weapons into the astonished defenders of Cap Nègre as they edged forward through the smoke and bullets toward the battery. Commando Nardeau and the dauntless Sergeant Daboussy had the honor of demolishing the first 3-inch gun with their rifle grenades.

'Take it easy, Pépion! Hey, that one's mine!' Nardeau shouted to Daboussy, who was already darting off to the second gun.

Amid the shower of tracer bullets now falling over the gun shelter, the first gun blew up with an ear-splitting explosion that spewed forth thick, blinding billows of acrid, suffocating smoke. Pépion, gasping and choking, stood swathed in a swirling storm of dust, and in the half-light he could barely make out the outlines of the target that he was preparing to attack.

Drowning out the sharp chatter of the machine guns, louder than the shrieking waves of shrapnel that were showering down over the battery, the roar of a Bangalore torpedo rent the night air. Pépion and five other commandos had just rammed home their explosive tube into the black muzzle of the heavy field gun, and the blast knocked all six men flat – but the battery had been demolished.

Around the wreckage of the guns, the firing and explosions gradually subsided and the heavy, stifling smoke cleared away. The Germans began surrendering, one after another. Their casualties totaled some twenty dead and wounded, while the French commandos had emerged from the brief fight with only two men slightly scratched. Ducournau's job on Cap Nègre was over. His next rendezvous was at the assembly point for all the commando demolition squads, the wooded heights of Mont Biscarre in the Monts des Maures. Barely twenty minutes had elapsed since his commandos had scrambled to the top of the cliff. The first battle of D-Day in Provence had been fought and won, despite the many errors, miscalculations, obstacles and tribulations that had so nearly doomed it to failure. Ducournau anxiously studied his watch. The time was 1.35 A.M. It had been touch and go there for a while.

About half an hour before, in Baudouvin, above Toulon, an alert had suddenly come through to the headquarters of Rear Admiral Heinrich Ruhfus, commanding the *Kriegsmarine*'s coastal defenses in Provence. The operations room of the land-based naval command had just received a message from the radio station at La Crau, near Hyères.

It read as follows:

'Enemy units attempting to land at Bormes.'

This was the signal that the headquarters staff had been awaiting, almost eagerly, for three days. For Ruhfus and his aide, Commander Rüling, who had been on duty there since the previous September, the long months of waiting were over. Just as everybody had felt certain it would, the second D-Day was going to come on 15 August.

5

THE THREE ISLANDS making up the Hyères group lie southeast of Toulon, some five miles out to sea. The two islands farthest from the coast are the easternmost ones, Port-Cros and the Ile du Levant. From the outset, the third island, Porquerolles, had been excluded from the D-Day attack plans because of its distance from the mainland invasion beaches – Porquerolles lies about twenty miles to the west. The task of storming and capturing Port-Cros and the Ile du Levant, which constituted a direct threat to the landing zone, was assigned to Colonel Edwin A. Walker's 2,000 American and Canadian troops of the First Special Service Force, a shock unit trained for special missions.

Twilight was falling by the time the men aboard the auxiliary ships of Force Sitka caught sight of the steep side of Port-Cros and the Ile du Levant rearing up dead ahead. From his vantage point on board the transport *Roper*, a Canadian sergeant, Bertie A. Clinton, of the Second Special Forces Regiment, watched the forbidding-looking rocky masses as the ship glided in closer. The troops had been given a briefing, during which they were informed that the islands had received a heavier pounding from aerial bombardments than they should normally have been able to stand – but the actual sight of the rocks brought Clinton the sharp realization that this attack was not going to be 'a piece of cake.'

Long before the famous 'mosaic' had been assembled in the Flambeau Building in Naples, aerial photographs taken by 12th Air Force reconnaissance planes had provided Walker with an accurate picture of the steep slopes of Port-Cros and the rocky ridge and the sheer drops on the Ile du Levant. The terrain on the seaward side looked particularly difficult and challenging. Yet it was this very spot that Walker had chosen, deliberately, for his troops to make their landing. He went so far as to send a submarine to reconnoiter the area, to glean whatever extra details might come in handy, and he listened attentively to the opinions of several people who had been familiar with the islands in prewar years. They were all agreed on one thing. Because of the landing area that he had decided on, Walker's plans amounted to nothing short of suicide. The difficulties presented by the terrain were considered insurmountable.

Seldom in his career had Edwin Walker felt as elated as he felt now, facing his bewildered staff.

'But that's why I want it!' he exulted. 'Don't you realize that the Germans have figured it out exactly the same way? In other words, there are ninety-nine chances out of a hundred that this area of the island is the most weakly defended – precisely because it's the hardest to attack!'

And Walker refused to back down.

On this evening of 14 August, the nearly 2,000 men in the three Special Forces regiments had been towed by Rear Admiral Theodore Chandler's assault ships to within half a mile of their objective. Now they were on their own, pulling on the oars in the small boats preceded by scout troops in kayaks whose job was to mark the landing sites. Like the African Commandos who were proceeding toward the mainland coast at that moment, these men were scheduled to occupy their positions far in advance of H-Hour. The plan was for the island defenses and the German garrison to be neutralized by at least one hour before daybreak, and the sun was expected to rise at about 5 A.M.

While the 650 men in Lieutenant Colonel J.F. Akehurst's First Regiment were landing on Port-Cros, the 1,300 troops of Lieutenant Colonel Robert S. Moore's Second Regiment and Lieutenant Colonel R.W. Becket's Third Regiment were scrambling ashore at the foot of the supposedly inaccessible rocks on the Ile du Levant. Between 1.35 A.M. and 2 A.M., all of Walker's men landed safely on both islands, thereby confirming his hunch. Not a single shot, neither bullet nor shell, had greeted the troops as they launched the opening phase of their attack. On both Port-Cros and the Ile du Levant the surprise was total. Subsequent interrogation of German prisoners further supported Walker's theory that, in the minds of the enemy, the high rocks plunging straight down into the water had considerably diminished the likelihood of an attack from that direction.

When Walker's men reached the top of the heights on the Ile du Levant – formed by a rocky crest some $2\frac{1}{2}$ miles long – they immediately deployed toward the far end of the island to the Titan lighthouse and battery, whose 6.5-inch guns had to be destroyed before all else. In fact, that was the express purpose of their landing.

Innumerable times and from every possible angle, Allied reconnaissance planes had photographed the four heavy guns at Titan that commanded the Alpha sector's beaches. When the invasion plans for Provence were being mapped out, the decision to land the American 3rd Division in the Cavalaire-sur-Mer area had finally been agreed on only on the condition that a preliminary attack on the Ile du Levant first knocked out the Titan guns. At the time, a heated controversy had begun – in fact, it was still going on – between General Patch's staff and a French naval officer, Commander Yann Le Hagre, who, as noted earlier, had had a hand in the installation and arming of the 13.4-inch battery at Saint-Mandrier, opposite Toulon, back in 1932. For six months Le Hagre had been the 'chaperon' of the Provence invasion for everything concerning the landing areas. In the face of strongly dissenting opinion among the Allied headquarters staff, the French officer stoutly maintained that the 6.5-inch guns on the Ile du Levant had been destroyed in 1942, at the time of the scuttling of the French fleet, and that they were no longer a threat to the troops who would be coming ashore at Cavalaire-sur-Mer.

However, intelligence reports from Allied agents seemed to contradict Le Hagre. In addition, there were the aerial reconnaissance photographs, in which the British and the Americans put all their faith. Yet the Allied experts were disturbed no little by the fact that none of this evidence shook Le Hagre's convictions. His only concession was to say that 'if the guns were still in place, they were incapable of firing.' He even volunteered to provide proof. On the night of 8 June, under a full moon, a French submarine, the *Casabianca*, cruised over just off the point of the Ile du Levant, opposite the battery with its four monstrous guns showing up starkly in the moonlight, their muzzles ostensibly aimed out to sea. That same night the *UJ-6078*, a ship of Commander Hermann Polenz's Sixth Security Fleet, was patrolling off the Iles d'Hyères. Aboard the *Casabianca*, Lieutenant Bellet detected the patrol ship's presence and issued orders to attack, but, in accordance with instructions, he did not submerge. Instead, he surfaced, thereby openly challenging the German ship with his own guns. In thirteen minutes, the *Casabianca* had fired forty-nine shots from her 4-inch gun and 420 from her 20-mm. cannon – and during the entire engagement the Titan guns had remained mysteriously silent.

So it looked as if Le Hagre might be right after all, although he still had only appearances in his favor. The invasion plans were not altered, and Allied headquarters continued on the theory that the guns on the Ile du Levant constituted a hazard for the entire left flank of the landing operation. The battery existed, and therefore it had to be destroyed.

Colonel Walker was personally responsible for all the details of this phase of D-Day, which was to be one of the decisive operations of the night. The Germans had been prodigal with mines, and had used them to line the approaches to the small coves of L'Ane and Le Liserot, as well as the adjacent wooded area. Despite this, the attackers overcame these hazards pretty well. A few minutes later, as they neared the Titan lighthouse (whose guardian, François Onorati, had fled a few hours earlier after having removed the fuses from the explosives), they were rewarded by the sight of the somber forms of the four guns silhouetted against the starlit sky.

All seemed quiet on the island; here, as elsewhere, the only sound was that of the surf, eddying and swirling among the rocks. The men got to work fast, and the attack on the battery went through without a hitch and was over in a flash. Apparently there was no one to defend it! But Walker's men did not allow themselves to judge from appearances only, and anyhow, there were the guns, big as life, their camouflaging now clearly visible to the reconnaissance patrol. Through the darkness the leaders made a rush toward the gunners standing at their posts, motion-less and presumably self-confident under their helmets, unaware that they might go down in history as among the first German casualties of the Second D-Day. As the attackers lunged, the sentries still did not move – for the very good reason that they were dummy figures! The Allied soldiers, suspecting a trap, hesitated briefly. Le Hagre had been correct – the sabotaged guns on the Ile du Levant had been out of commission since the French had blown them up in 1942. What looked like a battery and had been photographed so many times by the reconnaissance planes, was simply a set of fakes ingeniously contrived out of corrugated metal, wooden stakes, and ordinary drain pipes daubed with paint. Walker's men felt somehow cheated of their rightful reward when they saw what their so-called prize amounted to. They had just about changed their minds completely about those French islands that everybody had been chewing their ears off about and giving such a big build-up to. As far as they were concerned, their landing had not been much different from a routine night exercise over a smooth sea with a slight swell, with their bazookas the heaviest weapons they had. Just then the first shots ripped over the island.

The resistance of the German garrison on the Ile du Levant turned out to be sporadic and lacking in coordination – at least up to the moment when the Germans finally realized what was happening. By dawn, when the fighting was over, the score was a few light casualties among the men of the Second and Third Regiments, and the resistance put up by the Germans had amounted to a few shells lobbed pretty much at random.

Meanwhile, the First Regiment had also landed and established a beachhead on Port-Cros, encountering even less opposition. Colonel Akehurst and his 650 men entrenched themselves at vantage points and occupied a fair-sized ridge that provided an excellent observation post overlooking all the surrounding area. Gunners and sharpshooters automatically went about setting up positions on the sides of the ridge, and the reconnaissance patrols that had fanned out over the island returned without having encountered any fire or met one German soldier. Like their counterparts on the Ile du Levant, Akehurst's fighters also felt cheated, and it seemed to them that the night was taking unduly long about fading into light. They could not remember when the weird silence of the sea and the dawn had ever weighed so heavily upon them, except maybe in those long-ago days of peace. In any case, it was certainly nothing like Anzio and Nettuno seven months before. A lot of the men, exhausted by the night's work fell into a well-deserved slumber right at their posts, and it seemed to Akehurst that this was undoubtedly one of the strangest landings in which he and his troops had ever taken part.

Walker, Akehurst's superior, was in complete agreement.

'These damned islands weren't really important at all,' he concluded.

At 7.45 A.M. – fifteen minutes before H-Hour on the landing beaches – Walker announced that all his objectives had been taken. Less than an hour later, he further reported that 'the capture of Port-Cros and the Ile du Levant could be considered as definitely accomplished.' Walker had taken a few prisoners and was requesting further instructions. At about 9 A.M. the radio aboard the *Augusta* received the following message from the commader of the special forces that had landed successfully on the Iles d'Hyères:

'Islands utterly useless. Suggest immediate evacuation. Killed: none. Wounded: two. Prisoners: 240. Enemy batteries dummies. Request permission immediate departure.'

Walker's request could be granted only by General Patch and with the agreement of Admiral Hewitt, the commander of the invasion forces. If all went as planned, the three regiments of the First Special Service Force would leave the islands and take their prisoners with them. They would be replaced by French troops who were to occupy the islands until the return of the civilian populations.

Although Patch was impressed by Walker's expeditious conquest of the islands, on both of which the Allies had expected to meet stubborn resistance, he nevertheless ordered the impatient colonel to stay put for the time being. However, in view of the lightning-like speed with which Walker's mission had been accomplished, he decided to reduce by ninety per cent the French troops ready to land on Port-Cros – fifty men instead of the planned five hundred – where a big radar station was to be installed immediately.

Just as Patch was about to radio this decision, a new and radically different message was flashed in from Port-Cros, hastily dispatched by an alarmed Walker:

'Urgent. Request heavy bombardment on citadel (position 184). Under attack, having difficulties.'

Day and night without letup, men and equipment are loaded aboard waiting craft for the invasion of southern France. Here, 3rd Division troops line up to embark at a port in Italy on D-Day minus seven. (*Photo U.S. Army*)

Showers of leaflets rained on the French coast immediately prior to the D-Day in Provence landings. Pictured is a message to the French people from General Sir Henry Maitland Wilson, Allied commander in chief of the Mediterranean Theater of Operations. (*Photo courtesy Robert Laffont*)

AU PEUPLE DE FRANCE

Le général Sir H. MAITLAND WILSON
Commandant suprême allié. Zone de la Méditerran

ANNONCE,

Les armées des Nations Unies ont débarqué dans le M?...

Leur but est de chasser les Allemands et d'effectuer une jonction avec les armées alliées qui avancent de Normandie.

Les forces françaises participent à cette opération, aux côtés de leurs frères d'armes alliés, sur mer, sur terre, et dans les airs.

L'Armée française est à nouveau une réalité: elle combat sur son propre sol pour la libération de la Patrie, avec toutes ses traditions de victoire. Rappelez-vous 1918!

Tous les Français, civils aussi bien que militaires, ont leur rôle à jouer dans la campagne du Midi. Votre tâche vous sera expliquée: écoutez la radio alliée, lisez les avis et les tracts, transmettez les consignes de l'un à l'autre.

Mettons fin aussi rapidement que possible à la lutte, afin que toute la France puisse reprendre sa vie libre dans des conditions de paix et de sécurité.

La victoire est certaine.

Vive l'âme de la France, et tout ce qu'elle représente!

Commandant suprême allié. Zone de la Méditerranée.

FRANÇAIS Affichez cette déclaration où tout le monde pourra la voir.

In the distance, a portion of the invasion fleet lying off the coast of southern France a few hours after the initial landings were made. (*Photo U.S. Air Force*)

Marine Sergeant Raymond T. Kaiser aboard the *Augusta* could not believe his eyes, and Commander Le Hagre remembers the stupefaction registered by both Patch and Hewitt when Walker's message reached the *Catoctin*.

A French ensign, Georges Lasserre, who had landed as a guide with the island attack force, has related how two American soldiers in Akehurst's regiment gave the first alarm. They were 'idly ambling down to the seashore, after leaving their rifles behind.' At a bend in a path in the woods, they suddenly found themselves face to face with a German sentry, who was as scared as they were. Both sides took to their heels and spread the alarm in their respective camps.

The Ile de Port-Cros contained three small forts dating from the seventeenth and nineteenth centuries. In them a German garrison of fewer than sixty men had entrenched itself. The forts' thick vaulted ceiling provided a secure shelter – and these were what Walker had requested the bombardment for. But the *Augusta*'s 8-inch shells bounced off the forts like so many tennis balls. The battle for the Iles d'Hyères, which Walker had believed over, was just beginning. Fifteen hours later it was still raging.

6

THROUGH THE DARKENED SKY, the first Allied invasion planes were streaking toward the coast of Provence. They were only a small group – five Dakotas from General Saville's XII Tactical Air Command. Flying low over the Mediterranean, they came into sight of the bay at La Ciotat, eighteen miles east of Marseilles, and then dropped even lower, to under 1,600 feet, as if deliberately seeking to provoke German flak. The only result was a few uncertain burst of fire from the naval batteries guarding the small port.

And yet, as late as the evening of 14 August, the German coastal command had been positive that it was here in this very area, between Marseilles and Toulon, that the Allies would stage their landing. All of the 244th Infantry Division's occupation troops, and particularly the radar observation crews – that is, the crews of those radar stations that were still able to operate – had been placed on *Alarmstruffe I*, or top alert status; on the basis of intelligence obtained subsequent to the recent bombing raids, it appeared that the Allied planes had attacked the area

E

around La Ciotat with greater intensity than any other part of the coast.[1] For its part, the Allied staff had more than a good hunch that the Germans would interpret the situation exactly as they proceeded to do – and the Germans soon realized that this tactical ruse was only a tiny part of a vast over-all plan of deceit designed to fool them up to the very last minute about the exact area of the landings.

At the command post at La Ciotat, which was also an air-raid shelter, Lieutenant Christian Bick, commanding the port, could not even begin to think about turning in for the night.

Just before 2 A.M. he heard the first planes roaring over. By then the chaos had become widespread, not only in the threatened sector but also several miles away, at the various echelons of Army Group G. This group had been alerted by messages from Nineteenth Army headquarters, and in turn, shortly before midnight, had notified the Western Naval Group (*Marinegruppenkommando West*) in Paris, under Admiral Theodor Krancke, that 'Allied paratroops have just landed at Marseilles, at the submarine harbor, and also south of the city.' This item of intelligence eventually turned out to be without basis.[2] In fact, since 10 P.M., both the port and the center of Marseilles itself had been bombed almost uninterruptedly by Allied planes. By now it was obvious that, for the Germans in Provence, the wild night of 15 August had begun in earnest.

Bick waited inside the shelter. The antiaircraft batteries had gone into action the instant the planes began approaching, but the steady droning of the aircraft continued, without any bombs falling on either the port or the city. Bick was understandably surprised. He felt sure that more waves of planes would follow. Nothing of the sort happened except that, a few minutes later, the zone occupied by Colonel Westfal's regiment opened up with a brisk sustained ground fire. Bick's bafflement increased.

When they reached the coast, dodging the sporadic bursts of tracer bullets and flak, the C-47s had flown low over La Ciotat and followed the Nice-Marseilles railway tracks for a short distance before continuing on in a half-circle over the heights of Adouillet and the pine woods of Ceyreste. The five planes then descended to a low altitude and opened

---

[1] Proof of the Germans' conviction that the area of La Ciotat would be one of the landing objectives is explicitly recorded in the *Kriegsmarine* logbook for 14–15 August 1944 – 'Landings can be expected in this area on the day of August 15.'

[2] Captain Edo-Friedrich Dieckmann, former coast artillery commander of the Marseilles area, has provided an explanation for this error:

'We were convinced that it was a parachute attack, and to settle the matter I ordered flares shot from a 6-inch gun on Ratonneau island. This permitted us to ascertain that it was not troops, but rather bundles of leaflets that were being parachuted down. As the leaflets struck the ground, small explosive charges went off, scattering them to the winds.'

But since the ground units did not know that the flares had been fired by German guns, and that they were coming from out at sea, a certain amount of 'agitation' had ensued.

their doors. Each plane then released sixty heavily equipped parachutists. Over the outskirts of the town and the wooded hillsides of La Ciotat, three hundred early-blooming morning glories suddenly blossomed in the night sky. It was 1.55 A.M. These American paratroopers, the first to be sent in behind the German lines, were dressed in the regulation trappings of airborne troops, and they resembled so many black-faced ghosts. To the observers, they appeared to be falling like dead weights – Indeed, they somehow did not look very much alive. And there was nothing strange about that, either: for they were rubber dummies.

Some of these ghostly creatures from outer space exploded on contact with the ground, making the loud noise, like that of automatic weapons, that had so perplexed Bick. Just then his telephone shrilled out in the shelter:

'*Paratruppen*! *Paratruppen*!' a voice shouted from the receiver.

Bick dashed out of the shelter, but the night had settled back into a silence as uncomfortable as the preceding noise.

Meanwhile, the alarm had been sounded near Aubagne, at General Schaefer's command post, and between Cassis and Bandol, along the entire length of the sector defended by Westfal's regiment. Hans Schaefer, a wounded survivor of Bejelgorod, had formerly commanded the 252nd and 332nd divisions on the Russian front; since early 1944, for reasons of health, he had been in command of the 244th, occupying the area between Sanary and Port-de-Bouc, on either side of Marseilles. Schaefer had special orders from Hitler that Port-de-Bouc was to be 'defended to the last round.'

In the hills and woods around La Ciotat, the troops of Westfal's 932nd Battalion were closing in on the rubber 'paratroopers,' which lay motionless wherever they had fallen. Baffled, the Germans were attempting to encircle their 'enemy.' Finally, receiving no answering fire, they charged with fixed bayonets, whereupon the rubber dummies exploded their remaining charges. (In a newscast the following morning, Radio Berlin denounced the landing of the fake paratroopers at La Ciotat, branding it as 'one of the most dastardly devices used in the war,' and as something that 'could have been contrived only by the lowest and most sinister type of Anglo-Saxon mind.')

Nor were the trials of the Germans at La Ciotat at an end. While they were still grappling with the phony airborne figures, the C-47s had returned to their base at Ajaccio and were on their way back. This time they released near the shore wide strips of tinfoil, called 'windows,' designed to make the German radar screens register the effect of an entire air squadron – only this time again, it was only a phantom. Simultaneously, a small group of American and British launches commanded by Lieutenant Commander J.D.Bulkeley of the United States Navy had left the main fleet and was dashing at full speed toward the beach at La Ciotat. Two days earlier, four of the five radar stations under the command of Major Griffel, who in civilian life was a Hamburg bank clerk, had been knocked out by Allied bomber raids. However, Griffel's biggest radar screen, set up on the hill west of the Bec de l'Aigle at the entrance to La Ciotat bay, was still in working order. Its *Lichtspuker* (literally 'light spitter') suddenly began registering a tremendous echo, which attained an intensity unprecedented in the experience of any of the screen's veteran operators, greater even than any recorded in the recent massive air raids. Griffel's men were convinced that this time they were not up against an ordinary raid.

After threading its way through the dense concentration of mines in front of La Ciotat, a powerful 'naval force' was proceeding across the bay, and the Bec de l'Aigle radar station had speedily relayed the alarm to all the artillery batteries guarding the port. The German guns instantly went into action and began firing on the attackers—in the words of Griffel, a 'stupendous cluster of flames shot up over the water.' He felt satisfied with the system that he and his superior, Commander Edo-Friedrich Dieckmann, had carefully worked out. As Dieckmann described it, 'the batteries around La Ciotat commanded various grid squares of the water's surface marked out in accordance with radar indications based on the direction and speed of the enemy's ships; each grid square covered about one-fifth of a mile of shoreline.' Although tonight the enemy had remained out of range of the powerful searchlights and rocket flares of the coastal defense installations, Griffel felt certain that his artillery had hit home, and he immediately phoned Dieckmann's command post on the hill of Notre Dame de la Garde in Marseilles.

'Griffel? What's going on?'

'Attempted large-scale landing, commander, repulsed with heavy casualties,' replied Griffel.

Back in his shelter at La Ciotat, Lieutenant Bick was sharing the same opinion, and no one contested the 'attempted landing' at La Ciotat, not even the German radio announcer, who gloatingly pronounced it a failure some hours later.

Only Bulkeley knew what was what. For him, Operation Ferdinand was now over, and it had gone off without a hitch.

Still another diversionary operation was staged that night, at the opposite end of the landing area. This one was Rosie, directed by Lieutenant Commander Douglas Fairbanks, Jr., who, with a few PT boats and the British gunboats *Aphis* and *Scarab*, ventured in close to the shore near Cannes and fired a few rounds of 4-inch shells in the direction of the coastal highway. As Bulkeley had done at La Ciotat, Fairbanks was to stir up as big a commotion as possible and to create confusion among the Germans by simulating the approach of a substantial invasion fleet. Fairbanks managed to create quite a disturbance with his ships, and his mission, too, was rated one hundred per cent successful.

7

THE STACCATO BARK OF A SCHMEISSER sounded out in the darkness and two rocket flares – one red and one white – soared up over Pointe-de-l'Esquillon, west of Cannes. The white flare was a dud, and the Germans were unable to distinguish much of anything.

In their rubber rafts, the sixty-seven men in Commander Sériot's French Naval Assault Group took this opportunity to pull forward with all their might as they neared the Esterel rocks, and were soon scrambling ashore. They were coming in, eight hours before H-Hour, to protect the right flank of the assault zone by setting off demolitions along the highway from Cannes to Fréjus and from Cannes to Saint-Raphaël. Their purpose was to prevent German reinforcements reaching the sector of the invasion front where the going was likely to be roughest and where the most decisive fighting would take place. Each man's pack contained sixty pounds of mélinite, an individual arsenal of submachine guns and reserve ammunition – over ninety pounds a man. Some of these men were facing a march of $1\frac{1}{2}$ miles through thick underbrush to reach their destination.

Every one of them belonged to a regular French naval unit, and they were on their way to do a trained engineer's job. It was estimated that they would be isolated behind enemy lines for three days, during which time each man would have to survive on a half-pound bar of vitamin-fortified chocolate. These men had been carefully screened out of hundreds of volunteers and were part of an assault group set up in Corsica in 1943 by Rear Admiral Robert Battet.

It was 2 A.M., and they were behind schedule. Only three hours remained before daybreak.[1]

[1] The Naval Assault Group's landing got off to a bad start. A German plane had sighted the fleet of LCIs while they were still half a mile out at sea and began circling overhead and dropping rocket flares. As a result, the landing had to be postponed for over eighty precious minutes. The plane failed to reappear. But in the meantime, the Germans on the mainland were preparing their own special reception for the sixty-seven men in the assault group.

They began landing at 2.10 A.M. The first to come ashore on the dark purple patches of porphyry rock on the Esterel coast were the forty-two men of a section commanded by a thirty-nine year old lieutenant commander, Gérard Marche. This unit was to penetrate the farthest behind the German lines. Marche fully realized that the enemy was ready and waiting up there in the darkness for him and his men. Hefting and shifting their heavy gear, the forty-two Frenchmen started their slow and arduous climb up the rocks above the coves of La Figueirette, near Le Trayas. Seven hundred feet higher, the Saint-Raphaël coastal highway wound its way along the cliffs, and everywhere the night seemed calm and silent, with no tangible evidence of an enemy presence.

Within a few minutes, the lead officer, Christian Auboyneau, Reserve Officer, Interpreter Decoder unit, found out why there was no apparent sign of life coming from the German side. He suddenly saw, directly ahead of him, a large sign adorned with a skull and crossbones and bearing the warning '*Achtung! Minen!*' The very spot at which they had landed had turned out to be a mine field. Auboyneau took in this information slowly – he almost could not believe it.

He had excellent reasons for doubting what he saw. On the basis of the latest Allied intelligence report, which had been reconfirmed just before the group's departure, there could be no mine field at Pointe-de-l'Esquillon.[1] Any lingering doubts that Auboyneau may have had were dispelled in the next instant, when a tremendous explosion blasted the night. He and two men near him were hit – Auboyneau thought they had probably been killed. He himself had been struck in both legs and in the stomach, and one of his eyes had been torn out.

The explosion was so violent that Lucien Chaffiotte, an engineer, who was far in the rear, thought the Germans had launched a grenade attack.

Chaffiotte shouted through his walkie-talkie:

'Hit the ground!'

He immediately realized the futility of this order. Everywhere the men fell, the ground blew up beneath them.

François Andrei, a sailor, got entangled in a piece of wire and called out for help to Chaffiotte, who was lucky enough to find the wire without

[1] Actually, the mines had been laid only one or two days before. Part of my research for this book involved an investigation as to whether the local Resistance leaders had been able to find out about the laying of these mines and had tried to inform the Allied staff. Georges Dewaël, an intelligence agent for the *Mithridate* group, who knew the whole region from Cogolin to La Bocca, with every last German foxhole and battery, like the palm of his hand, told me that the 'entire coast along the Esterel heights as well as the offshore waters had been systematically and abundantly sown with mines, with one single exception – the beach at Le Dramont.' Dewaël was correct up to a certain point – the mine field at Pointe-de-l'Esquillon had been planted during the forty-eight hours before D-Day.

setting off the mine. Proceeding cautiously, a short distance farther on Chaffiotte stumbled over the bodies of the first two victims, a seaman named Pierre Fichefeux, with his carotid artery severed, and a warrant officer of the Colonial Engineers, Marius Arzellier. 'There was also a third man whom I couldn't identify right away,' Chaffiotte recalled later. 'He was lying across Arzellier's body.'

The survivors of the Naval Assault Group remained rooted to their positions and dug in as best they could, refusing to retreat, whispering to one another in the blackness. Almost all of these men had left France four years before, and now they were clinging desperately to this hostile patch of their native land, stubbornly determined to win a victory. But the minutes were ticking by, and Lieutenant Letonturier's second group of twenty-five men, who were to attack the coastal highway, still had not attained their objective.

And still the Germans remained hidden in the night, deliberately holding their fire, confident of their ability to repel this vanguard of the invasion force that had strayed across their path.

Chaffiotte heard the murmured words of Goulven Le Rouzic, an electrician's mate, one of the group's first volunteers:

'Those bastards really planned quite a party for us! And damned if I don't feel like I'm going to enjoy it!'

Obviously, few of his companions could say they shared his view.

And now, without a mine detector among them, literally inching along, the men began to thread their way through the mine-ridden crumbling rocks and thorny underbrush of this steep and deadly cliff. Completely at the mercy of a wayward fate in a nightmarish adventure, they gradually shortened the distance between themselves and the highway above. But now the shattering explosions were ringing out again on all sides and the screams and moans of wounded men rent the darkness, mingling with the death rattles of the victims of this suicidal mission.

After dragging himself along by his elbows, Ensign Pierre Servel decided to resume his advance, followed closely by Warrant Officer Cacaud, whom Servel told to plant his feet exactly where he was putting his own. Both men were blown into the air by a fiery concussion, their bodies riddled with metal fragments. Death was instantaneous. The mines continued to explode – it seemed as if they were everywhere – and soon five more men were hit. In the fury of the detonations, Chaffiotte recalls, there was one man with a shattered leg, screaming in pain and sobbing like a child, calling for his mother.

Letonturier bent down over the screaming man, who pleaded:

'Lieutenant, please help me! Cut my leg off!'

'Take it easy, Marchetti,' said Letonturier. 'Don't cry out, the Germans can hear you.'

Marchetti began moaning softly. He felt someone standing near him, feeling for his thigh, and recognized Corpsman Perraut, coming to give him a shot of morphine. A few minutes later Marchetti fell silent. For the rest of the night Perraut and two other corpsmen, Bertrand and Bénard, came and went tirelessly over the mine field with their sulfa kits and syringes, guided through the blackness by the hoarse cries of the wounded. Occasionally a survivor would whisper sadly that one of the others was dead.

'Don't worry about Mignot – it's all over for him,' Louis Billiemaz murmured to Bénard.

By now, Chaffiotte was only three hundred feet from the highway, the first of the group's two objectives.

He looked at his watch again, almost 4 A.M. Chaffiotte would have given anything to know where Commander Marche was and what Marche intended to do, but he could get no response to his repeated radio calls. With his mouth glued to the transmitter, Chaffiotte could get contact only with Letonturier.

And now Letonturier, his voice choked with pain and fury, was reporting that he had just been hit and that two other men in his detail had been killed by the mines. Of the sixty-seven men who had landed two hours earlier, ten were dead and nineteen seriously injured, including three of the five officers.

Just then a deep rumbling began sweeping in from over the sea, grow-to a loud roar as it approached the Esterel coast. The surviving men of the Naval Assault Group, fewer than fifteen of whom were still uninjured, gazed upward. Against the ceiling of stars, wave after wave of planes were winging their way in, engines throbbing steadily and signal lights flashing. They were the Dakotas bringing in the airborne troops to the Argens Valley, some eighteen miles away from the cliffs of Le Trayas.

Chaffiotte sighed bitterly. The noise of the planes was both reassuring and heartbreaking. The aerial invasion had begun, and after it would come the main body of troops wading ashore on the beaches.

There was no longer the faintest hope of the Naval Assault Group's carrying out its missions, which were to have preceded all the others. Not one of its objectives had been attained, and the plight of the survivors of the Point-de-l'Esquillon mine field was desperate. Even if they had been able to, it was impossible for them to evacuate their position. None of the assault troops would be coming to deliver them, and they had suffered such heavy casualties that they could not consider continuing the attack. Assuming that they might eventually extricate themselves and make it up to the highway, there were not even enough men left to carry a sufficient supply of explosives. The mission had to be rated a total failure.

When Chaffiotte finally made radio connections with Marche, he learned that the latter, too, had just been wounded. Chaffiotte was the only uninjured officer left.

The night sky suddenly lighted up as bright as day. Seaman Billiemaz, huddled against the rock, thought that 'this was it, the Jerries have made up their minds.' German flares streamed down, pinning the Frenchmen to the ground, and Chaffiotte was expecting 'the end to come quickly, badly, and at any moment.' He looked up to see 'all the round heads of the Germans lined up along the road above,' their rifles aimed down at the mine field.

There was no choice. With a sinking heart, Chaffiotte resigned himself to the most painful decision of his naval career. Surrounded by his dead and wounded men, amid the cries of the dying, he rose to his feet and called to the Germans, only in the hope of getting the remaining members of the group out of the mine field.

Dawn was just beginning to glimmer on the horizon, and Letonturier had no more illusions – he knew the game was up. Still, he wanted one last chance to accomplish his mission. On the lightening horizon he could make out the Cannes-Saint-Raphaël highway just 150 feet away.

Chaffiotte saw Letonturier take a great leap forward despite all his injuries, and knew what he was up to. Chaffiotte shouted:

'Hit the ground, Tontu! We haven't a chance!'

'I know,' Letonturier yelled, 'but I don't give a damn!'

Burdened with all his demolition gear, Letonturier had progressed a bare ten feet over the rocks when another mine exploded under him, blinding him, ripping his uniform to shreds, and shattering a leg. He collapsed to the ground just as Chaffiotte reached his side.

In the meantime another wounded officer of the Naval Assault Group, Commander Marche, was crawling over the mine field, but for a different reason. He was trying to make a get-away. Marche was carrying all the secret documents pertaining to the mission, and he was mainly concerned with not being captured. He had a wild notion that if he could make it back to the beach before the day had fully dawned, he might be able to get into one of the rubber rafts and row back to rejoin the fleet.

Marche did not live to be captured. When he got to within sixty feet of his objective, another explosion – probably the last of the mines – knocked him to the ground, fatally injured. With his last breath he called out to Chaffiote, and the men quickly set about destroying papers and maps. After they had finished, Marche had just enough strength to lift himself off the ground. A second later he began staggering, his body sagged, and he went crashing to the bottom of the cliff.

Peering through the yellowish light of dawn, Chaffiotte could see in the distance, fifteen miles out to sea, the silhouettes of two French war-ships with which he was thoroughly familiar, the heavy cruisers *Emile Bertin* and *Duguay Trouin*. In June 1940, aboard the *Emile Bertin*, Chaffiotte had participated in the evacuation of the gold from the Bank of France. The Allied ships lined up on the horizon had just opened fire on the coast in front of Saint-Raphaël.

Chaffiotte looked around him at the few of his remaining men who were still able to walk.

As he later recalled it, 'It might have been our last chance if we could have reached the shore fast enough and got into those rubber boats before the Jerries started shooting.'

But fate was really against them. Of the original sixty-seven, there were now only twenty-five who had survived without a scratch or were not too seriously injured. They were trying to steel themselves against the cries and appeals of their stricken comrades, who were begging not to be left behind but whom they could not take with them. The group did actually get back to the shore and was about to re-embark – and that was the precise moment at which luck abandoned it. Two British fighter planes flying over the coast zoomed out of the half-light and mistaking them for the enemy dived toward the pitiful band, strafing at point-blank range. Chaffiotte and his men leaped into the water in a mad scramble, trying to dodge the Mosquitoes' bullets, which were riccocheting all over the place.

This was the beginning of the end of this bloody odyssey, which had deteriorated into the first collective tragedy of the Second D-Day.The Germans standing on the road above began firing on the hapless men, who somehow managed to get back on the shore again. And while the first waves of the main invasion troops eight miles away were advancing in their LCIs and could just begin to see the outline of the Anthéor viaduct, as they braced themselves for the landing, the survivors of the French Naval Assault Group, with rage in their hearts, began their second climb up the steep face of the cliff. This time they were under the menace of German rifles as they made their way along the bitter road to captivity.

8

As COLONEL JOHN CARNY, a group commander in the United States Army Air Forces, gazed down around him, he could see the murky outline of the French coast gradually emerging out of the night. According to his watch, the planes were ahead of schedule, and in a few more minutes they would be over the dropping zone. The C-47s were flying low. Lieutenant Colonel William A. Tesch, an American officer with four airborne operations to his credit, was flying in another formation nearby. He noted that they had just lost sight of the light signals that had guided them in on their way from Corsica.

Around the formations lay the deep, starry Mediterranean night. An article by Ed Hogan, a war correspondent, relates that 'a thin sliver of moon had risen just as the first Allied planes began arriving over the coast.' These planes – a full squadron – were transporting the scout teams of the First Airborne Task Force. However, although General Frederick's vanguard did see the moon, it was only for a fleeting instant, at 3 A.M. Thirteen minutes later the planes began losing altitude and coming in low. As they did so, visibility became zero.

A thick layer of fog was carpeting the ground, covering all the drop zones around the sleepy hamlet of Le Muy, shrouding the field and wooded hills of the Argens Valley, a few miles from Draguignan. Their hands and faces smeared with black, yellow, and green greasepaint, the airborne scouts were floating down toward the dense, whitish land fog, scarcely able to discern their objectives. They were scheduled to hit the ground at 3.23 A.M., and were eight minutes early.

These twelve advance groups had slightly over an hour in which to reconnoiter, prepare, and plant signals around the drop-zones over an area of about twelve square miles. Here, during the night, the first units of the division would be landing – 5,000 infantrymen, artillerymen, and air force engineers, ferried over by 396 planes that had left Rome four hours earlier. During the ensuing hours – the deadline was set as the end of D-Day – more than 4,000 reinforcement troops, 213 mortars and anti-tank weapons from the supporting artillery, an equal number of light vehicles, a complete field hospital and service units were to be brought in by planes and gliders.

In the Allied invasion plans, the Argens Valley, which separates the

Monts des Maures from the Esterel chain, had been designated as the principal zone of action, the backbone of Operation Dragoon. The mission assigned to General Robert Tryon Frederick and his 10,000 paratroopers was to prevent the Germans from getting into this valley in the area around Le Muy, starting at H-Hour minus four. They were also to isolate the enemy troops that would be besieged on the beaches, by blocking all the roads and other means of access by which German reinforcements might possibly be sent in toward the beachhead. A secondary task had also been assigned to the paratroopers – to capture a German general and his entire staff, who were occupying a villa at Draguignan.

The every-day occupation of Le Muy's 3,000 inhabitants was in the local cork industry or in the vineyards. While the first airborne scouts were drifting down over the Argens Valley and the surrounding area, these peacefully sleeping citizens could hardly dream that their village was about to become a strategic center for the Second D-Day.

Through the heavy fog, the scouts were diligently trying to get their bearings as accurately as possible, with an eye to avoiding any major clashes with the Germans. The silent countryside, the vineyards, the pine and cork-oak forests, and the empty roads were suffused with a wan moonlight as the men moved quietly and efficiently about their business of installing ground lights and fluorescent markers. When this was accomplished, they waited noiselessly, this particular mission ended. Of the dozen groups of advance scouts, only one had been lucky enough to land within one hundred yards of its objective. Most of them hit far off course, and many had to trek several miles over unknown territory in order to reach their drop zone. Some became hopelessly lost, and among them were those paratroopers who were to mark the area on to which Colonel Rupert D. Graves and his three airborne infantry battalions of the 517th Parachute Regiment were to drop.

Meanwhile most of the airborne troops were steadily nearing the coast of Provence. In the second plane of the first wave, Captain William H. Young, a former detective sergeant from San Jose, California, was resolutely 'refusing to let myself get worked up over all this – not too much, anyhow.' Before joining the army, Young had also been a boxer, fighting under the name Billy Ryan, with an impressive record of bouts. As he stood waiting to bail out, he was thinking that 'this invasion wasn't going to be as exciting' as the fight of his young protégé Georgie Latka, a lightweight who had fought a draw with Sammy Angott in San Francisco. Captain Louis J. Vogel, commanding a field artillery battery in the 460th Parachute Battalion, was of the same frame of mind; Vogel felt almost certain that everything was going to go off as planned, 'without a hitch and probably a damned sight better than in Normandy.' Sergeant Harold E. Hand, on board the same plane – nicknamed the 'Skin Hound' – was firmly convinced that they were about to 'land Hitler a clout that would give him plenty of headaches.' A private first class from Minnesota, Norbert Bergstrom, observed that 'all the guys on the plane were good and relaxed – it was just like any other regular exercise.'

Aboard the Skin Hound, Vogel's men sat facing one another, their helmets and equipment held in their laps, while they calmly puffed on cigarettes and exchanged casual banter as if they had not a care in the world. Private Albert A. Callwas slept through most of the four-hour flight with his head resting on the shoulder of his friend, Ralph Olinger. Before the take-off, Corporal Cameron Gauthier had issued one last mail call, at 7.20 P.M. Callwas had not received any letters, but had consoled himself by swigging a final bottle of the pre-invasion beer that had been distributed to the men. Twenty minutes before jump time Olinger had roughly shaken him awake:

'Hey, Bert! Time to shove off!'

The aerial armada – nearly four hundred planes – appeared exactly on schedule for the rendezvous over the beach resort of Agay, east of Saint-Raphaël. At the same moment, the C-47's flew over and passed the coast on their way inland, formation after formation, powerful engines droning steadily. The 5,000 paratroopers on board were girding themselves for the leap, their eyes fixed on the green alert signal light to the rear of the cabins. Little did they know that, far below at Le Trayas, a forlorn group of French naval officers and men were clinging desperately and wearily to the hostile rocks, listening to the planes that could bring them no help, their souls barren of hope.

The 'flying boxcars' continued to thunder over the shore line, the stars twinkling high above them. Not a single antiaircraft battery opened fire, and the planes' occupants noticed only a few distant sparks that looked as if something was shooting somewhere. Although he could not be sure about it, the Skin Hound's twenty-two year old pilot, Captain Albert S. Harwell, 'thought that those shots might be coming from a couple of Allied ships standing by off the beaches.' (He was slightly mistaken about the time, but not about the source of the firing. It had indeed come from Allied ships, and he and the Skin Hound's crew had witnessed the only naval engagement of the Second D-Day.)

Colonel Tesch was feeling just a little bit cheated 'because I hadn't had a crack at anything, not even the meanest old German fighter plane.' The German planes were conspicuous by their absence, but this fact and the complete absence of flak did not surprise him even mildly, 'considering the load of bombs we'd been dumping around those parts for quite some days and weeks.' First Lieutenant Ronald H. Warrell, the Skin Hound's co-pilot, remembers making a bet with his navigator, Lieutenant Laurens H. Williams, that they would have a flight eighty per cent uneventful all the way to the drop zone. However, he admits that he was kind of amazed at winning his bet.

From his post on board the Skin Hound, Sergeant Hand could see 'that crazy flying boxcar's wing lights tearing through the sky.' Sixty seconds later the red lamp flashed on, and Vogel's men began bailing out into the night. Little clusters of parachutes floated down over a small wooded hillside, a neat spot tucked out of sight of prying eyes. By the time the last man of the stick had jumped, it was 4.22 A.M.

When the Skin Hound was empty, Harwell lifted the plane's nose sharply and 'gave her the gas.' The Dakota gave a growl and was off. As they circled their home base in Italy, the crew saw, in the glow of the sunrise, the waves of Waco and Horsa gliders being towed by the C-47s on their way to the drop zones.

9

THE STRIDENT, MOURNFUL WAIL of a siren sounded through the night at Le Muy, and the grinding roar of plane engines woke the members of the Stevens family, over a mile away. In compliance with the BBC's instructions, James Stevens did not move from the house. Hastily donning trousers and shirt, he sat down on the bed and began saying his prayers. He thought he heard the clatter of machine guns firing out on the plain in the direction of the Sorbine woods, where the Germans had a fuel and ammunition dump. Getting up, Stevens went over to the window and opened the shutters just a crack. But the only thing that greeted his eyes was the thick land fog that was blotting out the entire landscape. The fog was thick enough to slice with a knife, and so unusual for that time of year that most of the people who woke before daybreak thought it was an artificial fog.

André Lambrusco, a railway watchman, had just gone off duty at the station of Les Arcs and was walking home to Trans-en-Provence. His niece Mireille was anxiously awaiting his return – she, too, had been startled out of her sleep by the rumbling of the planes. Lambrusco reached his doorstep safely, but as he crossed the square in front of the church he saw rockets illuminating the dark sky, and it seemed to him that 'the house fronts were all brightly lit up as if by strong sunshine.' Twenty miles away, at Les-Tourrettes-de-Fayence, Lidia Airaud, worried over her husband's impending departure for the work camps in Germany, had slept scarcely a wink. As the first planes began coming over, she rushed to the window and saw parachutes drifting down like huge white mushrooms in the August night. (However, Fayence had not been one of the scheduled dropping zones.) Madame Airaud's first thought was that maybe her husband would not have to leave after all. The paratroopers she saw included a scout platoon from the 517th Regiment; its members were completely lost, victims of the blinding fog. They had been dropped far off course, a few dozen miles from their destination, and were groping around in an effort to get their bearings.

In the second wave of planes was a Dakota in which General Frederick, commander of the First Airborne Task Force, was getting ready to jump.

Frederick, a general at the age of thirty-seven, had been badly wounded in the battle of Rome, a slight inconvenience that had not kept him from popping up in the front lines again two days later. Right after the outbreak of the war, Frederick had collaborated with a British scientist in a 'suicide expedition' to Norway directed against the nuclear-experiment factories in which the Germans were stepping up their production of heavy water (water in which deuterium atoms replace hydrogen atoms). His force was composed of American and British paratroopers, and had been specially assembled for the Provence landings.

At 4.40 A.M., the green light went off and the red one flashed on inside the C-47. The general called out the familiar orders:

'Stand up and hook up! Sound off for equipment check! Stand in the door!'

Frederick flashed a final encouraging smile at the fifteen men in his stick. Jumping after him would be four officers of the divisional staff, followed by a French warrant officer, Schevenels, of the First Shock Battalion, one of the sixteen men who had been selected for their first-hand knowledge of the assault area. All of them were wearing silk scarves printed with green, brown and blue maps of the main road net in Provence. In addition to a cloth map of the region between Marseilles and Foggia, they also had an emergency fund of French, English and Italian currency.

The Dakota had already lost altitude and leveled off at a 40° angle when Schevenels heard Frederick bark out the jump order:

'Go!'

Exactly as at Anzio seven months before, the youthful paratrooper general was the first to plunge through the gaping opening into the night, with the ground spread out somewhere 2,000 feet below.

The other fifteen were right at his heels, as in some aerial game of follow the leader. Their faces covered with greasepaint, their bodies bunched up in heavy brown canvas jump suits, wearing their great boots and sturdy helmets and packing weapons and gear, they let themselves fall out into nothingness. Sixteen ripcords were pulled, and sixteen parachutes billowed forth in the night amid the hundreds already wafting down in the humid air over the combat zone. The oncoming waves of planes were unloading their human cargos at an unbelievable rate, as fast as they could.

The ace in the hole for this initial fraction of the 5,000 troops who were to be parachuted over Provence behind the German lines, was the element of surprise. As Schevenels slowly descended, he could see suspended in the murky darkness below him a 'wide whitish blanket perforated here and there by little black dots.' At first he thought he had been dropped too far to the south, probably over the water, and he got ready to cast off his parachute and inflate his Mae West jacket. However, as he began falling through the fog bank he spotted the ground just in time, and a minute later he was was rolling over in a vineyard. His first move was to draw his knife and free himself of his parachute harness.

While he was looking around for the right direction to head in, he heard a voice call out near him:

'Max! Max! *Achtung*!'

Schevenels froze in his tracks, holding his breath. His immediate concern was to get his bearings and proceed as quickly as possible to the farm at Le Mitan, north of Le Muy, where Frederick's command post would be set up. Five minutes later he heard the footsteps of two or three men making their way over the fields, and then the sound grew fainter as they reached a paved road. The Frenchman straightened up and set off in the direction of the footsteps. When he reached the first road sign, he realized it was going to take him quite some time to reach his assembly area. As a matter of fact, it was four hours before he met up with the first paratroopers of the 517th Regiment who had landed where they were supposed to. Schevenels resolutely set off on a long hike.

Instead of dissipating, the eerie fog seemed to have settled in for a long stay. It swirled through the wooded hills of the Var, nestled among the vineyards, hovered over the irrigation ditches and the planted fields, enveloping the strange 'asparagus stalks' of sharp spikes and pointed stakes. This particular touch of foresight, as with other obstacles set up wherever the Germans thought airborne troops or gliders might land, turned out to be mostly useless, or at best ineffective – and for a good reason. The French workers whom the Germans had recruited to set up the spikes had dutifully performed their task, and there were thousands of these stakes with their deadly points bristling up all over the land-scape. However, they had deliberately been placed either too far apart or too insecurely to constitute a serious hazard. As the result of these precautions, the over-all casualties among paratroopers when they landed amounted to less than three per cent of the total for the airborne forces.[1]

Frederick's paratroopers continued to drop, effortlessly and relent-lessly, in innumerable clusters of white blossoms. In the gathering light of dawn, the men hastened to assemble as best they could over a stretch of some twenty-five miles. Some found themselves totally isolated on landing, others grouped together in bands of six or eight, sometimes even fewer. Part of Lieutenant Colonel William P. Yarborough's 509th Para-chute Battalion hit the ground near the banks of the Nartuby river, a tributary of the Argens, near La Motte. By then it was 4.30 A.M. Five minutes later, Colonel W.J.Boyle and forty men from the 517th, who were cut off from the rest of their First Battalion, began landing in the gardens and vineyards around the hamlet of Les Arcs, where they were met by sustained machine-gun fire. The forty paratroopers and their leader deployed over the terrain and, although they had no supporting artillery, sent back strong answering fire. This marked the beginning of the first pitched battle of D-Day in Provence.

At 5.10 A.M., substantial detachments from the British Second Independent Parachute Brigade, the luckiest of all the airborne units, touched down in the hills of Le Rouet, east of the farm at Le Mitan, and the Second Battalion of the 517th, commanded by Colonel Richard J. Seitz, rushed toward Les Arcs to reinforce Boyle. At 5.14 A.M., the last of the 396 transport planes became a mere speck in the distance and vanished over the gray horizon, which was growing steadily lighter. The first phase of Operation Rugby had just been completed. More than 5,000 airborne infantrymen had been parachuted over Provence. The jumps were a remarkable achievement in precision timing, although their accuracy geographically left much to be desired. However, they were, by far, the most successful of the entire war.

A twenty-one year old American, Sergeant Joseph Blackwell of the 517th Parachute Regiment, had been entrusted with a ticklish assign-ment. He and his men, together with another squad of the Second Battalion, were scheduled to jump at about 4.30 A.M. over a secondary objective, and then proceed to the outskirts of Draguignan – specifically,

[1] Over the preceding three weeks in the area around Le Muy, Les Arcs, La Motte, Tran-en-Provence, Roquebrune, and throughout the Argens Valley, the Germans had not had time enough to rig these obstacles with barbed wire, electrified networks, or explosive charges, all of which had been included in the defense plans.

135

to a withdrawn and discreet-looking villa on the edge of town. Blackwell possessed detailed blueprints of the Villa Gladys, and had instructions to attack with grenades and rifles. At the same time, planes would begin bombing Draguignan in order to facilitate his task. As soon as the bombers had disappeared, the paratrooper would storm the villa and capture General Ferdinand Neuling, in command of the German army's LXII Corps, and his staff. Blackwell had memorized the names of the principal officers – Colonel Rudolf Meinshausen, Major Lademan, Major Fisher, and Captain Kurt Weyand. The plans had been elaborately laid, including provision for Blackwell's arriving early; in that case, he and his men were to knock at the house next door, where each morning Neuling ate a breakfast of coffee and lightly buttered toast. In fact, it was the lady of this house who had informed the local Resistance of the general's habits.

As Blackwell commented afterward, more than a bit ruefully:

'Everything should have gone off like clockwork.'

But as it turned out, everything went haywire.

Blackwell recalls that after he began parachuting toward the fog-shrouded ground, his very first feeling was that he was 'going to be engulfed in water.' Like many others, Blackwell thought he had been dropped over the Mediterranean, and this conviction was so strong that he could scarcely believe it when his feet actually touched solid ground. It was immediately obvious that only a small part of his outfit had landed anywhere near him. After considerable difficulty, he manged to assemble five or six men with their bazookas and ammunition, but the mortar that was to have been parachuted with them was nowhere in sight. The group set out blindly through the fog and crossed over a valley, one side wooded, the other not. At length, in the woolly mist, they made out a kind of road along which some more lost paratroopers, including Sergeant Richard Collester of the Second Battalion, were trying to find their way.

Shortly afterward, when the noise of shots rang out in some nearby woods, neither Collester nor Blackwell as yet had the vaguest idea of where they were. Eventually they came to a fork in the road, and both sprinted forward as they glimpsed a heaven-sent signpost. With disappointment they realized that the mission of which they had been so proud was doomed. The sign read '*Draguignan: 34 kilomètres.*' They were twenty miles off course.

Even if they could have overcome all the inevitable obstacles, they had not the slightest chance of reaching the Villa Gladys on time. Blackwell and Collester reluctantly decided that they might as well forget about continuing toward Draguignan and instead try to rendezvous with the rest of the Second Battalion.

As far as Blackwell could tell, the enemy's reactions were still uncertain, erratic, and isolated. The pre-dawn calm was racked sporadically with the far-off echoing of grenade explosions and the brisk rat-tat-tat of machine guns, succeeded once more by the somnolent silence of the dense mist creeping through fields and forests, making the realities of war seem nebulous and remote.

When they heard the rumble of engines approaching down the road, Blackwell and his men dived into the roadside ditches. A German motorized column slowly heaved into view out of the fog. As the sergeant was about to give the signal for an attack, he realized that 'they were just a few worthless old army trucks covered with branches, not worth a potshot.' The cumbersome vehicles crawled by less than three feet from the men crouching in the ditches, and after a moment that seemed like a century to Blackwell, they dissolved back into the pea-soup mist. As the men scrambled out and began continuing their march, one of them noticed a camouflaged ammunition and fuel dump hidden away in the woods, with no sentries around. 'Just for the hell of it,' Blackwell remembers, 'he tossed a grenade into the works, and his uniform caught on fire. We had no first-aid kits and no way of carrying him, and the poor devil had to keep on walking with shreds of burned skin hanging from his neck and hands.'

The gradually increasing opalescent light of the August morning disclosed hundred of limp, motionless parachutes strewn over the landscape like so many great, ungainly pale flowers. Down from the hilltops, out of the valleys, the orchards, the thickets, men lugging packs on their backs, staggering from the combined effect of exhaustion and the weight of their equipment, were steadily plodding. Some of them were still seeking their way, following the roads, reading the distance markers, and trying to locate on their maps whatever place names they came to.

Suddenly a human shape wobbled into sight out of the fog, right in front of Blackwell's column. It was a Frenchman riding a bicycle. Blackwell has described him as a 'burly guy with a big mustache. When he saw us he got so excited that he started laughing and crying at the same time. He let go of his handlebars, spread out his arms, and toppled off his bicycle. He got up and gave each of us a great bearhug, but he couldn't make a word come out.'

A few miles farther, the group – by now it had other scattered units following it – reached the assembly area, a junction of highways and railway tracks. This had now become the front line. Various outfits from the 517th had been holding the position for an hour and a half, and the Germans were steadily harassing them with small-arms fire and mortars. From behind a thick hedge at the edge of a pine woods, a German

137

blockhouse was firing a steady stream of tracer bullets. But through the air, already warm with the rising sun, a distant roar was sounding off to the south. It was continuous aerial bombing of the beaches, the prelude to H-Hour.

Just then, one of the *Wehrmacht*'s Mercedes convertibles, with four passengers inside, came racing along the still uncaptured stretch of highway between Trans-en-Provence and Vidauban. Blackwell's men, alerted by the lookouts, opened fire, and the car skidded clear across the road before turning over into a ditch amid a thick cloud of black smoke. The four passengers were killed outright – there was blood all over the coat of the German colonel who had been sitting up front with the driver, and he had a gaping hole where his forehead should have been.

It took some of the airborne units more than twenty-four hours – in a few cases, even several days – to reach their assembly areas. Others, including sizable contingents of the 509th Parachute Battalion and the 463rd Parachute Artillery Battalion, never did make it. But in most instances, as soon as they touched the ground, the paratroopers of the First Airborne Task Force were able to swing right into action and carry out the basic details of their missions – throwing up road blocks, setting up machine-gun positions, and snipping telephone wires wherever they found them. Part of their job also was to get runways ready for the gliders that would be bringing in vehicles and matériel, particularly the antitank weapons that were indispensable for any offensive action; these were due at 8 A.M. It had been assumed that by then the engineers would have had time to become fully operational and would be in complete control of the area adjacent to the Nartuby plain. Enemy ground resistance was on the whole instantaneous but weak. For at least the first hour after landing, Frederick's paratroopers encountered only sporadic machine-gun fire, proving that almost everywhere the Germans who were fighting against the units of the First Airborne had been taken by surprise.

The minute he hit the ground, Lieutenant Colonel Melvin Zais, commanding the Third Battalion of the 517th realized that he, too, was in the wrong place. The twenty-eight year old officer had been slated to jump near Le Muy and to proceed with his battalion of 540 men along *Route Nationale 7*, the main road to Fréjus and Saint-Raphaël, for the purpose of keeping German reinforcements from getting through to the sea before the troops of the 36th Division landed.

Like so many others on that fateful morning, Zais had made a successful jump at the right time – 4.40 A.M. – but had landed far from his drop zone. His parachute had gently deposited him east of Grasse, near the little village of Fayence, and about twenty miles of hills and forests lay between him and Nartuby. Zais did not know how many of his men had landed with him, but the landings had been marred by casualties. Several men had fallen on the stone retaining walls bordering the fields and gardens and had been injured. However, as they groped through the misty darkness, the paratroopers of the 517th met up with some members of the local Resistance who, although they had not exactly been expecting them, helped them to reassemble as best they could and joined them in waging the first of the battles of the liberation of southern France.

Spread across a farmyard in Les-Tourrettes-de-Fayence was an enormous white parachute with a red cross in the middle. The farm belonged to Lidia Airaud and her husband. It was not long before the farmyard was swarming with injured men, armed Resistance fighters, and a few American paratroopers who were thought to be Negroes because of their black greasepaint. It was nearly 9 A.M. when the paratroopers, who had managed to assemble amid confusion and difficult circumstances, began streaming into the village, whose capture had not even been included in their orders. By then the Germans had recovered from the shock of their first surprise and were retaliating. The garrison at Les-Tourrettes-de-Fayence put up stiff resistance that lasted late into the afternoon, until Allied air support finally had to be called in.

From the moment he touched down, Zais had been busy rounding up as many of the men in his battalion as he could. They had landed in three separate zones, scattered over eight miles in an area around Seillans, Fayence, and Callian. He cannot remember all the details of how he finally got them together, but says 'it was a long shot, a real piece of good luck.' With a few of the uninjured men, Aais had already covered three miles of wooded, hilly terrain when his second group unexpectedly appeared – eighty men from the British Second Brigade, who had landed in the same zone. While these men had been beating their way through the bushes in an attempt to reach the assembly area, they had managed – with bazookas and a few light weapons – to attack and destroy a German motorized column that was on its way to the landing beaches. But a long day and another night were to pass before this valiant unit, isolated in unknown territory, finally reached its destination. Just as it did so, the remaining men of Zais's battalion, who had been lost for thirty-six hours, began arriving from still another direction.

'It was a fantastic coincidence,' Zais remarked, 'because neither of the two columns had the slightest idea of the other's whereabouts, yet they came together at the same intersection and at the very same minute.'

The unluckiest of all the lost and strayed soldiers was probably Corporal Claude Jacquemet. His most cherished hope had just been dashed. Jacquemet was accompanying a stick of British paratroopers from the Second Brigade who were to land at a place that meant a great deal more to him than to them – his birthplace, Le Muy. He had so wished to give his parents the surprise of their lives.

As he hit the ground and took one look around him, the Frenchman knew he had fallen wide of the mark. He was not home yet – far from it! With the other men in his plane, he had come down twenty miles from Le Muy. They were near a château on the outskirts of Fayence. He had known this area ever since he was a boy, but that was no consolation for his not becoming the first French soldier among the Provence invasion troops to reach his home.[1]

Jacqueline Cézilly was a charming little girl with thick chestnut-colored curls crowning her impish face and sparkling hazel eyes. The night of 14 August was the most exciting in all her eleven years.

Her sister Michèle, two years older, had shaken her awake.

'Listen, Jacqueline! Hear the airplanes?'

The two girls pattered barefoot over to the window, but could not see a thing through the slits in the ancient wooden shutters of the château. Dawn had not yet broken, and the night sky over Sainte-Roseline was filled with the rumble of engines. Just then something else attracted their attention, the sound of voices coming from downstairs. The sisters exchanged a brief glance, gathered up their long nightgowns, and flew down the stairs. The dining room door stood ajar, and they could see their mother, the Baroness de Laval (Jacqueline and Michele were her daughters by her first marriage) pouring drinks for two men. Just the sight of the men was enough to bring the two youngsters skidding to a halt.

The two soldiers standing there in the dimly lighted room looked as if someone had taken a paintbrush and smeared them with black and green paint. Their machine guns were fearsome objects that struck awe in the children's hearts, and their helmets were covered with leafy foliage that added to the wildness of the scene. From the men's chests there dangled two big yellow 'eggs,' the 'shells' covered with little raised squares. Jacqueline subsequently learned that these were grenades.

'Who's that?' she whispered to her mother in the hallway.

[1] Claude Jacquemet did not make it to Le Muy until late the following afternoon, at the same time as Zais's men. His friend Jean Folliero de Righi described the scene to me: 'I was standing with his mother when Claude suddenly appeared, near the church in Le Muy. His joy and his parents' emotion are something I'll never forget.' Today, Mr and Mrs Jacquemet run a bakery in Le Muy. They still hope that Claude will come rushing around the corner again, just as he did on that long-ago evening of 16 August 1944. But Lieutenant Jacquemet, after volunteering in the Korean war in 1950, went on to fight in Indochina and was captured at Dien Bien Phu in May 1954. He never returned from captivity. His parents heard nothing more from him, but they refuse to admit that he is dead.

'They say that they're Americans,' Madame de Laval answered. 'One of them even called your father by his name . . .'

The child suddenly saw that her mother's eyes were filled with tears. Turning back to her husband, Madame de Laval said in a low voice:

'I still think they're really Germans, and that they're trying to make us believe there's been a landing or something, just to see how we react.'

At a gesture from his companion, the younger man walked to the other end of the room and cut the telephone wire.

The other man, who had 'a funny nose, all red and sort of bumpy,' according to the girls, invited Jacqueline to sit on his lap and gave her some chewing gum. Although she had forgotten what it tasted like, the gum dispelled any doubts that might have been lingering in Jacqueline's mind. These men were definitely Americans! And there really had been a landing! But the baroness was still not convinced.

By now the house was filling up with troops and the grounds around the building were strewn with dozens of parachutes colored red, blue, yellow, green and white. From a distance the acrid odor of smoke was blowing in, coming from the fuel dump that the soldier in Sergeant Blackwell's platoon had 'inadvertently' set on fire. It had just exploded, and the woods around it were burning.

The man with the chewing gum spread out on the table a huge aerial photograph shot a few weeks before, and the De Lavals noted with amazement that it revealed every detail of their property, including the remnants of a famous eleventh century monastery. Many months before, in the early stages of the Allied planning, the De Lavals's château had been selected to serve as the command post for a regiment of American paratroops during the night of 14 August.

Jacqueline and her sister giggled when they noticed that the American's mustache was 'half-black and half-green' under his hooked nose, which was 'all covered with scratches.' He explained that he had landed nose first in a grapevine, and introduced himself as Colonel Graves, in command of the 517th Parachute Regiment. At that moment, Graves's men were still widely scattered over a twenty-five mile area.

Another man was to have reached the château at the same time as Graves. Jean Blanc, one of the head Resistance leaders in the Var region, watched the American scouts land and saw the bulk of the airborne troops come in later. The evening before, he had been notified that paratroopers would be landing in his particularly crucial sector around Les Arcs in the early hours of 15 August. He also knew the password for the night – 'Napoleon' – and what his duties were. By the time the operation had begun, he was to have ensured complete control of the zone in which the Allied paratroopers would be landing. Blanc had alerted his men and made the necessary arrangements to get to Sainte-Roseline by 3 A.M. But his luck ran out, and at that hour he was swearing to himself as he bowled along in a truck, all lights out on a road north of Draguignan. With him were seven local gendarmes who were rallying to the side of the Resistance and two Allied officers, an American and a Frenchman, who had parachuted down twenty-four hours earlier. The ten of them had had their hands full, and they had given up all hope of arriving on time. First, they were attacked by an Allied plane, and then there was a series of encounters with German patrols. Now, as a crowning irony, they were right in the midst of the main paratroop operation, being fired on from the groves and forests by the very troops that they were to be on hand to meet.[1]

Dawn was already breaking.

At 6 A.M., on his regular morning round, Raymond, a Negro who had served as a corpsman with the colonial infantry, was delivering milk to the customers along his route in Le Muy, the cans dangling from his bicycle. Raymond had ridden about a mile through the countryside, and it had been an incredible experience, with bullets whizzing around his ears, multicolored rockets hailing down everywhere, and the fields full of strange, scarcely human-looking forms running in all directions.

Despite the danger, the milkman was fascinated by the show, and was hugely enjoying himself. He was looking forward to telling Dr Couve all about it. But when he reached the house, the physician was thunderstruck at seeing Raymond arrive.

'My God! How did you get here?' he exclaimed.

'You should see those Germans, doctor! They're getting crazier and crazier. Out there shooting up the whole countryside. They're even coming down in parachutes, way out in the vineyards, having a regular picnic...!'

The physician, marveling, went back into the house. Part of the building had been requisitioned by the Germans some time ago. For two hours, Dr Couve had been working uninterruptedly, with people bringing in wounded paratroopers from all directions or asking him to go out and give first aid.

All things considered, the German occupation at Le Muy, the strategic

[1] In addition to Captain Geoffrey M. T. Jones, of the First Airborne Task Force's G-2 section, and Major Allain, of the Free French Forces, I have been able to identify the other passengers in this truck, to whom one of the few coherent missions for the night of 14 August had been assigned. The seven gendarmes, belonging to the brigades of Les Arcs, Fréjus, and Draguignan, were Charles André, Emile Poutot, Lucien Bernard, André Toussaint, Pierre Dumas, Germain Courci, and Jean Castelain. Jones and Allain had made a special jump on the night of 13 August to help prepare for the arrival of the airborne troops.

center for Operation Rugby, the airborne assault, had not been much of an ordeal for the population. Of the seven thousand or eight thousand Germans originally stationed in the area (members of Panther and Tiger tank units assigned after the Italian capitulation), only two or three companies had remained since the Normandy landings. These were composed mostly of wounded men or of troops from the veteran ranks who had been withdrawn from the Channel front, a few detachments of motorized Tyrolese troops assigned to antiaircraft units, and part of the 932rd Regiment's infantry troops commanded by Captain Bruendel. The Austrians in the 'motorized' flak unit were now reduced to riding around on bicycles, and the local citizens had promptly dubbed them 'the cyclists.' Was it possible that the Allies had overestimated the enemy's defense forces in the area around Draguignan? This question was uppermost in the minds of the inhabitants of Le Muy, Les Arcs, La Motte, and Trans-en-Provence as they watched wave after wave of Frederick's 5,000 paratroopers drop into their midst. They were sure that the battle would be both unequal and short-lived. They were mistaken.

As the paratroopers had begun arriving over the villages, farmyards, and forests, Dr Couve had witnessed a surprising incident, one that had merely added to his other worries. The Austrian master sergeant billeted in the doctor's house had packed his belongings and gone out to the barn to hide in the hay until the time would be ripe for him to surrender. This spirit of resignation was not shared by the rest of the garrison troops, who continued to resist over the ensuing thirty-six hours and scored a high number of dead and wounded among both the military and the civilians.

During that long, dark night, people everywhere – in isolated farms, in the hamlets, in houses along the highway and out in the back country – were cautiously opening their shutters just a crack to try to see what was going on, peering through the obscurity that was punctuated by the staccato barking of nearby machine guns and deafening explosions deep in the woods. They could occasionally hear men's voices calling out in a foreign language, back behind the thickets, and these shouts were intermingled with the screams and moans of the wounded. The people living in La Motte, about a mile from Le Muy, had a hard time realizing that their tiny village was right in the thick of things and that the first inland combats of this Second D-Day in France were taking place in their area. They could not see much of the fighting. About all they could make out was a strange, spooky blanket of fog that swallowed up the fields, with here and there a lone cypress tree from which a parachute fluttered limply, the over-all effect very like a scarecrow.

Although there was something undeniably reassuring about this invisible combat, an undefinable uneasiness hovered in the air, partly because of the thick mist. Many of the villagers believed, with a member of the local Resistance named Ramella, that it was an artificial fog that the Allies had created to shield themselves against German air attacks.

Old Leycuras, La Motte's retired military tailor, had spent the entire evening making tricolor armbands for the Resistance fighters. When he heard the planes, he sprang out of bed, his hand instinctively groping for the lamp switch – only to discover that the Germans had shut off the current. His son Maurice had just left the house and Leycuras felt his way around in the darkness, cursing to himself.

It was a routine trick of the Germans to switch off the electricity whenever an alarm occurred. This time it turned out to be a stroke of luck for a paratrooper from the 509th Battalion. Maurice Leycuras and his fellow Resistance worker Ramella were walking through the center of town when something caused them to look up and stop. An American parachutist was struggling to disengage himself from his harness, caught in the high-tension wires that passed over the Chaberts' house. What happened next, after Ramella had helped untangle him, infuriated the Frenchmen. Assuming that his benefactors were Germans, the American had pointed his weapon at them. His two rescuers indignantly protested. Soon they were joined by more parachutists who had extricated themselves from various trees and rooftops and were trying to orient themselves. The whole group, with Leycuras and Ramella leading, was now proceeding toward the assembly area at the farm in Le Mitan.

The British had not fared too badly. Of all the airborne troops, they lost the least amount of time and had a maximum of good luck in parachuting into their assigned areas with relatively few casualties and little damage to equipment. The British scouts had done their job well in this region, particularly in the lightly wooded slopes around Le Mitan, which consisted of a few houses clustered along a brook between two main highways. The planes had dropped the troops with eighty per cent accuracy.

Roch Lombard, a French master sergeant who had jumped with the British troops, was among the first to reach the Lavagne farm, which had been chosen as the paratroopers' first headquarters. General Frederick had not been so lucky. First of all, Warrant Officer Schevenels, who was to have guided him as Lombard had guided the British, had not landed with him. Furthermore, in order to begin functioning, his scattered staff had set up operations in the ruins of an abandoned farmhouse. It was from there that the first orders were issued for the capture of the essential objectives that had to be taken before daybreak – the main intersections and all the junctions where side roads came in on *Route Nationale 7* on the way to Fréjus and Sainte-Maxime – to immobilize the enemy behind the landing areas.

By and large, this initial mission was successfully accomplished by the First Airborne Task Force. As night faded into day, only token opposition came from the Germans, who tried to put up a fight against André Bauchière's sturdy Resistance group. The Frenchmen had joined forces with an American unit, that of Colonel Yarborough and his 509th Battalion who had landed near La Motte. In fact, La Motte would be the first village in Provence liberated by the Allies in the early morning hours of Tuesday, 15 August.

Frederick finally reached the farm at Le Mitan just before 7 A.M. He had not yet learned that thirty-seven of the 396 Dakotas transporting his task force had failed to drop the paratroopers over the target area. His main hope was that the lack of moonlight over the drop zones and the fog blanketing the Argens Valley would not have any dire consequences for him and his men. On the whole, the steadily increasing number of partially regrouped units that found their way to the assembly areas every half-hour or so was encouraging. The sounds meeting Frederick's ears were mainly those of gliders bringing in the jeeps, mortars, antitank guns and reinforcements, and this meant that it was now 8 A.M. It was also H-Hour on the beaches, and the paratroopers behind the lines would no longer be alone in their fight for survival.

10

THE SIX HUNDRED FRENCHMEN huddled aboard their twenty LCIs under a darkened sky were slowly approaching the beach. Despite the eager anticipation of their long wait, they found themselves almost overwhelmed by the pungent scent of the eucalyptus and pine trees, of the plants and flowers that had basked under the August sun, by all the heavy night fragrance of the coast, the earthy odor of the soil of France to which they were at last returning.

Suddenly the flash of gunfire illuminated the sky over the beach, along the length of the African Commandos' landing zone. Lieutenant Colonel Georges-Régis Bouvet was straining through the blackness in a vain effort to locate the green signals that Major Rigaud was supposed to be flashing. He could see nothing. Deep apprehension gripped him. He remembered the tragic night of the capture of Elba and feared that Rigaud might have been taken prisoner. It was 1.30 A.M. off Rayol beach, the narrow landing area assigned to the troops making up Operation Romeo. Twenty interminable minutes dragged by before the guns ceased firing over Cap Nègre as suddenly as they had begun, and an oppressive silence draped the summer night.

The men of the Second and Third Commandos crouched in their barges were stricken with anxiety. Behind them was a unit of mortars heavy machine guns, and antitank artillery. No sound came from the shore except the rhythmic swish of the water against the sand. Lieutenant De Castelnau, a platoon leader in the Third Commandos, remembers 'an owl shrieking its wild hoot, like a mad thing,' somewhere back in the Faveirolle woods.

Standing in the lead assault craft, Bouvet decided to give the landing signal. The landing commander, a Canadian midshipman, shook his head resolutely. He was sorry, but he had orders to wait for Rigaud's beach signals before sending the men ashore. Uncontrollable anger welled up in Bouvet, and his African chauffeur, Yaya Archouni, who had been sticking to him like a shadow for the last two years, saw him suddenly pull out his pistol and jab it in the Canadian's ribs. The midshipman shrugged his shoulders and began obeying Bouvet's orders. The LCIs scraped up against the shore, the landing ramps dropped forward, and the commandos streamed out onto the beach.

And when finally they were treading on the soil of France, their emotion transcended anything these bold, battle-toughened veterans had ever experienced. Every minute counted, every fraction of a second was important for the six hundred men on this perilous mission. But even more important was the realization that at last they were back home in France, on the last lap of a long journey. As hundreds and thousands of their compatriots would be doing in the hours and days to come, these Frenchmen furtively reached down to scoop up a handful of the cool, damp sand, which they squeezed eagerly in their palms before pressing it to their lips.

They waded ashore, every man for himself, and reassembled by sections along the narrow strip of beach with the feeling that they were raising a fearful din. But, even before he landed, Bouvet knew that this was not the beach he had flown over a month earlier. He realized where they were – a mile to the west, at the foot of the Les Pradels heights, the very spot he had ruled out for his assault. For the moment, Bouvet's one desire was to get out of there, and quickly. So far, the Germans had not reacted, but it would not take long for them to be alerted. The officers hastily assembled their platoons, and everybody set off in the darkness under the pine trees of Le Canadel beach, toward the high, steep hills overlooking the sea.

Not an order had been spoken. The men knew exactly what they had to do, and few of them were aware that they had landed wide of the mark. Their job was to reach their objectives and to surprise the Germans, although the painstakingly prepared plans were now meaningless. As silently as they had approached the land, the LCIs were now edging back out to sea. Through the deep shadows the men could make out the roofs and walls of the sleeping houses nestled in their perfumed leafy bowers. Hubert Muller, a liaison officer with the Third Commando group, stumbled against a sign: '*Achtung! Minen!*' He gave the alarm, but the sign was a fake – the real mine field was a quarter of a mile to the left, and had no warning signs.

The Second and Third Commandos eventually reached the railway tracks of the small line that ran between Toulon and Saint-Raphaël. Captain Albert Thorel – who would be killed the following day – headed the Second Commandos. On the ground floor of Le Canadel's tiny depot, a typical saffron-colored Provençal railway station, Antoine Pergola was wide awake. When he heard the muffled footsteps of a large group approaching, he thought that perhaps it was a troop detachment trying to encircle the building, to take it by surprise. The next minute there came a soft but unmistakable tapping on the shutters of his room. The knocking became more insistent.

Pergola hesitated before speaking up:

'Who is it?'

The answer was barely whispered through the shutters:

'The African Army!'

Pergola was dumbfounded. He held his breath and did not make a move. It occurred to him that this might be another German ruse. The knocking on the shutters grew louder.

'Open up, for God's sake!' It was Thorel's voice again. 'We're French, all right – don't worry!'

It was Thorel's turn to be flabbergasted when the reply came from behind the shutters:

'I can't! My wife's having a baby!'

But Pergola finally did open the door of the station, but not without misgivings. And, following the familiar pattern of many other occasions on that eventful night when the Allied troops and the French civilians found themselves face to face, the first reaction was one of mutual hesitation and suspicion. In the darkness, the swarm of helmeted and armed men gathered around the station understandably looked rather like a bunch of thugs.

Thorel quickly briefed Pergola, explaining that he and his men had landed off course and required assistance in making their way through the enemy positions. He added that within a few hours the fleet would be shelling the coast and the main landings would begin.

Pergola shook his head.

'You mean you won't come with us? You refuse to help us?' Thorel snapped incredulously.

Pergola protested: 'No, it isn't that I'm refusing, but it's kind of complicated right now. You see ...'

And then Pergola stopped beating about the bush.

'What the hell!' he exclaimed. 'Let's get going – just a second! I'll be right there!'

Antoine Pergola ran back to his room, pulled on a shirt, jammed a beret over his forehead, and strode out into the night.[1]

Thorel and his commandos had not yet crossed the tracks on their way to the adjacent highway when the firing began back on the shore. A German machine gun, followed by a second and a third, went into action, their separate sounds blending into a discordant staccato as they fired into the blackness. The wild light of rocket flares bathed the wooded slopes near Mont Biscarre, the commandos' target for D-Day morning. One by one, the German positions took up the challenge and started shooting, and the night was strident with blasts of gunfire, hoarse shouts, and the screams and groans of the wounded.

The Germans – more specifically, one segment of Lieutenant Colonel Hasso Grundmann's 918th Grenadier Guards – had just realized that this was neither an isolated raid nor a random foray by the Resistance. The sky was suffused with the glow of artillery fire, and there was utter confusion everywhere. During these opening hours of the invasion, the Germans could not seem to find anything tangible in the way of attackers. The troops of the Fourth Battalion of Armenian volunteers assigned to defend the coastal batteries had been rudely awakened, and now they were dashing helter-skelter over the landscape, yelling out, imagining that they saw Allied troops everywhere at once – on the rocks, in the forest, at the highway junctions, under thickets and in the dense foliage of walled gardens. All they had really found were a few rubber boats abandoned on the shore and – more often – the bodies of their own troops. Out at sea, all was black and empty.

---

[1] Pergola had understandably feared a Gestapo trick, since they who stopped at nothing in their attempts to ferret out the French who were remaining loyal to France. In his initial refusal, he had used the first excuse that had occurred to him – his wife was not even pregnant, much less about to be delivered! Furthermore, Pergola was not a railway employee. The statiomaster at Le Canadel was Mme Silvan, with whom the Pergolas happened to be staying.

At the German command post in Bormes, near Le Lavandou, the messages were pouring in. An attempted attack against the heavily entrenched blockhouses along La Fossette point had apparently been repulsed, but the guns on Cap Nègre had been totally demolished. The commandos continued doggedly to carry out their mission, which was to keep the Germans baffled and panic-stricken until dawn. The commandos infiltrated in small groups, picking their way through the German defenses, skirting the mine fields, engaging in occasional skirmishes, and setting up ambushes all through the densely wooded slopes of the Monts des Maures.

Bouvet and his men had by now covered a considerable distance and were far inland. The sky was beginning to be tinged with the streaks of light heralding dawn. A familiar whining 'zing' accompanied the bursting mortar shells that were churning up great clouds of dirt and dust in the dry, sandy earth. Around the hamlet of La Môle, where Captain Bonnard's Third Commando had prudently set up an antitank defense, the crest of the ridge was beginning to take on a faintly yellow hue. The Second Commando was methodically mopping up every inch of ground in the tightly woven network of streets and gardens that constituted Rayol, barely one hundred feet from the spot where Major Rigaud had vainly watched for the first LCIs to land. A short distance away, Captain Farret's Fourth Commando was proceeding slowly and steadily toward Cavalière. Roger Font recalls moving in toward a village 'where there were two big palm trees at the entrance to the town' and then, with his submachine gun, 'mowing down two Germans at once with a single burst.' Font had just witnessed the death of a friend, Jacques Pancrazi, who had come face to face with a German pointing his pistol. The two men had fired simultaneously, and Pancrazi was killed outright. The German, his chest riddled with bullets, 'lay sprawled in the ditch, moaning – he finally died at dawn,' Font remembers.

Meanwhile, with their mission accomplished, Captain Ducournau and the survivors of the Cap Nègre attack were determinedly trying to find their way toward the assembly area where the main body of troops was to report. The captain and his group of thirty, including some wounded, were letting themselves be guided through the night by the noise of the German machine-gun fire coming from a position along the road to Cavalière. In the middle of the fighting area, at a turn in the road, Ducournau ran head-on into Lieutenant Fauchois's Fourth Commando platoon. Font, a member of the Fauchois group, has described the captain as they came upon him there, 'standing out in the middle of the road with the situation completely under control and his voice ringing out as strong and clear as ever.'

In the African Commandos' area, Bouvet, baton in hand, was leading his men as they climbed the trails on Mont Biscarre leading to the place where, in mid morning, ammunition, field rations and drinking water were to be parachuted down to tide the troops over and enable them to hold their positions while waiting to join up with the main landing forces.

Not until he reached the top of the hill did Bouvet notice that his life jacket was still dangling from his neck.

11

A FEW MINUTES AFTER 4 A.M. on the morning of 15 August, the German fast escort ship *SG-21* was in the Mediterranean, some thirteen miles south of Saint-Tropez, cruising through the darkness at her normal speed of twenty knots.

She had left Marseilles over five hours earlier. During the ensuing interval there had not been much to report, except that the *SG-21*, a former French sloop, had lost sight of her accompanying submarine chasers, the *UJ-6081* and the *UJ-6082*.

This fact was of no immediate concern to young Lieutenant Hans Joachim Metzenthin, commanding the *SG-21*. His own ship's speed was considerably faster than that of the other two. Metzenthin had kept clear of the waters near the Iles d'Hyères and was navigating parallel to the mainland, steering toward Cannes.

However, for quite a few minutes, Metzenthin had had a feeling that something was in the wind. He came back up on the bridge to keep the officer of the watch company.

It was not by chance that the *SG-21* was out patrolling in the offshore darkness. In Metzenthin's opinion, it was becoming daily more obvious that the Allies were getting ready to establish a second invasion front somewhere in France, and most likely in the Mediterranean area. All the top-secret reports that had come to his attention lately pointed emphatically to the fact that Allied troops and ships were assembling off Corsica, but that was the extent of his knowledge.

The previous evening, Metzenthin had not been at all surprised when he received an order, at about 9 P.M., from the Sixth Security Fleet to proceed to sea in the direction of Nice. The order further stipulated that, barring incident, he was to anchor at Nice by dawn. It was just another of the routine assignments to which the crew of the *SG-21* was accustomed.

French civilians rush to welcome the liberating troops. Here, tanks and infantrymen of the 45th Division find it difficult to make their way through the hilarious throng at Bourg, France. (*Photo U.S. Army*)

Amphibious tank and troops of the 3rd Division advance inland from the beach in the Saint-Tropez area. (*Photo U.S. Army*)

After landing in the Saint-Tropez area, troops of the 3rd Division cautiously move along a cleared mine strip on the beach toward their objective. (*Photo U.S. Army*)

Without waiting for a bridge to be built, American tank destroyers of the 45th Division cross the Durance River to Mirabeau in response to a call from partisans in that area. (*Photo U.S. Army*)

Metzenthin's orders for this particular night were not only strict, but they were also exceptionally stringent. But this was nothing new, either. For some time, the *Kriegsmarine* had been having to face the fact that it was no longer master of the sea in the Mediterranean or elsewhere, not even directly offshore from the coastal areas occupied by the *Wehrmacht*.

The *SG-21* was not equipped with a regular radar screen. Her only detecting instrument was a brand-new 'Matratze' radio system that made it possible to determine the direction and distance of another ship. Under no circumstances were messages by Morse code to be transmitted to other ships in the convoy. Metzenthin was authorized to send only a single alarm to the German installations on land. The *SG-21*'s captain was only too aware that if he ever had to send this one message, his chances of escaping destruction or capture were slim.

Metzenthin was standing on the deck of the *SG-21* with Lieutenant Günther Ahlers, who had just taken over the watch. The two men fell silent, scanning the horizon through their binoculars.

Through the dim darkness of the August night, a thin sliver of moon suddenly emerged from behind heavy clouds. Metzenthin later compared it to 'what you might see on a theater stage.' (This was one of those rare moments when the moon did become visible that night.) It was as if a curtain had parted, revealing a horizon bristling with motionless, ominous, shadowy silhouettes lined up over the calm sea.

For a split second Ahlers and Metzenthin were transfixed. The next instant, the ship's alarm system blurted out its frantic message:

'Alarm! Alarm!'

Riding at anchor less than three miles away, outlined against the background of the mainland, the shape of six or seven warships stood out sharply under the canopy of stars in the fickle, other-worldly light of a wayward moon. Metzenthin and Ahlers could make no mistake. The vanguard of the Allied invasion fleet was sitting directly in front of them. Seconds later the crew reached the deck, and every man was at his action station.

Metzenthin felt reasonably sure that the enemy destroyers had not yet detected his presence. He was right, but his assumption was short-lived. As he peered intently throught his binoculars at the line of Allied ships, the German lieutenant could see the sailors running to take up their gun positions. The *SG-21*'s crew was awaiting the order to fire, but Metzenthin had a more urgent task to perform. Now that his own ship had been detected, nothing prevented him from flashing a message to the headquarters on land. Furthermore, he had orders not to fight except as a last resort.

After noting the exact positions of the Allied ships, Metzenthin looked at his watch. It was 4.28 A.M. By using abbreviated alarm signals, the radio operator was able to transmit a maximum number of details with a minimum of letters and figures. The message was received directly by the headquarters in Aix-en-Provence of Vice Admiral Ernst Scheurlen, whose staff instantly alerted the Nineteenth Army at Avignon.

By then two Allied shells had struck the German ship. The first exploded against her engines, stopping her dead. The second wounded the radio operator and his assistant, who were still frantically transmitting the alert. Metzenthin first verified that the entire message had been sent, and then ordered that the dynamite on board be transferred to the fuel tanks. The ship was beginning to be flooded, but the firing from the Allied guns had stopped. The moon had just retreated behind the clouds.

Metzenthin and another officer hastily donned life belts and abandoned ship. The crew, together with Ahlers and the ship's engineer, Henry Meyer, had already jumped overboard and were bobbing around in the Mediterranean. A few minutes later, with all hands safely clear, the *SG-21* burst into flames, blew up, and sank.

The *SG-21* was not the only German ship abruptly confronted by vessels of the Allied fleet lined up off the landing beaches.

Since 2.50 A.M., Commander William C. Hughes, commanding the American destroyer *Somers*, had sensed that trouble was imminent and was tensing himself for action. For several minutes his radar screen had been insistently registering the unaccounted-for presence of two unidentified ships off the Ile du Levant. Neither had responded to the *Somers*'s signals, and Hughes was beginning to feel uneasy. It was necessary at all costs to avoid revealing the presence of the great armada spread out behind him, and he realized that he and his crew were fully vulnerable should the unknown ships – which he thought were probably submarine chasers – decide to let loose their torpedoes. When nearly an hour had gone by, Hughes could stand the suspense no longer.

Sergeant Raymond T. Kaiser of the Marines, on watch duty aboard the cruiser *Augusta*, nearly crashed his helmet against the bulwark as he leaped into the air from where he was standing at his observation post. He had just seen a gigantic tongue of flame lash forth over the polished black surface of the Mediterranean, describing it as 'like the sudden incandescence of a tremendous torch against a wall of basalt.' It was 3.45 A.M. (Allied time, an hour different from German time), and Hughes had decided to attack. He scored a neat bull's-eye. As the first shells from the *Somers* struck one of the two phantom ships broadside, she was literally lifted up out of the water before exploding. The other was hit by over forty shots from the *Somers*'s 5-inch guns, and its fate was scarcely more gentle, although its engines did continue to turn over for a short while.

The blasts shook the air as explosion after explosion tore the sinking German ships, casting a treacherous glow over the fleet assembly area from which the troops of the 3rd Infantry Division would soon be taking off. At dawn, Hughes was able to identify the *Somers*'s two victims. They were the auxiliary ship *Escaburt* and the *UJ-6081*, one of the three surface vessels attached to the Sixth Security Fleet that had set out from Marseilles a few hours before.

12

ABOUT TWELVE MILES AWAY on the mainland, in a pine forest south of Saint-Tropez, Captain Jess W.Walls of the 509th Parachute Battalion was fit to be tied. As far as he was concerned, the landing had got off to an extremely bad start. In spite of all the lighted signals out at sea, and in spite of the combined directional radar and radio guiding systems, he and his company of 115 men had parachuted into an unknown area a consider- able distance from their objective. Walls and his paratroopers had been scheduled to land with the rest of the 509th at a point twelve miles inland. Instead, from where they now stood, surrounded by wooded heights, they could see the Mediterranean close by and feel the soft sea breeze wafting up from the shore.

When Walls had jumped, he immediately noticed a sort of ethereal fog stretching out beneath him. But by the time he hit the ground, the mist had vanished. A few minutes later, it became evident that paratroopers from other companies of the 509th had landed in the same area and were coming in to join with his own men. One of the first persons Walls en- countered was Private Winifred D. Eason, from a different company, and he began to feel less anxious. He thought it likely that his friend, Captain Ralph R. Miller, in command of Eason's company, had also landed nearby, and was confident that, between the two of them, they would figure a way out of this hornets' nest. But Miller was nowhere to be seen.

Walls did not know how lucky he had been. Miller and all the others in his plane had been dropped over the Mediterranean, and nothing more was ever heard of them. Twenty-nine of the Dakota transports had released their troops near the Saint-Tropez peninsula, nearly twenty miles to the south. A miscalculation of 90° in the wind forecasts, and the factor of zero visibility from the time the planes reached the coast, were responsible for this tragic error. Two complete batteries and portions of two others of the 463rd Parachute Artillery Battalion were also victims of this same mistake.

Walls resolutely assumed command of the two companies and set out with them, still with no idea of where he was, how close the Germans might be, and – most important of all – how long it would take them to start showing some sign of life. By now it was almost 5 A.M. At that moment, Private First Class David H. Murphy, who had become separated from his own company of the 509th, heard a strange but far from unwelcome sound emanating from somewhere nearby. Somebody over there under the trees was whistling softly, and Murphy recognized the tune; it was the *Marseillaise*. The whistling came closer, and soon the grayish light of dawn brought into view a Frenchman wearing a reassuring tricolor armband. He was a member of the *Maures Brigade* Resistance group, one of the section chiefs who had been alerted by René Girard immediately after the BBC broadcast the previous evening.

In the lightening obscurity, a brief dialogue ensued:

'Le Muy?' Murphy asked.

'Oh! *Non, non*!' the Frenchman exclaimed.

Whereupon he added:

'Saint-Tropez!'

Murphy sighed dejectedly. This meant that Walls and his men – nearly half the troops of the 509th who were off course – would not make it in time to the combat area and to the objectives for which all that intensive training had just ended. Even if they had the time and means of transportation, getting there would mean crossing through the thickly wooded Monts des Maures, which were infested with Germans. Worse still, as Walls knew only too well, within an hour Allied planes would begin bombing and strafing the beaches. If the 250 men whom he had rounded up managed by some miracle to escape that assault, the gunfire from the ships lying offshore would surely not spare them. They were caught in the dead center of imminent aerial and naval bombardments, right next to the formidable coastal batteries that had to be wiped out before H-Hour and the landings.

While Walls was considering this grave predicament, Girard, too, was confronted by serious problems. Like everybody else, he had heard the planes but had been amazed to see the paratroopers touching down on the heights of Belle-Isnarde and Saint-Anne's Hill, barely a mile from Saint-Tropez. No one had informed Girard of a potential airborne attack in his area. He concluded that the Americans were probably aiming at setting up a beachhead before the mass landings got under way. Consequently, he had dispatched a few of his men to go out and meet the Allied paratroopers.

In Saint-Tropez, a German officer, First Lieutenant M.A.Heinsohn, had just received an order that he had given up expecting.

The execution of the order would mean blowing up all of Saint-Tropez's port facilities, and involved setting off sixty devastating mines – each containing twenty-five pounds of explosives – which had been laid along the mole and docks of Le Portalet. Six additional mines – even more powerful, amounting to one ton of explosives – would also be detonated along the eight hundred foot jetty. In the middle of the night, the mayor of Saint-Tropez had been instructed to evacuate all the inhabitants, many of whom had not waited to be told. Most of the town's population had already fled to the hills, lugging mattresses, blankets and food supplies for several days.

The entrances to Saint-Tropez were heavily defended by machine-gun positions and sentries, as if it were a fortified camp, which is about what the historic and charming little town had become by the early morning hours of Tuesday, 15 August 1944. Deserted were the sixteenth-century ramparts and citadel, the church with its steeple open to the sky, the Place des Lices planted with centuries-old plane trees, the narrow little streets with their venerable arcades. And the tightly shuttered and barred houses and shopfronts made the town look as if it were braced to be ravaged once again, as it had been all too frequently during its eventful history.[1]

René Girard recorded the explosion as occurring at about 5.45 A.M. In the dim, misty dawn, the sky over the entire city lit up like a flaming brazier. Gigantic clouds of smoke and dust obscured everything from sight, and the shock waves rocked the ground for several minutes. The people who had taken refuge in the nearby hills and woods watched helplessly as their shops and offices, their homes and monuments were sacrificed to the fury of the Germans.[2]

---

[1] Saint-Tropez is named after Torpes, a Christian centurion who suffered the double indignity of being decapitated by Nero and of having his name deformed. In the eighteenth century, Saint-Tropez also served as the home base for a renowned French naval hero, Pierro André de Suffren, more familiarly known as the Bailli de Suffren because of his high rank in the Order of the Knights of Malta.

[2] Not satisfied with blowing up the port facilities at Saint-Tropez, the Germans also demolished the town's main sewage disposal system, some 250 feet offshore and below sea-level; they possessed detailed blueprints of this installation. Its destruction meant an additional health hazard, a further complication in the already precarious situation of the town's inhabitants, who had suffered their full share of trials and privations resulting from the war and the occupation. The explosions also affected a considerable number of stores, commercial buildings and homes. According to the records on file at the Saint-Tropez City Hall, of the town's 1,024 buildings, 670 were damaged to the extent of 33⅓ per cent, 210 to the extent of 66 per cent and twelve were completely destroyed. Only 132 building escaped without some damage.

Girard and his men could only stand by while the earth shuddered and the leaping flames reached skyward, leaving a reddish afterglow. His morale had hit a new low after the brief hours of elation and excitement immediately following the previous evening's news broadcast. The Germans had foiled the plans of the Resistance by ordering the evacuation of the population. However, as Girard had just learned, the destruction of the port of Saint-Tropez also meant that, except for a greatly reduced garrison that would remain there, the *Wehrmacht* troops were withdrawing from the town. Girard tried to concentrate his thoughts on the prospect of the liberation of his city.

Many paratroopers had landed in the countryside around Saint-Tropez, in the gardens, on the farms – and sometimes right in the middle of the aviaries! Some touched down in the hills where the townspeople had fled. Madame Jugy, who operated a bakery in the center of Saint-Tropez, had thoughtfully brought a supply of loaves to Saint-Anne's Hill, and was busily distributing them. She recalls the frustration and disappointment on the faces of a few American paratroopers who were 'just sitting there under the trees, their rifles propped between their legs, not speaking, as if they had all been struck dumb.'

In the confusion and indecision of the moment, time was slipping by. Girard and his staunch band were eager for action. The unheralded descent of some three hundred Allied troops had by no means dampened their enthusiasm – far from it! The Resistance leader was hoping that the Americans would join forces with his underequipped group in an all-out effort to rid the town of the last remaining Germans. But Girard's initial proposal met with a blunt refusal from Captain Walls of the wandering 509th.

After laboriously assembling the scattered troops of the two isolated companies, Walls had made contact with a few men from the batteries of the 463rd Battalion, who had also landed in the same general area. However, he was acutely aware of his plight. There he was, in unknown territory, with no instructions to fall back on and without any communications, forced to rely on the resources at hand, and responsible for more men than he had ever commanded before. He was understandably reluctant to launch an attack outside his assigned area.

As Girard later described it, Walls 'yielded to persuasion only after a lengthy and involved discussion,' when the Frenchmen had shown the American the woefully inadequate equipment of the Resistance fighters, whose total armament consisted of a handful of decrepit French muskets and nine rifles taken from Italian prisoners.

Just when the American captain had agreed on a combined operation, all eyes were riveted to the sky as a thundering boom began sounding overhead.

Against the rays of the rising sun, wave after wave of Allied four-motor planes poured in. They were storming past in greater numbers and in more compact formations than the people of Saint-Tropez had ever seen, and their bombardiers and gunners were unleashing a furious attack along the entire length of the peninsula. Each minute the rumble and roar of the huge swarm grew louder, as the planes swept the skies from west to east, like some gigantic, endlessly breaking wave. H-Hour of the Second D-Day was here at last.

Part Three

THE DAY OF
15 AUGUST

1

THROUGH THE HAZY MORNING LIGHT, the shape of the coast was beginning to be discernible. In the foreground, a dark, tortuous fringe of earth ran along the water's foamy edge. Behind it, a deepening land fog reached out as if to swallow the blast-ridden shore. Thousands of erupting volcanoes seemed to be spewing up their furious fire. From the whole surface of the Mediterranean, incandescent columns shot skyward all along the coast of southern France from east to west, and the air and the ground were rent with concussions. At 5.50 A.M. the high-altitude bombers had swung into the deadly rhythm of their pounding, hammering at the thirty miles of sand, gravel, and rocks between Cavalaire-sur-Mer and Anthéor. The American, British, and French planes – 959 in all – were to attack the beaches of Provence for two hours before the landings and general assault began, but the persistent ground fog finally prevented about one-third of them from accomplishing their mission.

Every five minutes, a fresh wave of heavy and medium fighters and bombers flew over to bomb, rake and strafe. Aboard an LST of the American 3rd Division, the French liaison officer Jean-Pierre Aumont likened the shoreline to 'a read hemline,' as he gazed up at the myriad formations droning by 'like glistening drops of radium caught in the rays of the rising sun.' With the thousands of other participants in the Second D-Day, he had watched the implacable mechanism gather momentum and shift into high gear through the misty summer sky, had seen it soar high above the Allied fleet waiting out at sea, and stared as the tide of planes blended into a throbbing swarm of death-bearing insects. On the shore, in that maelstrom of flame, smoke, dust and fog, not one German flak battery had responded. The earth had been stricken dumb, stunned by the onslaught of shrieking shells and blazing braziers set afire by the deluge of bombs.

While flame was geysering up from the beaches, while the hills beyond began to sear and burn, while the shore writhed in an upheaval of metal and fire, a few lines of small Allied vessels had started their engines and were steering toward the mainland, oblivious of the zooming and swooping of the planes. These little ships were the mine sweepers, whose job was to clear the sea lanes leading to the three landing sectors for the hundreds of craft that would be bringing the troops ashore. Commander W. L. Messmer had his mine sweepers operating off the beaches of Cavalaire-sur-Mer and Pampelonne; Commander E. A. Ruth was doing the same off Sainte-Maxime; and Lieutenant Commander J. L. Maloney was assigned to the waters off Saint-Raphaël. Under the protective screen of destroyer escorts assembled farther out at sea, they had been the first vessels to get under way, at precisely 5.15 A.M., immediately after daybreak, and now they were parting the waves, proceeding toward the landing zones – Alpha, Delta and Camel. Some of the more mobile units had plunged boldly ahead and were within three hundred feet of the beaches.

The Allied armada, which had at last reached its destination after five days of sailing, was fanned out twelve miles offshore. The horizon was densely packed with hulls and superstructures, protected by an aerial forest of antiaircraft balloons. Directly behind the mine sweepers came the columns of small destroyers, ready and primed for battle. Next was the great pack of battleships and cruisers, and bringing up the rear were the convoys of troop transports. The convoys, which had to remain out of range of the German shore batteries, were already parceling out their clusters of armed men into the LCIs of the first assault waves.

Over the Mediterranean, gleaming dully like an expanse of lead, the banks of early morning mist still hovered tenaciously, occasionally dissolving here and there into reluctant patches as the sun rose. On the radar screens, the stretch of shoreline that at daybreak had shown up as only a series of whitish streaks had now become as clear and distinct as on a photograph. On the far left lay the distant masses of the Ile du Levant and Port-Cros, and the center was occupied by the Saint-Tropez peninsula, shaped like a great sprawling tortoise. To the right, still farther off, the sharp outline of the Esterel heights dwindled away, after one last sheer, plunging indentation, followed by the hills of Le Dramont and the cliffs of Le Trayas. This entire area made up the zone that the 90,000 troops of D-Day were preparing to assault.

The yellowish glow of the Mediterranean morning gradually deepened into a ripening brightness, despite the fog that was to linger for several hours, forming a screen between sea and land. The shore was a welter of flame, smoke and explosions. The A-20 attack planes of the American 47th Bombardment Group, the fighter planes of the 350th Fighter

Group, the Mitchells of the 57th Bombardment Wing, the British Spitfires, the P-38 Lightnings and the Thunderbolts of the 12th Air Force
had been joined by planes of the 15th Air Force, which had temporarily
deserted their oil-field targets at Ploesti, in Rumania. Together, they
were relentlessly ripping away at the shoreline fortifications, the pillboxes and dugouts on the beaches, the coastal batteries and the mine
fields. They were also dipping down into the back country to harass the
Germans along the roads and hills where they had entrenched themselves. According to Lieutenant General Jacob L. Devers, General
Wilson's deputy in the Mediterranean theater, the over-all score was one
of 'incredible and staggering accuracy' for all the targets concerned. The
total number of sorties from dawn to dusk on D-Day – including fighter
planes strafing the beaches, and heavy and medium bombers blasting
the fortifications and gun batteries – amounted to over 4,200; of these
3,939 were part of direct aerial support to troop landings in the morning
and afternoon of D-Day. With the exception of 216 planes belonging to
Rear Admiral T.H.Troubridge's nine British and American carriers at
anchor off the landing zones, all these planes took off from bases on
Corsica, to which they returned to take on fresh loads of bombs and
ammunition in order to renew the attack.

The day was already warm with the promise of Mediterranean heat.
The great blockbusters sent suffocating clouds of dust swirling up into
the clogged air. On the previous evening, most of the population along
the coast had scurried off to the hills and taken shelter in dried-up
streambeds, in ditches, small hollows and shallow holes, knowing that
they would at least escape death from collapsing walls, and, by remaining out in the open, hoping to emerge alive from the deadly air raids. The
hour they had long awaited, had long been apprehensive for, had at last
arrived, and all the way from Toulon to Agay every square yard of earth
was being plowed up by the bombs dropped by General Ira Eaker's
planes.

The minute the bombings began, Mme de Visme ran as fast as she
could out of her house, a few hundred yards from the beach at Cavalaire-
sur-Mer. In two world wars the old lady had lost a husband and a son.
Now, hastily flinging an old black coat over her nightgown and plumping
her son Serge's steel helmet down on to her forehead, she made a dash for
the narrow, shallow trench at the rear of her garden. She lay there for
several hours, stoically enduring the assault by the thousands of low-
flying planes roaring through the sky. It seemed to her that 'a deluge of
metal was pouring in from everywhere at once – from the sea, the air and
the earth.' At last, during a brief pause in the tumult, she cautiously
raised her head, and the scene that greeted her brought tears to her eyes.

The vast Allied fleet lay stretched out before her wondering gaze, surging up on the horizon and filling the entire bay of Cavalaire-sur-Mer.

Not far away, Paul Bureau, a prominent businessman, was stunned by the number and the concentration of ships. Shortly before the arrival of the first planes, he had been fascinated by the sight of some small vessels in groups of three, turning around and around in the bay. He realized that these must be the mine-sweepers, and stared almost hypnotized as they went about their business, describing huge semi-circles in the offshore waters. At the same time, Bureau felt both deeply apprehensive over what was about to happen and buoyed by an intense exultation. The sticks of bombs that soon began spiraling down snatched him out of his reverie. Hundred of planes were hurtling down on Cavalaire-sur-Mer, dive bombing their targets, raking the port and strafing the pine-covered hills of Les Pradels before turning around and starting back to sea. Their places were immediately taken by the next relay of squadrons flying in tightly packed formation. Every twenty or thirty seconds the cycle of noise was renewed, like a train drumming along on its tracks, gradually working up to a climax with the din of more bombs ripping giant furrows through the town and its outskirts. Bureau was more curious than cautious. He remembers being unable to tear his gaze from an Allied plane whose pilot, during the entire bombardment, concentrated on furiously attacking a small back-country road at Le-Cros-de-Mouton, a short white ribbon of highway winding through vineyards.

Robert Wuillequey and his family, who lived on a farm at Le-Cros-de-Mouton, a mile from the beach at Cavalaire-sur-Mer, were directly in the line of the aerial attack. When the first planes appeared, he and eleven other persons were busy carrying an eighty year old woman out to the farmyard and settling her in a trench lined with mattresses, tree branches and wooden planks. Wuillequey had caught a glimpse of the sea covered with warships and had seen the swarms of planes zooming over like demons in the direction of the coast. To the people huddled in the trench, which was also being shared by six Italian soldiers who had breathlessly run up at the last minute (they were 'prisoners' of the Germans), the bombardment was absolutely terrifying, and all were certain that their time had come. Everyone was saying his prayers, and the only person who insisted that she felt all right was the aged grandmother, lying with her hands placidly folded.

Feniglia, a shoemaker in Saint-Maxime had spent the night out of doors, under a spreading oak in the Bouillerettes woods, a few miles from town. His friend Fenouil and their two families had found refuge nearby in a broken-down shanty. Fenouil recalls that, as the sun began to rise, the sky 'had become heavily overcast,' and the fog soon became 'thick and seeping.' Suddenly a thunderous roar ripped apart the silence of the dawn glimmering through the trees. Fenouil could remember only one other sound like it, and he had heard that on the night of 14 July 1918, when the French army had opened fire on the German trenches along the Marne, as it began to repulse the Crown Prince's offensive. The frightening effect of shells crashing down in clusters and the agony of the earth's splitting open and settling back under the impact, had been the same. From where they stood, neither Fenouil nor Feniglia had a view of the landings or of the ships, but both realized, as Fenouil said, that 'the main feature was about to go on.'

Twenty miles to the east, near Le Trayas, the postmaster Canale – who had been so preoccupied with the demolition of the Anthéor viaduct – was with some friends who had taken refuge in the garden of a villa overlooking the sea. There were twelve persons gathered in this makeshift shelter, resolved to stick it out together no matter what happened. For these men and women awaiting their liberation, the night had passed in an atmosphere of mingled fear, hope, joy and fatalism. Despite the many strange and unusual noises coming from out the sea, and the flares rocketing up in the night sky (probably fired by the Allies), not one of them knew that one of the tragedies of this Second D-Day had taken place a few yards away – the ill-fated odyssey of the sixty-seven men in the French Naval Assault Group.

At 6.06 A.M., off Cavalaire-sur-Mer, Paul Bureau witnessed a blinding flash of flame, a ball of fire tearing through the screen of fog between the shore and the sea, and heard the salvos from a warship anchored far out chiming in with the uproar of the aerial bombardment. The guns of the British cruiser *Ajax*, in Rear Admiral J. M. Mansfield's support group, were the first to open fire on the coast, in the Alpha sector. But this was an isolated incident, and the majority of the Allied naval guns remained silent for another hour to give the planes time to finish pounding the three landing zones, at the saturation rate of one ton of bombs for every twenty yards.

The massive aerial assault did not end until 7.30 A.M. It had lasted more than an hour and a half. During the entire time, not one Stuka, Dornier, or Messerschmitt got off the ground, not a solitary swastika-bearing plane appeared over the landing beaches. The preliminary aerial bombardment begun ten days before was drawing to a close. And suddenly there were no planes over the beaches, no bombs crashing and exploding. The harsh barking of the machine guns of the Spitfires, the Lightnings and the Thunderbolts had stopped as abruptly as it had begun. Over the Provence beaches the sky seemed somehow empty, and the earth below was a mangled mass of torn-up, unrecognizable fragments, all pierced like a sieve. Now it was being given a brief respite.

One minute passed. The thick whorls of stifling dust subsided a bit, and the earth tried to catch its breath. In the next instant the air seemed to sob, the soil of Provence heaved convulsively and exploded as a fresh and even more terrible torrent of iron and steel spouted out over the coast. This time the attack sprang out of the sea, a fearsome tornado rolling from one end of the horizon to the other, with the four hundred guns of the invasion fleet unleashing their full fury on the beaches, the coastal highways, and the hills beyond.

Daybreak had brought the faint hint of a breeze. However, the fog continued, and, although not a serious hindrance to the complicated maneuvers of the fleets of LCIs, it concealed most of the shoreline, limiting visibility almost everywhere to three or four miles. General Patch was aboard the flagship *Catoctin*, which had switched off its engines ten miles south of Saint-Tropez. He had just received the first messages concerning the landings on Cap Nègre and the Iles d' Hyères, and news from General Frederick and the paratroopers who had landed in the Draguignan area. From the decks of the *Catoctin*, teeming with admirals and generals, the fresh blaze of fire kindled on the distant shore, and the tremendous volleys of artillery piercing the misty horizon, looked like little more than 'small patches of shuddering, quivering fog,' according to Signalman Jean Meirat.

The shells streaking around the *Catoctin* whistled and whined on their way out to send fiery geysers and opaque smoke clouds spewing up over the gutted beaches, torn and beaten as if by some monstrous flail. Along a thirty-five mile stretch, the ships' guns were spitting out their projectiles, chewing at the shore, and the troops waiting in the barges saw the sea as a churning, burning cauldron while the salvos continued to pour forth at a dizzy rate. As the minutes wore on, the pack of growling, snarling ships turned the horizon into an incandescent line, a fantastic rim of reddening foam sparked with hundreds of great gullets of fire, like dragons' nostrils snorting through the cowering mist.

On the cruiser *Emile Bertin*, off the Saint-Raphaël beach, a French gunner named Villechenoux, who was about to spend the day cooped up, had come on deck. Bracing himself against the recoil of the guns, he was taking a final look around and one last breath of air The mechanics and the stokers stayed in the engine rooms until sundown, the gunners and the electricians remained at their posts in the narrow steel cubbyholes, in the turrets and the holds. On the light cruiser *Le Terrible*, as the radio operator, Joseph Cochard, recalled later, 'very few of the men had been to bed since they left Bizerte.' Since the sounding of the dawn alert, the French sailors in their helmets and blue denim fatigues had been at their posts, but when the first rays of the sun pierced the fog, the helmets disappeared as if by prearranged signal and there was a spontaneous blossoming out of white caps with red pompoms on several thousand Gallic heads.

The waiting on board the fighting ships and the command vessels became more tense as the naval bombardment drew to a close. The time was 7.45 A.M., with only a quarter of an hour remaining before H-Hour. The guns of the Mediterranean Wall had stayed stubbornly silent. When were the enemy batteries going to open up and reveal their positions? What would finally make the Germans react? And where would their answering fire come from? Was the silence along the shore only a ruse, or had the fortifications, the blockhouses, the pillboxes, the bastions along the coast really been blasted out by the massive pounding from air and sea, by the incessant hail of shells that had been streaming down for the last two hours? Admiral André Lemonnier wished that he were a quarter of an hour older as he stood on the deck of the *Catoctin*, impatient to know the answers to these questions.

Until 7.47 A.M., the shore remained eerily silent, and the enemy's failure to respond had everyone in the Allied fleet on edge. But suddenly, from over the beach at Cavalaire-sur-Mer, on the left flank of the invasion zone, the first German shells came rumbling forth, aimed at the *Ajax* and at the French cruiser *Gloire*. By now, Paul Bureau had retreated to the relative security of a makeshift shelter built from worm-eaten planks. His tension mounted as he heard the German artillery belching furiously. The Allied naval guns were still firing into the bay, but now the batteries at La Môle, two miles inland, had also gone into action.

Rear Admiral Robert Jaujard was in the center of the invasion sector, alert for the first sign of answering fire. The two cruisers in his division, the *Montcalm* and the *Georges Leygues*, had orders to continue firing for only three more minutes. The admiral was vainly scrutinizing the shore through the veil of morning mist for the slightest indication of a response from the gutted beaches. Any minute, two of the main coastal batteries in his zone might start firing in his direction. He knew that they mounted at least twelve 6-inch guns, and he was less than six miles out at sea. From the intelligence reports that he had seen, Jaujard was aware that the precision firing of the powerful German guns off Pointe-de-Rabiou alone, at the far end of the Gulf of Saint-Tropez, could spell destruction for his ships. His concern increased as the minutes wore on – they seemed more like hours. No landing was planned at Saint-Tropez, and the troops that would be marching on it could not be expected to reach the batteries until that afternoon. If he could only have known it, the truth was that the guns on Pointe-de-Rabiou had been knocked out several days before by planes of the Strategic Air Command.

This was only one of Jaujard's worries. He had not had much sleep the previous night, partly because he was haunted by a gnawing obsession. For the second time since the Normandy landings seventy days before, he found himself compelled to issue orders to fire on his own country. Today, what he feared most was that the hail of Allied shells would touch off disastrous fires in the pine woods of the Provençal hills, where the tiniest spark falling into a thicket could touch off a blaze that the wind could fan to gigantic proportions. As it turned out, a providential rainfall a few days before had given the woods a good soaking. This, combined with the absence of wind over the mainland on 15 August, accounted for the remarkably few brush fires that were kindled during the fighting. However, all during the day, Jaujard suffered from what he later described as 'actual physical torment' over the possibility that the forest at Les Maures might go up in flames.

The steadily firing guns gradually shifted their range higher above the invasion beaches, and the naval bombardment reached its peak opposite the three attack sectors. Within a minute the ships would cease firing, and then perhaps the Germans would begin answering back. For a while, the persistent fog had prevented the naval gunners from sighting their targets clearly, forcing them to fire somewhat at random and to plot their firing on charts. Among other things, they used white tracer shells, which proved devastatingly effective. The veteran British battleship *Ramillies* lobbed its armor-piercing 15-inch shells into the most heavily fortified installations in the Pampelonne and Cavalaire-sur-Mer sectors. The *Nevada* and the *Texas*, two of Admiral Bryant's supporting ships, let loose terrific volleys of 14-inch shells against the beach of Sainte-Maxime, while the twelve great 12-inch guns on the battleship *Arkansas* and the heavy cruiser *Tuscaloosa* concentrated their fire on the Esterel coast, where the German positions were thought to be almost invulnerable.

During the last ten minutes of the firing, the destroyers in the three combat groups threw everything they had against the blockhouses and dugouts on the beach in which the German gunners from the besieged batteries would presumably have sought refuge. The ammunition used by the Allied ships during nineteen minutes of continuous firing reached the awesome total of 16,000 avenging shells, including 2,939 fired from large-bore guns of 12-inches and move.

It was now 7.50 A.M.

2

SUDDENLY EVERYTHING HALTED. A tomblike silence added its enveloping cloak to that of the fog that covered the twenty miles of assault front between Pointe-de-Cavalaire and the Argens river delta west of Saint-Raphël. The Germans waited in their concrete bunkers. The civilians huddled in their cellars and shelters along the coast. It was a few minutes before H-Hour for the Allied forces out at sea.

In the warm morning air, the silence seemed to last for ever. It was as if the entire living universe – plants, animals, humans – was listening to its own terrified heartbeat, taking its pulse, and trying to estimate the danger that threatened it. Only a few diehard birds raised their voices in tentative warblings over the petrified countryside, in the woods and vineyards near the coast. The hardware dealer Fenouil, waiting with his wife and daughter in the hills behind Sainte-Maxime, could hardly believe his ears. The little girl, frightened by the commotion, had been crying. Then, as Fenouil tells it, 'things quietened down as if by magic and the sky gradually cleared again; the smoke subsided, and we all thought that the fog covering the coast was an artificial screen.' To another local resident near Saint-Tropez named Temple, the 'unreal-appearing fog had the insipid taste of a pharmaceutical preparation.' Dr Jean Verdier in Saint-Maxime found that the fog 'made my eyes smart painfully.'

The silence extended out over the sea between the ships and the beaches and was broken only by the droning of the engines of the landing craft heading toward the shore. Emile Bresc, the French master sergeant with the 45th Division, recalls that 'the respite granted by the sky, the sea and the land' lasted but a fleeting moment – exactly five minutes, from 7.50 A.M. to 7.55 A.M., in accordance with the strict timing of Operation Dragoon.

Amid the general lull, the first invasion vessels that were speeding toward the smoke-shrouded shore carried not a single occupant.

In tight little groups, the buzzing swarm of Apex drone boats, remote-controlled from special landing craft, dashed for the beaches. The job of the explosives-laden drone boats was to complete the mine sweepers' task by blasting the last underwater obstacles and clearing the sea channels right up to the water line on the beaches, before the infantry began moving in.

A mile offshore, just behind the LCIs, teams of men clad in asbestos suits were awaiting the signal to swing into action. They had been trained for a final, brief but devastating mission, to be carried out on the flat-bottomed rocket ships. Each of these ships was armed with seven hundred rocket-firing tubes, which, when activated by a single switch, could sweep the beaches with still another round of murderous fire that would pass over the heads of the troops about to land. The rocket ships carried special crews whose sole duty consisted in keeping the decks hosed down during the firing, because of the intense heat generated by the rockets. A few minutes later, 30,000 tubes began sending forth their barrage of deadly metal.

The assault battalions crowded into the LCIs could hear the 'whoo-fuses,' as they were called, streak by overhead with a rushing roar far more terrifying than all the combined naval guns had been able to produce. According to Lieutenant Jackson, whose platoon would soon be landing on the Cavalaire-sur-Mer beach, the effect was as if 'the entire expanse of coast were being lashed by a mammoth whip.'

On board the *Catoctin*, a voice came over the loudspeaker, disrupting the watchful, waiting silence, to announce in English and in French:

'First wave, one hundred yards from the beaches.'

At Cavalaire-sur-Mer, at Pampelonne, at La Nartelle, at Pointe-des-Issambres and at Val d'Esquières, H-Hour was finally at hand.

Hundreds of LCIs ferrying troops, arms and ammunition, LCTs loaded with amphibious tanks and the first contingent of combat vehicles, shot off through the gray-white mist, which gradually lifted in the path of the landing craft to disclose the contours of the shoreline.

The men of the 45th Division in the middle, the 3rd on the left, and 36th on the right were hurling themselves onto the beaches of Provence. Their watches pointed to just before 8 A.M.

3

SQUEEZED INTO THEIR LCI, Captain Wright Hitt and thirty-five infantrymen of his 7th Regiment company were tensed for action. They fully expected at any minute to see and hear the guns of the Mediterranean Wall open fire on the fleets of landing craft, which were speeding in ever-increasing numbers closer to the beaches. So far there had been no reaction from the shore; the coast was maintaining its secret silence. As Lieutenant Jackson, one of Hitt's platoon leaders, observed later, this very silence and lack of response 'contributed more to the feeling of nervous expectancy than the certainty of danger.'

Hitt raised his head slightly to peer out over the side of the LCI. Around him lay spread out the bay of Cavalaire-sur Mer with its pine-covered slopes. Through the clouds of smoke, all he could see were the dark crests of Les Pradels, some 1,500 feet high, overlooking the beach. The 'whoofus' rockets continued to flail out, protecting the steadily advancing landing craft, methodically showering their fire on the three miles of coast and detonating the mines buried in the sand.

A few hundred yards away disaster was about to strike. Of the eighteen drone boats launched against the Cavalaire-sur-Mer beach to rid the waters of the last mines and obstacles, fifteen had performed properly, and two had failed to function. Now the panic-stricken occupants of an LCI saw one of the remote-controlled robot boats wheel abruptly from the shore and do a complete U-turn before it began charging straight at them. The lead LCIs maneuvered just in time to avoid the errant drone, but Commander Messmer's mine sweeper lay right in its path. The drone boat exploded amid the terrified men, close to one of the mine sweepers, which miraculously received only some damage to its engines and a few slight casualties.

Two miles offshore, on schedule, the LSTs of Commander O.F. Gregor's assault group had launched four of the 756th Battalion's amphibious tanks into the water. Their job was to support the first infantrymen landing in the Alpha Red sector – the left half of the 3rd Division's zone – in the center of the gently sloping beaches of the bay of Cavalaire-sur-Mer. As the bulky, slow-moving LSTs – weighing 350 tons each – dropped their landing ramps, they pushed away great walls of water, and the DD tanks,[1] buoyed by their watertight air-filled 'bubbles,' were now on their own as they plowed toward the beach. The eight-minute 'whoofus' barrage was about to end. Suddenly one of the leading tanks began to weave crazily, then righted itself, but a round of rocket fire fell short, killing the tank captain and wounding two of the crew. The driver managed to continue steering straight ahead, but within only a few yards of the beach the tank struck a floating mine and sank. The three other tanks got through without mishap, threading their way through the network of obstacles still submerged in the clear and relatively shallow water.

At 8 A.M. sharp, Colonel Wiley H. O'Mahundro's 154 élite troops – the

[1] Dual drive amphibious tanks.

sharpshooters and machine gunners of the first assault wave – hit the beach at Cavalaire-sur-Mer, leading a rifle company of the 7th Regiment. These men storming Alpha Red were all veterans of the battles of Sicily and of Anzio, and they leaped expertly, almost nonchalantly, out of the barges into the shoulder-high water, scarcely aware of their cumbersome equipment, with their life jackets floating out around them as they splashed ashore on to the hard-packed golden sand. In between the rising spirals of smoke, their eyes fell on a twisted gutted lunar landscape. Under the pale blue sky of the August morning, a few stray palm trees stood out amid the curtain of umbrella pines that reached to the water's edge, but the trunks had suffered heavily under the intense bombardments. Here, as everywhere else in the coastal forests, the Germans had made deep breaches, slashing great clearings to give their gunners fields of fire. Now those gunners steadfastly maintained their peculiar silence, showing no sign of life. The yellow walls and caved-in roof of what had once been a small restaurant were still visible near the beach.

The drenched and dripping men, bending under the weight of their packs, were now actually on the beach. No enemy fire greeted them, no machine-gun bullets or mortar shells disturbed the smoke-filled air. Not one of the pillboxes and blockhouses that theoretically should have already begun repelling the waves of invaders acknowledged the presence of O'Mahundro's advancing soldiers. The trenches that wound along for miles on the beaches, in the shade of the tamarisk bushes and the pine trees, were singularly empty. Presumably, anyone who had been in them had been mowed down by the preliminary artillery barrages or was in a state of shellshock; or perhaps had fled inland. The Americans who had landed at H-Hour entered a smoking, torn-up no man's land, a wilderness strewn with shattered tree trunks and stripped branches. A brooding silence hung over everything.

When the 154 men of the first wave, soaked to their shoulders, set foot on the sand, they immediately found themselves surrounded by a welter of destruction, and, more serious still, by concentrated networks of obstacles, including rows of stakes, as well as multiple obstructions and a jumble of barbed wire to which mines were hooked up. Along more than half the beach at Cavalaire-sur-Mer, the rockets had been duds, and their fire had lost most of its effectiveness, with the result that this sector had not been completely cleaned up. There were still many signposts printed with the '*Minen*!' warning, which the Germans either had not bothered to remove or had not had time to attend to. As far as the Americans were concerned, the silence could be largely accounted for by the jungle that they had to cut their way through before they could even get close to the concrete bunkers. In them, for all they knew, might be plenty of Germans, just waiting for the landing forces to attain sufficient numbers before they launched a counterattack.

But they did find the silence weird and unnerving, and it continued for some twenty minutes. The ensuing waves of LCIs were already covering the bay, coming up to the beach and unloading infantrymen, engineers and demolition squads, with tanks trailing them closely.

For the rest of her life, Andrée Riccioli would remember the incredible array of troop-laden vessels that greeted her eyes as she opened the windows of her house overlooking Cavalaire-sur-Mer. The bay, which had looked ominously empty when she had closed the shutters the previous evening, was now sparkling in the sunlight, and hundreds of landing boats were bearing down on the beaches, while over the vast fleet standing out at sea, she recalled 'thousands of silvery balloons floating, glinting in the clear sky.' But what struck Andrée, too, amid this enormous deployment of might, was 'the deep silence, so profound that not even a leaf seemed to be rustling.' What she saw next made her pulse quicken. The silhouettes of soldiers were appearing among the trees at a distance that 'made them look almost like ants in the shimmering sunlight that was sifting down around them.' And still the enemy had not given any sign. The venturesome Andrée immediately dashed down to the basement and wheeled out her bicycle. She pedaled off 'as fast as I could make those wheels go around,' hoping to meet the first arrivals. Andrée Riccioli was one of the first French people in Provence to realize that the landings had been successful.

This conviction was being shared a few miles out at sea by an American, Winston Miller, a pharmacist's mate, second class. Miller was on the transport attack ship *Samuel Chase*, which had seen action at four other successful landings – North Africa, Sicily, Salerno and Normandy – thereby earning the nickname the 'Lucky' *Chase*. Miller was certain that the events he had witnessed two months ago off the Channel beaches were not going to be repeated here. On this 15 August, Miller was with Captain E.H. Fritzsche of the United States Coast Guards, skipper of the *Samuel Chase*, at anchor off Cavalaire-sur-Mer and Pampelonne. On the mainland, Mike O'Daniel's fighting boys of the 3rd Division had just established a firm beachhead in front of their objectives.

Now the troops were literally pouring out all along the beach. Closely packed groups of men, dark clusters in the morning light, kept sloshing through the blue water. There was still not a trace of enemy retaliation. For many of the Americans in the early hours of D-Day, this attack on the French coast reminded them of a well-rehearsed piece of orchestration. To others, it was like a Sunday stroll through pine woods on a misty summer morning. However, for one group approaching Cavalaire-sur-Mer –

about sixty men in LCIs – there would be no time to reflect later about the landing or to compare it with those they had made in Sicily and at Anzio.

For these sixty soldiers, the landing was a disaster. Their LCI's struck the concrete tetrahedrons hidden beneath the water, which had not even been dented by the rockets or the naval artillery. The small vessels were shattered by the submerged mines, to become smoking, blood-spattered wreckage. Fewer than ten survivors, some of them injured, managed to swim the rest of the way to the beach among the torn bodies of their comrades floating in the surf. The LCIs that were close behind and were about to lower their landing ramps swerved immediately and swung off toward another sector. This was the only catastrophe that marred the landings on Alpha Red. Navy demolition squads promptly began clearing additional water lanes in anticipation of the arrival of the big LSTs, which would be bringing in the heavy supporting equipment and the reinforcement battalions.

In order to open the way for the infantry assault units, the engineers of the 36th Division began the painstaking task of clearing the obstructions that were blocking the advance. With their Bangalore torpedoes, they methodically blew up the bristling steel barriers and the land mines, until the assault troops were at last able to plunge over the sand and charge freely toward the coastal highway.

The Germans chose that moment to open fire. The first whizzing of bullets and whistling of shells began tearing the morning air which until now had seemed committed to eternal silence.

Shells from mortars and 88-mm. guns came crashing down from the adjacent hilltops, ripping through the adjoining pine woods on to the long, narrow strip of beach. Simultaneous bursts of machine-gun fire punched through the fringe of coastal forest. Aboard an LCI that was carrying part of an infantry company, Lieutenant Jackson found himself pinned down by the hail of fire. Projectiles were singing out over the water and howling around his boat, which was about to let down its ramp. Jackson ordered the men to keep their heads down well below the gunwale. He had his hands full – his craft had struck a submerged mine, and now he was responsible for getting his platoon, including several wounded men, ashore under this barrage, which seemed to be coming from everywhere and was concentrated on his landing site.

The LCI behind him, under Captain Hitt's command, was no better off. Hitt looked at his watch – 8.25 A.M.

The storm of bullets and shells had become fiercer, and the troops on the beaches were now sustaining a withering fire. The dazed and stunned Germans had finally emerged from the dugouts in which they had been cowering for the last two hours and, wherever possible, had raced to man their fighting posts.

But for them it was already too late.

4

A MILE FROM THE TOWN OF SAINTE-MAXIME, in the middle of the landing zone, a fortified wall ran the length of the beach. The wall was ten feet high and slightly over six feet thick. Neither the repeated aerial strikes nor the heavy bombardment by Admiral Bryant's warships had been able to inflict more than a few scars on this imposing concrete structure. The Allied firing had ceased, but the wall of La Nartelle was still squatting firmly in place, forming a continuous obstacle between the beach – which was barely thirty-five feet wide – and the wooded foothills beyond, opposite the position to be assaulted by General Eagles's 45th Division.

Because of the fog, through which the sun was just beginning to stab out little shafts here and there, it had been difficult for the troops to assess the nature and extent of the great fortified wall. And, in truth, few of the men in the 157th Regiment, who were spearheading the attack, even knew of its existence.

Like many of his comrades, Seaman First Class Frank D. Alt, aboard LCI 596, felt sure that the crushing strikes of the bombers and the big guns of the fleet 'must have bashed up all the damned blockhouses on the coast with all their occupants.' The apparent calm along the shore struck him as reassuring, and on LCI 596 the young sailor had a first-class observation post amid the swarm of 118 landing craft fanned out over the Mediterranean and streaking toward their destinations with the leaping and plunging motion peculiar to this type of vessel.

This portion of the assault zone, between Cap-des-Sardinaux and Pointe-des-Issambres, was the only one that had not been cleared by the drone boats. Commander Ruth's section of mine sweepers, partially shielded by the early morning fog screen, had systematically raked the approach channels and marked them with buoys. An officer commanding one of the mine sweepers had reported only a sprinking of underwater obstacles in the Bay of Bougnon (also called La Nartelle bay), and Ruth instructed a few light units to proceed towards the coast to evaluate the situation. A fierce volley of machine-gun fire greeted the small mine sweepers, which answered with their own guns. The officers in charge of the various vessels now confirmed the report that the three Delta beaches were not defended by any substantial submerged obstacles. On the strength of this information, Ruth decided not to order the drone boats into his sector.

At 7.49 A.M., as the rows of LCIs crammed with troops were nearing the shore, the blazing deluge of rockets was still pounding the nearly two miles of sand and rocks that line the Bay of Bougnon. The barrage was scheduled to continue until the landing craft of the two first-wave regiments, the 157th and the 180th, had approached to within a few yards of the beach.

No troops were to be sent in by sea at Saint-Tropez, whose haze-covered bay and wooded peninsula loomed up some five miles to the left. In the opinion of most of the Allied experts, a landing at that spot would have resulted in ninety-five per cent casualties. In addition, the supporting ships would have had to approach the coast through a zone that lay well outside their security limits. Consequently, the entire attack made by the 45th Division was to be carried out away from the danger zone, including the short stretch of coast between Sainte-Maxime and Cap-des-Sardinaux to the east.

The Germans were well aware of the possibilities of an invasion from this direction, and had fortified the highly vulnerable Bay of Bougnon. The only really important fortifications on the entire Riviera, the only defense installation that made the Mediterranean Wall worthy of its name, had been built along the full length of the wild, slightly curving beach at La Nartelle. The ominous mass of concrete ramparts towered behind the barriers and mined obstacles on the shore, protecting the troop dugouts, the pillboxes and the machine-gun positions. The veterans of Salerno and of the Volturno, the renowned 'Thunderbird' Division, were to land at this spot. Their mission was to destroy this key point of the invasion zone during the decisive minutes immediately after H-Hour.

The Delta sector, assigned to General Eagles's regiments, including two regiments in the assault waves, was actually the fulcrum on which the entire landing in Provence was balanced. It formed an enclave of about nine miles between the two other assault sectors of the American VI Corps – Alpha and Camel. Eagles did not have a minute to spare. His job was to move in as fast as possible and clean up his beaches, knock out the defense wall at Sainte-Maxime and capture the town itself. He would then march through fifteen miles of wooded country to an assembly area, where he would rendezvous with the troops who had been parachuted down at Le Muy.

Candide Bagnoud had just gone off night duty at the telephone exchange in the Sainte-Maxime post office. The sun was beginning to poke through the clouds as he shut the door and crossed the square. The town looked deserted. Along the empty, echoing streets the house doors and shutters were tightly closed. So far no shells had fallen. Bagnoud quickened his pace, feeling reasonably certain, although he possessed a special curfew pass, that no German patrol would stop to think twice before casually shooting down a lone French civilian.

The long hours of the night shift had been nerve-racking, and he felt uneasy. Until 4 A.M. everything had gone calmly enough, aside from the noise of German street patrols hammering the sidewalks with their boots. Bagnoud had listened anxiously as they passed through the maze of streets in the little town. Considering the number of arrests among the members of his Resistance group, Bagnoud fully expected to be apprehended at any moment. Despite the absence of moonlight, the night was clear, and the air remained warm, almost as if electrically charged. Bagnoud kept pacing back and forth, now and then opening the door to let in a gust of fresh air and to pause on the threshold for a few minutes. Each time, the penetrating fragrance of late-blooming summer flowers assailed his nostrils. At one point he thought he heard 'something like a far-off rumble a deep muffled roar, deadened by distance, rising up from the earth.'

A knock came at the door. Bagnoud gave a start and went to open up. Before him stood one of the *Kommandantur*'s sergeants, a man named Panzer, who occasionally dropped by at night with an interpreter to look things over. This time he had dispensed with the interpreter, but had brought along a few armed soldiers and a corporal. Bagnoud felt his blood run cold. He was sure that the game was up and that he had been betrayed.

But, after peering suspiciously around the room, the German sergeant suddenly turned toward Bagnoud, who by now had a clearer idea of what was going on. Outside in the night sky the roar of approaching planes was growing louder, and Bagnoud noticed great beads of perspiration dripping down the German's forehead.

The sergeant managed to bark out in bad French:

'Go get your chief! Fast!'

He paced restlessly up and down, nervously unsheathing his big pistol and shoving it back into his boot-top holster. Bagnoud took a deep breath and inquired casually:

'More terrorist attacks?'

Panzer shook his head. He was rolling his eyes wildly, and he appeared to be at a loss as he glanced wearily and helplessly around. At last he muttered:

'*Paratruppen*!'

Bagnoud felt his heart skip a beat as he ran off to rouse Boutet, the postmaster. Passing out into the courtyard, he realized that the drone of engines had diminished and was dying off in the direction opposite from which it had come.

With the German sergeant following, Bagnoud gazed up into the sky, and then he saw them. Above the Monts des Maures, over toward the winding valley of the Argens River, great white parachutes were billowing out into the night and studding the sky like poppies. He could not repress an exclamation:

'Americans!'

He instantly regretted his boldness. Glancing around at the sergeant, Bagnoud saw him blinking his eyes, looking furtively around. The German whispered hoarsely:

'*Ach*! Quiet!'

Several hours passed before the din resumed, this time with double the intensity, sounding as if it were directly in town. Because of the cape and the hill that stand between Sainte-Maxime and the beach at La Nartelle, only a muffled echo of explosions and shellbursts reached the center of town. And now, although it was considerably past daybreak as Bagnoud made his way through the streets, he did not see or hear a solitary German patrol. He continued on his way home along the road leading to the signal tower, east of town.

'When I reached home, the guns had been shooting for quite a while,' Bagnoud recounted. 'My family had taken shelter in a rock quarry close by, where everybody felt safe. We didn't speak a word – we couldn't. Everybody was crying, and we didn't even realize it. I think that as long as I live I'll never experience anything quite like it!'

Dr Jean Verdier had been awakened by the first roar of the planes, and he hurried over to a window to look out. From the terrace of his villa he could see out over the fog covered Gulf of Saint-Tropez, but through the mist, lightning-like flashes of flame were darting out from bulky black shapes at sea. His eyes were not deceiving him. One group of ships had advanced beyond the buoys at Basse Rabu and was firing at the shore. Four years ago, Dr Verdier had been at Dunkirk, 'until that morning of shame and surrender,' as he described it, and he had seen French villages burning over the heads of their defenders, devastated by dive-bombing Stukas in a sky where French and British planes had become fewer and fewer. For four years he had not been able to erase those scenes from his mind.

He hastily pulled on an old pair of trousers and a shirt and stole out of the house. He found himself almost racing through the streets – in which a few shadowy human forms were already beginning to appear – knocking on house shutters and rousing his friends. The young physician, beside himself with joy and excitement, had no intention of missing out on any of this triumphant assault on the coast after the tragic retreat into the sea in 1940. With a group of companions, including a few fishermen who were all as eager and impatient as he, Verdier was taking great, long steps, striding up the sides of the Petite Corse, a hill that looks out over the Sainte-Maxime signal tower. From there he could get a complete view.

Full daylight had not yet dawned, and through the mist the waves of bombers, hindered by poor visibility, were flying so low that they were almost touching the signal tower. The air was sending out its own shock and sound waves. The group on the hilltop could hear the faint chime of the Sainte-Maxime bell tower striking the hour far below. Along the beach, all the way from Cap-des-Sardinaux to Pointe-des-Issambres, explosive missiles were relentlessly hitting home, with dazzling flashes of light marking the continuous bombardment of the shore. This was the assault by the hundreds of rocket launches, all hurling forth their deadly fire. The explosions gradually became more sporadic and finally the heavy firing broke off completely. It yielded to the dry tac-tac of the machine guns of the 157th Regiment's Third Battalion, which had landed east of Cap-des-Sardinaux. The crackling of the American guns was drowning out the furious response from the German blockhouses, which, as Verdier gleefully noted, were gradually ceasing to fire. The doctor was in his glory, and along the entire length of the Bay of Bougnon the battle was in full swing. The banks of fog had now begun to dissolve into wisps.

Verdier felt certain that the wall of La Nartelle, the Germans' local pride, could not hold out for long against the overwhelming force of the invaders, whose tanks and armored vehicles were already piling ashore. He was right. During the first few minutes of the attack that was launched directly on it, the massive fortified structure was literally split apart. The swarm of infantrymen, still clad in life jackets, guns firing, their faces smudged with the grime of battle, plunged headlong through the gaping breach and fanned out along the highway, through the gardens, the vineyards and the pine woods.

At that moment, there was at least one Frenchman busily cursing all the Germans and the Americans and the Allies, as a matter of principle. Old Haby lay sprawled flat on his face in his field surrounded by grapevines, while bullets whined angrily over him. Haby who ran a butcher shop in Sainte-Maxime, had decided to take advantage of the 15 August holiday by setting out at dawn to attend to the country garden on his property at La Nartelle. The fog had already put him in a bad mood, and as if that were not enough, he had suddenly found himself knocked to the ground, with bombs and shells bursting all around him. This had scarcely let up when a fresh hail of bullets and all the uproar of the heat of battle let loose again. During a brief lull, the elderly butcher stood up and saw the first landing troops emerging out of the mist and heading for Sainte-Maxime. He promptly decided that it would be most expedient to head for home with all possible speed – even though he expected to find his house a mass of ruins. Haby beat the tanks and troops of the 157th Regiment's Third Battalion into town by barely a few minutes.

While the mortar fire on the beaches and hills continued to intensify – up to H-Hour the Allied fleet had lobbed 4,000 shells on the heights over the small valley at La Nartelle – the Fenouil family was staying put in its refuge in the Bouillerettes woods, a mile from Sainte-Maxime. Fenouil attempted to console his hysterical young wife.

'Don't cry,' he said gently. 'After all, we're at least safe up here. Think about our friends down below. They're probably not being so lucky.'

It was to be several hours before Fenouil learned what had happened in town. At a few minutes past 8 A.M., a strange, uncertain calm had settled over Sainte-Maxime. Father Célestin Buisson looked out and decided that he might be able to celebrate mass after all for the Feast of the Assumption, in the big hall of the casino. He still could not get into his church.

As the priest turned off the Avenue de la Gare and started along the beach road, he gazed out toward the sea. For a moment he could not believe his eyes. A sort of monstrous 'miracle of the fishes' had happened, and the bodies of thousands of dead fish, their multicolored scales glistening brilliantly in the soft light, were floating on the surface of the Mediterranean or being deposited on the sand. This sad piscatorial display included gray mullet, red mullet, sea perch, scorpaenas, sardines. The priest could not help thinking what a splendid *bouillabaisse* they would have made.

Stripped to the waist, Seaman Alt stood at his post near the loud-speaker on board LCI 596, ready to aim his 20-mm. cannon at any enemy planes that might venture over the beaches. As it turned out, Alt was not going to be called upon to fire his gun that morning.

While Captain R. E. Parker of the United States Navy was launching his assault group of six LCIs against Cap-des-Sardinaux, LCI 596 had cruised past the two venerable battleships, the British *Ramillies* and the French *Lorraine*, which were firing at the beaches for all they were worth.

Through the incandescent shroud of the explosions obscuring the shore, Alt witnessed a tragedy. On his left, an LCT[1] from another group literally split in two, with all aboard killed, after hitting a mine less than seventy yards from shore.

The sailor reflected what a 'rotten deal it was for them to have come all this way, and then catch it when they were so nearly there'.

As the troops on Alt's LCI debarked under continuous shelling by German 88-mm. guns, landing safely on the sand between two rows of mines, he was wondering 'just what the hell am I doing here, with all those poor, half-crazy guys?' His next thought was that 'maybe my next breath will be my last.'

When the men had all splashed ashore, Alt's LCI pulled up its two landing ramps and made an uneventful trip back to its station at sea. For the remainder of the day the LCIs stood off the beachhead, tirelessly pouring forth their cargoes of troops, equipment and ammunition. Alt was forced to concede that although some of the men had considered their intensive training as a 'lot of wasted time', it had nevertheless 'turned a bunch of griping civilian softies into top-notch sailors able to perform their duties efficiently, even under fire.'

As the land fog and the clouds of dust and smoke whipped up by the explosions slowly dissolved and settled along the shore, Admiral Bryant's battleships and heavy cruisers gradually proceeded farther out to sea, having completed their massive hammering of the coast. But even eight hours later, the ships of the French 4th and 10th Divisions, with several light cruisers, were standing by fairly close in (at 8.10 A.M. they were less than a mile from the beaches), their guns loaded and ready to respond to any call for assistance from the troops on land. The assault boats continued to ply back and forth amid the cluster of big ships – most of them veterans of all the Mediterranean operations since November 8, 1942 – and all other vessels, from the amphibious DUKWs and the mortar and tank vessels to the LCFs[2] and the special vessels that laid protective smoke screens. There was plenty of everything to impress even the hardened survivors of Salerno and Anzio, who thought they had already seen everything.

The converted seaplane tender *Biscayne* was flying the flag of Rear Admiral Bertram Rodgers, commanding the Delta invasion forces. From the bridge of the *Biscayne*, Rodgers was scanning the horizon

---

[1] LCT: Landing craft tank, one-tenth the size of an LST.
[2] LCF: Landing craft flak – special craft for transporting antiaircraft batteries.

through binoculars, observing the milling swarm of boats a few miles away as they went on their frenzied tasks.

As he later described it, 'the extreme concentration of the Delta zone beaches forced us to group the bulk of our transport and assault fleet in two narrow sectors. To complicate matters, there were more than fifteen battleships, cruisers and destroyers – an absolutely fantastic number for such a cramped space – moving around in the same lanes as the troop transports. Their lanes even intersected the one that the landing barges used going toward the shore.'

However, through a miracle, no collisions or incidents occurred to mar these landings. There was never any confusion among the oncoming landing craft as they made for the beaches, and the operation was executed to the letter.

A special detail of engineers had come in with the first wave of the main landing troops, and these men were now tackling the fortified wall along the long, pine-bordered La Nartelle beach.

Expertly wielding heavy wire cutters, and with a liberal use of Bangalore torpedoes, the engineers of the First Naval Beach Battalion set about removing the obstructions that the Germans had planted between the water's edge and the wall – *chevaux-de-frise*, metal stakes, lengths of mined rails buried in the sand – to impede the Allied advance. Within minutes the men of the 157th Infantry were pouring through the several paths that had been cleared for them, on their way to the wall.

Crawling on all fours with their mine-detectors, the demolition squads located and removed the fuses from the 'S' mines that the rockets had failed to detonate. Suddenly their officer shouted:

'Hit the ground!'

The men of the 40th Engineer Beach Group ducked into the nearest shell holes and bomb craters. They could feel the force of the shock waves whipping against their faces and sending giant handfuls of rock and metal fragments swirling around their bodies.

The first breach of some fifteen feet was opened in the wall below the wooded slope amid clouds of thick smoke, under a steady avalanche of German fire coming from the left side of the beach. Soon the wall had been pierced by great gashes at two more places. The assault troops – the 45th Division's 'beach jumpers' – piled through the gaps, hurling grenades as they ran. The tanks were right behind them, all primed for action.

A few feet away, the defense wall of La Nartelle was now serving as a shield for one of the division's small reconnaissance groups, which had already paid its toll of dead and wounded before H-Hour and was

A cloud of dust from trucks, just off the ships, and Red Cross trucks, arriving with wounded, rises over the beachhead in the Saint-Raphaël area. (*Photo U.S. Army*)

Members of the first RAF party to land in southern France waiting to step ashore from their invasion craft. (*Photo Imperial War Museum*)

Private W. D. Eason of Atlanta, Georgia, of the 509th Parachute Infantry Battalion, landed three and one-half hours before H-Hour, D-Day, August 15, 1944, for the invasion of southern France. Here he thanks Monsieur Marc Rainaut (left), leader of the French forces of the Interior of Saint-Tropez, who saved his life. Mademoiselle Nicola Celebonovitch (center) led the paratroopers to a group of hidden Germans. (*Photo U.S. Army*)

under fire from German light artillery. Even Lieutenant Rogers, the platoon leader, had not escaped unscathed. Just before dawn, with ten American soldiers and a twenty-two year old French sergeant from Provence, Jean Garnier, Rogers had set off on his mission to probe the defenses on Cap-des-Sardinaux. In the darkness their boat had run into concentrated machine-gun fire which had killed two men and wounded three others. Following orders, they had turned around and headed back. Now Rogers and his remaining men were waiting for a lull in the firing to dash through the breach in the wall, reach the highway, and hustle through the vineyards to the shelter of the pine woods.

Aside from sporadic shelling and machine-gun fire, enemy opposition by and large appeared to be weak. The American infantrymen were proceeding in Indian file – as a matter of fact, many hailed from New Mexico, Arizona, Oregon and Nevada, and they included a good number of full-blooded Apaches and Cherokees – and had soon secured a foothold on the soil of France without much trouble. Under the steadily rising sun, which was tentatively poking its shafts of light through the cloudy ceiling, the columns of infantrymen, jeeps and armored vehicles advanced to the coastal pine woods of Provence. The Third Battalion of the 157th Regiment, the first to land on Delta Red, and its First Battalion, which had come ashore on the adjacent beach of Delta Green, sprang to attack the low walls around the gardens surrounding the old summer villas, many now in flames. One of these buildings housed the German headquarters for La Nartelle, from which so many orders for plundering and methodical destruction had been issued, all bearing the signature of a simple-appearing but nonetheless dangerous warrant officer named Schmidt. The two assault battalions struck out over the countryside and cut across the vineyards, the fields and the wooded slopes, meeting only intermittent small-arms and artillery fire.

The bombardment had touched off a forest fire in this area, and dark smoke was spiraling up in the warm air above the dense patch of pines. Along the coastal highway, portions of which the Germans had tried to blow up, the low grinding roar of the half-tracks grew louder, until it drowned out the shrieking of the shells in a glorious, victorious tumult. The timing had been so perfect that a few units in the second and third waves had sped up from the beach and surged inland ahead of schedule.

As a routine precaution, some of the men in the lead company tossed a few grenades into the gun slits of the blockhouse. The only response was the empty echo of the exploding grenades and the acrid smoke pouring out through the openings. After a few minutes, when still nothing had happened and no one had emerged, the platoon leader decided that the fortification had probably been abandoned before their arrival.

The men of the 157th's First Battalion crept cautiously around behind the bunker, where they stumbled upon a small scene of slaughter. The still-warm bodies of five Germans lay sprawled under some trees. They had most likely been caught in the strafing fire of the fighter planes as they were trying to get away.

Suddenly a voice yelled:

'Hey, Mike! Look out!'

Mike Harrison jumped to one side and pivoted around just in time to see three German soldiers aiming at him. His friend beat him to the draw, cutting down the first two. Harrison shot the third German at almost point-blank range as he tried to run off toward the woods. The German's body was literally lifted off the ground by the shots before he slumped down against a tree, his rifle slipping from his grasp. The fusillade alerted their sergeant and the other men in the platoon, who began firing furiously. This time the German went down for the count, collapsing heavily to the ground amid the clatter of his gas mask and canteen and the two grenades dangling from his belt.

The blockhouse had been positioned to overlook a considerable portion of the Les Maures coast, and it made an ideal observation post. In particular, it dominated the three landing beaches of the Delta sector, as well as the entire Gulf of Saint-Tropez, clear over to the town in the distance.

Inside the bunker everything was a mad jumble. On the one table that had remained upright, the men of the First Battalion found an unfinished letter dated 15 August, 1944. In it, the unit's commander, an artillery lieutenant of the 242nd Division, had been sending his wife the latest news from the front, telling her that 'all was quiet, except for the usual bombardments.' His wife's name was Martha, and he sent his love to her and to their two children, Ferdi and Irmgard. Although the officer had not had time to sign his name, he had scrawled 'Heil Hitler!' at the bottom of the page. His body was not among those scattered around the bunker. In all likelihood, he had hastily broken off his letter on receiving the withdrawal order, one which affected the major portion of the German troops in that sector, some three companies spread out on a ten-mile front. The eight soldiers whose bodies were found there had been left behind as a rear guard.

Less than a hundred yards away, Dr Verdier had to rub his eyes before he could believe what he saw. When he realized that it was no optical illusion, he felt profoundly stirred. The star-spangled red, white, and blue flag of the United States had been firmly planted by soldiers of the 157th Regiment and was waving proudly in the breeze on the Sainte-Maxime railroad signal tower, in place of the sinister swastika-adorned red and black banner that had been hanging there for twenty months, until just about an hour before.

It was nearly 9 A.M. As Father Buisson was on his way to say mass, his path crossed that of one of the first Americans to enter Sainte-Maxime, a young sergeant from the Third Battalion. The priest paused, took the soldier's hand and held it a minute without saying a word, before quietly continuing toward the casino with great tears of emotion rolling down his smooth-shaven cheeks. When he had almost reached his destination, he heard the first sounds of battle coming from the town – exploding grenades and the rapid fire of machine guns. He stopped to make the sign of the cross, tightened his grip on his small case, and hurried into the casino.

Two battalions of the 157th had already attacked, the Third by way of the coast and the First over the wooded hills and slopes near the signal tower north of Sainte-Maxime. The infantry and tanks had then set off toward town as fast as they could in the face of ambushes, antitank guns and obstacles that the Germans had set up. All things considered, the troops of the 157th were making a sizable advance. They were shortly met by a small group of Resistance fighters who had escaped from the town and daringly slipped through the German lines. The French informed the Americans that the town was almost deserted. Through the morning mist, heavy German trucks and combat vehicles, under a forest of camouflage, had driven away with a detachment of some five hundred troops just before 8 A.M. However, as the men of the First Battalion began entering the town, they came up against a few pockets of diehard Germans. The house-to-house fighting continued for two hours.

The streets of Sainte-Maxime were empty, the house shutters were closed and the store fronts lowered. Along some of the sidewalks lay the bodies of dead or wounded German soldiers. One of the town's elderly inhabitants, Mme Audiffren, had stolen forth early in the morning to attend Assumption Day services. In the Rue de Verdun she came upon the body of a German lying on his back with his arms crossed, a gaping hole in his forehead. Someone had been there before her – the soldier's papers had been riffled through and his socks and boots had been taken. A snapshot of a young woman holding a child had slid out of his unbuttoned jacket. The name on his identification papers was Polish.

Sergeant Panzer of the local *Kommandantur* felt safe. When the trucks had pulled out of Sainte-Maxime, no one had paid any attention to him. He and a handful of soldiers had been hiding out for two hours behind a coal pile. They were unarmed; they had no equipment, not even a helmet. As far as Panzer was concerned, the war was finished and Germany had lost. The eager faith and enthusiasm that he had felt back in 1940 were shattered and gone. One comforting thought kept recurring to him – at least he would not have to look for the Americans so that he could surrender.

Upstairs, overlooking Panzer's hiding place, the Sainte-Maxime postmaster, a quiet man named Boutet, was gradually recovering from the surprise of recent events. In the early hours of the morning, his night clerk, Candide Bagnoud, had fetched him from his home, saying it was by order of the Germans. By the time Boutet had thrown on his clothes and rushed to the post office, the Germans had already settled themselves in the basement. For a while, Boutet had feared that they were going to blow up everything. Bagnoud had told him about the Allied landings, but neither man knew exactly where the soldiers were coming ashore; the clerk mentioned having seen hundreds of parachutes descending during the night, farther inland.

But Boutet's fears concerning the post office building were soon dispelled; in fact, he had barely been able to repress a smile when he learned what the Germans really wanted.

Panzer and his ten men had hastily removed their helmets and cartridge belts and dumped their rifles and bayonets on the floor. As he watched their strange behavior, Boutet could hardly believe that these same soldiers, by their appearance and guttural shouting, had once been able to strike terror in the hearts of the people of Sainte-Maxime. He was still watching, amazed, as they briskly descended to the basement and shut themselves in.

When the soldiers of the First Battalion of the 157th reached the town square and burst into the post office, they found the Mausers and helmets lying in a heap, where they had been left a few hours before. The Germans had remained in the basement all through the aerial and naval bombardments. The Americans tossed a few grenades into the switchboard room, but there was no response. Panzer had carefully thought matters out in order to avoid any fighting. However, his plans might be foiled now if he and his men remained in hiding too long. The sergeant finally decided that the time had come, and he was the first to emerge from behind the coal pile. As he and his men stepped on to the square in the morning light, bareheaded and hands held high, they were grinning broadly.

A mile away, the seventh assault wave had just disembarked its troops, and the Seabees were busy anchoring steel pontoons to the shore preparatory to setting up floating docks. Within an hour and a quarter after the landings had begun, five heavy cranes had gone into operation. They were unloading tanks from the LCTs and stacking up the crates of shells and ammunition which had not been scheduled for delivery until early afternoon. The winds of victory were blowing proudly over the sands of Sainte-Maxime, as if to push the Americans upward and onward, deeper into the interior. The DUKWs were now being used to unload the landing ships and to take fuel and equipment ashore, and the piles of shells and containers were mounting higher and higher in the shade of the pines along the blue Mediterranean.

Aboard the *Biscayne*, the commander of the 45th Division, General Eagles, was nervously polishing his gold-rimmed glasses.

'Well, Bill! Isn't it about time for you to stretch your legs and take a little stroll in France?' Admiral Rodgers asked with a sly smile.

German shells were falling in the middle of Delta sector and to the east, on the infantry as they grappled their way along the rocky strands and coves of La Garonnette and the Val d'Esquières.

The men continued to advance, doggedly firing, now crouching, now straightening up briefly, now dodging down again. During this initial phase, only five men were lost by the 180th Regiment's Second Battalion, and its escorting tanks started shooting the minute their heavy treads bit into the sand. After a while there was no more firing from the German machine guns and the 75-mm. cannon in the blockhouses, but one of the lead tanks struck a land mine on the beach and was destroyed. All the other tanks came through the danger zone untouched. Their unit commander had organized his attack so that while one tank would be rolling forward, those behind continued to batter the enemy positions. The Second Battalion quickly assembled beyond the beach and began its march over the Les Maures heights toward the little town of Vidauban, seven miles from Le Muy.

Off to the right, the assault wave of the First Battalion of Colonel Robert Dunaley's 180th Regiment landed without meeting serious resistance. However, its difficulties began with the scaling of the fortified concrete wall on the shore. Its four escorting tanks from the 191st Battalion struck out over a strip of land planted with mines, and all were blown up. Three minutes after the first men in the wave had waded ashore, the big German guns suddenly opened fire from over Pointe-des-Issambres, on the right flank of the 45th Division's landing zone.

A few weeks before, at the Eighth Fleet headquarters in Naples, a

French lieutenant commander named Raymond Payan had held out a photograph to Signalman Jean Meirat. The picture had been taken near Pointe-des Issambres, between Saint-Aygulf and Sainte-Maxime.

'See this, Meirat?' he asked. 'What do you make of it?'

For a minute or so, Meirat thought that Payan was trying to get a rise out of him. The scene looked like a typical tourist snapshot of cactus plants and palm trees, with just another Côte d'Azur villa plumped down amid the usual profusion of bougainvilleas, morning glories and rambler roses. But closer scrutiny of this apparently idyllic landscape revealed more than first met the eye. All those windows, shutters and shrubbery were actually outlines that had been painted on the walls of a building. And the innocent-appearing building itself was actually a formidable blockhouse with fake palm trees and flowering plants camouflaging an old but still vigorous 8.7-inch battery – manufactured in 1918 by the Bethlehem Steel Corporation for the French army!

The sinister 'villa' at Pointe-des-Issambres that had been spotted by the reconnaissance planes and cross-checked and identified by naval intelligence had received special treatment, from both the bombers and from the naval guns, ten minutes before H-hour. But, shortly before 8 A.M., it became clear that they had not completely put it out of action.

The French light cruiser *Le Malin*, less than five miles out at sea, observed the flashes coming from the 'villa' in the morning haze, and began concentrating her own 5½-inch guns against the block-house. Lieutenant-Commander Ballande's report states that 'after the eighteenth round, it was virtually impossible to take proper aim because the fog had thickened'. However, the *Malin* kept firing, and the German guns eventually fell silent. From the deck of the battleship *Texas*, Admiral Bryant had been observing the engagement. When the battery finally ceased firing, Bryant lowered his binoculars with a sigh of relief. His next gesture was to flash Ballande a brief but hearty message of congratulations.

Near Pointe-des-Issambres, Master Sergeant Emile Bresc had just landed on the beach at Val d'Esquières, less than ten miles from his home town, Roquebrune-sur-Argens. He was counting the hours and minutes until his homecoming. Hundreds of rockets had been whizzing over his head, battering the sand and rocks, but they had stopped when the 45th Division began landing. The warm air was thick with smoke, and there was an overpowering stench of powder. Except for some random shooting, the enemy's retaliation had been insignificant. For the first time, Bresc caught himself wondering whether his wife would even recognize him, particularly now that he was wearing an American uniform! He was eager to clasp her in his arms again, yet he could not restrain a gnawing concern. But his pride and happiness at the thought of his imminent return soon erased all worry.

Bresc and the rest of the troops in the First Battalion of the 180th Regiment scrambled up from the beach, crossed the railroad tracks and the highway, and began striding off through the woods in the Angélis hills. Wherever he looked, along the roadsides, in the forests and fields, at the deserted intersections, lay the signs of the German occupation and of the enemy's confused rout. As far as the eye could see, business buildings and family dwellings had been blasted and cleared away to give the German guns fields of fire. Now the batteries were mute, stripped of their gunners. The antiglider stakes and spikes had been planted all over the old sheep pastures, and Bresc has a vivid recollection of the 'hordes of abandoned bicycles that the Germans had left sprawled in the ditches and strewn over the roads', a scene reminiscent of the 'tragic retreat of 1940.'

Dunaley, the 'fighting colonel', and his two energetic staff officers, Fletcher and Stapleton, had advanced to a point overlooking the seaside resort of Saint-Aygulf, nestled at the entrance to the Bay of Fréjus. Two companies from the 180th deployed along the coast and attacked the enemy positions defending the approaches to the town. At the same time the 191st's tanks went into action. Saint-Aygulf was not completely secured until the following day. The battalion finally had to flash a request for naval gunfire in order to overcome the German resistance, which had become stiffer as the Allied invaders swept toward Saint-Raphaël.

During these hours, on this warm and unforgettable morning of 15 August, in a modest home in the heart of the Delta sector, a moving scene was taking place, one of perhaps a hundred other similar scenes. Its owner, a man named De la Fargue had opened his front door to welcome a few officers of the American Seventh Army, and to celebrate the occasion fittingly he had broken out his last few bottles from their hiding place behind the logs in his basement.

Since 1940, De la Fargue had not had any news of his son, François, a sea captain serving with the Free French. He was reasonably certain that if François were alive, he would soon be hearing the news. The shooting was still going on in the nearby woods and occasional shells were dropping on the beach. As De la Fargue was lifting his hand to clink glasses with the officers, he felt a light tap on his shoulder.

He turned to see a deeply tanned young officer in an American naval summer uniform, with a quizzical smile on his face. The two men gazed at each other until at last the officer exclaimed:

189

'Don't you recognize me, father?'

François de la Fargue had just landed at Cap-des Sardinaux with Admiral Rodgers's advance staff.

5

LONG AFTER THE GUNS along the beaches of Sainte-Maxime and Cavalaire-sur-Mer had been silenced, the Allied warships continued their rolling barrage. It was directed against the last and the toughest of all the invasion sectors, the three Camel zone beaches near Saint-Raphaël, on the right flank.

Despite the violent artillery barrage and the heavy screen of smoke and fog, a young American, Ensign Anson Piper of the Eighth Fleet, could make out 'the still pale surface of the Mediterranean', and just beyond it a cluster of steep pinnacles and sharply indented rocky promontories 'plunging in a sheer drop down into the water.' Private Don Nelson of the 36th Division was 'absolutely petrified' at the sight of the 'dizzy heights of the vertical walls that were coming closer to us and looked as if they went on and on for miles.' A navy medical corpsman second class, Richard G. Hayes, on board LST 1019 in Captain W. O. Bailey's assault group, was particularly struck by the odd color of these wild, barren eminences that had been carved out by the wind and the sea. As far as eighteen year old Private Sam Kibbey was concerned, this sight through the morning haze was 'unreal, spooky, something from another world.' Kibbey, who belonged to a mortar platoon in the 143d Regiment had not 'at all imagined France to look like that.' In his excitement and apprehension, Sam had firmly resolved to 'prove myself a man,' even though he 'didn't know how to pray or even swear properly.' He felt like 'an adolescent on my first blind date.'

The Esterel cliffs cover twenty-five miles of rugged French coast marked by the natural lacy patterns and peaks that only erosion by the elements can produce. As his landing craft drew nearer to this forbidding-looking mass, Sergeant Harold C. Dean of the 697th Engineer Petroleum Distribution Company figured that his chances of survival were pretty slim if, as the troops had been warned, the Germans were firmly entrenched there and just waiting for the Allies to assault these seemingly impregnable positions.

Since 6.50 A.M., from Fréjus to Trayas, the naval guns had been lash-ing out uninterruptedly. Rear-Admiral Morton L. Deyo's eighteen battleships, cruisers and destroyers had edged in to the beaches as close as they dared and continued their furious firing until 8 A.M., fifty minutes longer than in the other sectors. The time was now nearly 8.30 A.M., and the landing boats were chugging straight toward Saint-Raphaël and slightly to the right, where lay the formidable cliffs and rocky coves.

The men of the 141st Regiment huddled tensely in their LCIs under the bows of Lieutenant Commander L. R. Herring's five LSTs. When they were a few miles offshore, the small craft began swaying on their davits, dangled a moment over nothingness, and finally hit the water opposite the easternmost and narrowest of the three beaches in the Camel sector.

The troops in the landing boats were keeping up their spirits by whistling and singing military tunes and folk songs, the martial airs of the Texas Rangers alternating with the nostalgic refrains of cowboy laments. Some of the younger, inexperienced recruits were silent – they had barely ten weeks' training behind them and were about to go under fire for the first time. Many were physically ill from the four-day Mediterranean crossing, and were suffering from seasickness during these hours in the small, flat-bottomed landing boats. But all became serious and businesslike as they carefully checked their weapons for the last time. Whatever their capacity for stoicism and stamina, the troops of the 141st, down to the last man, were inordinately proud of their shoulder insignia – the letter 'T' of the Texas Division, General Dahlquist's valiant 36th. The grim fighting on the Italian front had depleted their ranks while at the same time making the world familiar with the names of glorious but gory battlefields – Salerno, Monte Cassino, Rapido, Velletri. Following the fall of Rome, the 36th had set forth for southern Italy, where, ten months earlier, it had first seen action. Dahlquist's men had then begun in earnest their preparations for the Mediterranean invasion. During their training period, from 8 to 22 July, the 142nd and 143rd Regiments spent fifteen hours a day concentrating on assault tactics, while the 141st specialized in scaling the roughest and steepest kind of rocks. As a final preliminary to the Provence landings, they had staged a dry run at Mondragone, near Naples. At the end, Dahlquist had gathered his men together to inform them that their assignment would involve what was probably the 'toughest, nastiest hunk of all.' The Argens Valley through which the troops of the 36th Division would be advancing was considered the main zone of action by the Allied staff, and the invasion planners had given careful attention to the details of conditions along the Camel sector beaches, from the mouth of the Argens River to the rocky mass of Cap Roux.

The Esterel pinnacles stood out, 1,000 to 2,000 feet high, against the pale blue sky. The smoke screen released by special craft gradually dissolved, and the men could see in front of them the deep purple rocks with their innumerable inlets and creeks – the *calanques* – studded with bristling points as sharp as steel spikes.

The unit commanders in Herring's group had been provided with topographic maps of Cap Roux, showing also the route that led to the cove, winding through a maze of mines and obstructions. At the end of the narrow passage, facing the landing craft, rose the nine arches of the Anthéor viaduct, which had been partially destroyed by aerial bombardment. This viaduct was the assault wave's target, the pivotal point of the attack. Beneath it lay the strategically important little beach of Camel Blue, barely a hundred yards long. Because of the prolonged bombardment of the beach before the land attack, H-Hour here was set for 8.30 A.M.

As the landing boats emerged from the protective smoke screen, the German blockhouses swung into action and began showering down a deadly hail of fire, the speed, brutality and accuracy of which amazed Herring, considering the pounding that this diminutive beach had been undergoing for the past two hours. The most concentrated fire came from the railway tracks on the viaduct, overlooking the beach. Storms of tracer bullets and shells burst around the entrance to the inlet, sending up huge geysers of water around the LCIs and hammering down on the lines of boats in the first and second waves.

This murderous reception forced Herring to retreat to sea in order to continue to direct the deployment of the fourteen vessels filled with troops and equipment that were his responsibility. Three of the fourteen were already on the verge of foundering.

Two German antitank guns had begun firing from the farthest projecting rocky point over the inlet and were scoring direct hits on the front-line LCIs. The boats behind managed to maneuver away from the direct line of fire and eventually made their way into the narrow passage. But they were still under fire from the machine guns and other batteries set up on the viaduct. At full throttle the LCIs took one great leap forward and made it to the sandy end of the inlet.

This phase of the Provence landings had been regarded as potentially one of the most critical of the battles along the Esterel cliffs. However, despite the smoking wreckage of the landing craft at the entrance to the inlet, the combined army and navy casualties sustained during these first few minutes were considerably lower than had been anticipated.

In addition to the usual assortment of mine fields, barbed-wire obstacles, and booby traps, the troops had expected to find themselves up
against heavily fortified blockhouses and bunkers, communications'
trenches, dugouts, and a solid belt of walls complete with firing slits and
earthworks. Ralph R. Steig, of the 141st Regiment, felt that, except for
the few 88-mm. shells ricocheting off the rocks and the sharp firing from
the viaduct, the Anthéor landing, which 'had been given such a big
build-up was on the whole relatively easy.'

The First Battalion's combat patrols wasted no time in leaping ashore
and deploying over the small but rugged parcel of land, which they
speedily captured.

The impressive hundred foot span of the viaduct – only two of its
arches had been destroyed by the bombing – dangled high above their
heads, its torn bits of railroad tracks twisting in space. Machine-gun fire
seemed to be pouring out from every corner and over every bit of the
beach at once. Steig landed with the first wave and, as he glanced
swiftly back, was amazed to see that the tanks and combat vehicles
were, 'after all, rolling right along behind the men.'

The tanks lurched ashore off the landing ramps, and dug into the
beach, their heavy treads rasping over the rough golden sand of the
Anthéor cove. The landing boats were scattered along seventy yards of
beach squeezed tightly between two steep rocky masses, and Steig remembers reflecting that if 'even a single German plane happened along
right then, their goose was really cooked.'

As the fourth assault wave succeeded in getting safely to land, the
enemy fire suddenly tapered off. Amid the great boulders and sheer
walls of the inlet, the barking of the German machine guns died down,
the din of the small-arms fire subsided, and, except for a few isolated
snipers, the shooting eventually stopped completely. The men of the
141st, who were busily answering back with their bazookas and light
machine guns, did not immediately realize what had happened, but it
was not going to take them long to find out.

Faster than any of the officers had dared hope, the 141st overran
Anthéor beach and swarmed on to the Cannes–Saint-Raphaël highway, which at this spot runs quite near the sea, close to the viaduct and
the cove. The men of the First Battalion prepared to mop up the surrounding area, crawling and sliding and slithering among the rocky
coves, and finally emerging at the main Anthéor defenses – only to find
them totally empty. Completely encircling the beach was a tight network of interconnecting trenches that led down to a honeycomb of
shelters and flame-thrower pits set far underground, along with arms
and ammunition depots. All this was still intact, in spite of the fact that

the beach had been the target for the heaviest concentration of Allied air raids and naval gunfire.

Dazed and stunned, their uniforms gray with dust, the defenders of Anthéor slowly stumbled out of their dugouts. Every one of them belonged to a Polish 'volunteer' outfit, and they had been 'recruited' from the ranks of war prisoners on the Eastern front. As far as they were concerned, the game had been up for a long time. Whatever vague interest they might temporarily have had in fighting to defend Adolf Hitler's Europe had long since evaporated. Ironically, these were the troops who had been entrusted with the task of repelling the invasion at this key point of the assault front. Had they felt like putting up serious resistance in this strategic place, which the German command had provided with formidable fortifications and defenses, the result could well have been a slaughter of the Allied forces who landed there.

Instead, these Polish soldiers were meekly filing out of their shelters. As they emerged, dazzled by the morning sunlight, they tossed down their weapons and raised their hands high over their heads.

6

THE TERRIFIC COMMOTION FILLING THE AIR could have only one meaning. The Allies were landing! Allen Dimmick, an American intelligence agent hiding out in Boulouris, had never dreamed that the landing would be on this particular morning, nor in the very area in which he had found refuge. Dimmick had not been out of doors for longer than he cared to remember. He had not dared so much as to come up for a breath of air, fully realizing that he would only meet the same fate as so many others who had been hauled off by the Gestapo and never heard from again – François Crucy, Hélène Vagliano . . .

But now he shed all caution and was dashing across the garden under the howl of the low-flying planes. He dropped into the trench shelter in which Mme de Morsier was already cowering.

'Relax, Irène!' he shouted. 'It's all over!'

In his elation, he seized Irène de Morsier by the hand and they ran back to the house. Jagged pieces of glass from the broken windows lay scattered everywhere. They went up to the third floor, half expecting the house to collapse around them at any minute under the impact of the bombing. The noise was deafening, as if thousands of planes were flying over.

Dimmick flung open the shutters and gazed eagerly out over the unruffled blue sea covered with ships.

'Look! Look, Irène!' he whispered excitedly. 'We are free now! *A présent nous sommes libres!*'

Irène de Morsier could only stand there pale and transfixed, tears streaming down her cheeks.

From another vantage point on the coast, Irène's nephew, Alain Born, a young Resistance fighter, was also staring at the invasion fleet, along with the desolate spectacle of the millions of dead fish heaped up all over the beach below him.

Between Boulouris and Le Dramont, shells were raining down on the coast, and it seemed as if projectiles were hitting every square inch of sand and rock. In La Péguière, Suzanne Born and her husband and mother had taken shelter in a railway tunnel through which a tiny stream of water trickled. They were accompanied by their two 'companions in misfortune', an ageing cocker spaniel named Steph and their precious goat Biquette, which had been their source of milk, butter and cheese during the German occupation. They were cramped and uncomfortable, with their feet trailing in the water, trying to shield their ears from the succession of exploding bombs. The Borns had abandoned all hope of finding their seaside villa intact – the Germans had been entrenched there for some time, and this morning fresh troops had arrived to reinforce the defense installations at La Péguière. But the Born family was finding solace in the thought that deliverance could not be far off now.

In Boulouris, Irène de Morsier had just started walking across the garden when she was startled to hear a stifled moan despite the roar of planes and bombs.

Through the tree branches crashing down and the unbreathable, nightmarish fog, she could see a young woman, a stranger, lying almost prostrate against the wall of her house, holding a wailing baby. Irène ran to see what she could do, but it was already too late. As she approached she could see that the mother was glassy-eyed, obviously near death. A minute later, her head slumped down and her body lay motionless. After making sure that the woman was dead, Irène snatched up the terrified infant and carried it to the shelter at the back of the garden. At that moment, with the bombs bursting and smoking all around, Irène de Morsier, clutching an unknown baby in her arms, came face to face with 'the first American troops, grimy, sweating and exhausted.' They were climbing a path leading up from the beach, their submachine guns at the ready.

At Le Dramont, Clementine Minara and her husband François, a stonecutter in the porphyry quarries, did not live to witness the landings. A bomb made a direct hit on their little house, which they had steadfastly refused to abandon, scorning the spacious shelter in the quarry that could accommodate all the local population. A short while later, during a lull, their neighbours discovered what had happened. They were able to lay the victims out on their bed, but fate had more in store for the unfortunate couple, even after death. This time a German shell crashed down on what was left of the Minaras' house, tearing a hole in the bedroom ceiling and shattering the bed on which the two bodies lay.

Mario Falco and his wife were probably the only people on the entire Provence coast who had spent the night at the very spot at which the Allied troops were to come ashore a few hours later. For the last fourteen years Mario and Clotilde had been the caretakers for the house belonging to Louis Marchand – the owner of the quarries at Le Dramont. The Falcos, with a few friends, including David Sturlèse, Natale, Daniel Garin, and a Saint-Tropez fisherman named Picot, had taken refuge for the night in a shelter built by the Indochinese construction workers of the Todt Organization, right on the beach.

As Mario Falco describes it, he was roused from his sleep (it was still quite dark) by the sound of boat engines offshore from the tip of Le Dramont. As a matter of fact, shortly before dawn a fast American launch carrying a 36th Division patrol had ventured in near the cape to sound out its defences. There had been no sign of life, and the launch had departed. A little later, Falco knew that something was going on when the fort at nearby Poussaï began firing furiously at the Allied ships out at sea. Leaping to his feet, he dashed to the shelter entrance, to see a tower of flames shooting up out of the fog, near the tower on the Ile d'Or. He watched while two ships – mine sweepers from the Camel Green sector under Lieutenant-Commander Maloney – fired back as they rapidly maneuvered out to sea. All this occurred at about 6.30 A.M.

Before going back inside the shelter, Falco gazed around. The German radar station and the signal tower at the top of the thickly wooded cape gave no evidence that anything unusual was happening. In the gray half-light, the silent quarry looked like an enormous abandoned excavation, its little train of tipple cars drawn up near the entrance to a shed. Along the beach, nothing was stirring except the sluggishly moving tide. The stark silhouette of the Ile d'Or stood out, crowned by its 'neo-medieval' crenellated tower. Everything seemed quiet and normal, except for the lingering fog that enveloped the coast.

Falco shivered slightly in the cool air before closing the shelter door and going back in.

Captain Robert Morris had attentively studied the foam-rubber model of the beach at Le Dramont. In a cove near Naples, the American naval officer had ordered a strenuous work-out for the crews and assault battalions of the eighty-four assorted ships in his landing fleet, making them rehearse the minutest details of everything they might conceivably have to do on D-Day. But the American officer did not want to believe that the landings might be as disastrous as he feared.

Precisely three minutes after the first assault troops had gone ashore at the far end of the Anthéor inlet, Morris and twenty-three of his LCIs were under the tip of the promontory at Le Dramont. The entire Camel Green sector covered a stretch of beach barely five hundred yards long, surmounted by steep rocks and hills. Aboard LCI 19, Morris couldn't repress a feeling of tenseness and perplexity, even though he knew the beach wasn't mined. He was chary of the guns here, and was afraid that there might be some pretty rough going.

The swarms of LCIs transporting the 141st Regiment's assault troops surged forward under a sky that was reddening with explosions. To the infantrymen of the Second and Third Battalions crouched low in the tossing boats, it seemed that, instead of dissolving, the coastal fog was even thicker close to the beach. But they plunged straight on into the woolly mass.

From his post aboard LCT 625, which was transporting part of the 753rd Tank Battalion, a young Royal Navy officer, Lieutenant T. R. Evans, could glimpse something looming up out of the fog, a weird silhouette that resembled a fortified tower. The eerie sight chilled his heart. Like Lady Macbeth's castle, the islet had abruptly jutted out of the mist, and Evans did not know whether it harboured any gun batteries. So far there had been no indication. As a precaution, the young lieutenant began issuing orders over the intercom to slow down to avoid the rock. The beach at Le Dramont was only a few hundred yards away, in front of the first lines of landing craft.

The keening sound of the rockets overhead had just ceased, and the LCIs were now proceeding amid an unnatural and ghostly silence. Not until they approached within fifty yards of the beach did the fog begin to show signs of drifting away. And still Le Dramont's guns were quiet.

When the entire flotilla of LCTs and LCIs finally emerged from the misty curtain, the enemy guns let loose from one end of the beach to the other. The battle had at last begun. As the landing ramps were being lowered, sharp bursts of ack-ack and a few scattered volleys from

75-mm. guns responded to the fire of the Allied troops' automatic weapons. Strangely enough, the redoubtable German heavy artillery remained silent. As they swarmed across the beach, 'without even having got their socks wet,' the men of the 141st made for the narrow rocky strip, not without the unnerving feeling that a trap was about to snap around them.

The engineers of the 540th Engineer Beach Group landed and began advancing under the protective fire of machine guns and sharpshooters. However, nothing of all that they had been led to expect was evident. There were no mine fields, no booby traps, no serious obstructions of any kind – only some barbed-wire networks and a few scattered metal barriers. The beach itself was a pebbly strand littered with fragments of crushed grey rock, the by-product of the porphyry quarries. This was the residue that the Germans had earmarked for use in building the Mediterranean Wall's fortifications. The delivery of the major part of this material had been successfully delayed by the skillful machinations of Louis Marchand, an SOE[1] agent.

The demolition squads quickly rammed home their Bangalore torpedoes and disposed of the barbed-wire entanglements planted at irregular intervals. The job turned out to be so simple and the men were so expert about it that the 540th's engineers were almost instantly in a position to assist the infantry, setting up their own heavy machine guns, firing grenades in response to the enemy's attacks, and generally supporting the two assault battalions in a sweep designed to wipe out the nests of Germans defending the exits from the beach.

Evans's uneasiness grew as he stood on the deck of his LCT. As the moments flitted by, the silence of Le Dramont's guns worried him increasingly. He refused to believe that they had all been knocked out by the bombardment. Mainly, he was afraid that he might get there just too late – after the guns had opened up and before he had had time to hit the beach and get his tanks ashore.

The infantry platoon leaders of the 141st Regiment, who were taking heavy fire along the shore, were awaiting the tanks with the same anxiety and impatience. They, too, were suspicious of the unnatural failure of the German blockhouses to respond. As the smoke from the bombs began to clear away over the beach, the men could clearly make out the positions of the guns and concrete turrets on the bunkers that ringed the greyish rocks, like a frowning, beetling brow overhanging

---

[1] Special Operation Executive. This was the most extensive of the Allied secret services, 'stretched out like a net over a world at war,' with its strands centered in its London headquarters. At its head was Major General Sir Colin Gubbins, who had led the British Expeditionary Force in the 1940 campaign in Norway.

the beach. Each man was wondering just when the Germans would decide to begin firing. They might easily have been spared all their anguish. The guns of Le Dramont, whose unreal silence was the cause of so much concern to these soldiers and sailors in the early hours of the Second D-Day, were not likely to open fire, for the simple reason that they did not exist.

The blockhouses designed to house the guns were empty. Not a German soldier was found in them, and the guns that were to have been installed there were still biding their time in Toulon. This was the vital intelligence that Marchand had transmitted to London. But for some reason he had not been able to convince the Allied experts of its accuracy.

A German navy warrant officer named Karl Heinz Riecken was stealthily crawling on all fours through the pine underbrush, heading toward a 75-mm. gun battery situated three hundred feet above the beach at Le Dramont. He was completely covered with grime and dust, his face and hands were bruised and scratched by rocks. In fact, Riecken felt that he should pinch himself to be sure that he was still alive. For an incalculable length of time, he and his few remaining gunners had sweated out the 'carpet of bombs.' Just when they thought that the aerial bombardment might be over; an awsome naval barrage had unleashed all its might, forcing the Germans to hug the ground again. Riecken knew that the ensuing lull was only a prelude to the real thing, with the certainty of sudden death stalking them. A feeling of desperate courage seized him, and he was determined to put up a good fight, at least to have the satisfaction of making the Allies pay dearly for his life.

The previous day, after the Allied planes had blasted his battery, Riecken and his men had gone to work grimly and furiously, and by dint of enormous effort had sifted through the wreckage. They had salvaged two of the four guns and somehow contrived to patch them together so that they were able to fire. The men, totally exhausted, had just returned to their shelters. Riecken himself was getting ready to turn in when the telephone in the blockhouse rang. The call was from division headquarters:

'All troops to be withdrawn immediately! Allied landings expected at dawn in your sector! Prepare demolition fuses and assign a few men to the battery. The charges must be set to explode only at the moment the enemy enters the battery. . . .'

The order broke off as abruptly as it had begun. It was a bleary-eyed and dejected Riecken who shook his men out of their sleep. He had no illusions about the withdrawal order. It would be impossible to execute it in the darkness in an area in which Resistance fighters were lurking everywhere.

With three volunteers, he set the explosive charges in place around the guns. The men then drew straws to see who would remain to blow up the battery. Finally, Riecken and the others – about twenty soldiers – started marching in the darkness along the coastal highway towards the nearest base of operations, the village of Le Dramont. Stooping under the weight of the arms and ammunition that he could not bring himself to abandon, staggering occasionally, and completely absorbed in his own gloomy thoughts, Riecken slogged along at the head of his small, silent column. Although they had only a few miles to go, it seemed to him afterwards that they had trudged for hours. He wondered whether this was a general retreat and whether any action was going to be taken against the invaders. He was so lost in thought that he did not hear the first planes approaching. When he finally realized what had happened, he was lying flat on his face in a ditch, with fragments of rock and steel whizzing around him. Riecken did not know how long he had remained prone along the roadside. His men had scattered in every direction, wherever they could find a semblance of shelter. The fighter planes seemed to be flying lower each time, and the bombs were falling thicker and faster. Each time Riecken tried to lift his head to assess the situation or to rise up to give first aid to his wounded men he was knocked down by the concussion from another cluster of bombs. The aerial fury finally slackened, and during this brief pause the straggling band of dazed and shaken survivors came within sight of the hills of Le Dramont. There Riecken hoped to find some troops who would be able to help him organize some sort of resistance. But just as they reached a blockhouse overlooking the beach, the air again shook violently and a deluge of naval shells began to batter the shore. Riecken knew then that things had really begun in earnest – the long-awaited landings were imminent, and he and his men were trapped in the heart of the invasion sector.

The bullets were flying and the bursts from the American machine guns crackled sharply in the heavy, moist air, literally shaving the needles off the pine trees in the grove in which Riecken had sought refuge. The bomb craters and the clouds of explosions from the rockets gave off a nauseating stench of rotten eggs. Suddenly a rift came in the fog, and from behind the smoke screen Riecken was able to see the fleet of landing craft, with rows of boats streaking toward the shore and still others coming in behind them – the most fantastic array of vessels he had ever seen. But the sight did not dampen his fighting spirit, and he felt no urge to call it quits.

Just as the ramps on the landing craft began lowering, Riecken raised his arm and let it drop, giving the signal for his men to open fire on the growing clusters of Allied troops on the beach below. From his observation post on the opposite side of the road, it seemed to Riecken that the ack-ack guns also started up and that there was a general fusillade. Under the hail of concentrated fire, the Allied soldiers on the beach began scattering, throwing themselves down and taking shelter wherever they could. Despite himself, Riecken had to admire their nerve under fire and had to admit that they could take it. He watched as the American engineers with their mine-detecting gear continued to advance, saw others coolly setting up their machine-gun positions without wasting a second, or taking aim and firing their bazookas across the beach toward the German positions. Behind these troops on the beach, new waves kept pouring in, and the waters of the small bay were crammed with miscellaneous vessels and amphibious craft.

The shooting from his own light artillery had begun to weaken, and Riecken now found himself directly in the line of Allied fire.

Half-crawling and half-running under the protective pines, he made his way to a big automatic gun concealed among the trees. For some reason the gun had jammed. Riecken saw a few of the gunners frantically working over the weapon, and others crouching in a trench. He dashed toward them, yelling furiously:

'What are you waiting for, you idiots? Load that gun and start shooting!'

Within a few seconds, 75-mm. shells again began raking the beach below. But Riecken was soon to regret his rashness. The LCTs were getting ready to unload their tanks, and after a few minutes of sporadic shooting, the one piece of heavy artillery that might have at least temporarily checked the Allied rush across the beach had exhausted its meagre supply of ammunition.

While Riecken was frantically squeezing the trigger of his submachine gun, the last artillery shell was fired. A few minutes later he was aghast to see an infantry master sergeant starting off toward the beach brandishing a white flag, a handkerchief knotted around the end of his bayonet. Angry and disgusted, Riecken dashed out and yanked the sergeant back, snatching the 'dirty rag' off his rifle. The German began to blubber as he blurted out:

'*Mensch! Es ist alles vorbei!*' 'It's all over! It's crazy to go on fighting!'

Riecken paid no attention to him, and ran back up to the blockhouse, where an interesting sight met his eyes.

In a deserted shelter, two of his men had just found two *panzerfaust* and were getting ready to fire them. In a frenzy of excitement, Riecken seized one of the weapons and pointed it toward the shore on which the American tanks were about to land.

From between the tree branches directly below him, Riecken could see an amphibious tank making steadily for the shore. He let it approach, and when it had come within ten yards of land, he took aim and fired.

A cloud of black smoke mushroomed up from the armoured turret, and the tank stopped dead. Riecken's men were shouting, pounding one another on the back.

'*Prima! Prima!*' 'Great!'

Flushed with triumph, Riecken immediately reloaded and began looking about for a second target.

One of the twenty-one LCTs – LCT 625, commanded by Lieutenant Evans of the Royal Navy – was maneuvering to land alongside the beach. As its ramp was being lowered, Riecken sighted and fired again. This time he aimed too high, and the shot missed the tanks, which continued advancing imperturbably. But it struck the bridge of the LCT.

Hearing the shriek of the oncoming missile, Evans ducked to one side, but it was too late. His helmet fell off and rolled at his feet as the Briton slumped forward, mortally wounded.[1]

The tank of the 753rd Battalion on which Riecken had scored a hit and which he thought had been destroyed, had a gaping hole in its armour, and the water that streamed in flooded the diesels. After working over them for half an hour, its crew succeeded in getting the tank on to dry land. It took some time before the seven other tanks of the 753rd, deployed along the narrow strip of rock, were finally able to neutralize all the defences at Le Dramont. When the enemy fire began to abate, the crews hauled themselves out of the turrets, removed the floating gear, and the tanks were ready to fight on land.

Now that they had come within six hundred yards of their landing sector, the 753rd's tankers were amazed to find themselves in a sector that had already been virtually conquered. The dry rattle of the Schmeissers and heavy machine guns was dying out, and in some places had totally stopped. A few stray shells ripped through the air, but there was no serious resistance as the tanks wound their unwieldy way through the village of Le Dramont. The quarries near the beach were conspicuously empty – not one German soldier remained in them. As one of the witnesses to the scene remarked later, 'After all that fuss on the beach, the quiet that followed was such that we might have been

[1] Evans was the only fatality of the Camel Green landing. Shortly afterward, his ammunition exhausted, Riecken surrendered.

taking a stroll out in the country.' Meanwhile, the sky had grown less mottled, and the heat was rising. A new kind of stridency greeted the ears of the advancing troops – the chirping of the first crickets of the day.

One of the tank units assigned to the 141st Regiment, lumbering along the road to Le Dramont, overtook a column of German prisoners who had been captured near the Camel Green sector. They were being marched to an open space in front of a small chapel, and among them were Warrant Officer Karl Heinz Riecken and the twenty men of his battery.

Not far away, Mario Falco was looking on as the prisoners filed past, their hands over their heads. He wiped his face and neck with his big checked handkerchief. Although he had scarcely slept the night before and had had his full share of excitement, he did not feel the least bit tired. Falco had been in the thick of all the bombardments. In his opinion, the most terrifying had been the lightning-like barrage of rockets fired at the beach – they had fallen right around his shelter. He felt that he had been 'more frightened by the landings than many of the Germans had.'

When the first troops of the 141st Regiment had leaped ashore under the enemy's fire, they had been amazed to find a French civilian waiting for them on the beach, on his head a beret perched at a jaunty angle. Since that dramatic moment, Falco had not been idle. He had guided a patrol of the Second Battalion through the wooded paths of Le Dramont, skilfully avoiding the mine fields, all the way to the radar station and the signal tower. Hands in pockets and cigarette between his lips, Falco had witnessed the spectacle of the Germans emerging from their shelter, and as they passed in front of him he kept tally, gloatingly – there were twenty-two of them.

The day was growing hotter as the sun climbed in the heavens. The room was smothered under a layer of fine powdery white dust, and a snarl of telephone wires cluttered the floor. The American two-star general leaning on the stone balustrade of a Provençal garden near the seaside was resting his eyes on the glowing flower beds and on a tree of Judah, near a bush of blooming oleanders. From time to time, the low growl of gunfire disturbed the air around the villa.

Removing a fine white Philippine linen handkerchief from his pocket, he slowly mopped his brow, turned from the garden, and strode back into the living-room. Underneath its heavy beamed ceiling, the room was teeming with the hustle and bustle of assorted staff personnel. A few men were perched on stools, tacking up on the wall a long relief map of the invasion sector. There was the endless coming and going of intelligence officers from regimental command posts, and division liaison officers kept rushing in and out through the double doors. The telephones never stopped ringing, and messages were pouring in and out, from and to every place at once.

The villa itself had been built during the early years of the Côte d'Azur's popularity, when the French Riviera had become the chic place to go. Now the house was serving as the first Allied headquarters on the coast of Provence. By a coincidence, it was the residence of Louis Marchand, but the Resistance leader was far away at the moment. In fact, he was in London listening to the BBC newscast announcing the landings at Le Dramont. He was sure that his house, which stood near the beach, had been completely destroyed.

Most of one wall in the living-room was occupied by a huge bookcase with glass doors, crammed with books, some of which, to judge from their mellow bindings, were fine early editions. Framed prints hung on either side of the bookcase, but no one had time to look at them.

General Dahlquist bent over the long oak table in the middle of the room and examined the map on which officers armed with blue and red grease pencils were marking the positions and movements of his 36th Division. Although Dahlquist felt optimistic, a long, hard day still lay ahead of him, exactly as he had been anticipating for some time. As soon as the first messages from the troops on land had reached him aboard the *Bayfield*, he knew that he could not stand it any longer and had informed Admiral Lewis that he was going ashore. Lewis, secretly envious, had wished him all the best. Although his troops had been the last to land, Dahlquist was the first division commander to set foot in Provence.

At Le Dramont, Dahlquist found himself in the middle of the assault zone. The town of Saint-Raphaël was a bare five miles to the left, and Anthéor lay at about the same distance to the right. By now, one of his three regiments, the 141st, had landed on the beaches near Anthéor and Le Dramont. The second, the 143rd, was in the process of landing a few dozen yards away, and the third, the 142nd, was still aboard the LCIs waiting to attack the formidable beaches of the Gulf of Fréjus. Its objective was Saint-Raphaël itself. The attack was scheduled for early afternoon.

The lead battalions of the Texas Division were thrusting deep into a large pocket of enemy resistance, which had turned out to be erratic; it was concentrated in spots, weak in others. Dahlquist watched as the red and blue lines on the map traced the steady advance of his men, right on schedule, occasionally even a bit ahead of the timetable. To

Dahlquist's mind the situation conjured up the image of a sharp scalpel slicing its way through a spongy abscess.

As the first interrogations of prisoners were to reveal, the German plan of defense for the Camel zone had been strangely lacking in coherence. The plan had relied largely on the fighting capacity of scattered units of unequal quality, all more or less left to their own devices. Moreover, their efficiency had been impaired by acts of sabotage and harassment by the Resistance. So far, the 36th Division's assault troops had reported no retaliation by the *Luftwaffe*. Not one German plane had yet appeared in the skies over the invasion area.

Dahlquist went back out through the French windows and leaned on Louis Marchand's garden balustrade.

He was satisfied with the developments, but the game, although well played up to this point, was far from won. Of this fact Dahlquist was sharply aware. Not for an instant did he have any doubts about the inevitability of the Allied victory, but he could not help worrying about the price his troops might have to pay for it. He could hear the reassuring rumble of the invasion from less than a hundred yards away, and he could see the tanks, the DUKWs, the parade of jeeps, trucks, ambulances, and bulldozers being unloaded on the sand. As the minutes slipped by, he also saw the silvery antiaircraft balloons rising and glittering in the sunlight in ever denser clusters, over the land and sea. From the shore out to the rim of the horizon, the Mediterranean was thronged with every possible type of vessel speeding toward the coast or back out to sea. It all had gone smoothly so far. But Dahlquist's thoughts dwelt anxiously on the nearly two miles of heavily defended beach from the mouth of the Argens river to the entrance to Saint-Raphaël.

The hands of the general's watch pointed to 10.15 A.M.

7

ON THE MORNING OF AUGUST 15, near the village of L'Isle-sur-la-Sorgue, near Avignon, Maurice Pons, a railway switchman, was strenuously pedaling his bicycle, trying to get home in a hurry. He had just gone off night duty at the Petit Palais station two miles away, and he was eager to reach his house in time for at least a quick nap. After all, it was a holiday, and his wife had invited some cousins for lunch. As he bent over the handlebars, Pons heard the sound of planes far off over the Durance and the Rhône rivers, and his fear of the Allied bombers, which had been mercilessly pounding the railways and highways, inspired him to double his speed. But the blue sky above him remained empty.

Reaching the outskirts of town, he saw little sheets of yellow paper fluttering in the morning breeze over the fields. Curious, he stopped to pick up what he imagined was some sort of advertisement. At first he did not grasp what it was all about.

The text was in French, and began: 'The armies of the United Nations have landed in southern France. Their objective is to drive out the Germans and to effect a junction with the Allied forces that are advancing through Normandy.' At the top of the sheet was a design of crossed American, French, and British flags. The statement was by General Sir Henry Maitland Wilson, the Allied commander-in-chief for the Mediterranean theater, and the leaflets had been dropped by planes during the night.

After a quick glance around to be sure that no one was looking, Pons furtively crammed the leaflet into his pocket, and raced the rest of the way to his home. At that hour the houses in L'Isle-sur-la-Sorgue were just beginning to thrust open their shutters to welcome the radiant sunshine. Inside their homes set among carefully tended gardens or hidden behind neatly trimmed cyprus hedges, many of the town's 6,920 inhabitants were preparing to attend the Assumption Day mass at the Church of Our Lady of the Angels. Although a German garrison had been stationed here, as everywhere else, the troops totaled fewer than a thousand.

Bursting through the door, Pons slammed the leaflet on the dining-room table and began reading it to his wife:

'The French forces are participating in this operation. They are fighting alongside their Allied comrades at arms, on the sea, on the ground and in the air. The French Army exists again. With all its past traditions of victory, it is battling for the liberation of its homeland. Remember 1918! All Frenchmen, civilians as well as military, have their parts to play in this campaign in southern France. Your role will be explained to you. Listen to the Allied broadcasts, read the posters and leaflets, pass the word along to your neighbour. Help us to bring the conflict to an end as quickly as possible.'

During the morning, copies of the leaflet were picked up by families on their way to church, by people going to other nearby villages, along the back roads, in the fields and gardens, on *Route Nationale 22* between Les Vignères and Caumont, and on the banks of the Durance river.

Still more were found the length of the Rhône valley, in the remote hamlets of Provence, over the whole of occupied southern France.

Additional leaflets in foreign languages – German, Russian, Czecho-slovak, Polish, Armenian – were released about 8 A.M. by the last waves of Allied planes flying over the Mediterranean coast and the Iles du Hyères. They were designed for the garrison troops of General Friedrich Wiese's Nineteenth Army.

On this same morning, the commander of the 57th Bombardment Wing radioed a message from his base on Corsica to the Office of War Information[1] at the American headquarters in Naples:

'Today, 15 August 1944, two million nickels released on to assigned targets.'

Oscar Dystel, a former magazine editor, was in charge of the propaganda leaflet section in Algiers. It was Dystel's first experience outside the United States, and it had taken the 1942 landings in North Africa to get him to Algeria. Although he spoke only English, he had at his disposal a carefully screened staff of some twenty British, American and French officers, as well as a team of experienced translators, including many civilian refugees from Germany and from the *Wehrmacht*-occupied countries. Since February, 1944, Dystel's section had been entrusted with the task of composing the leaflets that were to be dropped for D-Day in Provence. He was using printing presses in Algiers and in Bari, Italy, and was obliged to resort to all sorts of devious means to find the necessary paper, printer's ink, and material for illustrations. Above all, secrecy was of the essence. One misplaced copy of a text could compromise the entire invasion. Lieutenant Colonel V. C. Armitage was the officer in charge of security, responsible for surrounding everything with the most impenetrable veil of secrecy.

On Sunday, 13 August, an incident occurred that, years later, would still give the shivers to Dystel and his assistant, Stevens Salemson. The printing was finished in Algiers and Bari, and the leaflets for the Second D-Day were to be flown to Corsica to be placed in special containers for distribution to the pilots of the Bombardment Wing. In Salemson's presence, the containers were filled and then sealed with adhesive paper. He was responsible for their distribution, and was making a final inspection, item by item, before the B-25s took off.

'Suddenly,' as Salemson has described it, 'a great gust of wind ripped open one of the containers that had not been securely taped, and hundreds of leaflets went fluttering out over the airfield.'

Salemson immediately alerted the military police unit assigned to guard the planes, and the MPs managed to retrieve every copy of the

[1] The office of psycholgical warfare during World War II.

wayward leaflets. 'The soldiers were crawling around on all fours on the landing strips,' Salemson says, 'and I knew that if any one of these men who had involuntarily been let in on this secret talked, the invasion that was scheduled for only two days later would be a disaster.'

In addition to 'Jumbo' Wilson's message to the French people, the containers held two other leaflets advising everyone to 'keep the roads clear' and to 'collect every bit of pertinent information worth transmitting to the Allied troops.' The messages also urged sabotage by transport workers. Another set of papers that were dropped were 'surrender permits' for the *Wehrmacht* troops and for the foreign recruits who had been forcibly inducted into the German army. Maps were included, too, showing a simple, clear illustration of the entire invasion area. But for a long time, Salemson was haunted by nightmares of what might have happened if, through some unfortunate indiscretion, the contents of the OWI leaflets had been divulged to the wrong people.

The German leaflets dropped by the 57th Bombardment's Mitchells behind the Mediterranean Wall proclaimed:

'*Die Front in Süd Frankreich ist steht!*' ('The front in the south of France is now a reality!')

They provided the troops of the German Nineteenth Army with a wealth of details concerning the might of the Allied invasion forces, and the last line read: 'At this hour, the crucial question for you is to decide whether to die or to become prisoners of war.' The propaganda aimed at the Armenian troops exhorted them to 'stop fighting for Hitler and his clique.' On the night of 11 August, low-flying planes had dropped solemn warnings over the German positions:

'The time will soon be ripe for you to get clear of your present predicament. Be ready!'

The leaflets printed in Armenian had been Dystel's biggest headache. As he has explained, 'The nearest available special type for printing in Armenian was in Cairo. A copy of the text had to be sent to Egypt to be set up by the compositor, and the lead was then forwarded to Bari for final printing. Despite all these complicated steps, the secret remained well protected. However, the Armenian tracts, once they had been printed, were not, unlike the French and German texts, sealed and locked in the OWI's safes.

'Since the Armenian tracts were printed from special type, we figured that to a casual observer they might have looked like exotic recipes or even like excerpts from *Alice in Wonderland*. We didn't worry too much about them.'

Even among the German intelligence agents operating in Naples and Cairo, not everyone was capable of deciphering Armenian.

8

TEN MILES OUT AT SEA off Saint-Tropez, on the observation tower aboard the British destroyer *Kimberley*, Winston Churchill was scanning the horizon through binoculars. He could see line after line of landing craft filled with American troops steering steadily toward the French shore. After a while he put down the glasses, yielding his place to an American, General Brehon B. Somervell, and lighted up his sixth cigar of the morning, before going off to join Robert P. Patterson, the Under Secretary of War.

Although he had just about got over his resentment, Churchill still bore a slight grudge against the Allied staff. Two months earlier, on 6 June security people at SHAEF[1] had not allowed him to be in on the Normandy landings. Consequently, he had firmly resolved to make up for this slight by being present at those in Provence, whatever reservations he may still have had concerning Operation Dragoon. Churchill also sensed that he had a duty to discharge toward Operation Dragoon, a gesture of civility. As he had remarked to 'Jumbo' Wilson the previous day, it was not such a bad idea for him to show up at the scene of the very invasion that he had so stubbornly and vehemently opposed.

A Royal Naval officer, Captain G. R. G. Allen, hovered constantly at Churchill's elbow. Admiral Sir John Cunningham, who knew the intrepid Prime Minister only too well, had assigned a member of his staff to him. Allen's strict orders were not to let Churchill out of his sight for a single minute.

Cunningham had acted with good cause. After leaving Ajaccio at midnight, the *Kimberley* had steamed out to join the assembly of warships and other invasion vessels, reaching her destination just as the lethal fire of the naval guns began thundering down on the coast of Provence, fifteen miles away. The *Kimberley* had noticeably slackened speed, and Lt. Cdr. J. W. Rylands took pains to inform Churchill that he had been ordered not to approach closer than six miles from the beaches, because of the hundreds of floating mines. Churchill finally wangled it so that the destroyer did advance to within four miles of the shore.

The mainland looked as if it were buried beneath a solid layer of smoke, with tremendous explosions shaking the air and the earth. A

[1] Supreme Headquarters Allied Expeditionary Force.

continuous ribbon of flame wound from east to west, floating on the surface of the Mediterranean. The Allied guns had left off bombarding the beaches, and Churchill was biding his time. As far as he could judge, there had been no serious resistance against the landings, and the Provençal coast, at least for the moment, appeared to be devoid of any signs of the enemy. The steady streams of small fleets of boats and landing craft kept forming out at sea and heading for the shore, carrying troops, automatic weapons, tanks and ammunition.

Churchill had had his fill of all this. The burning questions for him now were 'How long will it take to reach Marseilles and go up the Rhône valley?' and 'How are these operations going to be combined with those in Normandy?' The *Kimberley* stayed around only a short while longer and then began slowly turning, weaving its way through the pack of cruisers and battleships, and headed back to Corsica.

The heavy morning air was calm and the thermometer was steadily rising. Churchill left the deck of the *Kimberley*, went down to the captain's cabin, and noticed a novel lying on Rylands's table. He picked it up and spent all five hours of the return voyage reading the book, which, he later commented 'kept me in good temper till I got back.' It was *Grand Hotel*, by Vicky Baum.

9

THE BEACH OF PAMPELONNE extends along two miles in the centre of the Saint-Tropez peninsula, about twelve miles from the bay at Cavalaire-Sur-Mer. The bay had been captured in less than an hour by Mike O'Daniel's battle-toughened veterans of the 3rd Division. On this summer's day, the fine golden sand sparkled invitingly in the sunlight, speckled with occasional tangled clumps of seaweed cast up by the tide. But this pretty spot had been saturated with mines, and was now punched full of craters. Shifting slightly in the faint sea breeze, the clouds of artificial smoke concealed from enemy eyes the troops swarming ashore, the teeming activity of the demolition squads inching along the beach with their mine detectors, and the continuous arrival of fresh convoys of reinforcements and supplies that were hitting the beach from one end to the other of Alpha Yellow.

The drone of an engine overhead partially drowned out the din of battle, and a plane resembling an enormous black, glistening insect tore through the moist air, to hover briefly over the water before diving down into the smoke curtain. One of Commodore C. D. Edgar's six LSTs had been converted into a sort of miniature aircraft carrier, complete with flight deck. It could accommodate four Piper Cubs, whose pilots were veterans of close-support reconnaissance missions. One of the Piper Cubs had just taken off, practically on the heels of the assault wave, and was now reconnoitering over enemy territory.

A squad of men from the 2nd Battalion of the 36th Engineer Beach Group heard the plane pass over as they kneeled at their work, groping their way forward, using the tips of their bayonets to detect the mines in the sand and remove the fuses. Farther away, Colonel Richard G. Thomas's men, who were forging their way inland, raised their heads at the sound of the plane soaring through the pale sky.

So far the going had not been too rough for the assault battalion of Thomas's 15th Regiment. The infantrymen had landed at H-Hour, trailed by the tanks of the 756th Tank Battalion and the 601st Tank Destroyer Battalion. In fact, everything had gone off in fine style. Within forty minutes of reaching land, the first two assault battalions, closely followed by a third which had quickly leaped ashore, had established a firm beachhead on the Pampelonne shore. They had easily disposed of the obstacles set up along this stretch of coast. The mine fields extended no farther than a quarter of a mile inshore. A few random shells did come hurtling down on the beach, and bullets sprayed out from the surrounding hills, but the enemy fire had practically ceased by the time the infantrymen and tanks left the beach and started off through the heavy brushwood and scrub, over land that had once been marshes and was still flat, but planted with occasional patches of trees. Even on the various roads, including the main highway to the two communities nearest this landing area – the old Provençal village of Ramatuelle on the west and Saint-Tropez on the east – the 15th Regiment encountered no major difficulties. Nor were there any serious obstacles to delay the advance of the tanks and armored vehicles. The first eight assault waves had discharged their cargos well within the allotted time, and coming in behind them were more troops, tanks, trucks, DUKWs with fuel and ammunition, LSTs loaded with pontoons ready to be set up by the engineers, all of them about to land on the beach. John Da Bell, a soldier of the 15th, recalls how amazed he was to stumble across a few perfectly harmless little cabanas still standing peacefully intact amid the clutter of barbed wire and mined traps at one end of Alpha Yellow. This place struck him as 'one of the unlikeliest sites for the battles being fought in an obscure corner of ancient Europe by the warriors from the New World.' To the habitués of the French Riviera, it was anything but obscure – it was their glamorous Tahiti Beach resort.

Meanwhile, the Piper Cub that had taken off from the LST was pursuing its course, without, however, flying over the interior of the peninsula. It had encountered no flak, and the pilot felt that it was safe to come down a little lower. As the plane lost altitude, it dipped one wing, and the pilot could see the impressive and majestic spectacle of the entire invasion front spread out below him, all the way from the yellow strand of the Alpha sector to the ominously protruding dark red cliffs of the Esterel beachhead, the whole pageant standing out starkly amid the fog and smoke. From time to time, part of the bedlam reached his ears – the clatter of machine guns, the muffled thunder of the big guns, the screech of shells seeking their target, all the inextricably mingled confusion of the artillery duels that were being fought in the valleys and among the hills behind the coast. Some columns twisted symmetrically up through the bluish air along the full length of the fighting front. The guns of the German shore fortifications, which had been expected to put up a fierce resistance to the invasion, maintained an ominous silence. Everywhere, over miles and miles of beaches and rocks, troops and supplies were spilling in at an unbelievable pace.

The plane remained aloft a few minutes more, plunging through the mist. The pilot leaned out once again.

Directly below, at a spot that was isolated from the main arena of combat, he saw the town of Saint-Tropez, with its majestic big white hotel, the fortified walls and moats of its ancient castle, and the steeple of its venerable church. The place looked empty and forsaken. As far as he could judge, the Germans were not showing much activity down there. Having noted the 'total absence of any enemy presence in the bay,' the pilot radioed his report to fleet headquarters and, almost reluctantly, turned back to rejoin his carrier.

For a moment Captain Jess Walls of the 509th Parachute Battalion thought that he had heard the noise of a plane motor high above him. When he looked up, he could see nothing and decided that it had been a delusion.

Although the situation had changed slightly since dawn, there had not been any significant improvement in Walls's predicament. Wandering with his three-hundred 'lost' paratroopers in the wooded Saint-Tropez peninsula, he still felt isolated and at a loss as to what he should do.

As he had expected, the landings a few miles away on the beach at Pampelonne had proceeded on schedule. But, before that, Walls and his men had sweated through two frightful hours of bombardment by their own planes and warships. Some of the paratroopers, including even the veterans of the heaviest fighting had begun to feel as if they might go out of their minds. Still, there had been no casualties. Winifred Eason, a paratrooper second class, believed it was 'a sheer miracle that they had been able to endure the snarling plane attacks, the hail of bullets and bombs, the vicious blasts from the big naval guns and still come out in one piece.' Now they were trying to estimate their distance from the sounds of far-off fighting along the beaches that echoed over the hillsides and through the pine trees. From time to time they were able to distinguish the long bursts of American machine guns answering the barks of German Schmeissers, now close by, now far off, almost swallowed up in the unknown region of deep woods and wild, untamed valleys. Shells erupted here and there, and through the hazy air a rash of brush fires was flaming up.

After some hesitation – he was without maps or orders – Walls had resolved to act on his own. He had no notion where the Germans might be holed up. It was possible that the nearest American troops had not even made it beyond the beaches. For all he knew, they might still be held up in the tangle of obstructions, threading their way through mine fields, and nailed to the ground by fire from the enemy pillboxes and batteries. Walls was forced to admit that even if he had succeeded in making himself visible to the pilot of the lone plane that he thought he had heard, it wouldn't have solved his problem. He reflected gloomily that he was caught in 'the damnedest hornets' nest that anybody had ever seen.'

René Girard, the local Free French leader, had not given up arguing with Walls, begging him to join forces with the Resistance fighters.

One of Girard's men, who had slipped through the enemy lines, came racing over from Saint-Tropez, breathless and exhausted, but elated. Walls would never forget the man's excitement and his exultant smile as he, too, joined in the discussion. He had brought a message of victory. After blowing up the port, most of the German troops had fled from Saint-Tropez, and the townspeople, who were gradually filtering back, were eagerly and impatiently awaiting the Allies' arrival.

The three men exchanged a long, silent glance.

Finally the American's response came. 'O.K.'

And Walls ordered his men to attack.

Later in the morning, the same messenger delivered his news to Colonel Thomas's infantrymen, who had landed on Pampelonne beach and were ready to attack the town from the coast.

Following their involuntary and unscheduled landings in the woods and fields around Saint-Tropez, the 'misplaced' gunners of the 463rd Parachute Artillery Battalion – victims of a navigational error and handicapped by poor visibility – had recovered the scattered pieces of their artillery and had assembled the guns. So far they had been able to set up five howitzers and had retrieved a fair amount of ammunition.

With Girard's Resistance fighters enthusiastically leading the way, the paratroopers of the two lost battalions and a few men from some other strayed outfits started marching toward Saint-Tropez, over the hills of Saint-Anne and Belle-Isnard, at about the same time as Walls and his two companies from the 509th. They had about two miles to cover. During this impromptu operation, the paratroopers of the First Airborne Task Force, almost without firing a shot, captured two German antiaircraft batteries intact and two other coastal batteries complete with all their gunners, who were in pretty much of a daze because of the rapid turn of events.

The men of the 463rd and 509th had firmly expected to meet some desperate last-ditch resistance from the German units left behind in the blockhouses and pillboxes to defend the entrances to Saint-Tropez. In the end, the paratroopers engaged in surprisingly little fighting. In fact, Walls was amazed to see the entrenched Germans emerging from their positions over the countryside, holding up their hands and letting themselves be disarmed with disconcerting ease.

For a great many of these German soldiers, surrender to the Allies spelled the end of their troubles; this much was clear from the remark they kept repeating: '*Krieg fertig!*' ('The war is over!').

Walls became obsessed by the sound of those two words, and when he learned their meaning, he felt a complete revulsion. As they continued their advance toward Saint-Tropez, the three hundred paratroops, still cut off from their units, gradually gathered a horde of some 240 prisoners of war, nearly as many willing captives as there were captors.

10

THE FIGHTING IN SAINTE-MAXIME was nearing an end. In the church belfry, the air became more suffocating every minute, but the twenty soldiers who had shut themselves up in it refused to surrender. Although they belonged to the oldest age group in the German army and were

NAVAL MESSAGE

PRINCE DAVID

From:

CTF 86.

17h45

Following received from CTF 86.

TO COLONEL BOUVET. THE OFFICERS AND MEN OF THE ALLIED NAVIES
ARE PROUD TO BE ASSOCIATED WITH YOU AND THE GROUP DE COMMANDOS
IN THIS BATTLE TOWARDS THE LIBERATION OF FRANCE. MAY GOD
BLESS YOU AND KEEP YOU. REAR ADMIRAL DAVIDSON.

141722B

COL.
SNOL.

LIGHT P /L   TO: 1725   PARKER.

*Pass to Prince Albert and Princess Beatrix
and return to Colonel Bouvet.*

Photograph of a message sent to Lieutenant Colonel Georges-Régis Bouvet,
commanding the African Commandos, the first group to be plunged into action on
the beaches of Provence. (*Photo courtesy Robert Laffont*)

Task Group 85-12 meets Convoy SFIA off the west coast of Corsica on August 14, 1944, to form Task Force 85 en route to the invasion of Provence. SFIA on the horizon is followed by the battleships *Texas* and *Nevada*; the French cruisers *Montcalm* and *Georges Leygues*; and the *Philadelphia*. (*Photo U.S. Navy*)

En route to the drop area, paratroopers smoke tranquilly as they approach the coast of France. (*Photo U.S. Information Services*)

battle-weary, they continued to hold out. The men belonged to a company of former customs officers who had been incorporated into the 242nd division. As recently as the previous day they had still formed an effective unit, serving as the vigilant slave-drivers for Italian war prisoners and French civilians requisitioned for the forced-labor gangs. And now here they were, defying the Americans in a last determined stand, squeezed together in the tight confines of a church tower, coughing and gasping with the dust and heat, many near collapse. Most significantly no more shots were being fired from the church.

The old church that the Germans had been using as an arsenal contained enough ammunition for a siege of several days. Voices from the square below shouted up at the embattled twenty to give themselves up. Through the wooden slats in the belfry, the soldiers were being treated to a grand spectacle – the tops of palm trees, a sun-drenched port and beach, a bay swarming with ships that were bearing down on a shore already teeming with Allied troops, and, on the right, the town hall with an American flag fluttering gently in the soft, sultry air. The church was still encircled by a dense network of barbed-wire entanglements. It was also now beginning to be surrounded by the local townspeople, who had emerged from their basements and shelters and were mingling with the American troops of the 157th Regiment. The Americans were leaning casually against the walls or sitting nonchalantly on the sidewalk, waiting. For the men of General Eagles's 45th Division who had just beaten their way through the wall at La Nartelle with hardly a scratch, their landing was beginning to seem more like a 'friendly little scrap, nothing to write home about.'

The Germans' position was hopeless, and they knew it. The twenty men were cramped into a space barely large enough for five. Over half of them were willing to show the white flag and get it over with, but a few diehards insisted on continuing to resist, threatening to blow up the church, with themselves in it.

By now it was past 10 A.M. Every once in a while an American of the 157th would get up, casually aim his rifle at the church tower, and a few brief shots would ring out. Then, since the Germans had ceased returning any fire, and since the church doors remained stubbornly closed, the soldier would sit down again, his rifle propped between his legs, and devote himself to munching peacefully on his chewing gum.

Suddenly, from the throng gathered in the adjacent streets, a white-haired old lady stepped forward and walked boldly out on to the square in front of the church. She looked enraged and determined. Her name was Olga de Rodzienko, and she was Tschaikovsky's grandniece. She spoke German fluently, with just the trace of a Russian accent.

'Idiots! Fools! Imbeciles!' she shouted as loudly as she could. 'Come down right now! You don't have a chance in the world! Come down here and get it over with! There's no use putting it off!'

But neither the old lady's shouts nor the jeering and heckling of the crowd were having the slightest effect on the Germans locked up in the church.

'Make it snappy! Move before it's too late!' Mme de Rodzienko, livid with indignation, was still yelling.

A tall, gangling sergeant from the 157th Regiment gently grasped the composer's grandniece by the elbow and led her away.

'Take it easy, grandma!' he admonished her gently, as he steered the furious woman toward a sheltered spot under an overhanging roof on the square.

It took the arrival of the tanks to make the stubborn Germans change their minds. Two heavy, low-slung, armored mastodons, their turrets open, came waddling over the worn paving stones. The first tank of the 191st Battalion did not even come all the way up to the church, but ground to a halt in front of the jetty. The other maneuvered ponderously under the palm trees and aimed the muzzle of its 76-mm. gun straight at the church tower, poised to fire. One second later, a white cloth was seen hanging from the slanted slats of the bell tower, and the church doors were flung open. A shabby little band of gray-haired, haggard old men began shuffling sheepishly out into the sunlight. Some of them had on their *Wehrmacht* cloth visor helmets, and the others wore big, square-cornered caps. The first German to emerge carried an old broom with a piece of white rag knotted around it, and another had tied a handkerchief on his wrist. They came out hands up, gazing furtively around amid the taunts and jeers of the onlookers. Olga de Rodzienko stared stonily and silently as they filed past her.

Only a hundred yards away, the fighting was still going on, and German shells were continuing to crash into the Bay of Sainte-Maxime.

Six desperate men, the defenders of the Tobruk gun position – so-called in commemoration of the desert fighting and the Afrika Korps, for which Rommel had designed its use – were jammed into the blockhouse at the end of the jetty. They had barely enough room to stand erect. The ammunition for their lone gun was running low, and yet they kept on firing, creating a flurry among the 45th Division's troops, who by then had secured virtually the entire town.

The Tobruk consisted of a mobile tank turret set into a reinforced concrete bunker. The crew manning the 3-inch gun were economizing on ammunition, firing at longer and longer intervals, but they knew that the end was near. The six men had no intention of capitulating. And then they saw the sergeant running toward them.

The sergeant, a stout, florid-faced Bavarian, was puffing and wheezing as he scurried frantically along the jetty, tripping in the holes and stumbling, slipping and sliding among the man-made obstructions and rubble heaps. The obstacles, designed to thwart the Allied advance, had been set in place a few weeks before, and were the handiwork of the engineers. The sergeant's stocky figure clambered awkwardly amid the masses of rock, and his short legs maneuvered laboriously through the maze of stone, barbed wire and potholes. The six men at the far end of the jetty, packed in behind the gun slit, could see the dense throng of French civilians and American soldiers, together with the tanks against the background of the town. And then they saw something else. The sergeant who was painstakingly making his way toward the Tobruk was wearing a band of white cloth attached to the sleeve of his uniform. They must have smiled grimly as they observed his progress.

The fat sergeant struggled out to the tip of the jetty, sweat streaming down over his broad face. As he inched his way along, the Tobruk's 3-inch gun resumed its firing, and the sergeant could feel the shock waves from the shells streaking past him and could see the smoke rising over the turret. He wondered how much longer his comrades in the Tobruk would try to hold out. Of one thing he felt fairly sure – his own chances of coming out alive were slim.

The Allied bombardments had succeeded in making only a few dents in the Tobruk position. Its six gunners were one of the last bastions of German resistance at Sainte-Maxime. His white streamer dangling from his arm, the sergeant, who had been sent as an intermediary to his fellow soldiers, finally reached the entrance to the turret. As he disappeared inside, the door swung shut behind him, and that was the last anyone ever saw of him.

Dr Verdier had joined the gathering crowd of spectators near the port, all wildly excited. He has described the entire scene, with the LCIs and LCTs continuing to land on the beach under the intermittent fire of the Tobruk's gun. Candide Bagnoud, the post-office clerk, was also present, standing near the pier. Like everyone else, Bagnoud was peering into the distance, waiting expectantly for the white flag to appear over the end of the jetty. But nothing of the sort was to happen.

Finally, a tank of the 191st Battalion slowly maneuvered into position, out of the Tobruk's line of fire. The tank's great turret revolved, its gunner aimed at the battery, only fifty yards away, and let loose two rounds that sped straight to their target. Out over the water a huge geyser of dismembered bodies, shattered weapons and twisted metal spouted up amid the explosions and the swirling smoke of the disintegrating concrete.

11

TWO HOURS WENT BY, perhaps three. The turmoil had abruptly subsided. A sudden calm had settled in the air and over the land. Along the thirty mile expanse of combat zone, on the fringe of the beaches, the blue wavelets of the Mediterranean nudged gently at the warm golden sand, the winding stretches of flat stones, the coves and patterned rocks carved out by the wind and water. Except for the occasional whine of shellfire and the distant mutter of machine guns, the enormous battle front seemed wrapped in a kind of hushed expectancy, as if marking a temporary truce. The sun was at its zenith, beating mercilessly down over Provence in a turbulence of sharp light with scarcely a hint of sea breeze to relieve the sultry heat. The haze of the early morning had grudgingly given way, and small, clear blue waves were chopping listlessly at the surface of the water.

On the beaches, dank clumps of seaweed had been reduced to a gluey consistency by the thick gray ashes deposited by the firing of the guns all along the churned up strand. The landscape to the east looked as if the earth's blood were flowing down from the brick-red tops of the mountains, streaming down between the verdant slopes suspended between the Technicolor-blue water and the pale azure sky. Under the searing daylight, waves of hot wind blowing in from the interior wafted the fragrances of the hills – the heavy scents of the forests of Les Maures and Esterel, the pungent odor of eucalyptus trees, lavender and thyme, the sweetly-perfumed gardens and fields full of flowers. And over it all, rising up through the torrid heat, came the persistent chirping of undaunted crickets. This was the Mediterranean shore at its fullest and finest, the hour at which the coast was preening itself in all its natural glory.

Jean-Pierre Aumont, who was with the 3rd Division near Cavalaire-sur-Mer, has stated that he was taken aback by the calm and silence on all sides, which contrasted so sharply with the clashing violence of the fighting that had filled the morning. Not far away, Robert Wuillequey, a farmer in the Var region, found himself thinking that it was almost as if 'the good old days were back again,' the peaceful time when the *boules*[1] players could placidly enjoy their game under the shade of the plane trees. However, the scene of desolation around him brought him back to reality with a sharp wrench. His own house in Cavalaire-sur-Mer had suffered considerable damage from the fighting, and everywhere in the little town it was the same nightmarish spectacle, as if everything had gone to wrack and ruin. Roof tops had been blown off, doors and windows sagged from their hinges, walls were shattered. The town square, the railway station and the tracks were a sorry jumble of twisted wreckage and ashes.

In Le Lavandou, just outside the main landing area, Luce Ergen, a civil service worker from Toulon, had been spending the holiday with friends. In the ordinary course of events, she should have been packing her suitcase and getting ready to say good-by, because she was due back at work on Wednesday morning. But the long four-day weekend was far from over. Since the previous night, she had been caught up in the feverish exodus of the population, and her troubles were only starting. In a few hours, Luce was to find herself among the group of hostages whom the Germans had rounded up to execute in the forest around Bormes.

12

THE PLIGHT OF THE GERMAN LXII CORPS in Draguignan was growing more critical by the hour. Although the town had not yet officially capitulated, General Frederick's 5,000 paratroopers, fully equipped with all the matériel, guns and vehicles brought in by the gliders, were steadily tightening their vice and preparing for the final blow. All attempts at a counteroffensive by random units of the German 148th and 157th Divisions had consistently met with defeat. Moreover, the scattered items of information that filtered through concerning the Allied landings were both incoherent and contradictory. However, of all the conflicting reports, one fact remained certain. By now all the roads to the coast had been blocked off by the Allied paratroopers. General Ferdinand Neuling, in command of the LXII Corps, nevertheless continued to make routine phone calls to his superior, General Friedrich Wiese, 125 miles away in Avignon.

---

[1] *Boules*, also known as *pétanque*. A bowling game played in France with small metal balls. (Translator's note.)

At 2 P.M., at Nineteenth Army headquarters in Avignon, the heat was oppressive, almost unbearable.

The chief of staff, General Walter Botsch, sat at his desk mopping his brow. He had not had any sleep for over thirty hours. Since the previous evening, reports and telephone calls had been pouring in at a staggering rate. For Botsch, the night had been one of the longest and most exhausting in his life – and one of the craziest. Although his adjutant, Lieutenant Colonel Schulz, had thoughtfully had a dinner tray sent over from the officers' mess, Botsch had not been able to bring himself to eat, and the food was still lying there untouched.

Two new reports had just come in. One concerned the air and sea bombardment of Saint-Raphaël, leading to the conclusion that a landing was imminent in the area. The other, submitted by Colonel Rudolf Meinshausen of the LXII Corps staff, described the general failure of the morning's counterattacks, staged in an attempt to ease the threat of encirclement by the Allied airborne troops around Draguignan.

Botsch rose from his desk and went into the adjoining office, where Wiese and another officer, Colonel Allert, were standing in front of the big map that covered one wall. As the messages arrived, a captain busied himself shifting the positions of the colored pins that indicated the continual changes in the Allied positions. Theoretically, he was supposed to await confirmation of each item of information, but by now he had no choice but to rely on the initial reports in the order in which they were received.

'The LXII Corps reports that paratroopers are advancing east and south of Draguignan,' said Botsch. 'According to Meinshausen, there are more than 6,000 troops. They're attacking with antitank guns and equipment flown in by glider. Meinshausen is hoping that the 148th Division can supply him with infantry and artillery to fight his way out.'

Wiese took a closer look at the map. He, too, had had scarcely any sleep since the day before. But today, as always, he was freshly shaven, his ash-blond hair was neatly trimmed, and, despite his troubles, he retained his courteous and energetic demeanor.

In a sense, Wiese felt almost relieved. The situation that had seemed so chaotic during the night – an Allied paratroop attack on Marseilles had been announced and later denied – had become considerably clearer, and there was no doubt now as to what the Allies' intentions and targets were. Wiese did not think there would be any further landings, either on the Italian beaches or in the Languedoc region, and the Allies were surely going to try to take Toulon and Marseilles as a preliminary step to advancing up the Rhône valley to join forces with the troops that had come ashore in Normandy.

Shortly after midnight, emergency messages had begun streaming in at the Avignon headquarters, and had continued hour after hour, often minute by minute. If Botsch had lent credence to everything that had been reported, he would have had to believe that the Allied forces were everywhere at once – at Marseilles, Nice, La Ciotat, Bormes, Cannes, the Iles d'Hyères.

Actually, the first reliable information had been transmitted by the *Kriegsmarine*'s general headquarters in southern France, over the direct line connecting Vice Admiral Ernst Scheurlen's Aix-en-Provence office with Botsch's.

Captain Carl Jacobi had reported the news to the chief of staff: 'Two ships of the 6th Security Fleet have sighted the Allied invasion fleet! Allied destroyers have attacked our ships ten miles south of Saint-Tropez and off the Hyères islands!'

That message had been flashed at 5 A.M. And Botsch had his own bit of news to tell Jacobi:

'The enemy,' Botsch announced in a neutral voice, 'is reported to have attempted a landing in La Ciotat bay. Paratroops have been dropped around the town, in the area of the 244th Division.'

Jacobi interrupted him. He already knew about that. A few minutes later he called back.

'The reports from our batteries at La Ciotat and from the Bec d'Aigle radar station are positive, General. The Allies did attempt something in the area, but they were repulsed. For the past two hours everything seems to have quieted down again. Strange, don't you think? In my opinion, they were merely trying to sound out our defenses, but it's also possible that there'll be landings in the daytime from that direction. . . . Unless,' he added, 'all this is just another maneuver to fool us.'

'What makes you say that?' Botsch asked.

'But I thought you'd been told, General!' Jacobi replied. 'The troops that were parachuted over La Ciotat were only dummies!'

While Botsch and Jacobi were ruminating over the possible places at which the Allies might be likely to land, 5,000 airborne troops were parachuting over the fog-covered fields and vineyards near Draguignan. And this time there were no rubber dummies – these were real flesh and blood troops.

None of the Germans in southern France – not even Wiese – had ever cherished the illusion that it would be possible to push the Allies back into the sea once they effected a landing. Even if the Nineteenth Army had had the necessary manpower, equipment, tanks and guns, it would have been wishful thinking to imagine that they could cope with the superiority of the Allies' combined naval and air strength. Information gathered by intelligence agents concerning the Allies' preparations, their troop movements and the assembling of the invasion fleet, had enabled the Germans to assess thoroughly all eventualities, from both the technical and strategic angles.

By the time the LXII Corps had announced the landing of the first airborne troops, the radar stations that were still operating after ten days of Allied bombardments had also reported the presence of Allied mine sweepers and other ships cruising near the coast. Following this report, the rest was silence as far as the remote inland command posts at all levels were concerned. For some of them, this was their last contact with the assault zone, communications having been entirely disrupted along a distance of sixty miles between Marseilles and Menton. And even those remote posts which had been set up in localities whose inhabitants, for the most part, did not even know of their existence, had had their share of lethal Allied bombardments for an hour and a half.

Neither Scheurlen's Avignon headquarters nor the Château Saint-Ange, at Montfavet, where the *Luftwaffe* headquarters was installed, had been spared, nor had the Nineteenth Army headquarters at Avignon, General Baptist Kniess's LXXXV Corps headquarters in Taillades, near Cavaillon, and the division command posts at Aubagne, Brignoles, and Grasse.

Secluded in his villa on the Boulevard Monclar, Wiese felt that his situation was comparable to that of a man who had lost both arms and both legs. He was forced to take part in an unequal combat, and there was no way out. However, disciplined soldier that he was, Wiese remained clear-headed throughout the storm. He could not even be certain about the troops under his command. They were poorly armed, scattered along a line of a few hundred miles, and dazed and exhausted by weeks of disastrous air raids. The few crack regiments on which he might rely would, he realized, quickly be engulfed by the avalanche of Allied divisions, which would not be confined to the beaches very long by the defense works and fortifications of the Mediterranean Wall.

Wiese sensed the folly of even hoping to hold out against the Allied armed potential and equipment, nor could he remotely contemplate the possibility of containing the Allied attacks against Toulon and Marseilles, which he knew would inevitably follow within a week or so – two weeks at the most. During the intervening period, French guerrilla fighters would not be giving a moment's respite to his troops. They would be attacking everywhere, on the coast and in the interior, in the woods and in the Provençal farms, in the back alleys and along the highways, around the railways, and in the towns and cities themselves. The Resistance fighters would be making the Germans pay dearly for all those long years of occupation during which the *Wehrmacht* garrisons had had the upper hand, for all the suffering and privation, the rationing of foodstuffs, the requisitioning of human beings, the crimes of the Gestapo, the executions of hostages, the deportations. Wiese was also fully aware that the fighting in the Rhône valley would not postpone for long the ultimate outcome of the gigantic pincers action – the eventual junction of the armies of Provence and Normandy. In the light of the vastly uneven match that was about to be played, with the small and scattered units at his disposal, the frantic orders that were being issued by the *OKW* and by Hitler – 'hold out at all costs!' – clearly appeared what they truly were – the wild blusterings of madmen.

The Nineteenth Army commander's calm behavior made a deep impression on his subordinate, General Botsch. In compliance with the specific orders for such circumstances, the bulk of the coastal garrisons had begun their withdrawal, even before the Allies had reached the beaches. Before abandoning their positions, the garrisons stationed a number of rear-guard, or covering, detachments, composed mostly of members of the *Ost Legion*. As they retreated toward the interior and attempted to elude both the Allied planes and the French Resistance, the regiments affected by the withdrawal orders were supposed – during the night or early morning – to effect a maximum amount of destruction and demolition in the various ports and in the abandoned fortifications and ammunition dumps. It would appear that these orders were carried out with varying degrees of thoroughness, or that they perhaps did not apply to all the units in the combat area.

Shortly before dawn, a German infantry general, Otto Fretter-Pico, commanding the 148th Division at Agay, near Menton, left his command post at Grasse to inspect units along the coast near Théoule. His heavy gray convertible was within a few miles of Le Trayas when the thunder of the Allied bombers and fighter planes began crashing down on the German positions in the Esterel mountains. Seeing that the planes were coming over in steady waves, Fretter-Pico and his aide-de-camp hastily abandoned the car and dived into the nearest command post, on the slopes of the Pic d'Aurelle, one of the highest mountains in the coastal chain. Captain Burckhardt, commanding the 661st Eastern Battalion, placed his shelter and telephone at Fretter-Pico's disposal. The general, inadvertently caught in the full fury of the American 36th Division's attacks, was the only officer of his rank in the Nineteenth Army to find himself provided with a grandstand seat from which to observe the various phases of the Allied landings.

At headquarters of Army Group G in Rouffiac, near Toulouse, no one had been surprised by the night's chain of events. Just before dawn, General Heinz von Gyldenfeldt had been awakened by a phone call from Nineteenth Army headquarters.

'The invasion fleet is approaching the coast off Saint-Tropez,' Botsch announced. 'Therefore, we feel certain that the landings will take place there.'

A few hours later, Botsch's message was confirmed by teletype. 'Violent air raids and continuous naval bombardments' were reported in the sectors of Le Dramont, around Saint-Raphaël, and on the Saint-Tropez peninsula. Shortly afterward, another report from Avignon headquarters stated that 'fierce fighting was going on twelve miles from Draguignan' between Allied paratroopers and the German garrison. Twenty minutes elapsed before another message arrived, from the LXII Corps, announcing the arrival of over two hundred Waco or Horsa-type glider planes in the same area.

At Rouffiac, the general feeling was that the date and location had been correctly pinpointed by the small group of clever forecasters on General Johannes Blaskowitz's staff. A good many of these cocky young officers exchanged formal congratulations with one another. Late in the morning, at 11.17 A.M., Commander Edo-Friedrich Dieckmann's 611th Artillery Group in Marseilles reported a 'formation of enemy mine sweepers clearly visible on the horizon inside the limits of the off-shore mine fields.' This was the last message received by the Army Group.

A few minutes later, communications were cut off between Blaskowitz and the Nineteenth Army. The telephone stopped ringing and the teletype machines ceased their chatter. The last telegraph lines and special cables connecting the Rouffiac headquarters with the attack area had just been cut, either by enemy bombs or by Resistance fighters, perhaps by both.

Sixty hours earlier, Blaskowitz had transmitted to General Wend von Wietersheim the *OKW* order to proceed with his 11th Panzer Division to the Nineteenth Army zone. Von Wietersheim had reached the banks of the Rhône on the previous evening, and by now he and his armored columns should be across the river and rolling at top speed toward the invasion area. Or so Blaskowitz hoped.

Neither he nor Wiese had any remaining doubts as to the Allies' intentions, and the maps clearly pointed to the direction that would be followed by the enemy divisions after they had established a solid beachhead.

Blaskowitz hastily convened his staff just before noon and summed up the events that had taken place since the night before. According to him, the Allied attack had almost completely removed the threat that had been hanging over the German First Army, which was defending the coasts of the Bay of Biscay.[1]

Now that all danger from that direction seemed to have vanished, Blaskowitz, after consulting with *OB West* at Saint-Germain-en-Laye, ordered his officers to remain on the alert, ready to move within two hours. Because of the increasing difficulty of keeping in contact with Wiese's army, he had decided to transfer his entire headquarters immediately to Avignon. If luck stayed with him, he might just be able to get across the Rhône before it was too late.

13

AT HITLER'S HEADQUARTERS in Eastern Prussia, noon was about to strike. On this 15 August, the Führer had arisen late, as was his custom, and was still in his bedroom when Field Marshal Wilhelm Keitel, General Alfred Jodl, and the other members of his staff began assembling for the military conference scheduled for late that morning. All was in readiness. But there was plenty to worry about in the reports that had been arriving during the last twelve hours concerning the over-all situation. And Hitler still had not put in an appearance.

When Hitler finally walked into the room, Jodl, the operations chief, was struck by 'the Führer's haggard look and his air of overwhelming distress,' clearly discernible in his expression. His complexion was sickly under his prematurely white hair, his face and body were racked with nervous tics. Now, more than ever before, his features betrayed the traces of the burns he had suffered in the attempt on his life of 20 July. The look in his deeply sunken eyes, that 'magnetic look' that had subjugated so many men and moved so many mobs, was tense, uneasy and feverish. When he had been awakened that morning by his aide-de-camp, General Rudolf Schmundt, Hitler had learned the news that the anticipated Allied invasion had been launched at dawn.

---

[1] It would appear that the German High Command had never taken this threat very seriously. Two days before, the First Army staff had been ordered to withdraw from the Bay of Biscay toward the Loire area and to assume responsibility for the front with the Seventh Army of SS Colonel General Paul Hausser in the Orléans area. However, it was still felt that an Allied landing might take place on the Atlantic coast, and the *Luftwaffe* staff continued to be haunted by this possibility, notably in the Bordeaux region, during the night of 15 to 16 August.

Jodl fully expected that Hitler would immediately start firing questions about the new landings. Instead, addressing himself to Keitel, he asked bluntly:

'Any news from Von Kluge?'

The answer was negative. Jodl decided to plunge into the first reports on the Allied attack in Provence.

Going over to the wall map, Hitler scrutinized it intently and silently. Then, turning toward Keitel once again, he said:

'Get *OB West* on the line right away! I must speak to Von Kluge immediately!'

Since midnight there had been no further sign of life from Field Marshal Günther von Kluge, the successor to Von Rundstedt and Rommel in the West. Hitler had good reason for concern regarding the sixty-one year old Von Kluge, and not only because of the extra responsibilities that he had been having to shoulder on the Normandy front over recent weeks. Hitler held Von Kluge personally accountable for the Allied successes following the breakthrough at Avranches, which the marshal had been powerless to prevent. During the last few hours, at Hitler's request, Jodl had had several telephone discussions with General Hans Speidel, the chief of staff of Army Group B, concerning the possibility that Von Kluge might defect to the enemy. According to General Walter Warlimont, the basis for these suspicions 'undoubtedly lay in the fact that Hitler had reason to believe that Von Kluge was personally involved in the 20 July plot.' The Führer had frankly unburdened himself of his doubts to the members of his entourage – Keitel, Jodl, and Schmundt – blurting out his insinuation of the 'likelihood of Von Kluge's trying to establish contact with the enemy in order to negotiate the cessation of hostilities in western France.'

For once Hitler's instinct was sound. The truth was that Von Kluge had driven around for an entire day in an unsuccessful attempt to locate the American lines and to surrender to General George S. Patton, Jr., commander of the United States Third Army. As a precautionary measure, Von Kluge had been personally ordered by Hitler not to remain near the front, and to continue directing the fighting from his command post. Since then, not a word had been heard from him.

Keitel left the room to try to get *OB West* on the phone. But as Warlimont, who was not himself at the meeting, later recorded, 'It was impossible to put a call through to the commander in chief, west.' This no doubt precipitated Hitler's decision to strip Von Kluge of his command and to order his immediate return to Germany. To replace Von Kluge as *OB West*, Hitler was planning to send one of the last remaining members of his stable of ready-made marshals, Walter Model. Model was the stocky, heavy-set, mastiff-jowled officer who had halted the Soviet offensive on the Vistula. More important, he was a loyal, reliable National Socialist, and following the July putsch, he had been one of the first to send Hitler a message vowing personal fidelity.[1]

Sitting hunched over in his chair, his left hand leaning on the table and his right arm dangling and twitching, Hitler listened impassively and almost without uttering a sound as Jodl read the reports from *OB West* concerning the Allied landings that had taken place during the preceding night and that morning.

'The main assault area,' Jodl explained, 'appears to be centered on Saint-Tropez. The LXII Corps has reported heavy paratroop landings about twenty miles inland, and Allied troops have set up positions in a few small towns east of Toulon. The 11th Panzer Division has been assigned to the Nineteenth Army and is now on its way toward the landing area, but is encountering serious difficulties in trying to cross the Rhône.'

Hitler, his gaze riveted on the map, only muttered to himself. He evinced neither surprise nor impatience, and continued to keep silent. Most amazing of all, he did not even fly into one of his customary ranting, raging tantrums.

Most of those present at the conference that morning, have agreed that Hitler's behavior was strangely apathetic and that his attitude was one of extreme weariness and indecision. Obviously, he had ample cause for anxiety. There were the Balkans, the Eastern front, Italy, and the battles raging in Normandy. And now a new front had been opened in southern France.

From noon until the conference ended forty-five minutes later, officers kept rushing into the room with the latest reports on the Provence landings. The Army headquarters of Group G had packed up and pulled out of the Toulouse area and was en route to Avignon. The destruction of port facilities at Saint-Tropez, Nice and Cannes had begun.

Jodl resumed reading:

'The reconnaissance reports submitted at 11.20 A.M. by the *Luftwaffe* state that the Allies have a fleet of more than two hundred battleships and combat vessels backing up the landing troops. Eight landing boats,

---

[1] Von Kluge had fewer than three days of life left. When he received the order relieving him of his command and instructing him to proceed immediately to Germany, he made his preparations, leaving on 18 August. Riding in his staff car near Metz, Von Kluge swallowed a vial of cyanide. A similar fate awaited his predecessor, Rommel, who killed himself two months later, on 14 October.

including several tank transports, have been sighted in flames off the beach at Cavalaire-sur-Mer, and one cruiser has been hit.'

A few of the French divisions that had set sail from Italy and North Africa were still some distance out at sea, waiting their chance to come ashore. The fighting in the Iles d'Hyères was still raging. The *Luftwaffe* operations section considered this 'probably only a secondary operation designed to disrupt the communications lines between France and the Italian front.' It also predicted that 'the main attack would be forth-coming either in the Bay of Biscay or the Bay of Marseilles.' The report added that, in this eventuality, there was every likelihood of further Allied landings in the Gironde area, and that special surveillance had been set up in the Bay of Biscay.

Jodl and the other officers expected the Führer to attempt to gal-vanize the troops in Provence by issuing another all-out appeal for resistance to the last man, as had been his unwavering custom on previous occasions when the Allies opened new fronts. But this time Hitler made no move to do anything of the sort.

Instead, he seemed to be closed off behind a wall of silence. At moments his jaws appeared to be working 'as if he were silently grind-ing his teeth over some obstacle.' At last he began to come out of his lethargy.

'Nothing,' he snapped, 'must be allowed to fall into the enemy's hands! Especially no fuel! Everything must be destroyed! The ports must be blocked, the ships scuttled! All the supplies must be moved into the blockhouses and the shelters!'

Within the iron ring in which the *Wehrmacht* now found itself, the new Mediterranean front did not appear to constitute an event of crucial importance. No one in the higher echelons of the German command seriously believed that this new Allied attack would have any decisive effect on the course of events – at least, not for the time being. On this morning, the Provence landings were merely one more worry to be added to the High Command's list of troubles.

Hitler was getting ready to adjourn the conference and to lock himself up in his apartment.

To quote Warlimont: 'Hitler was still clinging to the illusion that the *Wehrmacht* forces would be able to check the Allied landings.'

The Führer did not bother to explain just how he expected to repulse the invasion. By now, the Allies had established solid beachheads, and their tanks and artillery columns were speeding inland to join up with the 5,000 paratroopers, while the sky over Provence again became dark with Allied planes and the naval guns remained in position offshore, ready to intervene at any place on the invasion front. Even before the end of D-Day, three entire American divisions would have completed their landings, while a few miles out at sea 50,000 eager Frenchmen were awaiting their turn to come ashore.

As the meeting drew to a close, Hitler, standing with his horn-rimmed glasses in his hand, appeared lost in thought. He finally gestured to Jodl.

Hitler agreed to cancel the frantic orders that had been issued to Blaskowitz and Wiese in recent days, and – this was even more extraordinary – he expressed his willingness to 'consider the measures to be adopted in the eventuality that the situation in France should become unfavorable.'

Keitel and the others listened dumbfounded. Jodl merely bowed his head and repeated:

'*Ja wohl, mein Führer! Ja wohl, mein Führer!*'

In the opinion of everyone in the room, this sudden about-face on the part of Hitler – who was exhausted and depressed, and embittered by the treachery and defeatism that were insidiously setting in around him – was the outstanding proof of his disturbed state of mind on the morning of 15 August. For the German High Command, and for the strategic operations room at Rastenburg, the invasion of the Mediterranean coast that had now been going on for half a day was to produce within twenty-four hours consequences that were as yet undreamed of.

Returning to his own office, Jodl picked up the phone and called Warlimont at *Sperrkreiss II* – the second echelon of command – half a mile from Hitler's headquarters.

'Get over here right away!' he exclaimed excitedly. 'The Führer has approved the withdrawal plans for France!'

Twelve hundred miles away, the advance units of General Wietersheim's 11th Panzer Division, after their forced march, were finally reaching the banks of the Rhône. Storm clouds were gathering in the skies over Provence, and a light heat haze was rising up from the river. The air was sultry and oppressive. Colonel Stenkhoff's Panther tanks were following in scattered detachments, ahead of the remainder of the division.

Two nights and one stifling, interminable day had gone by since Hitler had signed the order authorizing the movement of the 11th Panzer. The entire trip from Albi and Carcassonne – and, for certain units, from Toulouse – had been harassing. The division had not stopped moving night or day, but General Werner Drews, the chief of staff, who had reached Remoulins on the evening of 14 August, did not expect the main body of his regiments to arrive much before the late afternoon or evening of 15 August.

Dawn found the first units of the division still fifteen miles from the Rhône. By then, Von Wietersheim had received a radio message informing him that the invasion had begun in the Saint-Tropez area, more than ninety miles away. Stenkhoff and his tanks continued their desperate race against time. Through the early morning mist of the summer day, the churches and towers of Avignon were looming up across the river. But Allied aerial bombardments had knocked out five of the six bridges that spanned the Rhône from the coast to a distance of thirty miles north. To the best of Von Wietersheim's knowledge, the bridge at Pont-Saint-Esprit was still intact, and he decided to head there to try his luck at getting across with his tanks.

A scout who had been sent ahead to reconnoiter came back with bad news. The last remaining bridge over the Rhône had been destroyed at dawn by Allied planes. If Hitler had issued his orders for the 11th Panzer only twelve hours sooner the day might still have been saved. The tanks would have rushed to the front and Von Wietersheim would have been in a position to counterattack at the beachhead, or, at least, would have been almost there.

And so, under the continuous bombing and strafing of Allied aircraft, the élite units of the 11th Panzer Division began their pitiful struggle to cross the Rhône river. The planes were roaring over the water, diving and turning, strafing both banks at once, but the German armor was determined to undertake a crossing.

With their leafy camouflage still in place, the trucks loaded with ammunition and fuel, the tanks, the motorized artillery and the staff vehicles ventured forth on their perilous task. They were ferried over on hastily assembled barges provided by the Nineteenth Army Engineers – as Drews described them, 'jerrybuilt barges thrown together with any old thing that happened to be handy.' By the time Von Wietersheim's tanks had been able to re-form between Carpentras and Avignon, five days had elapsed since the first units had begun crossing the Rhône. They arrived just in time to cover the Nineteenth Army's retreat, without having ever got anywhere near Marseilles.

14

IT WAS JUST BEFORE 1 P.M. at the farthest sector of the beachhead. Arrayed along and behind the waterfront directly ahead, rising up from the blue water amid green hills and red rocks, the landing troops could see the friendly, random collection of bell towers and domes, the many-windowed façades of great luxury hotels, the palm-lined boulevards, the gardens and rooftops of a white city, a port and a deep roadstead – in short, all that goes to make up Saint-Raphaël. To the left a long line of fine sand curved off to the edge of the marshes of the Argens river delta adjoining the airport and a seaplane base.

This was Fréjus beach, designated as Camel Red on the invasion maps, the most critical zone in the sector assigned to General Dahlquist's 36th Division. In fact, such stiff resistance was anticipated here that the attack had been scheduled six hours later than the ones on the other beaches. The 8 A.M. H-Hour did not apply to the 142nd Regiment, which was to launch this assault. Theirs was Z-Hour, H plus six. The Germans had a stranglehold at Fréjus.

Naturally, the shallow waters of the Gulf of Fréjus, which were less than fifteen feet deep three hundred yards offshore, had been thoroughly and efficiently mined. The zone was saturated with all types of under-water obstructions – stakes, railway spikes, concrete pyramids loaded with explosive charges, cement cylinders containing still more explosives, and segments of tracks on the forward part of the beach – as well as every imaginable kind of obstacle designed to hamper the landing boats. For ten months, fantastic amounts of barbed wire had been lavished on the beach, and the German engineers had blown up the last few remaining houses along the flat, treeless shore, whose barrenness was punctuated only by an occasional scrawny cluster of reeds. The Todt Organization's laborers had been forced to throw up a fortified chain of concrete blocks several miles long, designed to provide machine-gun positions for General Johannes Bässler's 242nd Infantry Division. The harmless-looking beach huts and refreshment stands behind the crenellated wall were actually a camouflage for powerful long-range batteries, complete with a warren of communication trenches connecting them with observation posts, underground ammunition stores and concrete dugouts. All along, the Germans had believed that, if a landing were ever attempted in the Saint-Raphaël area, it would take place here. Consequently, they had outdone themselves in providing a warm welcome for the invading forces, and were confidently awaiting the onslaught, ready for anything.

For this zone, more than for any other, the landing timetable had had to be calculated to the last minute. Nonetheless, it had been necessary to allow six extra hours for preparing the arrival of the last assault wave that would be landing on the Provençal coast. By 1.15 P.M. the 142nd Regiment's boats were waiting less than four miles off shore, ready to whip forward toward the beach. This would be the signal for the naval guns to open up on Saint-Raphaël and the redoubtable fortifications around the Gulf of Fréjus. For the second time in five years – the first time was the assault on Toulon in November, 1942 – the barely two-mile-long stretch of Camel Red would be subjected to the massive firing of American, French and British naval guns.

The flashes of flame grew in intensity as the guns fired in a wild rhythm, aboard the battleships, the cruisers and the destroyers, and their barrels glowed with heat. Maurice Villechenoux, a gunner aboard the *Emile Bertin*, which was flying Admiral Philippe Auboyneau's flag, could 'see my ammunition disappearing right in front of me.' On the command deck, Captain Ortoli was worried that if this terrific rate of firing continued, 'the three turrets might exhaust their ammunition within twenty minutes.' Captain Toussaint de Quiévrecourt, aboard the nearby cruiser *Duguay Trouin*, was thinking the same thing. On the same ship, Warrant Officer Maurice Champlan, was letting loose round after round of his 6-inch gun at a mad rate, and reflecting that 'if things kept up the way they were going, everything would soon be finished in this sector and the working day would be over.'

A young American sailor named Richard Hayes was on board a boat in Captain W. O. Bailey's fleet of LCIs and LCTs. He thought that 'the spectacle was certainly worth the trip' and that it was 'the biggest and most fantastic show I had ever seen.'

'The shells were fired off in howling clusters right on a level with our heads before they zoomed onto the shore', Hayes says. 'It was a real nightmare, like being in the midst of a volcano that was splitting up. We tried to console ourselves by telling ourselves that the Germans in their shelters were having the living daylights pounded out of them.'

However, on the shore things were quite different. The German blockhouses continued to thunder and boom, their volleys rent the air, and a hail of lethal fire rained down on the assault boats. For three nerve-racking hours, Lieutenant Commander Maloney's mine sweepers had been trying to clear channels for the landing craft. The zone was considered so dangerous that a submarine chaser, the *SC-1030*, and seven more escort vessels were protecting the mine sweepers, while Admiral Morton Deyo's destroyers covered their approach with uninterrupted fire. But when he got to within five hundred yards of the beach, Maloney was forced to turn back because of the intense fire from the German guns. The navy called for air support, and ninety-three Liberators stormed off to pound the beach, circling the enemy position. They dumped 187 tons of bombs on the blockhouses and on

Saint-Raphaël itself. The stolid, robust *Catoctin*, which was less than a mile away, suddenly began to tremble like a leaf in a storm.

Admiral André Lemonnier clearly recalls this episode.

'In less than a minute,' he declares, 'those planes were pouring 220-pound bombs out of their bellies just like ballast sand being dropped by a balloon pilot, twice as fast as a machine gun.'

Despite this murderous attack, the German guns still continued to fire. The time was now 12.45 P.M.

A quarter of an hour later, Maloney's agile little mine sweepers again darted off toward the beach. Once more, one after the other, they were forced to beat a retreat to get out of range of the German guns. For the troops tensed in the overloaded landing boats, unnerved by the racket of the exploding shells and heavy artillery fire, Z-Hour was less than sixty minutes away.

Finally, in one flaming red salvo, six hundred naval guns of all sizes, from the French 6-inches to the 12-inches on the battleship *Arkansas*, opened up and swept the entire shore of the Gulf of Fréjus, beating at the beach defenses and inundating the town of Saint-Raphaël with a barrage of shells. Now it was 1.15 P.M. From where he was standing at the railings of one of the command ships, Signalman Jean Meirat watched as the town became completely engulfed in smoke, while an opaque fog gathered over the coast from points where flames were rising. When the smoke clouds began to roll away, the Saint-Raphaël water tower, which was the reference point of the entire Allied fleet, gradually emerged, like a smoking saucepan forgotten on a stove. Yet the town was still holding out.

The townspeople had burrowed in wherever they could to escape the furious avalanche. Many felt that they were doomed to die in their cellars and were calling down all the curses of hell on Germans and Americans alike. Many kept their sanity by doing things that would have made no sense under ordinary circumstances. At the height of the turmoil, an Italian workman, who was a notorious Communist, burst out of the basement in which he had been huddling since the beginning of the bombardment and ran halfway across town under the murderous barrage. When he reached his house, he went straight into the bedroom, snatched a large crucifix off the wall, and ran back the way he had come, dashing into the shelter with the figure of Christ firmly clasped in his arms.

The firing was continuing out at sea, but luck was again deserting the besiegers. Under the volleys of protective fire, the steel umbrella of the naval guns, more drone boats were now being launched. The remote-controlled craft contained ten tons of explosives each, and their purpose was to rid the waters of the mines and mined obstacles that the mine sweepers had not been able to clear.

Richard Hayes, from aboard LST 1019, which was carrying tanks of the 753rd Battalion, watched as the special landing craft tow-boats released their two drones. Aghast he saw that the drone boats had scarcely been set loose 'when they began cutting up something awful.' A few escaped completely from the control of the special vessels and 'went whirling crazily like ducks with their heads cut off.' Others went far astray and overshot their targets before finally exploding. For a few minutes, it was touch and go whether they might head back toward the flotilla of landing craft, and one of them had to be sunk by a volley from the American destroyer *Ordronaux*. The result of these mishaps was that scuttlebutt soon began spreading the word that the Germans had 'loused up the radio system of the damned robots.'

By then it was two minutes before 2 P.M. The assault troops of the 142nd were awaiting the signal to begin heading for the beach. Many of the men in the more than a hundred LCIs did not have a clear idea of what was going on around them, and felt more reassured than not by the roar of the Liberators and the booming of the ships' guns. The Allied troops elsewhere had been making successful landings for several hours, and not far away, the 143rd Regiment, which had come ashore at Le Dramont, was preparing to attack Saint-Raphaël. But many of the officers in the 142nd feared that the casualties at Camel Red might be heavy.

The firing from the enemy batteries seemed to have diminished somewhat. But, contrary to optimistic predictions, the guns on the Gulf of Fréjus had still not been silenced. The fortifications and blockhouses had resisted the combined efforts of the heavy bombers and the guns of the *Arkansas* and the *Tuscaloosa*, the *Duguay Trouin*, the *Brooklyn*, the *Argonaut*, the *Marblehead*, and the *Emile Bertin*. Amid the whining and shrieking of the shells, the sharper and more threatening clamor of heavy automatic weapons could be heard. From their solidly entrenched positions along the shore, the German machine guns spouted forth an unbroken stream of bullets, firing from behind the beach wall and through the slits in the blockhouses.

At 1.59 P.M., the invasion fleet began releasing an awesome new storm. A great whip of steel lashed out to sting the shore. The rocket boats, which by now had been reloaded, had just gone back into action. During the naval bombardment, a few of the rocket boats had withdrawn to a position in front of Saint-Raphaël, out of the enemy's range. Sergeant Donald Robinson, an engineer aboard one of the 142nd's landing boats, found grim satisfaction in the thought that 'each one of those rockets, which were being fired twenty at a time, was causing as much damage as a 4-inch shell.' The deluge of rockets and the simultaneous explosions on the shore were making a signalman aboard a command ship four miles out at sea do a lot of fast work. His blinker signal device was clicking like a castenet. For a moment, the officers on the bridge of the *Catoctin* almost thought that it was not the Allied fleet that was firing, but rather that the Germans had evacuated Saint-Raphaël and were blowing up everything behind them.

But this was only a passing impression. Under the continuous German barrage, the waves of assault craft were edging toward shore, yard by yard. From the enemy fortifications, from the camouflaged batteries, the guns kept hammering away, the projectiles crashed and thundered, churning up the water around the landing craft, whistling furiously and exploding over the crouching men pressed against one another in the small boats. Under the beating rays of the afternoon sun the full heat of day was scorching. A few minutes earlier, the infantrymen, sweltering under their heavy helmets and cumbersome battle equipment, had been envying the crews of the LCIs and LCTs who were stripped to the waist. But now the fervent wish of every man in the 142nd was simply to escape alive from the hell that was erupting all around them.

At 2.05 P.M., Captain L. B. Schulten, the assistant commander of the first assault group, radioed a message to his superior, Captain Bailey.

'Wave being held back. Request instructions.'

Two months earlier, Bailey had commanded one of the 29th Division's assaults at Omaha Beach, in Normandy. He now described the situation to Rear Admiral Spencer Lewis, aboard the *Bayfield*.

After a brief silence, Lewis asked:

'What do you think, Bailey? Any suggestions?'

Without a moment's hesitation, Bill Bailey replied:

'We should go in, sir! As quickly as possible!'

Lewis looked at his watch. It showed 2.30 P.M. – half an hour later than had been allowed for. Lewis had participated in the fighting against the Japanese at Midway, in 1942. Although realizing that battles were often won by taking a gamble, this time he thought it wiser not to tempt fate. He wondered briefly what the unfortunate Don Moon would have done in his place. All things considered, the morning's events had not gone off too badly in his sector, and no significant reverses had occurred except here at Fréjus. This was the only real setback. Of all the combat zones, the one assigned to the 36th Division had been the first one on which an army general had landed, less than an hour and a half after the first assault wave. Lewis would have given anything to know where Dahlquist was at this minute – how he might resolve the problem now facing the admiral.

Lewis had to make a decision of supreme importance. The assault troops in the landing boats, kept at bay by the heavy, punishing German barrage, were trying to hold up under the nerve-racking ordeal and were tensely awaiting his orders. Lewis decided to disregard Bailey's advice.

A few minutes later – minutes that had seemed like hours to the men under enemy fire – the *Bayfield* flashed a message to Bailey.

'Beach 264-A to be abandoned. All assault groups proceed to 264-B. Order effective immediately.' (The landing beaches from Cavalaire-sur-Mer to Anthéor were numbered from 259 to 265; six miles separated Camel Red from Camel Green, and the mission assigned to the troops landing on these beaches was to clamp the town of Saint-Raphaël in a vicelike grip.)

With the speed of a trail of flaming gunpowder, the orders reached all of Bailey's eighty attack ships. Standing at the bow of LST 1019, Richard Hayes was stunned to see the landing craft about a mile off perform a kind of intricate ballet pattern as they started to back off from the shore to escape the steady downpour of shells and bullets from the Saint-Raphaël blockhouses. At first, Hayes could not imagine what they were up to. The waves of landing boats were falling back; they were in full retreat under the onslaught of the German artillery, and Hayes was stricken at the sight. But he had his own job to do, and quickly recovered from his momentary feeling of despair and mortification.

About six miles from Saint-Raphaël, on the wooded slopes of Mont Vinaigre – 'Vinegar Mountain,' the highest peak in the Esterel range – a small band of isolated paratroopers also watched the retreat of the assault craft and felt that all was lost as far as they were concerned. Since the previous night, they had remained dug into the sheer ravines and steep paths near the mountain refuge at Le Malpey, waiting to be delivered by their own troops. The area was infested with Germans, but these isolated soldiers had had the good fortune to meet up with a courageous Resistance leader, Marceau Honorat. With a few other underground fighters, Honorat had matter of factly gone about rescuing and assembling the paratroopers, who had been dropped twelve miles wide of their objective. From their precarious perch on the Esterel heights, the group had followed all the successive developments in the battle. But now there was no doubt about it – the fleet was withdrawing. The Allied paratroopers were horrified to see the lines of landing boats and transports slowly maneuvering out of the Bay of Fréjus and proceeding east towards Le Dramont.

The smoke and the dust clouds from the bursting shells and the last exploding rockets were beginning to dissolve over the Fréjus beach. The veteran gunners and lookouts of the German 242nd Division could scarcely believe their eyes as they watched the Allied assault flotilla turn about and start out to sea.

The firing from the German guns became intermittent. The machine-gun bursts subsided, and the weary, haggard men, who had been steadily at their posts for three hours, could finally raise their heads. When the full realization of what was happening dawned upon them, they broke out into lusty cheers and victorious shouts.

'*Heil Hitler!*' We did it!'

They tossed their helmets into the air. Oldtime German reservists and *Ost Legion* recruits alike slapped one another on the back, leaping and howling in their exhilaration, delirious with triumph.

'*Wir haben sie ins Meer zurückgewerfen!*' 'We've pushed them back into the sea!'

Shouting boisterously, General Bässler's exhausted, grimy men were convinced that they had repulsed the entire Mediterranean invasion all by themselves.

In the secret plans of the Allied invasion, Fréjus beach (Camel Red) bore the code number 264-A, and Le Dramont (Camel Green) was 264-B. If all worked out according to plan, after their landing the Camel Red troops were to capture the marshy Argens river delta, break through to the coastal highway, and take the main bridges. They would then proceed to the town of Fréjus itself, about a mile inland. It was anticipated that Fréjus would be captured by the end of the afternoon on the Second D-Day, and also that the troops who had been parachuted over Le Muy would by then have joined forces with the men of the 36th Division.

The failure of the landing on Camel Red upset this phase of the planning. The naval attack was resumed the following morning off Fréjus and was tenaciously and courageously carried out to fulfillment by Maloney's mine sweepers and underwater demolition squads. Maloney lost three ships in the operation, but refused to call it off until forty-eight hours later, after an exhausting mission that had lasted five days in all.

As Schulten and the retreating Camel Red assault fleet passed Boulouris, the time was 3.32 P.M. Two minutes later, at 3.34 P.M. the LCIs with the three battalions of the 142nd Regiment aboard reached the rockbound shores in front of Le Dramont. Most of the men in the

142nd crossed the beach so fast that they never learned its name, and even for those who did, it continued to be known simply as Quarry Beach, because of the great grayish slashes in the porphyry rock overhanging the shore.

Among the troops who had been unable to land at Fréjus and found themselves still out at sea, were a French general and his First Armored Combat Command. General Aimé Sudre's orders read that he was to follow the 142nd ashore, to the left of Saint-Raphaël. But the setback at Camel Red had drastically altered the situation.

Warrant Officer Roland Pomarès, a Frenchman from Algeria, was on the deck of the troop transport *John Brinkenridge*. With a detachment of American Negro soldiers, he had just received his baptism by fire from the violent barrage of the German shore batteries. Pomarès recalls the shells and shrapnel that were coming at him in a steady stream, and also 'all sorts of objects floating haphazardly around in the water.' Opposite the beach there was a downed airplane, 'half-sticking up out of the sea, with no sign of its pilot.'

Second Lieutenant Jacques Moine of the Second Squadron of the French 2nd Armored Regiment, was aboard one of the LSTs. He felt intensely moved as Lieutenant Colonel Durosoy spoke over the public address system:

'We shall all reassemble at a point on the French coast, and immediately begin the battle for liberation. Help all who come to your aid. Destroy everything and everyone who resists you. Let us never forget that we are fighting on the soil of France.'

The troops of the First Armored Combat Command aboard the attack boats still thought that they were going to land at Saint-Raphaël, behind the first American assault wave, as originally planned. But Sudre had just been informed that his objective had been changed. His convoy had already swung around far to the left at a considerable distance from its original destination, opposite Sainte-Maxime. Sudre's convoy and first troops formed the largest armored group that was landing with the assault force. He found himself forced to do a sharp about-face and to cope with an entirely new situation, abandoning all the plans he had carefully worked out with his superior, General Touzat du Vigier, commander of the 1st Armored Division and with his adjutant, Colonel de Montgaillard. Instead of supporting Dahlquist's 36th Division on the right, he would be supporting Eagles's 45th in the middle of the invasion area and would be making his drive through the Monts des Maures instead of the Esterel.

Since the departure from North Africa, there had been so many orders and counterorders that Charles Stiegler, an Alsatian volunteer in a tank-destroyer squad, was not at all surprised by the change in destination. He was profoundly stirred at the imminent prospect of being back in France, having fled in 1941 from his province of Alsace, which the Germans had annexed. A radio operator, Pierre Rigal, gazed around at his companions on the LCI that was conveying them toward the shore, and was struck by 'how down in the mouth everybody looked, they were so nervous and wrought up.' He particularly remembers that 'out of the dozen or so men crowded together on the landing barge, no one was cracking any of the casual, coarse jokes or trading the crude banter that is part of servicemen's conversation everywhere.'

General Lucian K. Truscott, in command of the American VI Corps, had issued orders to Sudre to land on the La Nartelle beach, six miles from his original destination, ending his message with the words:

'Good luck and good hunting!'

Sudre, too, was silent and taut as he watched the shoreline draw nearer. The heavy keels of the LSTs scraped along the bottom, and the forward ramps, after a sinister sliding movement, opened out and down on to the soil of France. Most of the men were undoubtedly experiencing the same emotions as Jacques Augarde:

'I kept my eyes closed so as not to be aware of too much happiness too soon, just as you might recite a prayer that you don't expect ever to be able to say again. And then I bent down and scooped up a handful of sand, with the feeling that what I was doing was a private act, separate from anybody else's. What you feel at a time like that is what you yourself have created for yourself, for the sole joy of taking greater pride in your duty and of being more resigned in the face of adversity.'

What Private Daniel Sanchez noticed first of all as he began cautiously making his way across the beach was 'the wreck of the big concrete wall of La Nartelle, all caved in with gaping holes.' He also recalls the pungent fragrance of resin coming from a wooded area just beyond the sand where his outfit had quickly assembled. Everything around appeared to be calm.

Lieutenant Moine's feet had scarcely touched the ground before he was running off to join the other officers in his squadron up on the highway. Although his friends were all weary and haggard, their faces revealed a secret inner joy at being home. At that point they did not know what else fate had in store. They were blissfully unaware that they would all be keeping appointments in Dijon, Colmar, Sigmaringen and Austria in the ensuing weeks and months.

Rigal, the radio operator, looked up into the bright sky and saw

great waves of planes flying over, towing gliders. By now it was
4.30 P.M.[1]

15

THE ALLIES WERE PURSUING THEIR OFFENSIVE in all directions
inside the beachhead – at Le Rayol on the way to Le Lavandou, at
Cavalaire-sur-Mer, at Sainte-Maxime, around Saint-Raphaël, at Agay
and at Anthéor, along the cliff highway on the Esterel heights leading
to Théoule, and in Cannes. American troops and French commandos
were relentlessly tracking down and harassing the German 242nd and
148th Divisions, forcing them to retreat along the highways and through
the villages, the hills and the forests. By and large, all the objectives of
this Second D-Day had either already been attained or were about to be.
Even the troops that were going to attack Fréjus were beginning to
make up for lost time on the extra ten miles of marching, which were a
result of the change in landing beaches. John Dahlquist, as dead-set
on his objective as ever, had radioed Lewis aboard the *Bayfield* that he
firmly expected to capture the town by evening.[2]

The tanks were spreading out over the conquered beaches, shedding
their watertight sheathings and casting off the thick coats of grease
that covered the engines. Jeeps, trucks, and half-tracks were spilling
out reinforcements, ammunition and heavy artillery, and were bowling
along the highways under the scorching Provençal sun. Out at sea, the
Emile Bertin flashed a message to the *Catoctin* to report that she had
exhausted her ammunition during the attack on Saint-Raphaël and was
proceeding back to Corsica for fresh supplies. By now nearly all the
generals had disembarked from the transports and were on their way
to their command posts on land – John Dahlquist had been the first,
and Mike O'Daniel and William Eagles were the next division commanders to rejoin their troops inland. The officers of the VI Corps had
to wait until the 157th Regiment had cleared the road to Beauvallon,

---

[1] Dahlquist learned only an hour later (he could not be reached earlier) of the failure of
the attempted landings at Camel Red and of Admiral Lewis's decision to transfer the Fréjus
landing troops to Le Dramont. Dahlquist highly approved of this step, and Truscott was the
only one to express displeasure at not having been consulted.
[2] The First Battalion of the 142nd reached the heights east of Fréjus toward nightfall.
However, the actual attack had to be postponed until dawn, and Fréjus did not finally
capitulate to the 36th Division until 1.55 P.M. on 16 August.

near Sainte-Maxime. A long-standing arrangement had provided for the setting up of staff headquarters in this locality, specifically in a rambling, comfortable-looking house of some twenty rooms that had attracted the attention of the aerial photographers. It was the residence of Henri Desgranges, the director of the magazine *L'Auto* and manager of the *Tour de France*.[1]

Long columns of bleary, dust-covered, grime-streaked prisoners straggled along the roads. Under the merciless sun, wounded Germans in field gray and khaki uniforms, outdistanced by the tank and infantry regiments, were helplessly waiting for someone to come to their rescue. Beyond the ridges, in the crater-riddled fields and valleys, the great guns could be heard booming out, the 77-mm. shells were keening and screeching, the machine guns clattered, grenades were bursting in excited clusters around scarred houses and ruined summer cabins, around the gutted belfries of Provençal churches. The roads were cluttered with parked vehicles – old Renaults and Citroëns, decrepit carts and wagons, piles of deserted bicycles. All of them had been requisitioned by the *Wehrmacht,* all were now mute evidence of the frantic rush with which the Germans had fled in the face of the Allied invasion. The American armored columns wound their way along highways and byways strewn with burning cars and dead bodies – those of German and Allied soldiers, and also of hapless French civilians caught in the fighting.

Joseph Cherrier, a gardener, watched the dying flames as the Grand Hotel, the pride of Le Canadel, between Cavalaire-sur-Mer and Le Lavandou, burned to the ground. The sight that made the deepest impression on Cherrier was the bodies of the sentries of an Armenian auxiliary battalion – their throats had been slit before they could even give the alarm, and their bodies lay in a ditch along the highway. At the village of Les Arcs, near Le Muy, the postman, Marius Novo, had an unexpected encounter. As he was going out of his house, he was hailed by a stray paratrooper. The village was still solidly in the grip of the Germans, and the men of the First Airborne Task Force had not been able to get a foothold yet. Mustering up his smattering of English, Novo went over to the soldier and whispered:

'Friend! O.K.!'

The postman nearly leaped into the air when the paratrooper, who happened to be one of the airborne forces French guides, answered:

'Cut it out! You're no more an American than me! *Sé voulés, vous parléi patoi?*' ('If you'd rather, we can talk patois.')

[1] The *Tour de France* is an annual bicycle race, lasting most of the month of July. (Translator's note.)

The German garrison at Le Muy was putting up a stubborn resistance. One officer had taken cover in the church tower and was maintaining a solitary vigil, firing at everything that moved. At the entrance to the village, on the road to Vidauban, another equally determined and fanatical captain had been fighting since dawn. His men had fallen one by one, leaving only the captain and his orderly, who continued to pass him the ammunition as he stuck to his post behind a machine gun. When at length it became obvious that it was useless to resist, the captain dashed back into his quarters. A few minutes later, he emerged, freshly shaven and in parade dress, to surrender to the 517th Regiment's paratroopers, whom he had been keeping at bay for several hours.

16

SHORTLY AFTER 4 P.M., a dull roar could be heard in the sky, gradually increasing in volume and drowning out the tumult of the battle, the racket of the machine guns, and the screaming of the shells.

General Otto Fretter-Pico, in command of the German 148th Division, and Captain Burckhardt, at the head of the 661st *Ost*-Battalion, were at their observation post in the Esterel mountains, on the tree-covered slopes of the Pic d'Aurelle. They gazed intently as a swarm of tiny black dots swerved up over the water. The onrushing planes appeared to be endless, and they looked somehow heavy and slow. Fretter-Pico, however, refused to believe that they were bombers, and Burckhardt was inclined to agree with him.

'Probably paratroop reinforcements,' the captain suggested.

The general stared steadily through his binoculars at the approaching planes, and was eventually able to distinguish successive formations of ten or twelve Dakotas towing gliders. Fretto-Pico wondered about General Neuling, who was sealed off and trying to put up resistance in Draguignan. At that moment, the LXII Corps was vainly attempting to reach Fretter-Pico and request reinforcements to aid in the defense of the encircled headquarters.

The gliders were also seen by Kurt Schroeder, a Berliner from the 148th Division. The day before he had been lazily sunbathing and swimming in the Mediterranean. Since midnight, he had been beating a retreat through the Argens valley, near Fréjus, laboriously picking his way northward. In a farmyard at Le Puget, he had just found an old French tractor, which he had used to recharge his radio batteries, and was now hastily transmitting a report to the division headquarters about the approaching gliders. As they came directly overhead, Schroeder thought he counted at least three hundred, flying toward the interior.

'Just when the fellows in Grasse were begging for more details,' Schroeder recalls, 'my batteries went dead for good.'[1]

Not far away, Private First Class Sam Kibbey, a member of a mortar platoon from the 143rd Regiment, attacking Saint-Raphaël, was scaling a steep hillside, with shells bursting all around. It seemed to Kibbey that he suddenly 'understood what war really meant' when, along a narrow path, in the bright daylight, he stumbled upon the twisted wreckage of a bicycle with 'bits of an arm and a leg scattered near it, and, still covered by a grimy gray uniform, a shapeless mass that had once been the body of a German soldier.' Despite his hatred of Hitler and the Nazi regime, Kibbey could not help feeling 'just a little sorry' for the dead soldier. 'Even a kraut,' he thought, 'deserves a death less horrible than what this man got.' The grisly mess made him sick to his stomach, and he averted his eyes. He could hear the drone of the planes 'zooming right along, deep into the interior.'

The gleaming waves of C-47s and gliders streaking past at two-minute intervals were now well past the coast, flying at an altitude of about 1,200 feet above the hills and fields, headed for Le Muy. As the great armada of over 370 gliders proceeded inland towards the positions occupied by the still isolated First Airborne Task Force, the German antiaircraft batteries reacted only sporadically. Not a German fighter plane appeared in the sky.

For the second time since dawn, reinforcements were being brought in for General Frederick's paratroopers, who were holding the positions they had captured to the south, the east and northeast of Draguignan. At 7 A.M. on the dot, a massive Allied air raid had been launched against the city. But Sergeant Joseph Blackwell and his special group from the 517th, who were to have synchronized with the bombardment by infiltrating the city and capturing General Neuling and his staff, had been parachuted too far away to accomplish their mission. The raid caused many casualties, and fires broke out over the city. A few bombs landed on the jail and enabled several French patriots who had been arrested by the Gestapo to make their escape.

---

[1] Schroeder miraculously made his way through the combat area without getting captured, escaping from both the paratroopers and the 36th Division. His route took him from Grasse to Vence, thence to Nice and Menton, and finally to Tende. Schroeder wound up the war on the Italian frontier.

The heavy ground fog had taken its time about clearing, but the sun finally broke through. The first wave of reinforcements – 138 gliders – had not been able to land until 9.30 A.M., nearly an hour and a half after the time scheduled for this operation. They were bringing in the first jeeps, mortars and antiaircraft guns, along with more machine guns, ammunition and supplies. The battle was raging around Le Muy, Les Arcs and Trans-en-Provence, and farther eastward along a combat front some twenty miles long, in places where the airborne troops had not been supposed to land, around Fayence and Saint-Paul-en-Forêt.

However, as the paratroopers passed through the tiny hamlet of Callas with its fields of olive groves, they saw worshippers calmly coming out of church after mass; life was going on as usual. At 5.30 A.M. that morning, Mme Imbert, whose husband was in the Monaco guard corps, had caught the Draguignan-bound train at Grasse. She was on her way to Callas with her two children, whom she was going to leave at their grandmother's for the rest of the summer vacation. She felt that they would be safer there than on the coast. She found seats in a coach where there were already about fifteen German soldiers and a warrant officer, on their way back to the Draguignan garrison. The train crossed over the plain outside Grasse, went through the Colle Noire forest, and it was not until they reached Fayence that Mme Imbert noticed the first parachutes draped in the trees and saw American troops firing nearby. Although the men of the 517th saw the train, they made no attempt to halt it. The Germans in the coach at first could not believe their eyes. When they realized the full significance of the situation, the soldiers quickly took refuge under the seats and in the train toilets, while the warrant officer pointed his Walther pistol at the civilian passengers. Mme Imbert drew a deep breath as she got her children safely into the station at Callas and watched the train pull out and continue calmly on its way.

By noon the Allied forces had cut off and were barring all the possible roads and junctions along which German reinforcements would have to pass in their attempt to stem the invasion and reach the coast around the Sainte-Maxime and Saint-Raphaël beachheads. The vicelike grip of the airborne troops – the British Second Brigade, the paratroopers of Lieutenant Colonel William P. Yarborough's 509th Battalion and Woody Joerg's 551st Regiment – was steadily tightening around Draguignan. Four hours later, the 602 Glider Field Artillery Battalion's pilots and the crews in the 12th Air Force's Dakotas that were towing them were gazing down on the rectangular patches of vineyards, the trim fields and wooded hills that were being held by the First Airborne Task Force. Scattered brush fires were blazing over the sun-baked countryside, and the intermittent smoke from exploding shells wafted gently up in the hot air along the back roads.

The Dakotas gradually lost altitude until they were less than 1,000 feet over the Nartuby plain. As the signal was given, the bellies of the C-47s opened up to release their clusters of paratroopers. Behind them the Waco gliders with their heavy loads began their own oblique descent to earth, shuddering and whirring in the wake of the tow planes, and the 602nd's troop-filled Horsas got ready to land. In each of the light wooden gliders the co-pilot, seated at the right front of the long, light wooden craft, checked the angle-indicator to make sure that he was either slightly above or below his tow plane, not directly behind it. Otherwise, he knew, the air currents would cause the glider to oscillate and the cables connecting it with the plane would snap.

One of those aboard a Waco glider in the second wave was Corporal Jean Folliero de Righi, who, the evening before, had been forced to yield his place to a war correspondent. An American military police sergeant had agreed to take the Frenchman on as excess baggage, and they had spent nearly five hours crossing the Mediterranean. Before the take-off from the Italian airbase, De Righi had given vent to his enthusiasm by scribbling on the glider fuselage the words '*Marseilles, mes amours.*' He was now bracing himself for the imminent scraping and splintering of wood that would accompany the Waco's landing.

The pilot released the cable, and the great wooden bird with the spindle-shaped wings plunged earthward, steering sharply down, plummeting like a rock. As it released its landing gear, the heavy craft began skimming over the tops of some pine trees, at about fifty miles an hour, and finally came to rest in the middle of a vineyard. De Righi picked himself up and crawled out, limping – in the confusion of the landing, he had been cut on the leg by his own knife. He limped to a nearby farmhouse, whose occupants were gathered in the doorway. They were overwhelmed with joy when the young paratrooper spoke to them in French, and everybody embraced him like a long-lost son. He got directions to the road to Le Mitan, the airborne command post, less than a mile away. There de Righi hoped he would find his friend Jacquemet, who had been parachuted the night before.

In Draguignan, a Resistance leader named Cazelles was cautiously making his way along the Rue des Minimes, hugging the walls, when he saw the paratroopers floating down and the gliders landing in the distance. The town was still holding out, and Cazelles scarcely expected it to capitulate before nightfall. What dismayed him the most was the prospect of further Allied air raids that would inflict more devastation on the city and more suffering on its sorely tried population. Still, he was buoyed with joy. Along with a few fellow Resistance workers, his friend Garrus, a veteran underground fighter who had been arrested and tortured by the Gestapo, had just been freed by the Allied bombs that had miraculously struck the jail a few hours earlier.

The steady waves of American and British gliders kept piling in. Some of them encountered concentrated German flak the minute they appeared on the horizon. Others landed amid a bucolic and somewhat disconcerting calm. The gliders were, as one observer saw it, 'packed together like a swarm of flies,' wing to wing, so that they occasionally wound up in tangled heaps, littering whole fields between the hills of Rouet and the villages of La Motte, Trans-en-Provence, Les Serres, Clastron, Les Esclans, and around Le Mitan and Le Muy. The planes dug up huge clouds of dust as they hit the ground. According to witnesses, the famous 'asparagus stalks,' the wooden stakes that the Germans had liberally planted over the countryside, in some cases actually helped the pilots to bring the gliders to a stop. But, some of the fragile craft were impaled on the filed sticks, the pyramids of sharp rocks and the grapevine stakes, and were completely shattered. Out of the crumpled fuselages, everything came rolling and spilling – equipment, weapons, the 75-mm. guns and ammunition eagerly awaited by the airborne troops who were ready to start closing in for the big push on Draguignan. There were jeeps, too, that would soon start rolling over the roads and picking up the wounded.

Over a hundred gliders had landed at Valbourgès, on James Stevens's property. Wrecked hulks, shreds of wings and fuselages lay strewn over his gardens and vineyards, in the fields and among the rows of plane trees near the château where, only twenty-four hours earlier, everything had been so calm and peaceful when Stevens took his last stroll of the day around the pool just before sunset. The château of Valbourgès had now become a mad beehive, buzzing with armed American soldiers and crammed with military vehicles and equipment. It was serving as both a hospital and a morgue for the casualties of the preceding night and morning.

At Saint-Roseline, the command post of Colonel Rupert Graves and the 517th Regiment, near one of the glider landing zones, little Jacqueline Cézilly, for the first time in her life, was staring at a dead body – that of a German soldier lying in a pool of blood near an ivy-covered wall. The same Germans who, only hours before, had been such a source of fear were now mere human wrecks, groaning with pain and begging for water as they lay helplessly under the scorching sun. The man had just died as she watched, and Jacqueline had felt a deep shock as she saw him become motionless and limp, his mouth

Major General John E. Dahlquist, commander of the 36th Division, was the first division commander to set foot in Provence. He debarked at 10 A.M. August 15, 1944, on the beach near Le Dramont. (*Photo courtesy Robert Laffont*)

Studying invasion plans on board the British destroyer *Kimberley*. *Left to right:* Lieutenant Commander J. W. Rylands (commander of the destroyer); Lieutenant D. S. Sanders (the navigator); Admiral Sir John D. Cunningham (C-in-C Mediterranean); and General Sir Henry Maitland Wilson (Supreme Commander Mediterranean Command). (*Photo Imperial War Museum*)

Allied troops and equipment pour ashore on the beaches of southern France. (*Photo courtesy Robert Laffont*)

gaping open. The appearance of the airplanes and the hundreds of parachutes floating in the blue sky brought a momentary diversion to the eleven year old girl, who had been so abruptly plunged into the fantastic and bewildering realities of war.

The screeching waves of oncoming gliders plummeting into the fields and on to tree tops brought more scenes of catastrophe and death. One glider struck an oak tree and crumpled, killing all its occupants instantly. Another fell amid a row of great cypresses that sheared off its wings, like an enormous guillotine, sending the fuselage crashing to the ground. Still others turned over several times before finally smashing against outlying buildings, or disgorged their cargoes pell-mell over the hedges and fields. The torn masses of dismembered gliders, like skeletons of giant birds stricken by bolts of lightning, covered the Nartuby plain, while the machine guns fired in the forests and shells continued to burst at irregular distances over the countryside. In the torrid afternoon heat at Saint-Roseline, the sounds of men moaning and groaning were audible from every direction and all through the house, and the kitchen had been converted into an operating theater. At Valbourgès, James Stevens and his family piled up great heaps of straw in the farmyard, away from the sun's rays, for the ever-increasing number of wounded men to lie on.

But by and large the casualties were light. Fewer than 175 men were killed or injured during these landings – representing two per cent of the total number of airborne troops brought in that day – and of the 407 gliders, 148 cracked up as they hit the ground or struck the obstacles set up by the Germans. By late afternoon, when the final wave of reinforcements arrived, General Frederick and his 9,000 combat troops had already captured five important towns. In addition to Draguignan itself, two of Operation Rugby's main targets, Le Muy and Les Arcs, both of them stubbornly defended by German garrisons, were not captured until the following day. By then, the paratroopers of the 509th Battalion, who had been fighting since dawn of the Second D-Day, had begun sending patrols off towards the coast and had joined up with the leading detachments of the 45th and 36th Divisions that had come ashore at Val d'Esquières and Le Dramont.

Meantime, the remaining men of Captain Jess Wall's 509th, together with the men of the 463rd Parachute Artillery who had strayed off course around Pampelonne, had gone into action and were attacking Saint-Tropez, north of the peninsula. For several hours the extreme heat was the main enemy of Walls's men and the troops of the 463rd. In the furnace-blast of mid-afternoon, paratroopers burdened with equipment were lugging the laboriously assembled matériel and ammunition that they had been carrying since morning and climbing up, down, and around the hairpin turns in the steep paths amid oak and pine forests filled with a concert created by the chirping and buzzing of thousands of insects.

Around 3 P.M. some of the units of Colonel Richard Thomas's 15th Regiment, which had landed at Pampelonne, came upon the paratroopers in the thick of a pitched battle. The airborne men, after pooling their resources with the local French Resistance, were tracking down the last few remaining Germans, and flushing out machine-gun nests and mopping up scattered German resistance points on the outskirts of Saint-Tropez and in the town itself. The hard-pressed but fanatical garrison was at bay, and had withdrawn behind the ramparts, deep moats and high walls of the sixteenth-century citadel. But by now, except for this one last patch of diehard defenders, the town had been almost liberated, and could ruefully contemplate its devastated dikes, the ruined port, and the extensive damage to its houses. There were still some long, grueling hours to be lived through, and it was not until 6.30 P.M. that a white flag was finally hoisted over the citadel and began fluttering in the evening breeze.

One man was especially reveling in this moment of triumph. René Girard felt that he had at last been rewarded for all the long weeks and months of torment, anguish and bitter disappointment. Standing with the excited crowds among the plane trees on the Place des Lices, Girard stared at the approaching column of German prisoners. They had come down from the citadel to surrender to the French, and at their head were the officers, stepping heavily, with the haggard, dazed look of the vanquished. A sudden silence fell, and the twilight calm was disrupted only by the cheerful warbling of hundreds of birds settling down for the night in the branches of the venerable trees.

17

BY MID-AFTERNOON OF THE SECOND D-DAY in France, the rejoicing was by no means widespread, and not everyone was exulting in the joy of sweet victory. At the far side of the Esterel mountains, more than thirty French prisoners of war were proceeding under heavy guard along the road from Mandelieu to Saint-Jacques-de-Grasse. They were the able-bodied survivors of the Naval Assault Group's disaster at

Pointe-de-l'Esquillon. Of the sixty-seven men who had landed the previous night on the Esterel rocks, eleven had met violent death and seventeen had been seriously wounded. The single able-bodied officer, Lucien Chaffiotte, and a naval gunner, Gilbert Chéry, had been taken under armed escort to the German division headquarters in Grasse.

After reaching the 148th Division command post, Chaffiotte and Chéry were searched and interrogated, and then locked up in a basement. Several hours later they were brought out for further questioning. After more than eight hours of fighting, the Germans were mainly concerned with finding out what the central point of the Allied landings was.

Chaffiotte had anticipated the question, and replied calmly:

'Port Vendres.'

The German officer gestured impatiently, and two heavy slaps shook the Frenchman's face.

'I warn you! Don't try to play the brave little soldier with us,' the officer snapped. 'Now – are you ready to talk?'

Chaffiotte kept silent.

'Very well,' said the German.

He snapped his fingers at a young lieutenant standing near the door.

The two Frenchmen were shoved out into a courtyard surrounded by a high wall drenched in blazing sunlight.

They heard the measured tread of a firing squad advancing as twelve German soldiers emerged from an archway. Led by a sergeant, they took their places in front of the wall, ten yards from the prisoners. Chaffiotte stared straight up into the blue sky, then closed his eyes as he heard the command:

'Squad halt!'

And then came the order: 'Ready! Aim!'

Chaffiotte felt as if his heart had stopped beating and as if 'everything had been finished and over with for a long, long time.' It was like an awakening from a nightmare when he opened his eyes. The German officer stepped toward him, burst into laughter, and exclaimed in excellent French:

'That's enough for today!'

Chaffiotte and Chéry were led off to the schoolhouse in Grasse and locked up in the toilets, where there were palliasses crawling with bugs. They stayed there for three days and three nights before being moved to Genoa, the Brenner Pass and Austria, finally winding up in a prisoner-of-war camp near Bremen.

In the meantime, the other survivors of the Naval Assault Group were being marched toward the village of Auribeau-sur-Siagne, about six miles from Grasse. The heat along the road was overpowering, and the men were suffering from an agonizing thirst, but they refrained from complaining in the presence of their captors. Above all else, they were sick at heart as they kept recalling the events of that nightmare on the Esterel rocks and mine fields.

Thus absorbed in gloom, the Frenchmen were not paying any particular attention to a peasant woman who was walking along behind them, trundling her crates and market baskets. Nor did she seem to be taking any heed of them. She looked completely indifferent to what was by now undoubtedly a familiar sight.

Just as the woman was catching up with the column and was about to pass it, one of her baskets suddenly fell to the ground, spilling out its load of tomatoes, onions, and thyme. When Pierre Ferrandi stooped down to help her pick up her scattered vegetables, he was startled to hear her whisper in his ear:

'Be prepared! There's going to be an attack in the forest to free you!'

Wailing and cursing, Mme Giordamengo, whose husband was a Resistance leader in Mandelieu, picked up the last of her load and disappeared around a bend in the road. Near Auribeau-sur-Siagne, six men armed with pistols rushed out of a thicket and attacked the Germans. In addition to Humbert Giordamengo, there were Francis and Fernand Tonner from La Bocca, and Raymond Bargeris, Pierre Borghèse, and Lucien Albis, all from La Roquette-sur-Siagne.

While bullets whizzed around them, ten of the prisoners made their getaway over a low wall that ran along the road. Besides Ferrandi, they were Dubois, Louis Billiemaz, Casabianca, Gardembas, Cury, Richard, Ducreux, Bollore and Huet, who was struck by a machine-gun burst just as he was entering the woods but kept on running.[1]

At about the same time that afternoon twenty-two men and women who had been arrested by the Gestapo were being marched out of their cells in the prison at Nice. Twenty-seven year old Hélène Vagliano was among them. She had the consolation of knowing that the landings had taken place and that her suffering had not been in vain. Her silence under torture had served the Allied cause. Now that she was about to die, she realized that it could only have ended this way for her.

---

[1] The ones who were left behind were not quite so lucky. A few days later they were taken to Nice and reunited with Chaffiotte. Despite an intensive manhunt, the ten escapees eluded recapture. They were given refuge by a Swiss, Jacques de Chaudens, who hid them until they were able to join forces with the First Battalion of the 141st Regiment. The men who had been wounded at Esquillon had comparable good luck. The Germans abandoned them in a shack on the Trayas highway. On the morning of 16 August, Christian Auboyneau, the interpreter-decoder, heard tanks approaching and succeeded in dragging himself outside. He and the other men were picked up by the United States 56th Medical Battalion.

She was in excruciating pain from injuries to her back. Heavy-booted German feet had kicked her, rifle butts had struck her, the SS guards had seared her flesh with white-hot irons, but nothing had made her talk. Hélène was not complaining. She was happy that she had been able to hold out. In less than three weeks, her hair had turned white and she had lost an enormous amount of weight from lack of food and from being shut up in dark, dank cellars. During seventeen days and nights punctuated with interrogations and torture, Hélène Vagliano had been dragged in and out of four prisons – in Cannes, Grasse, Cimiez, and now Nice. The fact that the Germans had removed her from her cell for execution only a few hours after the landings, clearly proved what a choice catch she represented. As she took her place in line with the others, Hélène let her thoughts rove back over her happy, carefree existence before the war. She thought about her family – her father was a well-to-do shipbuilder in Cannes – and also remembered the many Allied pilots whom she had rescued and helped to pass over the border into Spain, and all the reports and messages she had broadcast to the Allied headquarters over her clandestine transmitter – up to the end of July, when she had been betrayed.

The line of condemned prisoners emerged onto a barren lot in the Ariane quarter of Nice, and a volley of shots rang out in the steaming air. The twenty-two men and women fell to the ground. The clock on the Saint-Roch church, high above the old city of Nice, sounded four times.

18

SIXTY MILES AWAY, six hundred and fifty survivors of the first battles in Provence had taken seven hundred prisoners, and three hundred dead German bodies were strewn over the slopes of Mont Biscarre, the valley of La Môle, and the beaches between Le Rayol and Cap Nègre. The African Commandos, the first of the Allied invasion force to land, had eleven killed and fifty wounded. Over the last fourteen hours, Lieutenant Colonel Georges-Régis Bouvet's Frenchmen, all by themselves, had held a bridgehead two miles deep and over a mile long against the shells and machine-gun and rifle fire of the Armenian, Azerbaijan and Georgian gunners under the command of a few determined German officers of the 242nd Division.

Bouvet's chief concern after he got ashore had been whether he would receive fresh supplies in time to enable him to hold out until the arrival of the American 3rd Division infantrymen who had landed at Cavalaire-sur-Mer.

Late in the morning, Joseph Cherrier, a gardener in Le Canadel, saw a cluster of parachutes opening up in the sky over Mont Biscarre, but he could not make out whether there were men attached to them. Twenty bursts of yellow smoke rose up from the wooded mountain top, and while the 12th Air Force's Bostons circled overhead in the amber-coloured clouds, containers filled with food, as well as with ammunition for machine guns, light artillery and antitank guns, floated down to the isolated Frenchmen. (The only miscalculation involved a consignment of drinking water, impatiently awaited by the commandos, which fell behind the German lines, to the consternation of the French.)

Meanwhile, Captain Bonnard's Third Commando Group had marched on La Môle and captured the village. The first of the German batteries that had fired on the invasion fleet was now silenced. At about noon, the leading elements of American tanks and the 7th Regiment's jeep-transported troops, who had landed six hours earlier at Cavalaire-sur-Mer, established radio contact with Bouvet's 650 hard-pressed men.

A gruff, hearty voice crackled over the French officer's receiver. It was 'Iron Mike' O'Daniel, commanding the 3rd Division.

'Hello, Bouvet! Well, we made it. Are you holding out all right? If I'm any judge, your commandos are worth a whole bunch of infantry regiments!'

A faint smile crossed Bouvet's face. He was thinking of that memorable Sunday in Casablanca, on 8 November, 1942, when he had first found himself face to face with this American 7th Regiment, whose men had just met up with his today on a highway in France.

Immediately after landing, Mike O'Daniel had set up his command post in the barnyard of a Provençal farm near the village of Croiz-Valmer, less than a mile inland. While his jeep radio sputtered away, the local farmers were bringing out kegs of rosé wine to toast the victory. A steady stream of tanks and trucks was rumbling by on the highway, headed for Gassin to the east and for Cogolin and Grimaud to the northeast, the sector of Colonel Lionel McGarr's 30th Regiment.

O'Daniel's aide-de-camp, Lieutenant Newell, was standing with Jean-Pierre Aumont at the edge of the road, watching the flow of vehicles and equipment wending its way to the front lines.

Suddenly their gaze riveted on a strange sight. Under the burning sun, mingled with the stream of 2½-ton trucks, scout cars and jeeps, a bicycle, heavily loaded with bundles was being pushed, by a well-built, broad-hipped girl, her face brazenly made up. She was cursing sullenly at the bunch of jeering boys who were accompanying her.

Aumont asked a farmer's son what this was all about.

'Oh, nothing much!' he replied contemptuously, and then explained:

'She's just the local whore! They're taking her away. She was sleeping with the German officers.'

'If that's so, why don't they just shave her head?' the boy's sister exclaimed.

'What's the point?' replied the farmer's son, scornfully. 'Her hair would just grow again. No,' he continued, 'it's quite simple what they should do. They should just tattoo the word "whore" on her cheeks!'

Out at sea, off Cavalaire-sur-Mer and Cap Nègre, the fighting was still raging on the Iles d'Hyères – on Port-Cros and the Ile du Levant. Unable to raise Colonel Edwin Walker by radio, General Patch had decided to send an aide to Port-Cros to assess the situation.

Someone standing behind Patch spoke up:

'In that case, general, I wouldn't mind being in on the party. It'll give me a chance to stretch my legs.'

Patch turned and saw that the speaker was the usually taciturn Secretary of the Navy, James Forrestal. Most extraordinary of all, according to one witness, was the fact that Forrestal was actually smiling.

The situation on the islands was far from clear. On the Ile du Levant, after the unmasking of the famous dummy batteries at Le Titan, progress had not been any better than on Port-Cros, despite Walker's victorious reports. Part of the German garrison was putting up a last-ditch resistance, with a handful of officers and fewer than fifty men resolutely entrenched behind the island's heavy fortifications and counterattacking with artillery. They were holding off the 1,300 veteran Rangers of the Second and Third Special Forces Regiments.

As the hours went by, no significant change appeared to be developing. A barrage of 120 shells fired on the stronghold by the British destroyer *Lookout* had failed to make a dent or to discourage the fanatical Germans. At the same time, a few other German defenders who had holed up in the old Grand Avis jail were making things tough for Walker's special platoons. The fierce fighting continued there all afternoon, sixteen hours after the first landing. Later, when it was all over, fragments of dismembered bodies were found in the prison yard.

When Forrestal and the officer who accompanied him got to Port-Cros, they immediately realized that the situation was equally confusing, if not more so. The Fort at L'Estissac dating from the time of the seventeenth-century Marquis de Vauban, the fort of L'Eminence, and the small fort of La Vigie, built under Napoleon, remained impregnable. One of the important objectives of the Second D-Day was the capture of these forts, and Lieutenant Colonel J. F. Akehurst's First Regiment had been at it since dawn. The tenacious and stubborn resistance of the Germans behind these massive walls was delaying the installation of Allied radar equipment so urgently needed for subsequent operations.

The sun was sinking low over the horizon and still there was no appreciable change in the situation. It was not until 10.34 P.M. that the shells and Schmeissers ceased firing from the fortifications on the Ile du Levant. Lieutenant Colonel Robert S. Moore, commanding the Second Regiment, heaved a deep sigh of relief when his Rangers came out escorting the last Armenian soldiers, who were sheepishly pulling out of their pockets the leaflets that Oscar Dystel and the OWI in Algiers had been so concerned about. On Port-Cros, the furious fighting continued unabated throughout the following day and into the morning of Thursday, 17 August. The last of the three forts held by the Germans refused to give up until after twelve rounds of 15-inch shells had been poured into it by the British battleship *Ramillies*.[1]

19

THE EVENING SUN was setting in fiery splendor. James Forrestal was seated by a bush on Port-Cros watching the glow of colors come over the Mediterranean. The temperature began to drop almost immediately, and the air cooled off perceptibly as the earth entered into shade. Forrestal got to his feet and ambled over to Colonel Akehurst's command post a few yards away.

---

[1] The third and largest island of the Hyéres group, Porquerolles, was still in the hands of two hundred troops of the 242nd Division. However, the guns on Porquerolles did not constitute a threat to the landing beaches, and hence had not been included in the D-Day plans. All the beaches on the island had been conscientiously mined, and its civilian population evacuated, as at Port-Cros and the Ile du Levant. The exception was the lighthouse keeper, Dominique Pellegrino, now retired. Pellegrino prevented the Germans from blowing up the lighthouse, as they had been supposed to do in the event of an Allied landing. At dawn on 22 August, the Senegalese troops of General Magnan's Ninth Colonial Infantry Division landed on Porquerolles, while American ships with powerful loudspeakers cruised offshore calling on the Germans to surrender. Except for casualties caused by the mine fields, notably on Notre Dame beach on the east shore of the island, 'everything went off fast and smoothly.' according to a witness.

On the mainland, as dusk gathered over the highway on the Saint-Baume mountains north of Toulon, the roar of the German motorized columns, instead of abating, seemed to be growing in intensity. The gray *Wehrmacht* troop transport trucks, heavily camouflaged, were like a forest in motion. The troops inside, shaken and jostled by the lurching of the vehicles along the rough road, were for the most part strangely silent. They were not lustily singing the songs of their homeland, as they had been for four years while they paraded and strutted through the cities and towns of France. They were quiet as they sat or sprawled jammed together in the heavy trucks, sweat-stained and weary under their square helmets adorned with still more foliage. Some of the men had been in full retreat since morning, constantly on the go, with scarcely a moment's pause.

The interminable lines of sidecars and Hanomag trucks were not driving south, nor even toward the east. They were proceeding along *Route Nationale 560* in the opposite direction from the beachhead, speeding toward Aix-en-Provence and Marseilles in an onrushing uproar.

Except for this jarring din of impatient engines, there was nothing else to be heard or seen. In the deepening twilight, a twenty year old champion bicycle rider, Ida Renucci, watched them pass. At the sight of these somber-faced men, who looked somehow more ominous in defeat than in their time of conquest, she felt a kind of fear seizing her, a confused and inexplicable apprehension. Ida was pedaling her big Payan sports bicycle and was returning to Aix after having competed in the annual race at Nans-les-Pins. The race had gone off well, and Ida had made the acquaintance of a tall, handsome boy of Italian descent, Vasco Andreoni. The first trucks had not begun appearing until about six o'clock in the evening. By now the darkness was almost total, and the columns of vehicles dashing westward were like a procession of frantic caterpillars. In the wan glow cast by the camouflaged headlights, the men's faces looked sinister, like those of hunted criminals who had not slept for a week.

The massive withdrawal had Ida Renucci worried. No one knew for sure what had been happening at Cavalaire-sur-Mer and Saint-Tropez. It was not until she reached Aix that the girl finally heard the news about the landings. She had a date to meet Vasco the next day on the Gardanne road where she worked out, and this date was going to spell the end of her career as a champion cyclist. One week later, Vasco proposed, and Ida relinquished her sporting future in favor of running a restaurant.

At the far end of the beachhead, a different kind of throbbing was heard over the Esterel peaks, as if in answer to the rumble of the last salvos that the troops in the Saint-Raphaël sector had urgently requested of Admiral Deyo's warships just before nightfall. The naval guns ceased firing at about 8.30 P.M., and at 8.43 P.M. a wave of Dornier 217 and Ju-88 bombers suddenly soared into sight over the mountains. They were carrying out the *Luftwaffe*'s single offensive mission on D-Day in Provence.

The planes came in at an altitude of 13,000 feet and then dived to 6,000, describing a vast circle over the landing fleet anchored out at sea. The ship and shore antiaircraft batteries had not waited for the bombers to dive before opening fire, but the German planes up there in the night sky did not falter. Because of the limited number of planes remaining in the Second Air Fleet, the pilots had orders to attack the Allied beachhead at its nerve centre – the Camel Green beach. A few seconds later, bombs were hurtling down on the piles of the newly landed matériel, on vehicles, and on fuel and ammunition supplies stacked up on the shore and around the beach at Le Dramont.

At the end of the day, which had been a relatively uneventful one for his unit, Private Don Nelson of the 36th Division was horrified to see five of his friends hit – he had traveled with them all the way from the States via Casablanca and Palermo. Nelson was busy fixing himself 'a tasty little dish of fried eggs and tomatoes' – provisions carefully carried all the way from Naples. The shock of the explosions, he recalls, 'blasted my first meal in France to smithereens' before he had even finished cooking it. When Nelson picked himself up, the sky was as serene and empty as if absolutely nothing had happened.

Less than two hours later, the familiar whistle of a glider bomb could be clearly heard above the racket of the shells bursting over the crests around Camel Green. With unerring accuracy, the magnetic device streaked straight toward LST 282, which was anchored along the left edge of Le Dramont beach. The vessel was packed with troops and equipment. The result was forty casualties – killed and wounded – whom the rescuers did not finish pulling out of the flames until the early hours of the morning.

By that time, the over-all Allied losses for the preceding twenty-four hours amounted to about 1,000 killed and wounded, including the sailors and airmen. Casualties among the landing troops were highest in the 3rd Division, which suffered 264 losses, 203 of them at the Cavalaire-sur-Mer landing alone, including a substantial number caused by mines. Twenty-five assault ships, LSIs and LSTs, were sunk between Cavalaire-sur-Mer and Anthéor. And, of course, there had been hundreds of casualties on the beaches, in the interior, and occasionally in areas far removed from the actual invasion zone, among the civilian population, in its active or passive struggle for liberation. Of the estimated figure of 30,000 German troops who were in the invasion area on the morning of 15 August, 6,081 were taken prisoner. The biggest bag was credited to the 36th Division in the Esterel mountains, and the lowest – 205 Germans – captured in the Sainte-Maxime sector. Only forty per cent of the 1,600 enemy troops captured by the 3rd Division in and around Saint-Tropez were of pure German stock. For this same period, Allied warships had fired nearly 50,000 shells and planes had carried out 3,733 sorties, including nearly 1,000 for the transporting of airborne troops. Some 95,000 men of the Allied forces – Americans, Frenchmen, Britons and Canadians – had landed since the previous evening, by sea or by air.

At Stalag XI-B, near Gottingen, in Prussia, a French war prisoner named Albert Cola, from Toulon, was crouching furtively inside a dark garage at one end of the prison yard. While two of his fellow prisoners kept watch, Cola was tuning the radio in an Opel Kapitan belonging to one of the SS officers. The toilets were in the garage, and the three men had requested permission to use them as a pretext to get near the cars that were awaiting repairs and to listen to the broadcast from London. In civilian life, Cola was a perfume and cosmetics salesman. He had been taken prisoner four years earlier, on 20 May 1940, near Laon, after only three days of fighting.

On this evening, Albert Cola felt his heart beating a wild tattoo as he caught the BBC broadcast. He heard the following announcement:

'This morning, American and French troops supported by the Allied naval forces landed on the beaches of the Mediterranean coast near Toulon. Despite active enemy resistance, our troops have now established a firm beachhead on French soil.'

Cola heard no more. Emotion overwhelmed him as he stood there 'transfixed, picturing a sunswept French beach with its pine trees bending low as if to welcome France's own children back home.' He shut off the radio and joined his friends to deliver the news, but found that he could not utter a word. Only then did he realize that he was crying. His heart was bursting with pride, but at the same time he was worried about his parents; the fighting was probably going to lay waste their region of France. As he remarked, 'there had been the Normandy landing on 6 June, but they weren't the same thing.'

On this 15 August evening, Cola at last knew that 'the road back lay open, back to my homeland of sunshine, crickets and freedom.'

Nine hundred miles away, a warm, dark, fragrant night was enveloping the Provence battlefront. Private Sam Kibbey of the 36th Division was getting ready to enter Saint-Raphaël with his mortar squad. As he plodded along through the vineyards, he suddenly found himself 'thinking about Jesus in Gethsemane.'

For some of the D-Day troops, who were so exhausted that they could not feel their fatigue any more, the battle had been going on for twenty-four hours. Others, deserted by luck, had not lived to see the twilight of 15 August descend over the land. The moon was not showing itself, but late-rising stars, partially drowned in a drift of mist, were sprinkling the sky. Here and there, cottony clouds of smoke screens billowed up out of the shadows, along the edge of the landing beaches and around the ships at sea. In the far-off valleys, a few shots rang out occasionally. The Allied bridgehead already extended ten miles inland in certain places. Near the seashore and in the valleys of the Monts des Maures and the Esterel, whether the battle was near or remote, the villages of Provence had finally dropped off to sleep, tucked in amid their plane-tree bordered lanes, their cypress hedges and their pungent, palm-shaded gardens. The regular rhythm of the Mediterranean was lapping against the sand and the rocks.

Part Four

JUNCTION

1

THE TEMPERATURE HAD RISEN even higher than on the previous day. The waters of the Mediterranean blazed with golden light, and the fuzzy outline of the coast gradually came into sharp focus. For the troops of the French First Army, who had been at sea for five days – some even longer – the long vigil of arms was at last drawing to a close. The time was shortly before 5 P.M. on 16 August.

Aboard LST 306, Warrant Officer Eugène Ephantin was standing near a Packard Clipper. The car was the personal limousine of General Jean de Lattre de Tassigny, commander of the French First Army, and Ephantin was his chauffeur and bodyguard. The Polish troop transport *Batory* was flying the flag of the French general, with its five distinctive sable[1] stars, which had been presented to De Lattre by Rear Admiral Robert Jaujard as the general was boarding the *Batory*.

Clearly, Jean de Lattre – fifty-five years old – was a different kind of general. The officers on his various staffs had their reasons for bestowing upon him the nickname *le roi Jean*, 'King John.' When war broke out in 1939, he was the youngest general in the French army, and he was still 'young' – De Lattre had proved this, ten months before, in the early dawn of 18 October, 1943, when he had parachuted from an RAF plane on to the field at Tangmere, near Portsmouth, after his spectacular escape from the Riom prison.

Eight months later, on 18 June, 1944, in two nights and two days, De Lattre had conquered the island of Elba in the course of what the American naval experts considered to be 'the toughest of all the Allied landings in the Mediterranean.'

'Just a trial run,' was De Lattre's only comment before the landings in Provence.

[1] 'Sable' in the heraldic sense, the colour black produced by cross-hatched lines. (Translator's note.)

At 5 P.M. on Wednesday, 16 August, De Lattre's aide-de-camp had called the general over to look at the horizon through a pair of binoculars. Although no one could discern a reaction, De Lattre himself later admitted that he had felt deeply stirred at the sight.

His sharp gaze – one of his division captains has remarked that De Lattre's eyes, like Napoleon's, subjugated, pierced and ruthlessly 'stripped naked' everyone on whom they rested – roamed over the shoreline glimmering under the summer light. The mainland was still quite a distance off. For a fleeting moment, De Lattre indulged himself in the rueful realization that if only Giraud and De Gaulle had been able to plead their cause successfully with the Americans and the British, he himself, instead of Patch, would now be in command of the Allied invasion forces going to the attack on Provence. De Lattre was resolved that from then on the French divisions, which had reaped a harvest of victories on the Italian front, would completely expunge humiliating memories of 1940. He was also sharply aware of the fact that his men accounted for seventy per cent of the total invasion force.

De Lattre had been known to keep troops waiting for as long as two or three hours under a driving rain or a broiling sun, their weapons at the ready, before reviewing them – although this habit could not be predicted with any reliability. And his inspections struck terror in his staffs and regiments. Jean de Lattre had a diabolical knack for ferreting out everything that was the least bit out of line, and his resultant fits of wrath were as fearful as they were spectacular.

De Lattre had also been the only commander of the Vichy government forces to oppose the *Wehrmacht*'s armored divisions when they violated the armistice agreements on 11 November, 1942, and he had received a prison sentence. On the evening of the capture of Elba, standing near Napoleon's house at Porto Ferraïo, De Lattre had observed to Rear Admiral T. H. Troubridge that 18 June, 1944, was the anniversary of De Gaulle's historic appeal to the French people.

The Briton, who had good reason to remember the date, had replied softly:

'Yes, General, and it's also the anniversary of the battle of Waterloo.'

2

IN FRONT OF THE MAKESHIFT ALTAR on the upper deck of the *Circassia*, Chaplain Py knelt to celebrate the Elevation of the Host. It seemed to him that never before, not even during the battles of Monte Cassino and Rome, had he celebrated such a deeply moving ceremony.

The bugles blew, and the men bowed their heads. The 67th Artillery Regiment's flag was flying proudly from the bow, opposite the bridge where shone the three stars of General Joseph de Goislard de Monsabert – fifty-six years old, silver-haired with a bristling gray moustache. The commander of the 3rd Algerian Infantry Division, a veteran of the African Army, was one of the behind-the-scenes plotters of the British-American landings in November, 1942. After defending Tunisia against the tanks of Rommel's Afrika Korps, the division had fought in Italy's hostile mountains, waged fierce warfare for the conquest of the Rapido, Rome and Sienna, and had advanced three hundred miles, leaving behind 8,000 of its own dead. This was the valiant marching division of Constantine, descendant of the Numidian legions and of the centurions of the African proconsulate, the oldest of all the combat units of the very earliest French army. The majority of its officers came from French families who had lived in Algeria for a hundred years, and its shock troops were made up of the Kabyle mountain people, of Arabs and Tunisians from the *douars* and the towns. They had been mobilized en masse in 1943, and many of them had simply followed their civilian bosses into military life. For example, there was Lieutenant Génin, a Frenchman settled in the Aurès region, who had reported to the recruiting center with all his agricultural workers, his *fellaheen*, who in themselves were enough to form a complete infantry platoon.

Monsabert, a small, squarely built, robust man, had withdrawn into meditation and was quietly living through the most exhilarating hours of his career.

In his mind, the religious services on board the *Circassia* were identified with another mystical rite that he was on the verge of performing – the liberation of his humiliated fatherland. As they landed into the wind toward the coast of France, the nineteen ships of his division were, to him, 'a vivid resurrection of the Crusaders' galley ships bearing down on St John of Acre in the kingdom of Jerusalem.'

When mass was over, the troops listened to a brief address by Chaplain Chatoney, a Protestant.

Among the men was a native Algerian warrant officer, Philippe Manseur, attached to the division headquarters' 25th Company, who had been with Monsabert continuously and devotedly for the last five years. Although not a Catholic, he wore around his neck a gold chain with a medallion of the Virgin. He was the son of an Algerian railway employee, and he proudly drove Monsabert's jeep, equipped with screaming sirens and adorned with three stars, a vehicle that was by now almost legendary among the French troops in Italy.

At Taranto, when they were about to board the ship that would be returning them to France, Manseur had said to Monsabert:

'And now, General, it's life to the death!'

The general had smiled. Little did it occur to him as he stood there on the *Circassia* that this was the last time he would see Manseur alive. Chaplain Chatoney was finishing his talk about France and 'the great motherland of all of us, Moslems and Christians alike,' and Manseur was listening avidly, his eyes glowing. Manseur had only a few hours of life remaining. He was going to be the first man killed when the 3rd Algerian Division landed in France.

3

ABOARD THE CARGO SHIP *Sobieski*, which was leading the ships of his 1st Free French Division, a youthful and dynamic general, Diego Brosset, was seething with impatience.

Although motivated by the same emotions and fervor as Monsabert, Brosset expressed his feelings differently. He was so eager to set foot on the sandy shores of France that he would gladly have swum to the beach if necessary. The cloudless sky, the distant horizon of the beckoning mainland, the statuesque serenity of the convoys gliding through the calm water were a severe strain on the taut nerves of this muscular, athletically built man who was brimming with energy and vitality.

At the age of forty-five, this Free French general was a dynamo of energy. He paced restlessly around the deck of the *Sobieski*, clad in his customary attire, a pair of British-cut shorts and an open-collared shirt that revealed the strong muscles of his neck. Diego Brosset had been a rugby threequarter. He was also the son-in-law of that General Mangin who had distinguished himself at Verdun in 1916; he spoke fluent English, Spanish, Arabic and German, and had even written a novel. His officers claimed that he had been inspired and sustained by the famous 'reveries' on the art of warfare written by Maurice de Saxe, Louis XV's greatest general.

The barrel-chested Brosset, with his deeply tanned skin and his determined expression, had willingly accepted the title of 'the biggest daredevil' of all the impetuous lieutenants in his division in the days when he used to go careening along in his jeep at a wild sixty miles an hour! His division was now made up of the survivors of General Pierre-Joseph Koenig's 13th half-brigade, who had fought on the sands of Libya. They were the Tahitians, the West Indians, the Caledonians and the Senegalese of the infantry battalions, and the French marines of Bir Hakeim, Tobruck and El Alamein, for whom there had been no interruption in the 1940 war since the Norwegian campaign. Their ranks had been thinned by the loss of six hundred men, including forty-nine officers, killed in forty-two days of fighting on the Italian front.

Brosset was not the only one on board the ships who found time hanging heavy on his hands. A young nurse named Louise de Benoist had spent seven full days aboard the *Vollendam*, one of the transports in Brosset's division. She had learned only that morning that her 422nd Field Hospital was going to land in France. For Mlle de Benoist, aside from the inactivity, the crossing had not been too unpleasant. There were fifteen nurses in her group, and they were all crammed into one small cabin, but they did not mind, for they were enjoying the unaccustomed luxury of sleeping between sheets. And, Mlle de Benoist recalls, they were deeply relieved at no longer having to live 'in fear of invasion by the horrid spiders of the Italian fields, which, all things considered, were still less scary than their city-bred cousins.'

On board the same ship, Captain Henri de Guillebon, like many others, was trying to kill time. But this posed problems even for an adjutant of the division's quartermaster section. Lieutenant Henri Girard, of the 21st Infantry Battalion, had resolved the problem by spending the greater part of his nine days aboard ship sleeping on deck. On the *Staffordshire*, Jacques Sautreau, a young and well-organized midshipman of the same battalion's First Company, had 'grown tired of the endless discussion with my men concerning all the possible places at which we might be going to land.' He had made out his will and written a last letter to be sent home in case of accident, and had enclosed them in two carefully sealed envelopes. On board the *Sobieski*, Michel Colcanap, a tank crew captain in the First Marine Regiment, who had sustained serious head injuries from German machine-gun fire in Italy, had attended mass and taken communion. Then, with nothing better to do, he had begun thinking about the incredible night of the previous 11 May, on the Liri River, when 'with a single roar, the 2,000 guns of the Allied artillery had all begun firing simultaneously, and kept howling for two hours over our observation post before the launching of the big offensive.'

All the way from Taranto, Corporal René Maldant of the Fourth Infantry Battalion, aboard the *Durban Castle*, was fascinated by the gorgeous kilt worn by the stern Scottish skipper who, armed with a flashlight, minutely inspected every last inch of the cabins. For Mireille Hui, assigned to an army communications unit, the voyage from Italy, 'despite our heavy boots and thick uniforms in the searing heat,' was a pleasant interlude of *dolce far niente*, 'with France awaiting us at the end of the journey.' Dr Arthur Méplain, a lieutenant with the 7th African Light Armored Cavalry Regiment, faced the situation from the very beginning by taking on all comers at endless games of bridge. Aboard the *Fort Richelieu* was Captain Paul Camus, an intelligence officer attached to the same unit, who got involved in long discussions about Aristotle and Plato with an officer whose name he never discovered.

On most of the ships, mealtimes were the welcome distractions around which the long days at sea were organized. While waiting for the next lunch or dinner, 'we found ourselves a little nook or cranny on the fore or aft decks and stretched out until bugle call,' one young officer remembers. The French divisions, whose point of departure had been Italy, were under the greatest strain; their convoys had taken the longest and most drawn-out of the routes followed by the Allied armada. After they had sailed along the Sicilian coast, the troops experienced a fleeting moment of panic when they saw that their ships, beyond the island of Pantellaria, had begun heading toward Tunisia. The convoys continued along Cape Bon and cast anchor off Bizerte before proceeding on to Algeria.

Private First Class Georges Anoeff, of the 7th Algerian Infantry Regiment, traveling aboard the *Worcestershire*, could not believe his eyes, and turned to talk to his neighbors:

'I bet you Hitler has surrendered and we're on our way home!'

'You're crazy!'

'All right, suppose you tell me what we're doing here.'

His companion reflected for a moment.

'Maybe we're going to Gibraltar?'

Anoeff shrugged his shoulders and repeated, in a tone that precluded further discussion:

'I tell you, we're returning home!'

At about the same moment, on the heights of Bugeaud near Bône, a group of European and Arab children stopped their game and, shading their eyes with their hands, gazed out to sea.

'Look at all the boats! They're coming this way! Maybe the war's over!'

But after reaching the Cap de Garde, the convoys veered sharply and set their course due north. Anoeff watched the cliffs of Algeria fade in the distance. The farthest thing from his thoughts at that minute was that he would be the first Allied soldier to enter Marseilles.

4

AT 5 P.M. ON 16 AUGUST, the United States transport *James Parker* entered French territorial waters. The converted cargo ship was gliding over a pearly film of sea, the opalescent coloring of which merged indistinguishably with the horizon. It was carrying the entire staff of General Touzet du Vigier's 1st Armored Division and some detachments of his 2,400 troops. Another part of this division, the First Combat Command, had landed on Sainte-Maxime beach with the American VI Corps.

Since embarking at Oran a week earlier, Jacques Le Tilly, the division's chaplain, had been watching over a precious suitcase stored in his cabin. When the coast of France at last loomed into view, he unlocked the suitcase and removed a large French flag. Five minutes later, the tricolor was flying proudly from the mast of the *James Parker*, under the bemused gaze of the ship's American captain. There were few men on board whose eyes did not fill with tears. Among them was Colonel Rousset, in command of the division artillery, whom death was shortly to overtake in the outskirts of Marseilles, his carotid artery severed by a German bullet. The flag that was now fluttering aboard the *James Parker* was going to be used in the ensuing nine months to drape the coffins of the division's dead.

In the filtered golden light, a fine dust could be seen rising over the mainland shore, dimly discernible as if in a dream. The 'dream' was being anticipated in different ways by the men of the 1st Armored. Some of them had never before been in France; a few came from General Maxime Weygand's post-armistice army, the token force the Nazis had allowed; and still others had escaped by way of the Pyrenees and been jailed by Franco before finally making their way to Morocco and Algeria. For the great majority of them, the war would be really beginning here in Provence.

A far-off moan of sirens cleaved the sultry air. De Lattre was on the poop deck of the *Batory* with his principal officers, General Maurice-Marcel Carpentier and General Dromard, and the commander of the French I Army Corps, General René-Marie De Larminat, who was wearing a deflated life jacket slung casually over one shoulder. Squinting through binoculars toward the clearest stretch of shoreline, De Lattre was able to see the fires burning in the forest of Les Maures.

The troops aboard the *Circassia* could hear the firing on the mainland, and their tense, waiting silence was broken by Monsabert's hoarse voice, husky with emotion:

'We're in France!'

No further signal was needed. As if by prearrangement, thousands of voices burst into song, and the immortal words of *La Marseillaise* were lifted on the evening air – '*Amour sacré de la patrie . . .*' On board dozens of ships, from the passageways, the decks and the packed railings, Frenchmen standing to attention joined in the refrain of their national anthem.

The sloop *Commandant Bory* was escorting the French transports, on the lookout for submarines. On its deck, Gabriel Battut, a radio operator, stood overcome with emotion as the stirring music poured out, and realized that the long exile was now almost over. So far, Battut's only glimpse of France had been an ochre rock on a silvery horizon, and the *Commandant Bory* was due to turn around and head back to Naples to convoy more transports.

Admiral Jaujard, aboard the *Montcalm*, requested permission from his superior, Admiral Carleton F. Bryant, to sail in closer to the French convoys. As the cruisers of the 4th Division going in the opposite direction passed the *Batory*, the combined crews on the *Georges Leygues* and the *Montcalm* gave vent in perfect unison to their emotion by whistling American style, three fingers in their mouths.

If Jaujard experienced a momentary uneasiness about how De Lattre might take this far from orthodox demonstration, he was quickly reassured. As he saluted the general, Jaujard saw that De Lattre was beaming.

5

On the mainland, near Le Lavandou, a few German soldiers were roughly rounding up the town's eight hundred inhabitants who had fled to the woods during the early morning hours of 15 August. The sound of shooting could be heard in the distance. A few brave people had managed to sneak through the enemy lines to bring back news of the landings, and the townspeople were eagerly awaiting the arrival of the Allied troops.

The sudden appearance of the Germans doused their spirits.

'Watch out,' Dr Brachet warned the others. 'They look mean. Don't try to get funny with them.'

Indeed, the Germans were behaving as if they were possessed, bellowing orders, loudly clicking their heels and clanking their rifle butts. Luce Ergen mingled with the crowd and, like the others, she was anxiously wondering what was happening, or might be going to happen.

In the normal course of events, Luce should have been back at her job in Toulon long ago. It was four days since she had bought her ticket at the little station near the port before getting on the train to spend the holiday weekend with her friends in Le Lavandou. Sunday and Monday had passed without too much excitement except for the continual air-raid alerts. Things had not really begun to get alarming until the night of 14 August. At about 2 A.M., Luce had been roused from sleep by the tolling of the church bell alerting the slumbering villagers.

Father Hélin, at the presbytery, had been awakened by the noise of knocking on his door.

'Arthur! Hurry up! They're ringing the alarm!' It was the voice of his sister, Mme Dermaut, crying out.

Mme Calvet, alone and asleep in her house, was roused in the same way by one of her neighbors. Several people had heard the bell, and were up and dressed – Mlle Philip, the church organist, and her parents, the Faeddas, Mme Dermaut, Mme Regniat, and others. A key to the church had been left at the town hall, and it was the duty of the municipal guards to sound the alert. However, various witnesses disagree on what actually happened. One of the guards, Grégoire

Costa, and a Resistance fighter, Ulysse Richard, heard neither bells nor bugles, but were startled awake by the voices of guards, who were running through the streets and shouting to everyone to get out.

Mme Calvet heard someone calling, 'Hurry, hurry! You've got fifteen minutes to clear out of town!'

Mayor Bluzet, who was also treasurer of the Department of the Var, was doing everything he could to ensure the safety of his people, although there was as yet no sound of planes in the night sky. The *Kommandantur* had just ordered him to evacuate the entire population. Within a few minutes, everyone, with the exception of some thirty elderly or infirm persons who could not walk or be moved, had rushed out to the hill path toward the cemetery. Luce Ergen was stumbling along with them through the blackness.

During all of 15 August and the next day as well, most of the people from Le Lavandou stuck to their refuges wherever they had found them, away from the strafing and bombing – in the woods, under the cypress trees in the old cemetery, even in the big family funeral monuments. Back in the deserted town, the nervous Germans did not know which way to turn. The bullets had begun coming their way, fired by the Resistance fighters who were closing in on the occupiers. When Mme Calvet ran home to get some food, she was astounded to find a big French flag planted right out in the middle of everything. Some distance away, on the sidewalk in front of the Morlet printing plant, the body of the policeman Olagnon lay sprawled in a pool of blood. He had triggered off the local hostilities by firing at the captain of the Saint-Clair battery as he rode by on a motorcycle. And the Germans in Le Lavandou had had their full share of casualties.

It did not take long for the enemy to retaliate. When Luce Ergen saw the patrol approaching the cemetery, she failed to realize immediately what it was all about. Soon she found herself being shoved along with a lot of other people – men and women of all ages, including a sprinkling of children – with machine guns and rifle butts thrust in their backs to urge them on faster.

A German officer held his pistol pointed as he kept shouting:

'Hostages! Hostages!'

The Germans stopped counting when they had assembled three hundred people. One man was carrying his aged mother on his back, and a ten year old girl, Josette Bono, was walking along uncomprehendingly between her father and mother.

The stunned, silent group of hostages formed into a column and began trudging off over the steep paths of the Moulin district. While the roaring waves of Allied planes surged overhead, the straggly procession continued its long trek up to a village perched on the sheer side of a hillside carpeted with mimosa trees. Night was already beginning to fall when they reached the outskirts of Bormes. They were to be shot at dawn, and Luce Ergen seriously doubted whether the Allied troops could get there in time to rescue them.

6

THROUGH THE GATHERING DUSK a launch was skimming over the water toward the shore, churning up a foamy wake in the darkening water. A flag surrounded by an honor guard fluttered from its stern. On the hills a few hundred yards inland, the pine-tree forests were blazing, and the air was rocked with the shock waves set off by the explosions of the mines that the engineers were detonating in the Gulf of Saint-Tropez.

As the launch was being tied up, the long, melancholy notes of a bugle sounding *Aux Morts*, taps, rang out in the evening air. In the bow of the launch a French general stood stiffly to attention. A French war correspondent, Pierre Ichac, recognized Monsabert.

It was exactly 7.40 P.M. It did not take the peppery general more than ten minutes to glean from the Americans all the information he needed concerning the situation on the mainland and the location of the front lines before he headed back to sea to report to General De Lattre, waiting aboard the *Batory*. Monsabert left some of his staff on land, including Philippe Manseur, his chauffeur.

As Monsabert's launch reached the *Batory*, he recognized the sound of planes droning over the shore. A minute later, a wave of German planes, probably Focke-Wulfe 190s that had ventured out on a random sortie, began dive-bombing the convoys in the Saint-Tropez roadstead. Jacques Sautreau, of the First Free French Division, recalls watching as 'all the powerful searchlights that had been illuminating the big white identifying numbers on the ships as bright as daylight' snapped off simultaneously. A gun began firing excitedly, and soon 'all the ack-ack got into the act.' Hundreds of tracer bullets streaked through the darkening sky, and the 40-mm. shells of the Bofors guns were hurtling forth 'in thundering unison.' A thirty-six year old Algerian warrant officer, Maklouf Arfi, assigned to the Seventh Algerian Infantry Battalion, 'had never witnessed such a mad hullabaloo in all my life.'

Master Sergeant Jacques Sames of the Free French Forces recalls that it was 'as if a luminous steel arch were curving up over Saint-Tropez bay.' Lieutenant Henri Girard watched as one of the planes was hit and went spiraling down in flames into the water. Warrant Officer Albert Valz, of the 67th Artillery Regiment, has described how 'in a few brief instants the ships put up a thick white smoke screen that hid them completely from view.' Louise de Benoist, the nurse on the *Vollendam*, remembers the 'shouting and commotion' on board, with the guns firing in all directions and the thick artificial smoke 'giving an unearthly aspect to the landing.'

Light bombs and aerial grenades[1] had landed on the *Batory*'s bow without inflicting any appreciable damage. But on the beach of La Foux at the entrance to Saint-Tropez, eighty men lay dead or wounded. In the half-darkness, the troops began coming ashore at Sylvabelle, in the bay of Cavalaire-sur-Mer and in the Gulf of Saint-Tropez. Long columns of helmeted soldiers, rifles slung over their shoulders, packs on their backs, wound their way through the mine fields along the trails blazed by the bulldozers. The infantrymen of the Third Algerian Division, groping their way through the unfamiliar territory of their mother country, had to keep to the shoulders of the highways because of the roaring columns of American vehicles racing through the bridge-head sector. They managed to re-form into some semblance of order and began marching toward a small Provençal hamlet just over a mile away. The twisting road crept along between two stately rows of plane trees, and peaceful houses stood out from the night shadows. The sudden shower that chose that particular moment to unleash its pent-up fury could not dampen the spirits and joyful shouts and songs of the marching men.

Shutters were hastily flung back, and windows opened wide to welcome the mounting clamor. Pierre Ichac remembers seeing people appearing in doorways, 'clad in their nightclothes, with coats flung over their shoulders and carrying lighted candles.'

A voice at the head of the column yelled out:

'Is this Cogolin?'

'Yes! Oh, yes! We're so glad to see you!'

Men, women and children stepped out on to the balconies of the old houses, and excited laughter mingled with loud cheers filled the night. Everybody was telling everybody else:

'Here they are! Our army's arrived!'

---

[1] These were particularly devastating devices, pineapple shaped, equipped with long, supersensitive fuses that enabled them to explode on the slightest contact and to scatter hundreds of fragments of shrapnel.

Shortly after reporting back to the *Batory*, Monsabert returned to the mainland and went ashore at La Foux. The news was good, and the battle for Provence was already twenty-four hours ahead of the timetable. The entire schedule was changed, and the general felt rejoicing in his heart.

Near the beach he stumbled upon the first casualties of his division. Even in the darkness, he had no difficulty recognizing the limp, lifeless body of Philippe Manseur, lying as if he were asleep on the sand, his forehead shattered by shrapnel. So many times Monsabert had wondered which of them, Manseur or himself, possessed the *baraka*, which of them brought luck to the other. Tonight he knew. The grieving officer sighed deeply and sadly. Part of the past had vanished forever. Never again would he be calling out impatiently, 'Faster, Manseur, faster! Step on it!' as he hurtled along with sirens blaring. Never again would the speeding jeep with Philippe at the wheel overtake and streak past the columns of tanks and trucks, straight toward the front lines. Fate had availed itself of that brief hour of separation to strike Manseur. The general reflected ironically that he himself did not have so much as a scratch.

He felt suddenly weary. The members of his staff were scattered. An officer handed him his writing pad riddled with bullet holes – it had been found near Manseur's body. Monsabert did not even wait for his jeep to come ashore. He hailed a passing American amphibious vehicle; the DUKW ground to a halt and the general climbed aboard. From the church tower in Cogolin the bells were pealing out the sounds of victory. Monsabert did not bother to count the strokes.

7

THE DUROSNE FARM had not suffered too greatly from the war and the years of occupation. It stood near the fork where the local highway intersected *Route Nationale 562*, between Callas and Le Muy. The day before, the Resistance had blown up the bridge at Garron two miles away, thereby sealing off a column of German trucks that was attempting to break through to Draguignan.

By dawn on Thursday, 17 August, with the help of infantrymen, German engineers had performed makeshift repairs on the bridge. It was just beginning to grow light when the muffled chug of engines was heard approaching from a distance, coming toward the Durosne farm. The German column had just succeeded in crossing the river.

At that instant, a jeepload of seven Scottish paratroopers bounced through the gateway and jerked to a halt in the Durosne farmyard. A colonel, probably no more than thirty-five years old, jumped out, his submachine gun at the ready. These were the first Allied troops that Durosne had seen.

'Any Germans been around here recently?' the Scot asked.

'Not recently,' Durosne replied laconically, 'but it won't be long. Listen . . .'

Since the previous evening, Durosne had realized that if most of the troops who had been parachuted over La Motte to the south did not overtake the Germans in time, the Boche, harassed and at bay, would overrun Callas and Claviers, the nearest localities. But now he was breathing more easily – the vanguard of the paratroopers seemed to be arriving in time.

But he vainly searched the horizon for any sign of life in the woods of Garidelle and La Clue. The seven Scots, members of the British Second Brigade who had been dropped over the area of Les Esclans forty-eight hours earlier, did not appear to be expecting any reinforcements. In the distance, the drone of the engines was growing steadily louder and more insistent along the Fayence road.

Durosne did not have time to inquire what the colonel's plans were. The seven men had removed their battle tunics and were now stripped to the waist, ready to attack.

'Go to it, boys!' the colonel called.

Durosne watched with eyes bulging as the paratroopers, armed with three Sten guns and a few hand grenades, casually spread out behind the hedges along the road a short distance from his property.

The farmer listened as the sound of the trucks drew nearer. Finally he saw them. They were rolling slowly uncamouflaged and unprotected, with two long lines of troops marching on either side of the vehicles. Durosne thought his heart would stop beating. He felt almost relieved when the fresh morning breeze brought him the sharp retort of the opening machine gun-bursts. The seven Scots had opened fire on the column.

The shooting was all over in three or four minutes. One of the lead trucks had been hit head-on by a well-tossed grenade. The road was littered with the bodies of some sixty German soldiers who had been felled by the Sten guns and grenades. By the time the remainder of the column had recovered from the shock and realized what was going on, while the demoralized Germans were scrambling around, getting their machine guns set up and shooting in every direction, the seven paratroopers made a neat getaway, with their intrepid colonel at the wheel. The jeep was quickly swallowed up in the Garidelle forest and disappeared along the road to Le Muy, eight miles away.

The disrupted column hastily reassembled and resumed its advance. Durosne knew only too well what was going to happen next. Three of the trucks shuddered to a halt in front of his farm, and a mob of furious troops piled out and stormed into the barnyard.

Their retaliation was swift and thorough. (Years later, Durosne was still amazed at having survived, and never was able to understand by what quirk of fate his life had been spared.) With the farmer looking on helplessly, fully expecting to be shot at any moment, the Germans methodically went about setting the barns on fire, burning the harvested crops, staving in the wine casks in the cellar, slaughtering livestock – they shot down the horse as it stood in the stable – and sacking the house with every piece of furniture in it. When finally their vengeance had been wreaked, the battalion commander and his men clambered back into the trucks and got under way. They did not have far to go. A few miles farther on, the column came under attack from a combination of a few local Resistance fighters and the Allied artillery – all the officers were killed, and what remained was finished off by aerial bombing and strafing.

In the Villa Gladys at Draguignan early this same morning, General Ferdinand Neuling, in command of the German LXII Corps, was waiting for the clock on the mantel to strike seven. He still did not know whether General Otto Fretter-Pico had been able to send the reinforcements that he had requested in the hope of fighting his way out. In any case, nothing had turned up.

Something else that Neuling did not know either was that Fretter-Pico himself, after spending all of 15 August in a forward command post in the Esterel mountains, had barely escaped from the advance elements of the American 141st Regiment, which was bearing down on Théoule. Neuling's reinforcements had been sent all right. They consisted of a motorized battalion of the Eighth Grenadiers under Major Tornow, and an artillery battalion. The trouble was that they had not been able to break through the steel ring that was being steadily tightened by the British and American forces encircling Draguignan. By dawn on 17 August, these German reinforcements had laboriously progressed to within five miles of Draguignan. In all likelihood this was the column that laid waste the Durosne farm.

By then, ninety per cent of Draguignan, which was General Frederick's number one objective, was in the hands of the Allied paratroopers, actively supported by local Resistance units. Neuling's situation was hopeless. His radio contact with the 148th Division, the only unit that might have been able to come to his rescue, had been broken off, as had all the other communications with the Nineteenth Army.

The fifty-nine year old general sat calmly looking on as the hands of the clock on the old Provençal mantel moved inexorably forward. The sun had already begun its climb, announcing still another hot day, and out in the garden the birds were chirping excitedly. Neuling's listless gaze shifted from the clock and settled on the leafy shrubbery that surrounded the house. It was this villa, set back in a bower of foliage, that the paratroopers of the 517th Regiment were to have attacked forty-eight hours earlier – if their planes had dropped them at the right place.

Neuling had strict orders to resist to the last round, and he had every intention of complying, in full awareness of the consequences. Since the previous day, the Americans and the local Resistance troops had been methodically closing in on the Villa Gladys. In a few more minutes the ultimatum delivered to Neuling by Captain Evans of the First Airborne Task Force would expire, but Neuling had no idea of surrendering.

Warrant Officer Schevenels, standing near the house, was also anxiously consulting his watch. Captain Evans was beside him. Neither man spoke; they had given up wondering out loud whether the German general would capitulate. Whatever happened, everything was in readiness to force Neuling out of the villa. Evans's first invitation to surrender had been met with a disdainful and scathing refusal. This time there would be no fooling around.

'All right,' Evans had said, shrugging his shoulders. 'Tomorrow at seven o'clock we blow the place up! Those damned fools have asked for it!'

The clock in St Michael's Church slowly chimed the hour. A few seconds later, the old timepiece in the villa also struck seven times. Neuling and his staff were gathered in the living room. He had spent the night in meditation, and now felt calm and at peace with himself. He had thought a long time about his wife, Margarete, in Germany. Perhaps she would never see him again, but he did not want to give her cause to be ashamed of him.

Outside, Evans signaled to the jeep driver, who turned the radio loudspeaker on full blast. Schevenels began speaking in German into the microphone:

'This is our final ultimatum! Your time is up! You have one minute in which to surrender! Come out one at a time, holding a white flag, the general first, your hands over your heads!'

The living-room windows remained open as the minutes ticked by, but there was no sign that Neuling had changed his mind. Evans issued orders over the radio transmitter to the mortar batteries, which were zeroed in on the villa, and to the paratroopers with their bazookas, who were spread out around the building, to open fire. The shells and explosions tore through the early morning air. And as the smoke began to settle, Evans saw Neuling, his uniform and helmet covered with dust, appear alone at the doorway and start down the garden path, walking mechanically, like a man in a trance. After him, one by one, came a few more generals and a sizable group of staff officers.

8

UNDER COVER OF DARKNESS, two platoons of Lieutenant Colonel Georges-Régis Bouvet's African Commandos had just reached the outskirts of Le Lavandou and were approaching the first houses at the edge of town. Master Sergeant Giuseppi and the men of the Second Commandos had shot down nine Germans in an ambush and had learned from the local residents that hostages were to be executed at dawn. Bouvet had decided to attack the village at daybreak and had ordered his men to get ready.

Luce Ergens was near the quarries at Bormes, watching as the first flush of dawn streaked the sky. She had given up all hope. The night had seemed strangely short. Sounds of firing could be heard in every direction, but – or at least so it seemed to her – at greater distances than on the previous day, as if the three hundred hostages had really been forgotten by everyone and were being abandoned to their fate. Actually, a mad race against time was going on that very minute a few miles away, and Bouvet was desperately hoping that he would not be too late.

About 6 A.M., Luce received a shock. She grabbed her friend's hand and held it tight.

'Look!' she whispered. 'Over there!'

The two girls distinctly saw the silhouette of a helmeted soldier outlined against the gathering light of the summer sky, followed by still others, and then by many more.

Rifle barrels gleamed in the rays of the rising sun. The girls suddenly realized that the Germans had disappeared. Luce knew then that the hostages were safe and that there was nothing more to fear.

The newly arrived troops were not Bouvet's African Commandos – they were from the American 3rd Division. They had been unaware of the peril – or even of the existence – of the hostages, and it was by sheer chance that they had come upon them on their way from Cavalaire-sur-Mer, along the paths and roadways of the Dom forest.

At about this time, the French commandos who were proceeding along the coast from Cap Nègre to Cap Bénat, had cracked the German defenses at the entrance to Le Lavandou and were overrunning the town. Joseph, the local street superintendent, was the first of the residents to meet a Second Commando detail headed by a young midshipman named Arnoult. During the night, Captain Albert Thorel, the leader of the commando group, who had so unceremoniously mustered the services of the man he thought was the Le Canadel station master, had been killed in an attack on a strongly defended *Kreigsmarine* battery on the cape at La Fossette.

Little Josette Bono was walking down from the Bormes hills with her parents and the other liberated hostages. Halfway down they met Bouvet's commandos. The general rejoicing and relief on both sides was, to one observer's eyes, 'delirious and indescribable – soldiers and civilians were falling into one another's arms, embracing, shouting, weeping.' At that moment, Luce Ergen was too much in a state of shock and exhaustion to notice, among the African Commandos, a tall, lanky blond young man who was soon to become her husband.

9

DURING THE MORNING of 17 August, the situation changed in many respects for the Germans, in Provence as well as in the rest of France. This was a decisive date for the Allies, perhaps the most important since the 6 June landings in Normandy.

'An enormous, restless wave of troops of all ranks[1]' from all the branches and units of the *Wehrmacht* was fleeing through the north and south of France, shedding all semblance of the discipline that had so far marked the orderly withdrawal of the German troops who stood to be

[1] Eisenhower.

caught in the Allied trap. General George S. Patton's Third Army, to which was attached General Philippe Leclerc's French Second Armored Division, had already entered Orléans, and Allied troops were in Chartres and Dreux, steadily advancing on Paris. Over the last two days of the gigantic battle the enemy had lost more than five hundred tanks. The German soldiers who had thus far escaped death and destruction had been in full flight since the decisive fighting at Avranches, and were being mercilessly tracked down night and day by the Allied planes. On the Provençal front, General Friedrich Wiese was attempting to hold back six powerful American and French divisions that were attacking everywhere at once – on the Italian frontier, thrusting toward the Alps, and along the Rhône valley.

Hitler, in Rastenburg, reached a major decision, one that he had been mulling over since the previous afternoon. After the countless hesitations, refusals and muffed chances of the preceding days and weeks, General Alfred Jodl and the German High Command were making a final effort to prevent those divisions of the Nineteenth Army that were still almost intact from being mauled and from meeting the same fate as the ones in Normandy.

General Warlimont once again covered the half-mile that separated his headquarters from the *Wolfschantze*. Hitler listened silently as Jodl, his operations chief, propounded the emergency plan that he had worked out in great detail over many weeks. Then Hitler sighed, grasped the stack of papers, and, after a last swift scanning of the contents, scrawled his signature, thereby making the plan one of his own general orders. A number was assigned to the order: No. 772916. Warlimont bowed, clicked his heels, and went out.

Within moments, the teletype keys were busily chattering messages to France and Italy. The alert was issued simultaneously to *OB West*, to General Johannes Blaskowitz, and to Field Marshal Albert Kesselring. Before it became too late, all the troops and matériel that Blaskowitz could still muster in southern and central France were to be rushed to the support of the harassed armies retreating from Normandy. In the Rhône valley, the tanks of General Wend von Wietersheim's 11th Panzer Division had not arrived in time to forestall the irresistible Allied advance beyond the bridgeheads of Cavalaire-sur-Mer and Saint-Tropez. Theirs was the sole offensive mission of the entire German withdrawal order – 'to ensure by any and all means and with all the forces at their disposal' the protection of the Nineteenth Army units that were retreating northward. To the east, the 148th and 157th Divisions of General Fretter-Pico and General Karl Pflaum were withdrawing toward the Alps.

For reasons that have never been completely explained, probably because of communications difficulties, the Nineteenth Army in Avignon failed to receive its orders until late in the afternoon – the orders that, considering the urgency of the circumstances, the *Wehrmacht* and *Kriegsmarine* commands in southern France had been expecting for a long time.

The troops of Wiese's army, who had idled away so many pleasant carefree days along the balmy shores of the Riviera, received strict orders to leave nothing intact. The military installations in southern France, the railroads, the airbases, the construction and repair facilities, the power plants, the ports and basins, the ships at anchor – everything was to be ruthlessly destroyed, nothing was to be spared. A maximum supply of food and ammunition was to be transferred to the two fortified strongholds of the Provençal front, Toulon and Marseilles, and the garrisons of these cities were ordered to dig in for a long siege. Like the garrisons in Brest, Lorient and Saint-Nazaire, they were to defend themselves to the last man and the last bullet.

Needless to say, Hitler had not signed and issued these orders light-heartedly. Never had he admitted that the *Wehrmacht* might have to withdraw – not after Moscow, not even after Stalingrad, Monte Cassino and Normandy – but now the hard facts stared him in the face. The most bitter pill of all to swallow was the giving up of France, his proudest conquest.

Those present at the Rastenburg headquarters on Thursday, 17 August, 1944, have all agreed that Hitler, when he found himself forced to prepare the evacuation plans for the French territory that his troops had been occupying for four years, was 'in a bitter mood of melancholy resignation.'

10

THE PRISONER WAS OF AVERAGE HEIGHT and medium build. He had been stoutly bound to a pine tree near Bormes. With his hands tied behind him, he coolly maintained his composure under Colonel Bouvet's scathing look of contempt and disgust. Ten of the commandos were standing a few yards away awaiting the colonel's order to settle accounts with the prisoner. But despite the revulsion that he felt for the man, Bouvet had still not given the signal.

The captive was a soldier from an *Ost Legion* battalion, which had been giving the commandos a bad time since the night of their landing. He was a stockily built Armenian with dark skin and thick lips. He wore the long-visored *Wehrmacht* helmet, and a plain short-sleeved undershirt, the tail of which was hanging over his trousers. His uniform jacket lay crumpled at his feet.

It was this jacket that had drawn the commandos' attention to the man. He had vigorously resisted all attempts to search him. It had finally taken three strapping fellows to hold him down while his pockets were emptied. Their contents were horrifying proof of murder and theft. They included women's wristwatches and gold rings, and, most gruesome of all, an assortment of severed human fingers – exclusively ring fingers, with the wedding bands still on them.

The Armenian had been discovered living in a nearby barn, and an officer together with a few men had been detailed to search the building. They had scarcely gone inside when the lieutenant dashed out and ran to Bouvet's command post.

'Colonel! Sir, I think you'd better come investigate this yourself!'

Bouvet hastened to the barn where, as he has described it, he was met with 'the most appalling sight I had ever seen in my entire life.' The crucified corpse of a baby only a few weeks old had been nailed to one wall, impaled like a dead bat against the inner side of the door.

The colonel had immediately assembled the captured German officers and addressed them in German, stating that 'the German army had disgraced itself by such revolting conduct.' It would therefore not be possible to judge the offender as a soldier. He could be considered only as a plunderer and a murderer.

Bouvet felt nauseated as, with loathing in his heart, he turned and walked away. As he reached his command post, he heard the shots ring out.

On the same day, at about the same hour, Commando Corporal Charles Patin, astride his heavy Harley-Davidson motorcycle, was coming within sight of the first houses on the outskirts of Le Lavandou when his engine suddenly coughed and died. It was merely a routine breakdown, and Patin had experienced plenty just like it. This one, however, was going to take on a special significance in his life. The villa in front of which his motorcycle had spluttered to a stop was named Le Bastidoun. Its walls were built of great stones, and it had a wooden gateway. The villa's residents were only too happy to lend a hand to the young soldier. Among them was a girl named Luce Ergen, the office employee from Toulon, who still had not fully recovered from her harrowing experience as a hostage of the Germans. Within the year, Charles Patin and Luce Ergen had become man and wife.

11

REAR ADMIRAL HEINRICH RUHFUS had given up trying to keep track of how many days and nights had elapsed since he had hastily been forced to abandon his naval headquarters at Baudouvin near Toulon. He was no longer even sure whether it had been on 21 or 22 August. Ruhfus had barely made his getaway as the first Allied forces – the troops and tanks of the French First Army – began approaching. In the night his car had careened crazily through the sleeping city and suburbs of Toulon, and the final lap of his journey had been a frantic trip by motorboat across the roadstead to the Saint-Mandrier peninsula opposite the city. Since then, the attack had become an inferno.

The intensive barrage of naval shells and of 1,000- and 2,000-pound bombs continued all day and every day, without let-up except between sundown and sunrise. The ground shuddered, shook and rumbled as if the globe were about to split open and disgorge its entrails. At the crack of dawn the planes began soaring over the peninsula and releasing their loads. The battleships and cruisers fired their relentless volleys from less than twelve miles offshore. During brief respites from the naval assault, there was the continuous screech of falling bombs, the planes roaring over in waves of thirty and forty, diving almost straight down on to the narrow strip of land amid a hail of explosions, shrapnel and steel. The incessant noise was in itself enough to drive a man out of his mind.

The steady pounding of the blockbusters had plowed up the ground and sucked up the buildings. It had chewed to bits the vital electric cables of the firing batteries – those cables that had been laid deep beneath the earth's surface, below the concrete blockhouses, around the notorious and redoubtable 13.4-inch battery on Cap Cépet, which had weighed heavily in the Allies' decisions regarding the location of the landing beaches, and was even now continuing to worry the Allied staff.

The basic structure of the fortifications included two thick-walled, heavily reinforced turrets, which pivoted on a turntable sunk into a solid twenty foot thick concrete mass. The guns covered the entire twenty mile coastal area between Le Lavandou and La Ciotat. By now only one of the turrets was still in working order. However, not one of the 250 shells that had been fired since 16 August by the Allied naval artillery had scored a bull's-eye on this vital target. The battery, which was set on a rocky platcau planted with pine woods, was practically invisible from the sea, and was difficult even for the bombardiers flying overhead to distinguish accurately. Still, in nine days of intensive aerial pounding, three of its four 13.4-inch guns had been put out of commission. With its formidable underground organization, the battery constituted a complete sunken factory, with powder magazines, ammunition stores, central command posts and bunkers thrust deep in the earth at a considerable distance from the guns. Despite all this, the awesome old monster was now gasping its last. But the Allies had no conclusive evidence that the battery was nearing its end.

The outlook was hopeless for Ruhfus's gunners. For three days the half-crazed men, punch-drunk from the bombing and shelling, had been in a state of virtual mutiny, refusing to man their posts. Hail-storms of shrapnel, debris and steel drenched the gun pits. The ammunition stores had all been blown up, most of the undergound bunkers had been ripped to pieces, and the men were unnerved to breaking point. They had dug in and taken refuge in what they could salvage from the remaining shelters.

As one of the captured German officers afterward admitted, 'It had become absolutely impossible for us to stay at our posts in the Saint-Mandrier battery while the Allied artillery was firing on us.'

Grand Admiral Karl Doenitz, commander-in-chief of the *Kriegs-marine*, had sent Ruhfus a personal message of encouragement, reminding him that 'all Germany is looking to you and your men,' and that the 'battle for Toulon will become immortal in history, as will your heroic deeds.' But Ruhfus realized that the battle was already lost. The last bastions of resistance in Toulon itself, the old forts defending the entrenched camp, had all surrendered – Lamalgue, Malbousquet, La Poudrière. Of the 25,000 garrison troops, for whom capitulation was something unheard of, many had been killed, some had escaped and were in headlong flight, and most of the others had been taken prisoner. A handful were still resisting in the Saint-Mandrier peninsula, around the battery.

On the sunny morning of Sunday, 27 August, amid the bursting shells and the drone of the planes, Ruhfus could hear voices wildly cheering the arrival of the Allied troops. The sound was borne to him on the breeze blowing over from the far side of the roadstead. And the 1,800 soldiers still on Saint-Mandrier could scarcely believe their ears when, blended with the acclamations of the crowd, they recognized the victorious notes of bugles and trumpets and the rhythmic beat of a military band.

Around them stretched a scarred landscape, with burned or burning trees, the scattered wreckage of downed planes, and an infinite expanse of ground pockmarked with craters – some of them thirty feet wide – and strewn with jagged heaps of rubble and hillocks of dirt that had spewed out in the wake of the explosions. The pine forest that had surrounded the battery was a vast cemetery of scarred and battered tree trunks, twisted bare stumps reaching toward the summer sky as if in vain supplication. In the middle of this wilderness, the ugly muzzles of the four huge guns jutted out their ominous shapes, and random shots continued to be fired out to sea by the last one still operating.

Once again the bombers swamed over Cap Cépet, around the vast mine fields designed to thwart any airborne landings; once again the flak guns began reacting vigorously – that is what was left of the original seventy-one antiaircraft guns, the 105s, and the 88s and the 37s, resumed their furious barking and spitting. A pilot of the 12th Air Force has described the density of the ack-ack over Toulon as 'the equivalent of what we encountered over Berlin at the beginning of the war.'

At dusk, Ruhfus's aide-de-camp stiffly ushered in Major Pierre de la Brosse of the Ninth Colonial Infantry. The French officer was there to demand the surrender of the Saint-Mandrier battery and of the troops occupying the peninsula, which was connected to the mainland by a narrow sandy isthmus.

The Moroccan Colonial Infantry's reconnaissance unit under Lieutenant Colonel Le Puloch had just reached the isthmus after occupying the beach of Les Sablettes. Fierce fighting had occurred near the Tamaris, less than a mile away, in which one French company had lost one-third of its men in a bayonet charge. It was now nearing 8 P.M.

At Ruhfus's headquarters, the exchange of words was brief and to the point. The last lane of retreat or escape that had been open to the surviving gunners and the 1,800 *Kriegsmarine* troops defending the Saint-Mandrier pocket had been sealed off. The French officer summed up the situation in a few short, incisive sentences.

'What are the conditions?' Ruhfus asked.

'There are no conditions,' De la Brosse replied. 'Toulon has capitulated. All the forts are in our hands.'

Shortly before midnight, Ruhfus gave his answer. He was surrendering.

12

FIFTY MILES AWAY, a fantastic and almost incredible poker game that had begun five days earlier was drawing to a close. Bluffing, bravery and foolhardiness had been carried to the extreme.

Early in the afternoon of Wednesday, 23 August, in the underground command post at Marseilles, the phone had rung in the office of General Hans Schaefer. The aide-de-camp picked up the receiver, and the infantry general watched as his subordinate's face paled. He inquired anxiously:

'What's happened, Kurt?'

Kurt Bouveret handed the receiver to the general.

'I think you'd better listen to this yourself, sir,' he replied.

The next instant, Schaefer almost bounded out of his chair.

'Impossible!' he screamed into the mouthpiece. 'You're mad, Merz! You must be mistaken!'

The telephone clicked, and then a voice came over the line, speaking in perfect German:

'This call is coming from the headquarters of General de Monsabert commanding the French Third Division.'

Schaefer stiffened, and his face became ashen.

'Where are you calling from?' he asked.

The voice replied calmly and coolly:

'From Marseilles, of course.'

Schaefer, livid, could only stare straight ahead at the canvas curtain that hung at the entrance to his office at the far end of the shelter.

At last he managed to ask:

'Where is your general?'

This information was supplied instantly. Monsabert and his staff were occupying the offices of the military district, in the center of Marseilles. And, without giving the German time to regain his composure, the voice resumed:

'Issue orders for a truce to begin at 3 P.M. We will respect it. General de Monsabert will expect you at 4 P.M. to negotiate the surrender of your garrison.'

Schaefer's entire body shuddered, and he half-rose from his chair as he snapped into the phone:

'Are you insane? Do you really expect me to go there?'

And, lest the voice misinterpret his meaning, he hastened to explain: 'The French civilians would murder me on the way!'

The telephone line buzzed and crackled. Schaefer was breathing heavily as he wiped the beads of perspiration from his forehead.

The heat was stifling in the foul air of the underground shelter, which had been hewn into the cliffs on Cap Janet, opposite the gigantic concrete blockhouses that had been thrown up to protect the submarines. Schaefer had been extremely reluctant to leave his former headquarters in a pleasant villa – the property of a man called Dor – in La Valentine, on the road to Aubagne, to assume the defense of Marseilles in this complex warren of airless stairways and passageways, dozens of yards underground. Despite the installation of a ventilation system, the heat was fearful, and most of the rooms and cubicles in the nearly deserted shelter were in darkness. The flickering light of a few candles hesitantly pierced the blackness here and there. The only brightly lighted office was Schaefer's.

At the moment, his desk contained a large map of Marseilles, two telephones, a dish of cheese, and a telegram dated 20 August and signed by Colonel von Hanstein, commanding the Marseilles defense sector:

'As per instructions received from the LXXXV Army Corps Headquarters, Division General Schaefer is appointed to command the ground, naval and air forces engaged in the battle for Marseilles. As chief of the defense sector, I hereby solemnly swear in General Schaefer for this mission, in which he is to hold out to the last, in conformity with the Führer's explicit order.'

Schaefer hung up the phone and began to reflect.

'Check out that intelligence!' he ordered his chief of staff, Major Walter Merz. 'They claim the Allies have their tanks and troops moving up the Boulevard de la Canebière, and that they've already occupied the Prefecture Quarter!'

Since he refused to venture into the city, Schaefer had been ordered to meet his adversary, General de Monsabert, at 6 P.M. that evening in front of the postern gate of Fort Saint-John, at the entrance to the Old Port.

13

OUTSIDE, THE CITY WAS SIMMERING under sultry and oppressive heat. The sirocco had been blowing for three days over Marseilles, unleashing its fiery breath over streets that were already feverish with fighting. And as if that were not enough, the many oil-processing plants in the suburbs had caught fire during the last air raids. Now, with the strong wind blowing, they were belching out clouds of thick, oily smoke that spread over the city in a heavy blanket of suffocating air.

Captain Jean Crosia of the infantry took a deep breath as he put down the phone. He had just played the wildest and boldest bluff in his life, after rushing into a military switchboard center full of armed Germans and explaining that he had to make an emergency phone call. Crosia was an intelligence officer with the Seventh Infantry Regiment. When he was not in uniform, he wore a cassock, Crosia was the village priest in a small Lorraine parish near Metz.

When he had reached Marseilles with the regimental staff, it had occurred to him that the telephone service was still working. He had hit upon the idea of trying a subscriber line to put through a call to German headquarters. He had bet on a long shot by counting on Schaefer's state of shock in hearing – undoubtedly for the first time in his four years of war – an enemy officer speaking over the wire. And Crosia had guessed right. His mad 'practical joke' had succeeded beyond his wildest hopes.

Early that morning, Private First Class Georges Anoeff, who at one point had feared he would never get to France, was marching at the head of his infantry platoon through the still slumbering streets of Marseilles, his trigger finger at the ready. The men were hugging the walls, their eyes riveted on the rooftops, but so far the Germans had not reacted. At various houses along the way, front doors were suddenly flung open, shutters flew wide, and the incredulous and joyous people of Marseilles, clad in their nightclothes, their hair still rumpled, stood in their doorways or gazed from their windows.

Gradually, the people came streaming out of the buildings, shouting and cheering, rushing up to fling their arms around the marching soldiers. Major Martel's First Battalion of the 7th Algerian Infantry Regiment and the Sherman tanks of the French 2nd Armored Division's

Fourth Squadron had been under way since before dawn, and were now cautiously infiltrating the city, headed toward the Old Port. Along the expanses of wide sloping boulevards, the 88-mm. shells began whistling over the troops and tanks that were mingled with the ever-growing crowds, and exploded on the sidewalks, where the news stands were still tightly shut. The German batteries at Fort Saint-Nicholas, recovering from their surprise, swung into action. Anoeff and his men took refuge inside a clothing store, and as he waited and watched, he remembers, he saw 'rows of carefully dressed display dummies falling nearby, like the figures in a shooting gallery at a street fair.'

A different sound was now making itself heard over the noise of the machine guns and the exploding shells. The sound grew louder, and the people in the Quartier des Réformés and along the Canebière, Marseilles's famous main boulevard, paused in their tracks as a jeep came barging into view, hurtling along fast and furiously. Jean Labregère, the proprietor of a hotel at the corner of the Rue des Feuillants, remembers the screaming wail of the siren and the blue cap perched on the head of the diminutive French general seated alongside the driver. Behind the wheel was Warrant Officer Eugène Dustou, a former soccer player from the town of Félix Faure, in Algeria, who had replaced the unfortunate Manseur. In the best tradition of his predecessor, Dustou had his foot firmly on the accelerator and was pushing it practically through the floorboard, with Monsabert urging him on.

The tires squeaked as the jeep came bowling around a bend on two wheels and screeched to a halt near a Dodge command car. Standing beside it, Colonel Chappuis, commander of the 7th Algerian Regiment, was poring over a map. He looked up casually.

'Everything seems to be under control, General,' he announced. 'Shall we carry on?'

'Go to it, Chappuis,' was Monsabert's reply.

Incredible as it may now seem, the strength of the 3rd Algerian Infantry Division at that moment totaled only some eight hundred troops, whereas the Germans still had 16,000 men in the vicinity. The French artillery had not even reached Marseilles, and there were only twenty armored vehicles accompanying the infantry.

Furthermore, Monsabert had no orders to attack the city:

The evening before, a dramatic and turbulent council of war had been held in Gémenos, twelve miles from Marseilles, at the improvised French headquarters housed in Mme Marignane's hotel, the Relais de la Madeleine. The meeting was attended by De Lattre and his principal generals, Larminat, Monsabert, Sudre and Augustin Guillaume.

Monsabert had been in particularly violent disagreement with his chief. He was his usual impetuous and impulsive self, itching to attack Marseilles without wasting another minute. For several hours, the people in the city had been in a state of insurrection against the occupiers, and were firing pistols at isolated German cars and stray patrols and erecting barricades with paving stones torn up from the streets. According to couriers who had recently returned from behind the lines, French civilians were now occupying the center of Marseilles, the strategic Prefecture Quarter.

'Just let me take over a few intersections,' Monsabert pleaded, 'and I'll have the whole situation under control.'

De Lattre slowly shook his head. There was ample reason to have misgivings, and he was absolutely against venturing, as he put it, 'into the welter and confusion of a city that was in the throes of an insurrection.' Moreover, the fighting was still heavy in Toulon, and according to intelligence from G-2, everything pointed to the determination of the German garrison in Marseilles to hold out to the bitter end. De Lattre also reminded the assembled officers of the German defenses, which represented an impressive total. There were 10,000 troops in Schaefer's 244th Division; 5,000 *Kriegsmarine* specialists in the coastal batteries and forts on the islands of Pomègues and Ratonneau; an assortment of 4-inch and 9-inch guns ready to whirl around to attack the city itself, and fifty other artillery batteries, gun pits, fortified dugouts and blockhouses. Nor did De Lattre fail to mention sunken tank turrets and flame-throwers everywhere – in the harbor, and on the heights of Notre Dame-de-la-Garde and the Prado – and innumerable antiaircraft batteries and abundantly sown mine fields protecting the city.

Monsabert merely shrugged his shoulders. None of this was news to him, and he brought his fist crashing down on the table.

'Today's 22 August. Are you willing to bet that by the day after tomorrow at the latest I'll be drinking a *pastis* on the Canebière?' His tone was defiant.

The high-spirited general was going to win his bet, or at least come very close to it. De Lattre was impressed, but far from convinced. Although he did not pursue the matter any further, neither did he appear to have changed his mind.

'Don't worry, *mon cher* Monsabert,' he declared firmly. 'We're going to take Marseilles, all right, but only after further orders. . .'

The little general made no more comment, and soon ushered De Lattre out to his waiting car.

Chappuis was waiting on the hotel terrace for the conference to end. A battalion of his 7th Algerian Regiment and some of the tanks from General du Vigier's 1st Armored Division were already rushing on, headed for Marseilles, and taking prisoners as they went. Chappuis had just been informed by radio that the First Battalion had reached the small suburbs of Saint-Julien, just over a mile from the center of town.

Monsabert gestured from across the terrace to Chappuis, and it seemed to the colonel that his general looked a little bit put out.

'No luck. We're strictly forbidden to try for Marseilles,' was the general's wry comment.

Chappuis's eager expression turned to one of dismay, and he made no attempt to conceal his disappointment.

Monsabert continued:

'I'm afraid that's that. Those are the orders for today. But,' he added, looking Chappuis straight in the eye, with just a hint of a sly smile glinting around his silvery mustache, 'if you should by the merest chance happen to have an opportunity. . . .'

The colonel needed no further explanation.

Less than twenty-four hours later, Pierre Ichac, the French war correspondent, witnessed a memorable sight. As he described it:

'A little French general, the quintessence of what the world expects a French army general to look like, straight out of a bandbox – with his cap, gray mustache, breeches, leggings and baton – was standing waiting with four other officers in front of the postern gate at Fort Saint-John, at the entrance to the Old Port in Marseilles.'

The silence was impressive. Newsreel cameras were busily whirring from on top of a nearby wall. Surrounded by a heavily armed bodyguard, his boots rapping sharply against the cobblestones, General Hans Schaefer was stepping stiffly forward to where Monsabert stood. Chappuis was struck by this peculiar stiffness, which to him 'made Schaefer look exactly like a toy soldier who had been wound up with a key and released from his case.' The time was 6 P.M. on 23 August. However, since receiving Captain Crosia's telephone call, Schaefer had been thinking things over and had taken a grip on himself.

The meeting of the two generals was brief, their exchange of words was curt. The short-lived truce was shattered, and throughout Marseilles both sides resumed hostilities.

14

WHILE THE BATTLE CONTINUED TO RAGE, while a flood of motorized columns, long lines of tanks, artillery, trucks, jeeps and scout cars, was pouring over the highways and side roads, a strange-looking group of fighting men, almost figures from another world, converged on Marseilles. They had covered the twenty miles from La Ciotat by leaping and running, clambering over the sheer rocks, the limestone cliffs and the goat paths through the still-burning forests of Carpiagne and La Gineste. North of the city, the columns of flat-helmeted men loped along over the jagged crests and chalky peaks of the Chaîne de l'Estague before plunging abruptly down to the shores of the Etang de Berre and finally toward the sea, after carrying out successful raids along some twenty-five miles of the enemy's rear.

These troops were proceeding on foot, unaccompanied by a single motor vehicle. Instead, they had long trains of mules – their *brels*. Their 'uniforms' were a far cry from anything remotely resembling the regulation army issue. Since 1943, these men had been fighting bravely and fiercely on most of the Mediterranean battlefields – Tunisia, Corsica, Elba and Italy.

They had the coppery complexions of African fighting men, and they wore the thick woolen robes, the dark-striped, hooded *djellaba* of their native Morocco. Most of them had bearded fringes, and when they were not in actual combat, a thick twist of wool – the *kiout* – wound around their heads covered their smooth-shaven skulls. Over the last eight months, General Guillaume's indefatigable Goumier troops had seen action in nearly half the mountains of Italy, from the Volturno to Sienna. At Patton's request, the Fourth Moroccan Tabor – the equivalent of an infantry battalion – had taken part in the Allied landings in Sicily. And yet, they had been nearly ruled out of the landings in France, partly because of their indispensable mule trains, which required special transports and also because of what reports prudishly referred to as the Goumiers' 'violent instincts, which it would be regrettable to let them satisfy in France.' De Lattre and Guillaume, thoroughly enraged at this judgment, had insisted and finally won out. By noon on 20 August, the last Goumiers had come safely ashore at Sainte-Maxime and Cavalaire-sur-Mer. The following day,

American 2½-ton trucks carried them and their precious mules to within a few miles of Aubagne, and on 22 August these Moroccan warriors began their dash to Marseilles. They captured General Boïe, head of the city's *Kommandantur*, and nine of the colonels in his garrison.

Their advance under the broiling sun had been continuing for three days. While Monsabert was returning to his headquarters after the futile meeting with Schaefer at Fort Saint-John, Guillaume was turning loose his entire contingent of doughty Goumiers – 6,000 in all – with orders to capture all the strategic heights overlooking the roads leading into Marseilles.

Through barrages of mortar and 88-mm. shells, striding along rough dusty trails, hurtling over the bluish rocky plateaus, the boxed-in canyons and the *garrigues*,[1] winding between defiles and through passes, going through old abandoned sheepfolds, past isolated Provençal farms with parched walls, stepping over wild brush, gliding through the sheltering olive groves amid the clamor of thousands of crickets, the three battalions commanded by Colonels Leblanc, Boyer de la Tour, and Massiet du Biest forged steadily ahead. Some of the Goumiers met death in the mine fields or were wounded in the attacks on German blockhouses and batteries. Others fell into ambushes. Several times they charged with fixed bayonets. But wherever they went they sealed off all the possible routes by which the enemy might escape.

And at last, in the hazy dawn of a summer morning, they saw stretched out at their feet the maze of streets and the tangle of rooftops that is Marseilles, the sprawling, besieged city.

15

AT DUSK ON SUNDAY, 27 August, while Ruhfus in Toulon was still pondering his hopeless situation, a Marseilles policeman, wearing the identifying helmet of the civil defense and carrying a revolver in his holster, suddenly saw the French flag hoisted in the waning light, over the ancient walls of Fort Saint-Nicholas, one of the two bastions that dominate the Old Port. At the corner of Pharo Boulevard, a shell exploded against a building, and flames began leaping out of the windows and through the roof. The troops of Major Méric's Firs

---

[1] The patches of new forest undergrowth in southern France. (Translator's note.)

Moroccan Tabor had just flushed out the Roucas Blanc and the Malmaousque districts, and were now taking up positions on the highway running along the Catalans cliff, and storming the fort directly opposite Schaefer's last remaining defenses. For the Goumiers, the fighting was drawing to a close. In five days of unrelieved combat, they had captured 6,000 prisoners, over half of the total troops in the German 244th Division.

Schaefer also saw the French flag floating in the evening breeze, and knew the time had come for grim resignation. He summoned Merz, and in a flat, weary voice began dictating a letter addressed to the little French general with whom he had had the fruitless meeting four days earlier.

One hour later, General de Monsabert ripped open the envelope that had been delivered by a colonel from the 244th Division. His eyes rapidly scanned the page:

'As a result of the fighting that has taken place over the last few days, since our conversation of 23 August, the situation of my forces has changed completely. I feel that it would be purposeless to continue a battle which could lead only to the total annihilation of my remaining troops. I hereby request, as of today, an armistice containing a provision enabling me to prepare a surrender under honorable conditions for the morning of 28 August. Failing this, I am prepared to order my men to resist to the end.'

Monsabert tossed the letter on to his desk and uttered a sigh of relief. Chappuis heard him murmur:

'At last! For the first time since we began attacking Marseilles, my forces finally outnumber the enemy!'

In the warm night air, amid a silence unmarred by the sound of shots, the French general began slowly pacing in his office.

At dawn the next morning, a jeep took Major Andolenko of the 3rd Algerian Infantry Division to the port area. The driver had to skirt carefully the small 'Goliath' robot tanks loaded with explosives, their cables coiled on winding drums.

Schaefer stepped out of his underground shelter and carefully read the surrender papers that Andolenko handed him. The French officer noted that the German general 'looked haggard and pale-faced, hollow-eyed from fatigue and worry; even his nose seemed excessively long.' Now it was Schaefer's turn to sigh. He groped in his tunic for a pen, and then realized that he had forgotten to bring one.

Andolenko lent him his, and after spreading the papers out on the hood of the jeep, the German signed the capitulation.

Thirteen days had passed since the Allied divisions had landed on the Second D-Day in France. The troops were one month ahead of their timetable, and the battle of Provence was reaching its conclusion. What now lay ahead was the final mission – the junction with the armies that had landed in Normandy.

16

ON ROUTE NATIONALE 71 between Troyes and Dijon, 150 miles south of Paris, a detachment from General Leclerc's 2nd Armored Division was rolling serenely along between broad fields that were as empty as the road ahead, and meeting no sign of enemy resistance. A tank out in front was protecting the column, which consisted of light vehicles, with two armoured cars bringing up the rear.

Captain Gaudet of the 12th Armored Regiment felt uneasy as he wondered where the Germans might be lurking. And what were the other Allied troops doing? He had orders to thrust through to Chamesson, a village between Châtillon and Dijon. With a good ten miles to go, Gaudet found himself surrounded by deserted countryside. There was absolutely nothing in sight except the fields.

While Gaudet was trying to fathom the situation, he noticed in the distance a man and a woman coming toward him on bicycles. Gaston Merle and his wife ran a tobacco shop in Nod-sur-Seine. This morning, as they did every ten days, they were on their way to Châtillon to purchase supplies with the ration tickets belonging to the village's 260 inhabitants. They, too, were wondering just what the Germans might be up to. Although Nod-sur-Seine lay off the beaten track, the Merles had learned of the Allied landings and knew that American and French troops were fighting near Dijon. They thought that by now the city might even have been captured. Anyhow, realizing that the liberation could not be too far off, Merle was counting on getting a little extra tobacco from the wholesale dealer in Châtillon.

It was about 9 A.M. when they met up with the armored column. The vehicles by no means resembled any of the German ones that they were accustomed to seeing. Merle's eyes opened wide when he realized that this might indeed be the vanguard of the Allied troops. But he had been expecting them to arrive from the south, and here they were bearing down from the north! His excitement and amazement reached a peak when he saw a French officer alight and start walking over to him.

Gaudet explained that his division had landed in Normandy and that it had just liberated Paris. He told the Merles that his instructions were to go as far as Chamesson, and asked them what the situation was.

'Oh!' Louise Merle quickly replied. 'You won't have any trouble getting through at least as far as Nod-sur-Seine! There isn't a single German left around here.'

At the same time, another French officer, Captain Guérard of the 1st Free French Division, was proceeding north on *Route Nationale 71*. With two officers of the First Marine Regiment, Colmay and Morel – veterans of Bir Hakeim – he had set out from Arnay le Duc, between Autun and Sombernon. The machine gunners on his three scout cars and the twenty men in his patrol were all at their posts, their gaze alertly scanning the horizon in all directions. But there were apparently no Germans left in this area either. In any case, Guérard had seen no reason to slacken his speed.

The jeep at the front of the column was bowling along the steep, winding road when Guérard came in sight of the village of Nod-sur-Seine, where the river is a relatively narrow stream. The village church and its cluster of houses, against a background of flourishing fruit orchards, were set slightly back from the main road.

Pierre Garnier, the local architect, was standing at his window overlooking the highway. He heard the loudspeaker of the 2nd Armored Division's radio car announce the arrival of the other column and began exchanging messages with Guérard and the troops of the 1st Free French Division. A flying leap brought Garnier right out on the road.

The mayor of Nod-sur-Seine, Bernard Huguenin, who was also its quarrier and stonecutter, shut off his ancient battery radio set, which had just broadcast a speech by General de Gaulle. Straightening his collar as he ran, he began tearing through the village streets with the entire population at his heels. The old church bell was pealing for all it was worth, sending the exultant chimes of victory rolling over the countryside. Still running, Huguenin turned around and looked back. Two nimble figures were scrambling up the ladder to the top of the belfry. One minute later, the tricolor was proudly floating in the summer sky.

The mayor and his flock reached the highway in time to see two French officers who had never before met shaking hands vigorously under the welcoming shade of a venerable elm. One of the officers had landed on a beach in Provence and the other had come ashore in

Normandy. The date was 12 September, 1944, three months and one week after the first Allied soldier had set foot on the soil of France. The long-awaited junction betwen Operation Overlord and Operation Dragoon had become part of history.

Sources and Acknowledgements

To the best of my knowledge, there has been no publication covering the invasion of Provence other than fragmentary or summary descriptions, personal reminiscences and memoirs by generals and admirals, eyewitness accounts, and, of course, military reports at various echelons covering the operations. Especially helpful were those military reports providing an over-all view of events on 15 August, 1944, and the days following, as well as those pertaining to isolated parts of the period and others that enabled me to recapture the atmosphere of a specific happening or moment. My most important research source by far was the work published in the United States in 1959 by Admiral Samuel Eliot Morison in his fifteen volume *History of United States Naval Operations in World War II* (Boston 1947–62). Other material led me back to the period before the invasion in Provence, giving me insight into what had been the Free Nations' original plans for the Second D-Day in France, how they eventually brought it off, and, most important, why it took place.

This information, most of which stems from material published in France and the United States, has of course been verified and supplemented either through personal research through files, or research performed for me by qualified organizations and agencies, both official and unofficial. On all sides I encountered understanding, ready compliance and interest in my task.

First of all, I wish to express my thanks to Hervé Cras, head of the French Naval History Department, who, under the pen name Jacques Mordal, is well known as the author of widely respected publications. Monsieur Cras has given me the benefit of his experience and advice. He oriented my research, considerably facilitated my work, and saved me an enormous amount of time by carrying out investigations on my behalf, checking facts, and answering my many questions on even the most out-of-the-way matters with inexhaustible and commendable patience. Throughout my work, including the final correction of the manuscript, he remained a devoted friend, a sound adviser, and an able historian responsible for the solving of many thorny problems. Without his invaluable assistance, this book would never have seen the light of day. I want to convey to him my keen and friendly gratitude.

Various agencies, both official and private, in France, the United States, Germany, Britain and Canada, made their files available to me. These include the French Army's History Section at Vincennes, under General de Cossé-Brissac; the French Naval History Section in Paris, through Monsieur Golaz; the French Air Force's Historical Section in Versailles, through Captain Cadilhon; the United States Army General Headquarters and the Office of the Chief of Military History in the Department of the Army in Washington, D.C.; the Military History Research Office in Fribourg; the Institute for Defense Analysis in Munich; the German Veterans Association in Bonn; the Naval Officers' Aid Society in Krefeld; and, in Canada, the Army Headquarters Historical Section, Ottawa.

Among the principal publications that I consulted, Admiral Morison's *The Invasion of France and Germany* (Boston, 1959) proved valuable because of its wealth of information on the various phases of the Second D-Day naval operations, the composition of the fleet and the identities of its leaders; United States Seventh Army records enabled me to pinpoint troop movements from the moment the men landed on the Provençal beaches. In addition to these two main sources, there are the long report by General Sir Henry Maitland Wilson, addressed to the Combined Chiefs of Staff, on the operations in Southern France, and another equally detailed report by Vice Admiral H. Kent Hewitt, who commanded the United States Eighth Fleet; there are also the personal recollections, entitled *Command Mission* (New York, 1954), of General Lucian K. Truscott, Jr., leader of the United States VI Corps, and General Eisenhower's *Crusade in Europe* (Garden City, N.Y., 1948). Elliott Roosevelt's *As He Saw It* (New York, 1946) recaptured for me the behind-the-scenes atmosphere of the Teheran Conference in November, 1943, and *Invasion 1944* (Chicago, 1950), by General Hans Speidel, Rommel's chief of staff, enabled me to retrace the unfolding events in the German High Command in the West, beginning with Rommel's exit from the scene and leading up to Von Kluge's suicide.

Numerous other references deserve special mention. The files of the various divisions and regiments were kindly made available to me by their record sections. Marshal Jean-Marie de Lattre de Tassigny's

Histoire de la Première Armée française contains an over-all description – with all the indispensable details – of France's role in the Allied coalition against Nazi Germany. I gained valuable information from *Ouvriers de la première heure* (1954), by General Georges-Régis Bouvet, who was then a colonel; *Nous marchions vers la France*, by Pierre Ichac; *Tabor*, by Jacques Augarde; and *La Marine française dans la seconde guerre mondiale*, by Admiral Paul Auphan and Jacques Mordal. The book *Cap sur la Provence*, by Admiral André Lemonnier, former French Naval Chief of Staff and naval deputy to General Eisenhower at the North Atlantic Treaty Organization, furnished interesting material on French naval participation, along with personal observations. Finally, Raymond Aron's *Histoire de la Libération de la France* guided my choice of anecdote relating to the historic joining of forces that occurred on 12 September, 1944, between the troops from Normandy and those advancing from Provence.

Other lesser-known but equally essential accounts further assisted me. Among contributions of a local nature, I particularly wish to mention Robert Bailly's *Avignon meurtrie* (a day-by-day account) and Gustave Roux's *Histoire de l'occupation de la région d'Hyères*. These writers also kindly agreed to undertake extensive additional research for my own book. In his *Marseille 1944, victoire française*, Captain Jean Crosia retraces the moves in his gigantic poker game of 23 August, 1944. I am indebted to Honoré Isnard, of the Cannes Scientific and Literary Society, for details concerning the escape of members of the French Naval Assault Group.

Mention must also be made of the reports drawn up at the request of the U.S. Army by General Georg von Sodenstern, commander of the German Nineteenth Army in Southern France; by General Edgar Theilsen, a staff officer of Army Group G; by General Johannes Blaskowitz, who commanded Army Group G; and by General Walter Botsch, General Wiese's chief of staff in Avignon. This list is certainly incomplete, but would be even more so without Sir Winston Churchill's *Triumph and Tragedy* in his six-volume history *The Second World War*, (Cassell) which describes in detail the political preparations for Operation Anvil and the British Prime Minister's many desperate attempts to prevent this operation from taking place.

Such, then, were the main bases of my book – and such were the elements that largely made it possible to fit together the many pieces making up the events of 15 August, 1944.

I hereby acknowledge my gratitude to the French National Radio's record library and to my friend Pierre Ichac, who patiently played for me the tapes of his broadcast commemorating the Provence landings –

a remarkable program featuring the participation of numerous veterans of the Second D-Day. Special thanks go to Jean Meirat, who obligingly turned over to me his unpublished manuscript, *Le Journal d'un Timonier de 1942 à 1945*, and provided answers to my questions about the events in which he was involved; to Léon Metz, who gave generously of his time, and without whose testimony the story of the landing at Dramont would be incomplete; to Robert Chiglion-Fontange, who also contributed unstintingly of his time to locate and interrogate eyewitnesses, retrace routes, draw maps and assemble material; to General Joseph de Monsabert, commander of the Third Algerian Infantry, who reconstructed for me the taking of Toulon and the gamble that preceded his capture of Marseilles; to General Bouvet, who supplemented his own book with additional information uncomplainingly answered my long lists of questions, and accompanied me back to the scene to relive the landing of the African Commandos and the fighting on Cap Nègre.

I also wish to thank Vice Admiral Robert Jaujard, who assisted me in innumerable ways and compared for me his impressions of the two 1944 landings, 6 June and 15 August; and Admiral Yann Le Hagre, who placed his notes, written observations and records at my disposal. In addition, acknowledgment is due to General Augustin Guillaume, General Touzet du Vigier, and General Aimé Sudre; to Jean-Pierre Aumont, former officer in the First Free French Division, for his cooperation; to Marie-Madeleine Fourcade, with whom I exchanged a voluminous and fascinating correspondence; to Jean Cazeneuve, who helped conjure up the details of the Second D-Day beaches and to Commander Morazzani of the Toulon Port Library, former captain of the *Tempête*.

Former Lieutenant-Colonel Melvin Zais, now a major general commanding the 101st Airborne Division in Vietnam, spared neither time nor effort in locating the officers and men of the 517th Parachute Regiment, who had jumped with him during the night of the Second D-Day minus one. Among the German officers, special acknowledgment to General Franz Halder, the *Wehrmacht*'s Chief of the General Staff; General Walter Warlimont, the *OKW*'s Chief of Staff for Operations; General Heinz von Gyldenfeldt, chief of staff of Army Group G; General Walter Botsch, chief of staff of the Nineteenth Army; General Wend von Wietersheim, who headed the 11th Panzer Division, and General Werner Drews, his chief of staff; General Otto Fretter-Pico, who commanded the 148th Division and General Hans Schaefer, who commanded the 244th. Once again, I thank Captain Hans Joachim Metzenthin, who removed the veil of obscurity surrounding the sinking of the *SG-21* and the circumstances under which she found herself opposite the Allied fleet a few hours before the Second D-Day. Thanks are also extended to Captain Hermann Polenz, who headed the Sixth Security Fleet, and to Captain Karl von Kutzleben, both of whom energetically tracked down the *SG-21*'s survivors and provided me with invaluable material concerning this unpublicized episode.

My old friend Major Robert Bonne also contributed to this work. Three other persons deserve outstanding recognition – Robert Laffont, Michael Bouis and Jacques Peuchmaurd, thanks to whom my book actually got published. I am indebted to them for many memorable moments, much anguish and torment, many sleepless nights – and some of my happiest memories. Throughout the long period of preparation, Monique Touzard of the Laffont editing staff provided efficient assistance; she contributed to my research, wrote letters, interviewed people, made phone calls, sorted and routed mountains of correspondence, had countless letters translated, sent out reminders to lax correspondents – and still found time to offer words of solace.

The most arduous part of my task was the locating of the surviving actors in and witnesses to the invasion of Provence, sixteen years later. I should like to pay tribute to all those who aided me in the search, and specifically to James O. Mays and Colette Gaudin of the United States Embassy in Paris, who lent me their constant warm support. West Germany's diplomatic services in France also cooperated admirably, notwithstanding the nature of the book. Numerous other groups, agencies and associations in Europe, Britain and America furthered my efforts to find the survivors whose stories have made it possible for this book to appear.

I am extremely grateful to Mme de Lattre de Tassigny, to the Rhine and Danube Association, to veterans' associations in France, Germany, Canada, the United States and Britain, and to former Resistance fighters for their cooperation. Grateful acknowledgment is extended to local administrative authorities in Southern France, to Raymond Haas-Picard in Marseilles and to Monsieur Berthet in Draguignan, and to the sixty-two town halls in the communes of Provence that distributed the questionnaires that were sent them.

Newspapers in France and elsewhere publicized our appeal to veterans and civilian witnesses of the 1944 fighting. Similar services were rendered by radio and television stations – the ORTF[1] in Paris, Marseilles and Algiers; Radio Luxembourg, Europe No. 1, and Radio Monte Carlo, thanks to which I received my first eyewitness accounts.

Nearly a thousand people answered my questions and supplied me

[1] *Office de Radio-Télévision Française.*

with a great variety of material and information, in the form of notes, personal papers, letters, bundles of yellowed documents, maps, photographs, pamphlets, old newspapers, logbooks, diaries, etc. My debt to them is staggering. It is with the deepest emotion that I thank all these people, the chief protagonists in the story – including two who wish to remain anonymous – the men and women who so generously gave their assistance to my work.

Index

Maldant, Corporal René, 266
Maloney, Lt.-Cdr., J.L., commanding minesweepers, 162, 196, 232–3, 237
Mamy, Capt., 55
Manseur, Philippe, Algerian warrant officer, 264, 271, 288; killed in German air attack, 273
Mansfield, Rear-Admiral J.M., 165
Marchand, Louis, SOE agent, 196, 199, 204, 205; prevents mining of Le Dramont beach, 62–3, 198
Marche, Lt.-Cdr. Gérard: at Pointe-de-l'Esquillon, 124, 126; wounded and killed, 127–8
Marchesi, Théotime, Resistance sector chief, 61
Marseilles: importance as port, 14; principal objective of landings, 14; French enter city, 287–8; short-lived truce, 290, 292; Goumier troops advance on city, 291–2; German capitulation, 293
Marshall, General George C., U.S. Army Chief of Staff, 13
Massel, Father Joseph, 48
Massiet du Biest, Col., 292
Maures Brigade Resistance group, 154
Maury, Midshipman Albert, 91, 95
Meinshausen, Col. Rudolf, German staff officer, 220
Meirat, Jean, French naval signalman, 4, 64, 69, 78n., 166, 188, 233
Méplain, Lt. Arthur, 266
Méric, Major, 293
Méric, Marie-Madeleine, Resistance leader, 58
Merle, Gaston and Louise, 294–5
Merz, Major Walter, chief of staff to Gen. Schaefer, 286, 293
Messmer, Commander W.L., 162
Metzenthin, Lt. Hans Joachim, 150–2
Meyer, Henry, 152
Michelet, Master Sgt. René, 22, 74
Middleton, Capt. G.B. (Royal Navy), 77
Miller, Capt. Ralph R., lost in parachute jump, 153
Miller, Winston, 173
Minara, Clementine and François, 196
Minesweepers, 162, 196, 232–3, 237
Mithridate Resistance group, 58, 83, 124n.
Model, Gen. Walter, 227

Moine, 2nd Lt. Jacques, 74, 238, 239
Mont Biscarre reached by commandos, 150
Montcalm, French cruiser, 69, 75, 167; 268
Moon, Rear-Admiral Don P., 235; anxiety over Operation Dragoon, 21; commits suicide, 21, 88n.
Moore, Lt.-Col. Robert S., commanding Second Special Forces Regt., 254
Morieux, Jacques, 18–20
Morris, Capt. Robert, assault group commander, 48, 72; and Le Dramont landing, 197
Morse, Rear-Admiral John, 5–7
Muller, Herbert, 147
Murphy, Pte. David H., 154
Mussolini, Benito, 25

Navascuès, Manuel, 75–6
Nelson, Pte. Don, 190, 256
Neuling, Gen. Ferdinand, commanding German LXII Corps, 61, 136, 219, 242, 243; and surrender of Draguignan, 275–7
Nevada, U.S. battleship, 77, 168
Newell, Lt., A.D.C. to O'Daniel, 252
Nod-sur-Seine, French troops from north and south meet at (Sept. 12), 294–6
Novo, Marius, 241

O'Daniel, Maj.-Gen. John W. ('Iron Mike'), commanding U.S. 3rd Division, 7, 84n., 173, 210, 240; links with Bouvet and sets up command post, 252
Olinger, Ralph, 131
O'Mahundro, Capt. Wiley H., 171–2
Onorati, François, removes detonators on Ile du Levant, 51–2, 116
Operation Anvil: decided on (Dec. 1943), 12; importance of Marseilles, 14; choice of landing sites, 14–15; detailed planning, 16–17; shortage of LSTs, 18; separated from Overlord, 18
Operation Dragoon, Anvil becomes, 20
Operation Ferdinand (diversionary operation), 119–23
Operation Overlord, 12, 16; separated from Anvil, 18; 'D' Day, 18–19
Operation Rosie (diversionary operation), 122–3

Tito, Marshal (Josip Broz), visits Churchill in Naples, 5, 29
Todt Organization, 66, 196, 231; fails to mine Le Dramont beach, 62–3
Tonner, Francis and Fernand, 250
Toop, Lt., 87
Tornow, Major, 275
Toulon capitulates, 283, 284
Toussaint de Quièvrecourt, Capt, 232
Touzet du Vigier, Gen., commanding French 1st Armored Division, 238, 267, 280
Troubridge, Rear-Admiral T.H. (Royal Navy), commanding aircraft carriers, 17, 73, 163, 262
Truscott, Lt.-Gen. Lucian K., Jr., 7, 239, 240n.
Tuscaloosa, U.S. cruiser, 77–8, 168, 234
Twelfth Tactical Air Command, 16, 37–9, 71, 252; and raid on La Ciotat, 119–23

U.S. Air Force units, 37
U.S. Army:
  Third Army, 226; enters Orléans (Aug. 17), 279
  Divisions:
    3rd Infantry, 20, 73, 77, 84n., 99, 161, 170, 218, 252; embarks at Naples, 6–7; landing at Pampelonne, 212; links up with Commandos, 252; casualties, 256; German prisoners taken, 257; rescues hostages at Le Lavandou, 278
    9th Colonial Infantry, 254n.
    36th Texas, 20, 73, 78, 99, 138, 170, 190–1, 204, 205, 223, 231, 235, 238, 240n., 247, 257; casualties, 256; German prisoners taken, 257
    45th Infantry, 20, 73, 78, 86, 99, 169, 170, 238, 247; landing at La Nartelle, 175, 176, 182, 215; landing at Val d'Esquières, 188; in Sainte-Maxime, 215, 216
    88th Infantry, 19
  Regiments, etc.:
    2nd and 3rd Special Forces Regts., in fighting on Iles d'Hyères, 115–19, 253–4
    7th Regt., 170, 172, 252

15th Regt., at Pampelonne, 211; captures Saint-Tropez, 248
30th Regt., 252
36th Engineer Beach Group, at Pampelonne, 211
40th Engineer Beach Group, 182
141st Regt., 191, 250n., 275; at Anthéor, 193, 204; at Le Dramont, 198, 203, 204
142nd Regt., 191, 204, 240n.; and assault on Fréjus, 231, 234, 235; lands at Le Dramont, 237–8
143rd Regt., 190, 191, 204, 234, 243
157th Infantry Regt., 175, 240; landings, 179, 180, 182, 183–7; in Saint-Maxime, 185, 215, 216; clears road to Beauvallon, 240
180th Infantry Regt., 86; landings, 187, 189
191st Tank Battalion, 189, 216, 217
540th Engineer Beach Group, 198
601st Tank Destroyer Battalion, at Pampelonne, 211
753rd Tank Battalion, at Le Dramont, 197, 202–3
756th Tank Battalion, 171; at Pampelonne, 211
See also Airborne troops

Vagliano, Hélène, 194; put to death by Gestapo, 250–1
Val d'Esquière beach (Delta Blue), 87; landing at, 188–9
Valz, W.O. Albert, 272
Vercellino, Gen. Mario, commanding Italian Fourth Army, 25, 65
Verdier, Dr. Jean, 38, 169, 184, 217
Villechenoux, Maurice, French naval gunner, 232
Vilmot, Bosun's Mate, 97
Vogel, Capt. Louis J., 130
Vollendam, transport, 265, 272

Walker, Col. Edwin A., commanding First Special Service Force, 73, 90, 91n., 253; plans for landing on Iles d'Hyères, 114–15; and unexpected resistance on Port-Cros, 118–19
Waller, Capt. J.B.W., 78
Walls, Capt. Jess W.: makes parachute landing near Saint-Tropez, 153–4,